ENGLISH REBELS

AND

REVOLUTIONARIES

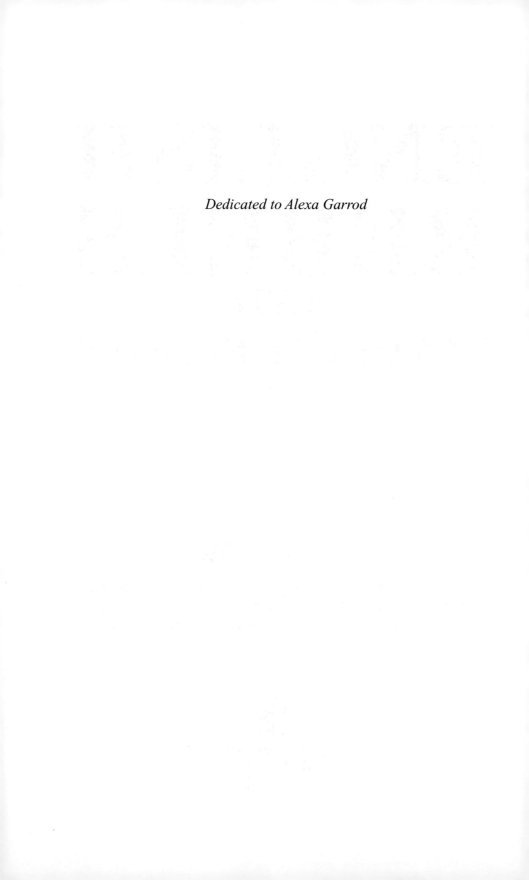

Dedicated to Alexa Garrod

ENGLISH REBELS
AND
REVOLUTIONARIES

STEPHEN BASDEO

WITH ESSAYS BY ANNE ANDERSON, STEPHEN BASDEO, DI DRUMMOND,
ANGELO CALFO, FRANCES CHIU, SHELDON GOLDFARB, ALEXANDER
KAUFMAN, REBECCA NESVET, SAM QUILL, AND JOSEPH SAUNDERS

PEN & SWORD
HISTORY
AN IMPRINT OF PEN & SWORD BOOKS LTD.
YORKSHIRE – PHILADELPHIA

First published in Great Britain in 2022 by
PEN AND SWORD HISTORY
An imprint of
Pen & Sword Books Ltd
Yorkshire - Philadelphia

ISBN: 978 1 52678 590 9

A CIP catalogue record for this book is available from the British Library.

Typeset in Times New Roman 10/12 by
SJmagic DESIGN SERVICES, India.
Printed and bound in the UK by CPI Group (UK) Ltd.

Pen & Sword Books Ltd incorporates the Imprints of Pen & Sword Books
Archaeology, Atlas, Aviation, Battleground, Discovery, Family History, History,
Maritime, Military, Naval, Politics, Railways, Select, Transport, True Crime,
Fiction, Frontline Books, Leo Cooper, Praetorian Press, Seaforth Publishing,
Wharncliffe and White Owl.

For a complete list of Pen & Sword titles please contact
PEN & SWORD BOOKS LIMITED
47 Church Street, Barnsley, South Yorkshire, S70 2AS, England
E-mail: enquiries@pen-and-sword.co.uk
Website: www.pen-and-sword.co.uk

Or
PEN AND SWORD BOOKS
1950 Lawrence Rd, Havertown, PA 19083, USA
E-mail: Uspen-and-sword@casematepublishers.com
Website: www.penandswordbooks.com

Contents

List of Contributors

With a first degree in archaeology and a PhD in English, **Anne Anderson** was a senior lecturer in Art and Design History at Southampton Solent University for fourteen years. She has curated three national exhibitions: The Truth About Faeries (2011), Under the Greenwood: Picturing the British Tree (2013) and Beyond the Brotherhood: the Pre-Raphaelite Legacy (2019-20). Anne has held several prestigious American fellowships including Fellow of the Huntington Library, CA and Fellow of the Henry Francis DuPont Winterthur Library and Museum. A tutor for the V&A Learning Academy, Anne specialises in Art Nouveau and the Arts and Crafts movement. Her career as an international speaker has taken her all over the world. Her recent books include *Edward Burne-Jones* (2018) and *Beyond the Brotherhood: the Pre-Raphaelite Legacy* (2019). Her book on Art Nouveau Architecture will be published in 2020.

Stephen Basdeo completed his PhD in 2017 and specializes in the history of medieval outlaws and rebels. Recent publications include *The Life and Legend of a Rebel Leader: Wat Tyler* (2018), *The History of the Most Noted Highwaymen, Rogues, and Murderers* (2018), and *Robin Hood: The Life and Legend of an Outlaw* (2019). Recent academic articles include commentaries on the life and work of the radical Victorian journalist and crime novelist G.W.M. Reynolds (1814–79). At the time of writing, Basdeo is also writing a monograph on Reynolds's political philosophy. Stephen lives in Leeds and is owned by a cat named Robin, named after Robin Hood. Stephen has also collaborated on another chapter in this collection with **Angelo Calfo**, a BA student whose essay, while he took one of Stephen's classes at Richmond University, forms the basis of the chapter titled 'Politics in the Age of Equipoise'.

Frances Chiu teaches history and literature at The New School, a university located in New York City. She has published in *Eighteenth-century Life, Notes and Queries*, and *Romanticism on the Net*. She has also prepared the first modern editions of Ann Radcliffe's *Gaston de Blondeville* and J. Sheridan LeFanu's *Rose and the Key* for Valancourt Books. More recently, she has published *Paine's Rights of Man* (Routledge, May 2020), the first full-length study of that classic text. She is currently working on a monograph for Manchester University Press, *Reading the Gothic: Matthew Lewis' Monk*. Chiu is an advisory editor for Anthem Press Gothic Studies and for the new MUP *Reading the Gothic* series. Not least, she is the dedicated servant of two shaded silver Persian cats, Sir Charles Fox and Duchess Georgiana, known simply as Charlie and Georgie.

Di Drummond was formerly Reader in Modern History in the Leeds Centre for Victorian Studies, Leeds Trinity University. Her chapter in this book stems from her teaching a module, 'Votes for Women', an exploration of the campaign for female suffrage in Britain, 1866-1918, for over twenty years. Best known for her publications on railways (e.g. *Tracing Your Railway Ancestors*, Pen and Sword, 2010 and *Crewe: Railway Town, Company and People*, Scolar Press, Aldershot, 1995), Di also made a significant contribution to a history of the University of Birmingham. Publications since retirement include; 'Borders and Margins? The Formation of Discourses on race, imperialism, and British overseas railway building, 1830-1930', Amina Alyal, Susan Anderson and Rosemary Mitchell (eds.), *Victorian Cultures of Liminality: Borders and Margins* (Cambridge Scholars Publishing, 2018) and 'Pure and Applied Science at the University of Birmingham', in J. Mussell and G. Gooday (eds.), *A Pioneer of Connection: Recovering the Life and Work of Oliver Lodge* (University of Pittsburgh Press, 2020). Di gained her PhD from Royal Holloway, University of London, some point during the last century! She continued in academia in order to keep various cats in the manner to which they were accustomed! Thanks to husband Ian for all his love and support in enabling her to do that, and in writing this chapter.

Sheldon Goldfarb is the Archivist for the Alma Mater Society at the University of British Columbia in Vancouver. He has published academic work on William Makepeace Thackeray, a historical novel that was nominated for a Canadian crime writing award, and a history of student life (including student protests) at UBC. His most recent work has been on Sherlock Holmes, but long ago before his graduate degrees in English literature, he pursued the history of the English Civil War, studying in Manchester with Brian Manning, a student of Christopher Hill's.

Alexander L. Kaufman is the Reed D. Voran Distinguished Professor of Humanities and Professor of English at Ball State University where he teaches in the Honors College. He is the author of *The Historical Literature of the Jack Cade Rebellion* (Ashgate 2009; repr. Routledge, 2016), co-editor of *Telling Tales and Crafting Books: Essays in Honor of Thomas H. Ohlgren* (Medieval Institute Publication, 2016), *Robin Hood and the Outlaw/ed Literary Canon* (Routledge, 2019) and *Food and Feast in Modern Outlaw Tales* (Routledge, 2019), and editor of *British Outlaws of Literature and History: Essays on Medieval and Early Modern Figures from Robin Hood to Twm Shon Catty* (McFarland, 2011) and *The Jack Cade Rebellion of 1450: A Sourcebook* (Lexington, 2020). He co-founded the journal *The Bulletin of the International Association for Robin Hood Studies* and also serves as co-administrator for the scholarly blog Robin Hood Scholars: IARHS on the Web. He is also a general editor of the series *Outlaws in Literature, History, and Culture* for Routledge Publishing. His research and teaching interests include outlaws from the medieval period to the present day, the Robin Hood tradition, historical writing and medieval chronicles, Chaucer, Arthuriana, and medievalisms.

Rebecca Nesvet, Associate Professor of English, University of Wisconsin, Green Bay, writes about Romantic and Victorian literature. She has published in journals including *Nineteenth Century Studies, Victorian Popular Fictions Journal, Victorian Network, Notes and Queries, Scholarly Editing: The Journal of the Association for Documentary Editing, The Keats-Shelley Journal*, and *Women's Writing*, and anthologies on Oscar Wilde, Rousseau and British Romanticism, Mary Hays, and the teaching of Victorian literature in the twenty-first century. Her current and forthcoming projects concern James Malcolm Rymer's penny serials *Varney, the Vampyre, The Lady in Black*, and *A Mystery in Scarle*t; Oscar Wilde's friend Julia Constance Fletcher; Victorian vegetarians; and Jane Williams, player of 'Shelley's guitar'.

Sam Quill received his PhD in 2019 from Queen Mary University of London. A musician and scholar of Romanticism, he completed a thesis on Romantic literature, Percy Bysshe Shelley, and philosophical necessity, titled 'The Question of Cause: Influence, Necessity and Change in Radical Thought and Romantic Poetics'. He has also published poetry in *PN Review* and *The Next Review*.

Joseph Saunders has a postgraduate degree from the University of Glasgow, where he wrote his thesis on the English print trade in the era of the Civil War. His research interests include the middling and lower sorts of early modern England, particularly the printers and booksellers of seventeenth century London. He is also interested in the reception of print amongst ordinary people and the relationship between print and popular culture. A long-standing desire is to find out what drove men to fight and die in the Civil War and to advocate for our understanding of this important period in English history. Joseph has been a tour guide and is a freelance historical researcher. He works mainly on genealogies and house histories but has investigated medieval castles, the lives of First World War soldiers and everything in between. Most recently, he has been working on a seventeenth century house in the Yorkshire Dales. Born and raised in Essex, he currently lives in the Pennines with his family and dogs.

Introduction

Oh for the swords of former time!
Oh for the men who bore them,
When, arm'd for Right, they stood sublime,
And tyrants crouch'd before them.

When free yet, ere courts began
With honours to enslave him,
The best honours worn by Man
Were those which Virtue gave him.

–Thomas Moore

The work of an early twentieth century historian named Joseph Clayton (1867–1943) is fascinating reading for any student of radical history. Educated at Worcester College, Oxford, he later moved to Leeds where he became a member of the local Independent Labour Party in 1896.[1] He considered himself a Christian Socialist and, throughout his life, wrote a number of articles on various left-wing matters, including advocating for the extension of the franchise to women, and he also wrote several history books on the radical tradition in England. His first notable work in this area was *Robert Owen, Pioneer of Social Reforms* (1908), a biography of one of the more enlightened factory owners in the nineteenth century. After this followed, in quick succession, the following: *Wat Tyler and the Peasants' Revolt* (1909) and *The True Story of Jack Cade* (1910).

However, two further books by Clayton really caught my eye as I was perusing his work: *Leaders of the People* (1910) and *The Rise of the Democracy* (1911). These two books were an account of every prominent radical society and rebel leader that ever graced the annals of English history, and the great march of democracy in the country. In Clayton's opinion, British democracy was the envy of the world:

> Our business here is to give some plain account of the movement towards democracy in England, only touching incidentally on the progress of that movement in other parts of the world. Mainly through British influences the movement has become worldwide; and the desire for national self-government, and the adoption of the political instruments of democracy— popular enfranchisement and the rule of elected representatives—are still the aspirations of civilised man in East and West. The knowledge that

these forms of democratic government have by no means at all times and in all places proved successful does not check the movement. As the British Parliament and the British Constitution have in the past been accepted as a model in countries seeking free political institutions, so to-day our Parliament and our Constitutional Government are still quoted with approval and admiration in those lands where these institutions are yet to be tried.[2]

That was certainly a very patriotic view of the development of British democracy and was certainly influenced by the Whig tradition of history, in which history is the story of progress. And while many of the peoples of the British Empire did indeed desire self-government, it was not always granted willingly. The British response to Gandhi's campaigns for independence, which were almost contemporary to Clayton's writings, was to lock up Gandhi up in prison. Clayton's work is now rather dated. There have been numerous advances in historical scholarship since he wrote *The Rise of the Democracy*, while Clayton's works were targeted towards young adult readers. I felt, therefore, it was time to produce an updated similar work, with a more mature audience in mind, with a slightly different theme.

The overall theme of this volume is therefore to give an account of *some* of the major events, and the actions of famous English radicals from the medieval period to the nineteenth century. The question remains to be asked, then: what does it mean to be radical? There are of course many definitions of the term and there are many forms of radicalism. I take the definition of radicalism offered by the historian Michael J. Turner: this does not seek to impose a specific ideology on to the idea of radicalism—for radicals come from across the political spectrum—but rather it can be applied to any actors or ideology which seeks a fundamental change in the constitution of society, and argues that the root of society's social and economic problems is political. The problems facing society are usually attributed to the operations of a corrupt state and selfish elite who legislate for policies that worked in their favour to the detriment of the people. Yet it is not enough for radicals simply to moan about the status quo; they also have to present an appealing vision of a better, future society to their readers and work towards it.[3]

That being said, the history of English radicalism is much broader than one book could ever hope to treat in depth. Had I had my own way, the book would probably have totalled about a million words and sold in several volumes containing the lives of every British freedom fighter and radical intellectual, from Boudicca to the poll tax rioters under Margaret Thatcher. As it is, for a book of the scope commissioned by a commercial history publisher, it was necessary to narrow the book's focus somewhat. The book, therefore, presents short histories of the people who fought for political rights, from the medieval period to the granting of women's suffrage in 1918. And when we say 'fought for', readers should take that to mean that we are discussing the lives of people who took part in direct action and protests. Another volume on the theme of revolutionary thinkers is planned for the future, although as this volume shows those categories are by no means mutually exclusive. In this volume, there are several

Sceau de Guillaume le Conquérant (face).

The seal of William
the Conqueror.
(British Library, Public
Domain)

figures who straddle both categories, such as the Duke of Richmond, Thomas Paine, G.W.M. Reynolds, and William Morris, to name but a few. Yet still some characters and events have had to be omitted or referred to only tangentially, while religiously-inspired rebellions such as the Pilgrimage of Grace are not included. However, readers will find that although several chapters, on the surface, deal with the lives and exploits of just *one* major figure, authors in this volume have used the events of that figure's life to illuminate a wider history of the people, places, and events in which those radicals took part.

A Norman Yoke

In the eighteenth century Robert Ferguson declared that:

> In all our histories of Great Britain and Ireland, we meet with nothing more frequent than mobs and insurrections, which tho' they have always terminated in the destruction of the ring leaders and the principal abettors, yet we still find that the madness of the people has fatally spread itself from one age to another, and is become even at this day, no less dangerous and infectious than it was at the very beginning.[4]

Ferguson was a Jacobite, a member of a group who, while not radical or revolutionary, did seek to depose the reigning monarch, George I, and reinstall a member of the Stuart dynasty to the throne.[5] Whatever his personal politics, however, Ferguson was right: There have indeed been rebellions in Britain since time immemorial. When the Norman William the Conqueror invaded England with his army in 1066 and defeated King Harold Godwinson, William assumed the English throne. It was not a smooth succession. A chronicler named William of Poitiers gives the impression that the Norman conqueror and his local representatives attempted at first to placate the English:

> They paid the greatest respect to justice, as the king had admonished, so that fierce men and enemies might be corrected and brought into friendship. The lesser officials were equally zealous in the castles where each had been placed. But neither benefits nor fear could sufficiently force the English to prefer peace and quiet to changes and revolts.[6]

That was certainly an interpretation of events that was very friendly to the Normans. The English indeed were not quite ready to make peace with their conquerors, especially as the grievances of the English people fell on deaf ears, as Oderic Vitalis explained:

> The king's vice regents, were so swollen with pride that they would not deign to hear the reasonable plea of the English or give them impartial judgement. When their men-at-arms were guilty of plunder and rape they protected them by force, and wreaked their wrath all the more violently upon those who complained of the cruel wrongs they suffered. And so the English groaned aloud for their lost liberty and plotted ceaselessly to find some way of shaking off a yoke that was so intolerable and unaccustomed.[7]

Shortly after Godwinson's death, the Witengamot (the early form of parliament, or national council) elected Edgar Ætheling to be king instead of William. Ætheling encouraged the English people to rise up against their new overlords and many people did as he commanded, with the help of local nobles and foreign allies. Allied with the Welsh, an English thegn named Eadric 'the Wild' launched quick raids in and around Hereford before scarpering back to Wales. In 1067, a thegn named Hereward the Wake was busy fighting, with the assistance of the Danes, what is best termed a guerrilla war against the Normans in the east of England. At one point the Danes even sent an army to England and William had to pay them to return home. The north of England was also a hotbed of resistance; led by English nobles such as Gospatric, Earl of Northumbria and Edwin, Earl of Mercia, and enlisting the help of foreign soldiers, the people in the north of England might well have succeeded in ousting their foreign conquerors. Yet it was not to be. William turned nasty. He decided to punish people in the north of England by starving them out and enacting what we would now call a 'scorched earth' policy. These actions in the late 1060s, which have acquired the name of 'The Harrying of the North' were described by Vitalis:

Nowhere else had William shown such cruelty. Shamefully he succumbed to this vice, for he made no effort to restrain his fury and punished the innocent with the guilty. In his anger he commanded that all crops and herds, chattels and food of every kind should be brought together and burned to ashes with consuming fire, so that the whole region north of the Humber might be stripped of all means of sustenance. In consequence so serious a scarcity was felt in England, and so terrible a famine fell upon the humble and defenceless populace, that more than one hundred thousand Christian folk of both sexes, young and old alike, perished of hunger. My narrative has frequently had occasion to praise William, but for this act which condemned the innocent and the guilty alike to die by slow starvation I cannot commend him.[8]

We may take the number of 100,000 deaths to be a bit exaggerated but still, whatever the numbers, many people did die. It was clear that after a brutal series of repressive measures the English rising was crushed. Ætheling's election was quietly set aside and the would-be young king was forced to bend the knee to William.

Magna Carta. (from a facsimile in Stephen Basdeo's personal collection)

The Battle for Magna Carta

Disputes over who should wear the crown followed after William's death, notably the civil war between King Stephen and Matilda. But the next major revolt, with consequences which reverberate even unto our own times, was the Barons' War against King John. Having ascended the throne after the death of his more popular brother, Richard the Lionheart, John proved to be a bad ruler. The Normans and, later, the Angevins, not only ruled England but also held extensive lands in France. John's father, Henry II, held lands in England, Normandy, Maine, Anjou, Brittany, and Wales. Yet during John's reign, the king of France had steadily made inroads into these domains and by 1204, most of John's ancestral lands in France had been conquered by Philip II of France. John attempted to regain these lands but the disastrous military expeditions came at a high cost and to fund these John arbitrarily raised taxes without the consent of the barons. English monarchs had, until John, always counted themselves as above the law, although most kings accepted that it was good practice to rule *in accordance with* the law. The best expression of this was the signing of the Charter of Liberties by Henry I upon his accession in 1100, which, among other things, declared that the raising of feudal dues should be kept within reasonable limits. However, subsequent monarchs largely ignored this charter and John was no different. He needed money and he wanted his French lands back.

Between February and October 1214, John suffered another ignominious defeat in attempting to reconquer his French domains. It was costly. All the money that he had spent from the taxes raised appeared to have been pointlessly squandered. The English barons were angry. John had also fallen afoul of the Catholic Church. He refused to accept Pope Innocent III's nomination for the position of Archbishop of Canterbury and the pope was so incensed at John's obstinacy that in 1208 he placed the entire realm of England under an interdict. The barons had had enough and they decided to renounce their allegiance to John and named Robert Fitz Walter as their leader. A baronial rebellion had begun. The

The barons' meeting with King John. (from Joseph Clayton's *Rise of the Democracy*)

rebel barons' demanded that the king reaffirm his pledge to abide by the provisions of the Charter of Liberties and on 17 May 1215, the rebels were welcomed into the city of London by the inhabitants.

John decided to face the music and meet with the rebels on 10 June at Runnymede meadow on the banks of the Thames. The barons had drawn up a new charter which was even more wide-ranging than the Charter of Liberties from Henry I's era: The Articles of the Barons. This document set out numerous conditions which they expected John to agree to before they would again pledge their allegiance to him. After some days of negotiations, King John affixed his seal to a new document — Magna Carta (the 'great charter') — and accepted all of its terms. There were sixty-three provisions dealing with the collections of taxes, the 'ancient rights' of boroughs and liberties, and even fishing rights. Most famously there was also a provision in clause 39 setting out in clear terms who could be arrested and how, once brought to trial, a person might be judged:

> No free man shall be seized, imprisoned, dispossessed, outlawed, exiled or ruined in any way, nor in any way proceeded against, except by the lawful judgement of his peers and the law of the land.[9]

Contrary to popular belief, this was not actually the foundation of *habeas corpus*, for that originated in the Assize of Clarendon in 1166.[10] The provision in Magna Carta merely built upon an existing idea which held that, if the authorities wanted to arrest someone, there had to be sufficient evidence of wrongdoing before they were allowed to. Hence clause 38 of Magna Carta: 'In future no official shall place a man on trial upon his own unsupported statement, without producing credible witnesses to the truth of it'.[11]

On 15 June 1215, King John accepted the terms of the Magna Carta and set his seal upon a draft of it. Four days later the barons pledged their allegiance to John again. The king now had to act within the law.

Or so the barons thought.

John had made amends with Pope Innocent III two years earlier by accepting Stephen Langton, the Pope's choice, as Archbishop of Canterbury. John got the interdict lifted and submitted to ruling England as a Papal Fief, with England forced to pay an annual tribute to the pope. Having signed Magna Carta, John appealed to Innocent and asked him to annul Magna Carta because it had been signed under duress. The Pope promptly took John's side and on 7 July 1215, the pontiff excommunicated all of the barons who rebelled against their king and on 25 August, the pope formally declared Magna Carta null and void.

Yet the barons would have their way. In September 1215, they rebelled against John again. But it was to be a short rebellion for on 16 October, King John died at Newark. Twelve days later, Henry III was crowned King of England at Gloucester and on 12 November, Magna Carta was reissued by young Henry's government, with some minor changes, and a third version was issued again on 6 November 1217, again with some minor changes. However, in the summer of 1224, the King of France invaded La Rochelle and Poitu—what was left of the Angevin domains in France—which required a new war, and new taxes, to fund its defence. Nevertheless, the English were expelled from these regions were formally incorporated into the French royal lands. However, this event did mean that in 1225 Henry III had to once again publicly signal his intention to abide by the terms of Magna Carta.

The De Montfort Rebellion

A young French nobleman arrived in England in 1229 and sought an audience with the king. His name was Simon de Montfort. Born in the early part of the century, de Montfort relinquished the rights to his lands in France, thereby absolving himself of any allegiance to the French king, and petitioned Henry III to be given an English inheritance. Land was granted to de Montfort and he even married the king's sister Eleanor. A fervent, bigoted Christian, he expelled the Jewish people from his land in Leicester which won him a lot of popularity in the eyes of the locals.[12] Yet he made a bit of a blunder—he was in debt to Thomas II of Savoy and, without consulting his brother-in-law Henry III, listed the king as a guarantor of his debt. The king was furious. De Montfort, perhaps wisely, decided to leave England for a bit and go on crusade.

By 1254, de Montfort was back in England, having made a somewhat frosty reconciliation with the king. In the same year, the king demanded more subsidies from the nobles in order to pay the Pope, who, after receiving payment, would allow Henry III's son to inherit the throne of Sicily. When the king summoned the nobles to a parliament in 1258 to deliberate on the king's financial matters, de Montfort was one of the leading voices who were opposed to granting the king more money. The parliament agreed the Provisions of Oxford which placed limits on the power of the king by appointing a privy council—comprising twelve of the king's men and twelve of the reformers' men—to oversee the king's government. The two chief ministers of this council, the Justiciar and the Chancellor, were to be chosen by its members. The Privy Council would then be accountable to the nobles when parliaments were convened.

The king granted the money to pay the Pope but the nobles still wanted Henry III to be accountable to them through the Privy Council. Tensions were brewing because the king wanted to completely scrap the Provisions of Oxford. The Pope formally annulled the Provisions of Oxford in 1261. This did not go down well with the nobles and, frustrated, de Montfort left England. He left a country on the brink of civil war.

For two years the remaining barons tried to persuade the king to pledge his support again to the Provisions of Oxford. Frustrated with the king's stubbornness, when de Montfort returned in 1263, the barons asked him to lead a rebellion with the sole aim of compelling the king to agree to abide by the terms of the Provisions of Oxford. An army was raised and the de Montfort's forces began attacking the estates of the king's allies. Into the fray, the King of France stepped forth as a supposedly impartial adjudicator. Having listened to the arguments of both sides he ruled in Henry's favour. This did not satisfy either de Montfort or the barons and further skirmishes ensued. At the Battle of Lewes on 14 May 1264, the king was captured and forced to sign the Mise of Lewes which, although this document no longer survives, compelled the king to pardon the rebels and abide by the terms of the Provisions of Oxford. In the words of

Adrian Jobson, the king was now 'little more than a figurehead'.[13] The king's son Prince Edward was also taken by the barons as a hostage—an extra incentive for the king to keep his word.

De Montfort was effectively England's ruler, although he claimed power in the king's name. He summoned a parliament to confirm the terms of his government but, upon hearing of widespread discontent across the country and with the support of the barons ebbing away now the king had been brought to heel, de Montfort tried to win legitimacy for his administration by summoning another parliament in 1265. Parliaments had been summoned before this but de Montfort's 1265 convening of parliament was truly innovative. He summoned the nobles, bishops and the knights as usual but also—something which had never happened before—representatives of the non-noble burgesses. Commoners were now being given a voice in the affairs of government. Let us not fall into the trap of believing this to be some sort of non-partisan and democratic assembly, however, for de Montfort made sure to stuff this new parliament with those who were friendly to his cause.[14]

De Montfort's parliament offered a temporary reprieve for the unrest in the country but several of the nobles now began to oppose him. There were rumours that he was enriching himself at the expense of the public. He did indeed gain a handsome fortune at this time. To add to de Montfort's woes Prince Edward escaped and, vowing to put an end to de Montfort's rule, raised an army and went into battle with de Montfort at the Battle of Evesham on 4 August 1265. De Montfort fell in battle here. His body was found on the battlefield and was decapitated. His testicles, his hands, and his feet were also dismembered.[15]

DEATH OF SIMON DE MONTFORT.

The reforms which de Montfort introduced would outlast him, however. Successive parliaments summoned by Henry III sometimes included non-nobles or representatives of the 'commons'. His son Edward, when he ascended the throne in 1272, actually continued de Montfort's practice of summoning both nobles and representatives of the commons to parliament. In the next century, the representatives of the nobles and the commons were split into two 'houses'. The House of Commons and the House of Lords were born, although England was by no means democratic in any sense of the word.

The Death of Simon de Montfort. (British Library, Public Domain)

The commons had been 'invited' to have a say in the affairs of the government because a discontented nobleman, de Montfort, needed to win legitimacy for his administration. Yet neither de Montfort's rebellion, nor the First Barons' War against King John were 'popular' rebellions. That is to say that, in spite of their importance, in neither case did the people rise up and demand their rights. The first time this would happen in England would be in the fourteenth century, and so I begin this collection of essays with an account of perhaps the most famous 'popular' rebellion in English history: The Peasants' Revolt of 1381.

Notes

1. "Clayton, Joseph," in *The Catholic Encyclopedia and Its Makers*, ed. Charles Herbermann et al (New York, the Encyclopedia Press, 1917), 30

2. Joseph Clayton, *The Rise of the Democracy* (London: Cassell, 1911), accessed 15 April 2020, http://www.gutenberg.org/files/19609/19609-h/19609-h.htm

3. Michael J. Turner, *Independent Radicalism in Early Victorian Britain* (Westport, CT: Praegar, 2004), 2–4.

4. Robert Ferguson, *The History of all the Mobs, Tumults, and Insurrections in Great Britain, from William the Conqueror to the Present Time. To Which is Added, The Act of Parliament and Proclamation Lately Publish'd for Punishing Rioters* (London: Printed for J. Moore near St. Paul's, 1715), i.

5. Melinda S. Zook, "Turncoats and Double Agents in Restoration and Revolutionary England: The Case of Robert Ferguson, the Plotter," *Eighteenth-Century Studies* 42 no. 3 (2009): 363-378.

6. William of Poitiers, *Gesta Guillelmi*, ed. R.H.C Davis and Marjorie Chibnall (Oxford: Oxford University Press, 1998), 46.

7. Oderic Vitalis, *Historia Ecclesiastica*, trans. Auguste le Provoste, 5 vols. (Paris: Société de l'histoire de France, 1838–1855), II, 46.

8. Vitalis, *Historia Ecclesiastica*, vol. 2, 195–96.

9. UK Parliament, "The contents of Magna Carta," accessed April 4, 2020. Available at: www.parliament.uk.

10. "Assize of Clarendon, 1166," in *Select Historical Documents of the Middle Ages*, ed. Ernest F. Henderson (London: George Bell and Sons, 1896), 146.

11. British Library, "Magna Carta," accessed April 1, 2020. Available at: www.bl.uk.

12. Oliver Harris, "Jews, jurats and the Jewry Wall: a name in context," *Transactions of the Leicestershire Archaeological and Historical Society* 82 (2008): 113–33 (129–31).

13. Adrian Jobson, *The First English Revolution: Simon de Montfort, Henry III and the Barons' War* (London: Bloomsbury, 2012), 117–122.

14. Jeffrey Hamilton, *The Plantagenets: History of a Dynasty* (London: Continuum, 2010), 46.

15. J.R. Maddicott, *Simon de Montfort* (Cambridge: Cambridge University Press, 1994), 342.

Section One

The Medieval Period

The Peasants' Revolt of 1381

Stephen Basdeo

In 1377, John Gower put his quill upon a parchment and began writing a poem entitled 'Mirrour de l'homme'.[1] Something about the general state of the nation had made him uneasy—the ruling class had to be on their guard against 'the folly of the common people … Which is too violent in nature'.[2] Gower saw the people as one of the raging elements—prone to violence, destructive, and unstoppable. Yet the year 1377 had, at first glance, been a rather peaceful one. Early in the year, there had been protests in Wiltshire, Surrey, and Devon—isolated incidents of unrest as some rural labourers went on strike and refused to perform their required labour services for the local landowners.[3] The strikes and the protests never amounted to anything significant; it seemed as though it was business as usual. Although a new boy king, Richard II, had been crowned on 16 July that same year, the business of government would continue with the king ruling under the supervision of a set of handpicked advisors. Yet Gower's poem might as well have been a prophecy for just four years later, in the summer of 1381, the

people of England rose up and, with an army of almost 60,000, marched on London with a set of demands calling principally for the abolition of the hated poll tax and the end of serfdom.

We are indebted for our knowledge of the Peasants' Revolt to some of the vernacular poetry which has survived in manuscript form, like 'Tax has tenet us alle' ('Tax has ruined us all'). However, historians' main sources for the study of the rebellion come from the many chroniclers who wrote about it, including Jean Froissart, Thomas Walsingham, Henry Knighton, and

King Richard II. (Stephen Basdeo's Personal Collection)

John Gower. Other chronicles were anonymously written, such as the *Anonimalle Chronicle* which was described by R.B. Dobson as 'the single most important source for the history of the rising'.[4] Most of these chronicles are what we might term 'hostile witnesses' because they had little sympathy with the rebels and their aims. The chroniclers did not celebrate the rebels as rising up and demanding their rights, even if they disagreed with the poll tax in principle. Instead, the rebels were cast as an unruly and frightening 'mob' and the events of that summer of 1381 were bewailed as 'a great and unexpected calamity not experienced by previous ages'.[5]

Context

But how did English society get to a state in 1381 where its people were willing to rise up and defy the law and the government and march on London? To answer this question, we must go further back into the mid-fourteenth century. In 1346, news reached Europe of some strange and tragic events occurring in China; there had been floods and earthquakes in the region in preceding years, but in 1345, many people began dying of a frightening 'new' disease. This disease was, to give it its scientific name *Yersinia pestis*, or what we today call the Black Death. The disease soon reached Europe. By 1347, it had reached Constantinople. Cases were found in Italy, France, Greece, and northern parts of Africa by 1348. In 1349, it reached England. Contemporary accounts are almost apocalyptic in tone, relating the disappearance of whole towns and the burying of people in mass graves.[6] Its symptoms were truly horrific, as Giovanni Boccaccio revealed tumours grew in the groin and the armpits, some as large as apples, while black spots appeared all over the body.[7] These symptoms were accompanied by a high fever and vomiting up of blood and the victim usually died between forty-eight hours and a week after first contracting symptoms. The death toll in Europe was truly staggering.[8] With an eighty per cent mortality rate, the Black Death is estimated to have killed between seventy-five and 200 million people in Eurasia, or thirty to sixty per cent of the population.[9]

The poor suffered most although there were plenty of deaths among the richer classes of society to show that the Black Death was no respecter of titles or status. Yet if a person managed to avoid contracting the disease, then they

John of Gaunt. (Stephen Basdeo's Personal Collection)

3

might take advantage of the shortage of labour to improve their condition. English society in the fourteenth century was, at least in theory, a feudal society. At the top of the pyramid was the monarch, to whom the clergy and the nobility under him were obliged to pay taxes and/or provide services. Underneath these were the peasants—usually families who possessed the means of agricultural production and worked on small landholdings, leased from the local lord, who provided the lord with rent payments and a portion of their agricultural produce, while also keeping some produce for their subsistence. Alongside these peasants were certain free labourers who did not own any land but worked on the land for a small wage, and who can also be classed as part of the peasant class.[10] At the very bottom of society were the serfs or villeins—these people were considered as the personal property of their lord who were bound to perform labour services essentially for free or for a very small wage, and serfs could neither rent nor emigrate from the village without the lord's permission. A lord might even impose fines on the serf at will.[11] A common saying was that serfs 'owned nothing but their belly' and their only legal protection against the whims of their lord was that they might not be killed or mutilated without a proper trial.

This social structure was well-suited for an agrarian economy but the feudal system came under increasing strain in the first half of the fourteenth century, not least because it could not easily accommodate the increasing economic and political importance of the town-based mercantile classes. After all, we have seen how after Simon de Montfort's rebellion subsequent monarchs felt obliged to call representatives of the burgesses to parliament. As a result of the Black Death, there was a shortage of labour. The peasants and some free labourers began to demand higher wages and got them while some serfs likewise began clamouring for a wage and certain rights. The shortage of labour even extended to the church as there were not enough priests to perform basic functions such as burial rites, and even chaplains began to demand more money for performing basic liturgical services.[12] Edward III's government responded to demands for higher wages by passing the Statute of Labourers in 1351 to combat 'the malice of servants who were idle and unwilling to serve after the pestilence without taking outrageous wages'.[13] It is hard for any government to successfully enforce any rules against the law of supply and demand and the successful enforcement of the Statute of Labourers was, to put it mildly, haphazard and in some areas. Particularly in the north of England, it had barely any effect at all. It was, however, enforced successfully in the south of England for some decades, and the coincidence that the Peasants' Revolt began in areas that applied the law to its fullest extent have been remarked upon by one historian as one potential factor in the outbreak of the rebellion.[14] Overall, as A.E. Levett remarked: 'the Black Death did not, in any strictly economic sense cause the Peasants' Revolt or the break-down of villeinage, but it gave birth, in many cases, to a smouldering feeling of discontent, which found its outlet in the rising of 1381'.[15]

There were people who were only too ready to stoke these 'smouldering feelings of discontent'. One man, in particular, was the bane of the establishment: John Ball. A mendicant priest, he travelled from town to town, village to village, preaching a

John Ball preaching to the Commons, from Froissart's *Chronicles*. (Stephen Basdeo's Personal Collection)

radical message of equality. To Ball, there were essentially two classes in society: the rich and the poor, the haves and the have-nots. The one enjoyed life and lived upon the produce of the labour of the have-nots, the poor had nothing:

The ryche maketh myry,	The rich make merry
Sed vulgus collacrematur;	*But the common people weep;*
The pepulle ys wery,	The people are weary
Quia ferme depopulator	*Since the land is nearly laid waste.*[16]

After church on a Sunday, Ball would gather people around him and begin preaching his message. Froissart recorded one of his typical speeches and, in what was quite a radical message for the age, advocated for the common ownership of property and the abolition of social distinctions:

> Good people, things cannot go right in England and never will, until goods are held in common and there are no more villeins and gentlefolk, but we are all one and the same. In what way are those whom we call lords greater masters than ourselves? How have they deserved it? Why do

5

they hold us in bondage? If we all spring from a single father and mother, Adam and Eve, how can they claim or prove that they are lords more than us, except by making us produce and grow the wealth which they spend? They are clad in velvet and camlet lined with squirrel and ermine, while we go dressed in coarse cloth. They have the wines, the spices and the good bread: we have the rye, the husks and the straw, and we drink water. They have shelter and ease in their fine manors, and we have hardship and toil, the wind and the rain in the fields. And from us must come, from our labour, the things which keep them in luxury. We are called serfs and beaten if we are slow in our service to them, yet we have no sovereign lord we can complain to, none to hear us and do us justice.[17]

Whether this speech was wholly made up by Froissart is difficult to say but it certainly encapsulated Ball's ideology. Some historians have speculated that Ball was a Lollard—a follower of John Wycliffe (c.1320–84). Wycliffe was a religious radical who protested against the many abuses of the Roman Catholic Church, including the sale of indulgences and the practice of private confession. The Lollards also held that praying to saints was a form of idolatry and argued that the Bible should be read in English so all people could understand its message, in opposition to the Church's official position that the Bible should be read out in Latin. Ball may have been associated with the Lollards at some point, although the only explicit connection between Ball and Wycliffe comes from a contrived confession written after Ball's death.[18] Whether he was a Lollard or not is immaterial; Ball's own religious sentiments may indeed have corresponded with those espoused by the Lollards, yet the Lollards were concerned primarily with religious reform. It was relatively uncontroversial to criticise corruption in the church. William Langland's allegorical poem *Piers Plowman* (c.1377) criticised the Roman Catholic Church on several issues and some scholars have argued that the poem is 'proto-Protestant'.[19] Even Wycliffe had allies in high places; the 'power behind the throne' in Richard II's days, John of Gaunt, was said to be a follower of John Wycliffe. Ball, in contrast, aimed at political and social reform. He used the teachings of the Bible to justify his egalitarian message and that made him dangerous. He first came to the authorities' notice in 1364 when he was arrested for 'preaching articles of faith contrary to the faith of the church to the peril of his soul and the souls of others, especially of laymen'.[20] Although he was eventually released, he was a thorn in the side of the religious and political establishment and further periodical spells in prison in the lead up to the revolt were to occur.

As well as disease and economic oppression, another feature of the 'smouldering discontent' was opposition to the government's continuation of a costly war against France. This was the era of the Hundred Years' War (1337–1453). Instead of seeing this as one long period of warfare, it was actually a number of intermittent conflicts between England and France fought with the aim of who should rule territory in the latter country. William the Conqueror was the Duke of Normandy and subsequent English monarchs laid claim to and ruled various territories in France. Due to various conflicts, by the war's beginning in 1337, the only English domain which remained in

France was Gascony. Tensions arose when the French throne passed to Phillip, Count of Valois, who confiscated England's remaining possessions in France, which then prompted Edward III to pursue England's historic claims to the territory of Aquitaine.

The English had some notable successes early on in the war, such as the Battle of Crecy and the capture of Calais—which English monarchs would rule until 1500—but by the 1370s, the war was going badly for the English. John of Gaunt and John de Montford led a 9,000 men strong army through a disastrous *chavauchée* ('scorched earth') campaign in 1373. A year before this, the naval Battle of La Rochelle resulted in a French victory and ended England's naval supremacy.[21] To people back in England, the entire war seemed 'ill-managed and expensive'.[22] To add to the nation's demoralisation, England's star warrior, Edward of Woodstock, 'The Black Prince', was suffering from a debilitating illness and died in 1376 and a year later King Edward III also died. The throne of England, therefore, passed to the Black Prince's son, the ten-year-old Richard of Bordeaux, who was crowned on 16 July 1377 as Richard II. Parliament decided that a regency should be established until Richard reached the age of majority—this was common when the ruling monarch was deemed too young to shoulder the burden of running the state. Richard's uncle, John of Gaunt, was widely disliked among the ruling elites. One of the wealthiest men in England, his hold over the government had increased since the early 1370s because of Edward III's old age and the Black Prince's death. Parliament wanted Gaunt to be involved as little as possible with the business of government, fearing that he might attempt to overthrow the boy king and place himself on the throne. Nevertheless, in spite of parliament's efforts to exclude him from high office, he still retained a lot of influence over the king himself.

Gaunt was also unpopular with the people at large because he advocated the continuance of the war and seemed to be demanding ever more men and money to be given to him for the cause. In view of the war's increasing cost, in 1377, it was Gaunt who convinced parliament to levy the first-ever poll tax in England: every person over the age of fourteen would be required to pay one groat (4d) in tax. Gaunt hardly endeared himself to the population when he initiated this tax, and further to this there was the ill-fated expedition of 5,000 men the following year where, under Gaunt's command, the English laid siege to St Malo but suffered a humiliating defeat. It seemed as though ever more men and increasing amounts of money were needed for this ill-managed war. The revenue from the first poll tax earned the government £22,000; the ill-fated Breton campaign had cost the government £5,000. And the government was planning another attack on France the year following Gaunt's disastrous expedition.[23] Thus, in their wisdom, in 1379, the government decided that a fresh poll tax was needed to meet the nation's military cost. This time somewhat fairer, the tax was graduated according to a person's status, meaning that the rich paid more than the poor, and only persons over sixteen years old had to pay it. A franklin in Wath, Yorkshire, for example, was liable to pay 40d; one Roger Bacon and his wife Emma had to pay 12d; Robert Hesilheued and Margaret his wife were required to cough up 6d, and the single woman Johanna Bythewater paid just 4d.[24] Vagrants and the destitute had always been exempt from poll taxes and this time was no different.[25] Yet even this tax could not satisfy the government's needs and the total returns were much lower than in 1377. The people were partly to blame for this—medieval people up and down the country were very good at finding ways to avoid paying their taxes, while there is some evidence to suggest that during the collection of the first poll tax, some tax gatherers themselves did not bother to collect taxes from some poorer people in spite of the fact that, technically according to the law, they should have been able to pay.[26]

With low returns and tax evasion rife, in Northampton on 5 November 1380, parliament decided that another poll tax would be collected. This decision came in the wake of a particularly bad harvest and a harsh winter, and the government now meant business. The age of eligibility was lowered to fifteen and the tax applied to all men and women whether they were single or married. All would have to pay a tax of 12d. There would be very few exemptions; not even those craftsmen and labourers who worked for the church would be exempt, as they were previously. And it would have to be collected quickly: two-thirds of the money was to be collected by the end of January 1381 and the rest had to be paid by June the same year. To give the government the benefit of the doubt, we should note that the government expected each town and parish to forward to the exchequer a set amount, and their advice was that this generally worked out at a flat fee of 12d per head.[27] How it was to be collected, however, was left up to the discretion of tax collectors.

The winter was harsh and the harvest had been bad. The war was being lost and it seemed as though it was too expensive to pursue. Grievances about poll tax emanated from the lips of the poor, the peasants and tradesmen. In light of this, the authorities deemed it prudent to imprison the troublesome priest John Ball once again in April 1381. Even parliament was suspicious of the ends to which the tax was going to be used, and some in parliament viewed this third and latest tax as simply another ruse for John of Gaunt to fill his coffers. The government had calculated that £110,000 needed to be raised for the nation's defence. The Archbishop and Chancellor of the Exchequer, Simon Sudbury, had requested £160,000 and the justification for the extra amount seemed rather flimsy. At any rate, parliament granted the government's request for a new tax, even though its representatives knew that it would be extremely unpopular with people. Parliament even exempted members of their own class from the responsibility of collecting it, whereas before its members would have served as collectors—an important condition which parliament attached to the granting of the poll tax was that 'the knights, citizens, and burgesses who have come to this present parliament are by no means to be made collectors or controllers of the aforesaid sums'.[28] The responsibility for collecting the new tax was therefore delegated to an assortment of bailiffs, constables, mayors, and two men from each village and township who had been specifically appointed to the position of tax gatherer because of their local knowledge.

The Spark

People still managed to evade the new tax and the government was exasperated with the situation. Special commissioners were appointed by the government to travel to each village and township and investigate why the revenue collected was different to the calculations which the government had expected. One such commissioner was Thomas de Bamptoun (called John in some accounts). On 30 May, Bamptoun travelled to Brentwood in Essex. He summoned before him all the villagers of Fobbing, Corringham, and Standford-le-Hope and demanded that they all pay the tax immediately. The villagers, who had chosen as their spokesman one Thomas Baker, declared that they would not be paying because they had already paid the tax and could prove it by showing him receipts. Bamptoun had two armed soldiers with him and ordered the arrest of those who refused to pay but the crowd grew angry and attempts to arrest those who refused to pay up were futile—the crowd protected the ringleaders and refused to let them be arrested. Bamptoun and his men hastily withdrew from Brentwood and went back to London with their tails between their legs.

The revolt had started.

The people of Fobbing, Corringham, and Standford-le-Hope sent messengers to the surrounding towns and villages urging people to rise up against their lords and the poll tax collectors. News of what happened at Brentwood travelled fast throughout Hertfordshire, Sussex, Essex, and Kent. The rebels were not illiterate brutes but included people who could read and write. These people were used, as Steven Justice points out, to write messages on parchment urging people to rise up. These written messages which the rebels made use of were called *escrowez* or *schedulae*—according to Steven Justice the closest equivalent we have in our own time is broadside: a single sheet of paper containing urgent public announcements or news. These broadsides were then mounted in public spaces in nearby villages and towns.[29] Some of the richer townsfolk who decided against joining in the rebellion had their houses destroyed, and one man in Maidstone was even beheaded for his refusal.[30] The rebels' next act on 6 June was to rescue a serf named Robert Belling from Rochester gaol, who had been imprisoned there at the behest of Sir Simon de Burley, one of the Knights of the King's Household.[31] Although the rebels laid siege to the castle for a day and a half, the constable decided that it would just be easier to set the man free and open the castle. The rebels then entered and freed all of the prisoners.

By 7 June, the rebels of Kent appointed a man named Wat Tyler as their leader. Little is known of Wat Tyler's early life, where he was born, who his parents were, or even whether he had any children. Some sources suggest that he may have been a soldier who had served in France during the wars and was appointed because of his experience in leading soldiers. Other sources allege that he was a blacksmith, or that his surname, Tyler, indicated his trade — that he was a tiler. Another source, written much later by John Stow, titled *A Summarie of English Chronicles* (1566), alleges that Tyler—who was renamed John Tiler in this source—was moved to lead the revolt after a tax collector visited Tyler's home. The tax collector, not believing that Tyler's daughter was a minor, attempted to indecently search her. In the words of another later source that repeated these claims, the tax collector 'pulled up his daughter's cloaths [sic] to see if she was arrived at the age of puberty'.[32] According to Stow's account, this enraged Tyler who, being a blacksmith, took his hammer and smote the tax collector, killing him stone dead. This particular narrative was repeated in many later novels, plays, and history books during the eighteenth and nineteenth centuries, to the point where people viewed

The rebels await an audience with Richard II, from Froissart's *Chronicles*. (Stephen Basdeo's Personal Collection)

it as a historical fact. However, there are no primary sources that relate this occurrence and it almost certainly never happened.

Prior to June, John Ball had once again found himself on the wrong side of the Church authorities and he was currently imprisoned in Maidstone. Under Wat Tyler's command, the rebels besieged Maidstone gaol, freed all of the prisoners, including John Ball. Yet it wasn't men who had all the fun. Sylvia Federico has also uncovered the stories of a number of women who took a leading role in the rebellion.[33] A woman named Julia Pouchere came to Maidstone and by all accounts took a leading role in laying siege to the gaol.[34] John Ball being freed, the rebels asked him to accompany them on their planned march to London, where they would take their grievances directly to the king. They also promised to appoint Ball as the Archbishop. The fact that the rebels thought to free John Ball testifies to the man's fame and popularity—he had of course first been arrested in 1364 and the message which he preached must surely have been popular with people who had seen their rights eroded, their wages stagnate, and their income decimated with three successive poll taxes. After Ball's liberation from Maidstone gaol, the rebels began their march on Canterbury on 9 June. Four thousand men entered the city on the following day, and many of them attended Mass at St Thomas' Mother Church. The castle and the Archbishop of Canterbury's palace were then ransacked. Afterwards, the Mayor, bailiffs, and the common people of the town were then assembled before the rebels. Those present were asked to swear 'to be faithful to King Richard and the loyal commons of England'.[35] Still the rebels, it will be noted, found no fault with the king. They merely resolved 'to get rid of all lords, archbishops, bishops, abbots and priors, as well as most of the monks and canons'. How convenient, then, that the rebels had Ball with them—a man of God from among their own ranks whom they could elevate to the position of an archbishop.[36] Indeed, the rebels were not a mindless mob. As we shall see shortly, they had a well-thought-out list of demands. As one of the rebels' demands was an end to serfdom, while the mob was at Canterbury, they entered the houses of several local nobles and destroyed any documents that might confirm whether a person was a bondman or not.

The next day, 11 June, Tyler and the people began their march from Canterbury to London. On the way, they came across twelve lawyers and twelve knights, accosting them and forcing them to swear allegiance to their cause upon pain of death. Also along the way, they ransacked the houses of several nobles. The *Anonimalle Chronicle* records that they did the most damage to the house of Thomas de Heseldene, one of Gaunt's men, by razing his house to the ground and stealing his livestock.[37] By this time the king had heard of the uprising, and on their way to London on 11 June the rebels were met by some of the king's messengers who asked the rebels why they were acting thus. The rebels replied that they were rising up 'to save [the King] and to destroy traitors to him and his kingdom'.[38] The king's messengers then informed the rebels that Richard would meet with them and hear their demands. It is also said by Froissart—*only* by Froissart, it should be noted—that the Queen Mother, Joan of Kent (1328–85), the wife of Edward the Black Prince, was returning from a pilgrimage to Canterbury and ran into the rebels. Froissart records that the insurgents treated her in a very disrespectful manner:

> She was in great jeopardy to have been lost, for these people came to her chare [sic] and dealt rudely with her, whereof the good lady was in great doubt lest they would have done some villainy to her or to her damosels. Howbeit, God kept her, and she came in one day from Canterbury to London, for she never durst tarry by the way.[39]

This 'fact' deserves to be taken with a pinch of salt; given the fact that throughout the whole affair the rebels repeatedly emphasised their loyalty to the king, it seems unlikely that they would have 'dealt rudely' with the queen mother.

The following day, the rebels from Kent arrived at Blackheath. According to Thomas Walsingham, it was here that John Ball addressed a sermon to the assembled multitude with the famous theme, 'whan Adam dalf and Eve span, Wo was thanne a gentilman?'[40] Meantime, the rebels from Essex made camp at Mile End, while more rebels were arriving from Surrey, Sussex, Norfolk, Cambridgeshire, Buckinghamshire, and Hertfordshire. It is estimated that the number of the rebels now amounted to 50,000 people according to some accounts, with 30,000 alone being in Wat Tyler's army.

The country was erupting in violence. While the rebels from Kent and the surrounding counties were beginning their march upon London, riots occurred in other towns and cities. At Cambridge on 14 June, rebels invaded the university and ransacked the library. Yet they were not, as might be supposed, an unhinged mob who sought only to destroy. They had a great respect for learning and the university's library containing rare Bibles, prayer books, chronicles, and manuscripts from time immemorial were spared. The rebels only destroyed court rolls and muniments (title deeds that proved a lord's right to a certain patch of land or an estate).[41] This was a well-thought-out strategy; in fourteenth century court cases, if a dispute arose between a lord and a tenant, the lord had to be able to give evidence that the tenant owed him a particular service or rent-in-kind.

At this point, on 13 June, the king, who only had 520 soldiers with him, retreated to the Tower of London along with Sudbury and Robert Hales, the Lord High Treasurer. The high walls and heavy fortifications of the Tower would, of course, have provided some protection against any sudden turn in the rebels' disposition toward him. Upon hearing that the king had retreated to the Tower, Wat Tyler sent a message to the king, asking to meet him at Rotherhithe. The king agreed to this, and by the afternoon he boarded a barge and travelled the short way down the Thames to meet Tyler and the

The rebels execute the Archbishop of Canterbury, from Froissart's *Chronicles*. (Stephen Basdeo's Personal Collection)

rebels. This was quite a brave act for the young king, as the sight of the rebels lining the banks of the Thames while he was sailing down it to meet with Tyler must have been a daunting one. Accompanying the now fourteen-year-old king was Sudbury and Hales. It might have been better for the young king to go alone, all things considered, for when the people saw the two hated officials in the barge with Richard the crowd became incensed, calling them traitors. It was these two men, after all, who had first proposed the 1381 poll tax. Perhaps wisely considering the circumstances, Richard decided not to disembark and after ten minutes he decided to return to the Tower.

On the afternoon of the same day, rebels from Kent arrived at the Southwark entrance to London. The rebels enjoyed a significant degree of support from the residents of London as well. After all, those in London were also liable to pay the poll tax, just as those from the country had been. Thus, some of the rebels' supporters from inside the city lowered the drawbridge and opened the gates to allow them to enter. The rebels' hatred of John of Gaunt meant that one of their first acts, when they managed to get inside the walls, was to rob and then set fire to Gaunt's palace at the Savoy. According to Froissart, the sacking of Gaunt's residence was done under the instruction and supervision of Wat Tyler, John Ball, and Jack Straw.[42] It is more likely, however, that the destruction of Gaunt's palace was carried out at the instigation of John Farringdon, a rebel from Essex. This was the man who, on the same evening, led the rebels into the Hospitallers' Priory at Clerkenwell. There they beheaded the master of the order, and burned the building and several of the surrounding edifices to the ground.[43] The rebels of course were not saints and sadly, if Froissart and other chroniclers are to be believed, some of the rebels did turn nasty, for it is reported in Froissart's account that some of them began attacking the houses of the Lombards, an immigrant community in London.[44] Some of the other rebels also used the disturbances to enrich themselves and settle scores against their neighbours at the same time. This is what we see, for example, in the records of the Court of Common Pleas: Joan Aleyn stole 2s 6d from her neighbour; Agnes Stevenage burgled the house of John Brode, an *escheator* in Kent, although an *escheator* was a royal official charged with, among other things, collecting taxes, so perhaps her actions were way of her getting revenge on the government *and* enriching herself.[45] Furthering the rebels' aims while taking a little for herself is also what a woman named Johanna did while Gaunt's palace was being attacked. Johanna took a chest containing over £1000 from Gaunt's palace, then took a boat to Southwark where she divided the spoils between herself and her friends.[46]

Although Tyler had wanted to meet with the king on the same morning, it will be remembered that the young king, perhaps wisely though not very bravely, sped away back to the Tower in his barge. It was not until the following day around 8.00 am that Tyler came face to face with the boy king at Mile End. Knighton says that most of the king's knights left him to face the mob alone, '[having] completely lost their courage and showed, sad to say, no spirit whatsoever; they seemed to be struck by womanly fears and dared not leave but stayed within the Tower'.[47] It was here that Wat Tyler put the rebels' reasonable grievances before the king: the abolition of the poll tax, end of all feudal services, the freedom to buy and sell goods (serfs at this time could not freely sell the surplus produce of their labour in the marketplace), and a general pardon for all offences that had been committed during the rebellion. Wat Tyler also accused those responsible for the poll tax as being guilty of corruption and he demanded that they should be executed. The king agreed to the first set of demands by granting a charter confirming them.[48] However, Richard said that his people could be confident that, if any of his advisors were guilty of corruption then they would be punished to the full extent of the law. The granting of the charter, and Richard's assurances, appeared to placate much of the mob for the moment and many rebels agreed to withdraw.

Gilbert á Beckett once joked: 'Whether or no Wat suspected the worthlessness of charters, which might be sworn to one day and treated as waste paper the next, he refused to be satisfied'.[49] Although writing with his tongue firmly in his cheek, Beckett was right: the rebels, while they respected the king, had little trust in the government who they suspected would, in a heartbeat, renege on the pledges enshrined in the charter. Tyler, Straw, Ball and quite a few of the rebels must have suspected this, and while many rebels returned home, Tyler decamped to Smithfield with about 30,000 of his men.[50]

While Tyler was with the king at Mile End, a contingent of rebels remained near the Tower. Led by John Starling, this group gained admittance to the castle, and there they laid hands upon Sudbury. They dragged him to Tower Hill where he was beheaded. His head was then placed upon a spike, and paraded through the city of London. It is here also that Robert Hales, the King's Treasurer, and John Legge (who along with Sudbury was instrumental in bringing about the hated tax) met their ends in a similar manner.

On the following day, the king expressed a desire to meet with Wat Tyler again at Smithfield. The king arrived with a number of armed retainers, and inquired why, when the charters had been granted, the rebels were still in London. According to the *Eulogium Historiarum*, when the king arrived Tyler refused to dismount from his horse or remove his cap, and according to some accounts he spoke to the sovereign in a surly manner.[51] Tyler reiterated his previous demands to the king, as well as adding several new ones, some of which were undoubtedly inspired by the teachings of John Ball: the end of tithes, the abolition of bishops, the redistribution of wealth, equality before the law, and the freedom to kill animals in the forest. At this point, Wat Tyler noticed that one of the king's squires was bearing a dagger, and Tyler demanded that the dagger be given to him. The king ordered his squire to do as Tyler commanded. Tyler then demanded the sword that the squire was carrying. It is at that this point that the villain of the story emerges from the shadows. William Walworth (d. 1385), the Mayor of London, had also arrived at Smithfield with several armed men. Upon seeing that Tyler had not been giving due deference to the king, Walworth began to quarrel with Tyler, at which Walworth exclaimed:

> Thou false stinking knave, shalt thou speak thus in the presence of the King my natural Lord? I commit never to live, without thou shalt dearly abye it.[52]

Walworth then drew forth his dagger and struck Tyler in the neck, causing him to fall from his horse. The next instant, one of the king's squires, John Cavendish (or Ralph Standish in some accounts), alighted from his horse and stabbed Tyler in the stomach.[53] This was the fatal blow, and Tyler did not recover from this murderous act.[54] The rebels

14

grew angry that Walworth had killed their leader, crying, 'Ah, our captain is slain, let us go and slay them all.'[55] Perhaps sensing a bloodbath, the King addressed the rebels:

'Sirs, what aileth you? Ye shall have no captain but me: I am your King: be all in peace'. And so the most part of the people that heard the King speak and saw him among them, were shamefast and began to wax peaceable and to depart.[56]

The king then turned to his advisors and asked them what should be done with the remaining rebels. Richard was advised to allow them to withdraw by Walworth, with a proviso that they should pursue them afterwards. Afterwards, Tyler's body was decapitated in Smithfield and his head was placed upon a spike, carried through London, and set atop London Bridge as a warning to others who might dare defy the established order.

Predictably, Richard annulled all of the charters that he had granted previously. His army pursued some of the rebels on their way out of London, and a battle was fought between the king's soldiers and the Essex men on 28 June. On that day, approximately 500 of the rebels were killed. One by one, former leading figures in the rebellion were hunted down. Thomas Baker and his comrades from Fobbing were executed at Chelmsford. John Ball was arrested in Coventry and taken to St Albans where he

The death of Wat Tyler, from Froissart's *Chronicles*. (Stephen Basdeo's Personal Collection)

suffered the horrific punishment of being hung, drawn, and quartered on 15 July. The rebel movement, without its key central figures, effectively collapsed. Further afield, in places such as Yorkshire, Lincolnshire, and Suffolk, other rebel leaders were hunted down and dealt with in the manner of the times.

Jack Straw was also taken afterwards. He was also sentenced to a traitor's death but his case is interesting because we have his supposed last speech. The gist of this, when loosely translated into English, is as follows:

> We would have murdered all the knights, esquires, and gentlemen in his retinue and to have led the king royally used, up and down, that with the sight of him, so that the common people would have followed us, and when we had got together an innumerable multitude, we would have suddenly put to death in every country, the Lords and masters of the common people, who might have resisted us, and we would have destroyed the Knights of Saint John, lastly we would have killed the king himself, and all bishops, monks, canons, parsons. We would only have spared the beggar friars in order that they might administer the sacraments. We would have made kings: Wat Tyler in Kent, and we would have appointed other kings in other counties.[57]

After this short speech, Straw was executed and his head was placed on top of London Bridge alongside that of his fellow rebel leader, Wat Tyler. It is likely that the other parts of Straw's body, as well as Tyler and Ball's, were sent to be displayed in public spaces in other cities, although none of the accounts of the revolt tell us where.

Yet the young king would eventually receive his comeuppance. Perhaps the manner in which he dealt with the rebels made him paranoid about any perceived threats to his authority. Many nobles were unhappy with the way in which Richard went on to abuse his power later in life, so much so that, in 1388, a group of nobles sought to impeach the king's favourite advisors in an attempt to curb what was widely perceived as an increasingly tyrannical reign. The nobles who challenged Richard were led by none other than John of Gaunt's son, Henry Bolingbroke (1367–1413). In response to the nobles' challenging of his power, at a parliament called in Shrewsbury in 1399, Richard effectively declared himself above the law, and placed all parliamentary power into the hands of twelve Lords and six commoners who, needless to say, were loyal to him. He was now to all intents and purposes an absolute ruler.

Enough was enough. In 1399, Bolingbroke, whose father's estate had been seized by Richard upon his death earlier in the year, returned to England from France with a view to regaining his lands and titles. Although Bolingbroke insisted that this was all that he wanted to do, the small band of followers that arrived with him when he first landed at Yorkshire soon swelled. Richard at this moment was in Ireland, so as Bolingbroke and his army progressed through England, they encountered little resistance. When Richard returned to England, upon seeing that Bolingbroke had the support of the nobles and that, militarily, he held the upper hand, he surrendered to Henry at Flint Castle. From there, Richard was taken to Pontefract Castle and imprisoned. The circumstances of his death are very unclear, although it appears to be generally agreed amongst historians that Richard simply starved to death in the vaults of the castle.[58]

There are many 'what ifs' in history, and, in spite of Wat Tyler's death, had the king kept his word, and not annulled the charters granted to the bondmen, his reign might have gone down as an example of good government. But it was not to be.

Legacy of the Peasants' Revolt

The Peasants' Revolt itself achieved very little. The rebels' demands remained, as we have seen, unrealised. The king reneged on his promises after Tyler's execution at Smithfield. The Peasants' Revolt did not end feudalism but was rather a symptom of the strain that the feudal system was undergoing. Even at the beginning of the century increasing numbers of people were working for wages and, in spite of the Statute of Labourers, both free men and serfs were increasingly able to demand wages for service. The Black Death was a shock to the feudal system and precipitated its decline even further. Even after the Black Death and the Peasants' Revolt, in villages where a manorial lord was unwilling to pay wages and insisted upon imposing his feudal rights, serfs simply absconded to the cities where they could work for a wage. Yet the revolt was important because it was the first time that the people themselves had risen up against the ruling class. There had been revolts before, of course. The Barons' Rebellion which led to King John signing Magna Carta in 1215, or Simon de Montfort's Rebellion in 1265 immediately spring to mind. But these were rebellions led by disaffected noblemen. Not so with the Peasants' Revolt—this truly was a revolt by the people.

The fact that in 1381 the people attempted to take power to themselves is probably why Wat Tyler and the events of that year would be remembered throughout succeeding ages, being an inspiration to revolutionaries, Chartists, and socialists.[59] Thomas Paine's *Common Sense* (1776)—a book which advocated independence for the Thirteen American Colonies from Great Britain—heaped praise on Tyler and argued that his actions merited a monument at Smithfield:

Robert Southey, author of Wat Tyler: A Dramatic Poem (1794). (Stephen Basdeo's Personal Collection)

Tyler appears to have been an intrepid and disinterested man, with respect to himself. All his proposals made to Richard, were on a more just and public ground, than those which had been made to [King] John by the Barons; and notwithstanding the sycophancy of historians, and men like Mr. Burke, who seek to gloss over a base action of the Court by traducing Tyler, his fame will outlive their falsehood. If the Barons merited a monument at Runnymede, Tyler merits one in Smithfield.[60]

At the beginning of the French Revolution in 1789, many radicals in Britain were inspired by the French who had finally, it seemed, put the final nail in feudalism's coffin. They wished for a similar revolution to take place in England. Among them was Robert Southey who wrote, in 1794, a short poem titled *Wat Tyler*, in which the politics of Britain in the 1790s were superimposed onto England in 1381. In this poem, Wat is a freedom fighter, taking up the country's cause against the unjust taxes that have been levied to finance Richard II's wars (with a message for his own day regarding the war against Revolutionary France):

> Think you we do not feel the wrongs we suffer?
> The hour of retribution is at hand,
> And tyrants tremble – mark me, King of England.[61]

There appears to have been a trend at this point for radicals appropriating figures from England's medieval past: one year after Southey was writing there appeared Joseph Ritson's *Robin Hood: A Collection of All the Ancient Poems, Songs, and Ballads* (1795) which portrayed the outlaw as a medieval Thomas Paine.[62]

Perhaps the greatest fictional account of Wat Tyler's life comes from Pierce Egan the Younger's *Wat Tyler, or, the Rebellion of 1381* (1841). In this novel, Tyler is truly allowed to live up to his potential. Thomas Paine held him up as a working-class hero, while Robert Southey envisioned him as a man who fought for 'Liberty! Liberty!' Circumstances had changed when Egan was writing, and Britain saw the emergence of Chartism between 1838 and 1858. It was a working-class political reform movement which sought to establish a People's Charter: A vote for every man twenty-one years of age, of sound mind, and not undergoing punishment for a crime; the Secret Ballot; no Property Qualification for MPs; Payment of MPs, thus enabling an honest working man to serve a constituency; equally-sized constituencies, securing the same amount of representation for the same number of electors, instead of allowing small constituencies to swamp the votes of large ones; and annual parliamentary elections.

In Egan's novel, Tyler is a man who fights for a medieval form of a People's Charter (the Chartists even had a Wat Tyler Brigade). Egan borrows the Saxon versus Norman theme from Walter Scott's *Ivanhoe* (1819). The Normans represent the nineteenth century political establishment, while Tyler—who is of Saxon descent in the novel—represents the British working classes. Egan's Tyler attempts to obtain the end of serfdom for the Anglo-Saxons (which means enfranchisement

Pierce Egan the Younger and illustrations from his epic novel *Wat Tyler: The Rebellion of 1381.*
(Stephen Basdeo's Personal Collection)

for the nineteenth century working classes) through 'petitions' but to no avail. Tyler then leads a peasants' revolt in order to obtain 'a code of laws or charter'.[63] Egan's retelling of the revolt is largely faithful to the historical record, with the exception that Tyler is conveyed to his home after the events at Smithfield and there dies in his bed.

Tyler was a great source of inspiration to the Chartists. His name was invoked in order to inspire activists to never lose hope in the great work they were trying to achieve. An oft-reprinted Chartist poem titled 'A Song for the Next Rebellion', which first appeared in *The Odd Fellow* in 1841 and made successive appearances in the *Northern Star* and other Chartist publications, depicted Tyler as the first in a long line of brave revolutionaries whose legacy was being continued by themselves:

> Up! Up! Ye English peasantry, for whom Wat Tyler bled;
> Up! Citied serfs, whose sturdy sires Cade and Archamber led;
> Up! Up! For equal rights and laws: your cause is all as good
> As when in the presence of the Smith a traitor monarch stood.[64]

Previous rebels such as Tyler, Cade, and Archamber may have failed, but victory is sure to belong to the 'citied serfs'—the factory workers, the seamstresses, the coal miners. The poem continued:

> Up! Up! If ye are Englishmen; be mindful of the day,
> When Cromwell strode o'er Worcester's fields, and scared a King away.
> Though Cade and Ket and Tyler failed, the 'crowning mercy' came: -
> Hurrah for England's stalwart one! Your fortune be the same!
> [...]
> Up! Up! Ye toil-worn English slaves: if blood must needs be shed,
> Let it be England's tyrant lords, and not the famine-sped!
> Ay, hand-to-hand, and foot to foot, grapple with tyranny! –
> Our Saxon Thor is Lord again: Our England shall be free![65]

To the Chartists, Tyler was 'Our Saxon Thor'—a semi-godlike revolutionary—indicative of the high esteem in which they held his memory. Of course, the aims of the Chartists would not be realised. In spite of three successive petitions, open-air mass meetings, and support from some MPs and high profile journalists like G.W.M. Reynolds (1814–79) the government ignored their demands.

However, although the movement failed, all but one of the Chartists' demands were implemented—annual elections being deemed too impractical. In 1867, the right to vote was extended to the 'respectable' working class. In 1918, the franchise was extended further to all men and some women, while in 1928, all women were granted the right to vote. During this time, famous socialist activists like William Morris became the custodians, if you will, of Tyler's memory. Morris's *A Dream of John Ball* (1886) depicted the Peasants' Revolt as the precursor to the emergence of socialism in England.

Thus, Tyler's name could inspire hope and provide historical legitimacy to their political actions in the present. Many of the reformers and revolutionaries featured in this book looked back to Tyler for inspiration. Even within the living memory of many today, during the Poll Tax Riots at Trafalgar Square in the 1980s, people carried placards bearing the words: 'Avenge Wat Tyler'.

Notes

1. An early version of this chapter, which has been significantly expanded upon here, has been published in a previous book of mine: Stephen Basdeo, *The Life and Legend of a Rebel Leader: Wat Tyler* (Barnsley: Pen and Sword, 2018). For this, I would like to thank Barnaby Blacker, who proofread the original chapter.
2. John Gower, "John Gower Foresees the Peasants' Revolt," in *The Peasants' Revolt of 1381*, ed. R.B. Dobson (London: MacMillan, 1970), 95-96.
3. Rosamond Faith, "The 'Great Rumour' of 1377 and Peasant Ideology," in *The English Rising of 1381*, ed. Rodney Hilton and T.H. Alton (Cambridge: Cambridge University Press, 1987), 43–73.

4. R. B. Dobson, "Introduction to *Anonimalle Chronicle*," in *The Peasants' Revolt of 1381*, ed. R.B. Dobson (London: MacMillan, 1970), 123.

5. Thomas Walsingham, "The Outbreak of the Revolt according to Thomas Walsingham," in Dobson, 132.

6. Ole J. Benedictow, "The Black Death: The Greatest Catastrophe Ever," *History Today* March 3, 2005. Accessed February 23, 2020. https://www.historytoday.com/archive/black-death-greatest-catastrophe-ever

7. Giovanni Boccaccio, *The Decameron*, M. Rigg, trans. vol. 1 (London: David Campbell, 1921), 5-11

8. C.J. Duncan and S. Scott, "What Caused the Black Death?" *Postgraduate Medical Journal* no. 81 (2005): 315–20: The traditional interpretation, of course, is that the Black Death was a variant of Yersinia pestis. However, new theories have been advanced in the twenty-first century which offer differing explanations of what the disease was. Samuel Klein Cohn in *The Black Death Transformed* (2002) argued that the disease was not, in fact, caused by a strain of the aforementioned bacteria, although Cohn never offered an alternative to Yersinia pestis. However, since Cohn, there is some speculation from some scientists like Scott and Duncan that the Black Death was not Bubonic Plague, as is often assumed, but was actually related to the Ebola virus.

9. Suzanne Austin Alchon, *A Pest in the Land: New World Epidemics in a Global Perspective* (Albuquerque: University of New Mexico Press, 2003), 21.

10. Rodney Hilton, *The English Peasantry of the Later Middle Ages* (Oxford: Clarendon Press, 1975), 13.

11. Christopher Dyer, *An Age of Transition? Economy and Society in England in the Later Middle Ages* (Oxford: Clarendon Press, 2005), 34.

12. Knighton, "The Black Death of 1348-1329," 61.

13. "The Statute of Labourers," in Dobson, 64.

14. R. B. Dobson, "The Enforcement of the Statute of Labourers," in Dobson, 68.

15. A.E. Levett, *Studies in Manorial History* (Oxford: Oxford University Press, 1938), 134.

16. John Ball, "On the Times," in *Medieval English Political Writings* ed. James M. Dean (Kalamazoo, MI: Medieval Institute Publications, 1996), 141. Middle English is translated by me.

17. Jean Froissart, *Chronicles*, Geoffrey Brereton, trans. (London: Penguin, 1968), 212.

18. Margaret Aston, "Corpus Christi and Corpus Regni: Heresy and the Peasants' Revolt," *Past & Present* 143 (1994), 36.

19. James Simpson, *Piers Plowman: An Introduction*, 2nd ed. (Exeter: University of Exeter Press, 2007), 38–44; Mary Carruthers, *The Search for St. Truth: A Study of Meaning in Piers Plowman* (Evanston, IL: Northwestern University Press, 1973), 167.

20. Cited in Juliet Barker, *England Arise: The People, the King, and the Great Revolt of 1381* (London: Abacus, 2014), 428.

21. L. J. Andrew Villalon & Donald J. Kagay, *The Hundred Years War: a Wider Focus* (Leiden: Brill, 2005), 36.

22. Dan Jones, "The Peasants' Revolt," *History Today* June 2009, 34.
23. Dobson, *The Peasants' Revolt of 1381*, 111
24. Tithe, Constable and Various accounts, 1379-1782. [Microfilm]. Salt Lake City, Utah, Genealogical Society of Utah, 1988.
25. Carolyn C. Fenwick, "Introduction," in *The Poll Taxes of 1377, 1379, and 1381 Part 1: Bedfordshire* (Oxford: Oxford University Press, 1998), xxvi.
26. Fenwick, "Introduction," xxvi.
27. Christian Drummond Liddy, *War, Politics and Finance in Late Medieval English Towns: Bristol, York and the Crown, 1350–1400* (Woodbridge: Boydell, 2005), 93.
28. Barker, *England Arise*, 32.
29. Steven Justice, *Writing and Rebellion: England in 1381* (Berkeley and Los Angeles: University of California Press, 1994), 29.
30. "The Outbreak of the Revolt according to the "Anonimalle Chronicle," in Dobson, 127.
31. Ibid, 127n: although the *Anonimalle Chronicle* says that Burley was present and took an active part in arresting Belling, he was actually away in France negotiating Richard II's marriage with Anne of Bohemia.
32. Anon, "London and its Environs Described (1761)," *Project Gutenberg*, accessed April 2, 2020, www.projectgutenberg.org.
33. Sylvia Federico, "The Imaginary Society: Women in 1381," *Journal of British Studies* 40 no. 2 (2001): 159–83.
34. Federico, 167.
35. 'The Outbreak of the Revolt according to the "Anonimalle Chronicle"' in Dobson, 127-128.
36. Ibid.
37. Ibid.
38. Ibid.
39. Jean Froissart, "Wat Tyler's Rebellion," in *The Harvard Classics: Chronicle and Romance – Froissart, Malory, Holinshead. With Introductions, Notes, and Illustrations* ed. by Charles W. Elliot (New York: Collier, 1910) [Internet <https://www.gutenberg.org/files/13674/13674-h/13674-h.htm> Accessed 27 March 2017].
40. Thomas Walsingham, "John Ball's Sermon Theme," in *Medieval English Political Writings* ed. by James M. Dean (Kalamazoo, MI: Medieval Institute Publications, 1996), 140.
41. Justice, *Writing and Rebellion*, 44.
42. Jean Froissart, "The Rebels in London according to Froissart," in *The Peasants' Revolt of 1381* ed. by R. B. Dobson (London: MacMillan, 1970), 188.
43. Helen Nicholson, "The Hospitallers and the "Peasants' Revolt" of 1381 Revisited," in *The Military Orders Volume 3: History and Heritage* ed. Victor Mallia Milanes (Aldershot: Ashgate, 2007), 225.
44. Froissart, "The Rebels in London according to Froissart," 189: it is also said at this point that Wat Tyler had a former master of his, one Richard Lyon, killed. That Lyon was killed is evident in other accounts. However, his being a former master of Wat Tyler's is attested by no other source but Froissart's.

45. Federico, 165.

46. Ibid, 168.

47. Henry Knighton, "The Rebels in London according to Henry Knighton," in *The Peasants' Revolt of 1381* ed. R. B. Dobson (London: MacMillan, 1970), 185.

48. Knighton, "The Rebels in London according to Henry Knighton," 183.

49. Gilbert á Beckett, *The Comic History of England* (London: John Dicks [n.d.]), 112.

50. Froissart, 'The Rebels in London according to Froissart' in Dobson, 195.

51. 'The Peasants' Revolt according to the Continuator of the "Eulogium Historiarum"', in *The Peasants' Revolt of 1381* ed. by R. B. Dobson (London: MacMillan, 1970), 207.

52. Froissart, "The Rebels in London according to Froissart," 196.

53. Ibid.

54. Thomas James Benningfield, *London, 1900–1964: Armorial Bearings and Regalia of the London County Council, the Corporation of London and the Metropolitan Boroughs* (London: J Burrow & Co., 1964). pp. 21-23; throughout the early modern and modern periods, the dagger on the coat of arms of the city of London was said to commemorate the stabbing of Wat Tyler. However, research has shown that the arms were in use before 1381.

55. Froissart, "The Rebels in London according to Froissart," in Dobson 196.

56. Ibid.

57. Translations of this supposed last dying speech can be found in any one of the following works: Dobson, The Peasants' Revolt of 1381, 365-66; David Preest and James G. Clark, *The Chronica Maiora of Thomas Walsingham* (Woodbridge: Boydell, 2005); H. T. Riley, ed., *Chronica Monasterii S. Albani: Thomae Walsingham, Quondam Monachi S. Albani, Historia Anglicana*, London Rolls Series, 2 vols (London: Longman, 1872), I: x; Ralph Holinshed, et al., *The Chronicles of England*, 4 vols (London: Lucas Harrison, 1577), IV, 1036; John Stow, *A Summarie of the Chronicles of England* (London: Richard Bradocke, 1598), 149; Ferguson, Robert, *The History of All the Mobs, Tumults, and Insurrections in Great Britain* (London: J. Moore, 1715)

58. Anthony Tuck, 'Richard II (1367–1400)', in *The Oxford Dictionary of National Biography* (Oxford: Oxford University Press, 2004; Online Edn. 2008) [Internet <www.oxforddnb.com> Accessed 12 March 2017].

59. A complete history of Wat Tyler's post-medieval portrayals in popular culture is given in my book, cited above.

60. Thomas Paine, *Common Sense* (London, 1776), 112

61. Robert Southey, *Wat Tyler: A Dramatic Poem in Three Acts* (London: Sherwin, 1813), 10-11

62. See Stephen Basdeo, *Robin Hood: The Life and Legend of an Outlaw* (Barnsley: Pen and Sword, 2019)

63. Pierce Egan, *Wat Tyler, or, The Rebellion of 1381* (London: G. Pierce, 1847), 835

64. "Hymns for the Unenfranchised: A Song for the Next Rebellion", *The Odd Fellow* 21 August 1841, 3.

65. Ibid.

The 'Gentlemen' of the Jack Cade Rebellion

Alexander L. Kaufman

It would be wholly appropriate to consider how persons from the twenty-first century would consider any seditious activity to be the product of lesser beings. After all, in the current state of mass media's saturation of our lives with images of revolt, rebellion, and protest, so often the picture that emerges in static print and moveable digital files that reside online and on television is one of a mass of unsophisticated, brutish, and crazed communities. Civility, it would appear, is at a premium. However, and thankfully, social scientists, historians, and cultural studies scholars are often the ones who, through their research and analysis, observe that most events of social unrest are more complicated than they might initially appear and are the product of deep systemic problems within a country.

While riots, revolts, and rebellions may at first glance appear to be spontaneous events, more often than not the origins of these uprisings have been present for many years, with those in power ignoring the pleas or valid arguments of the underclass, the disenfranchised, or the minority political, ethnic, religious, racial, or national faction. The Jack Cade Rebellion of 1450 was one of those popular revolts where tensions were simmering under the surface for some time, and the rebellion, when it commenced, was the result of a series of interconnected incidents.

Moreover, the rebellion was an event in which conceptions and representations of gentlemanly behaviour and actions were being negotiated on the ground and within written records. The Jack Cade Rebellion, thus, can be read as an event that was populated by England's 'middle class' of the gentry and yeomen, and engaged with concerns that were of prime interest to the gentlemen and women (114 females are listed on the general pardon) of the country's southeast. Those who wrote about the rebellion in the fifteenth century were themselves keenly interested in the ways in which the insurgents were depicted, and the historical literature of the rebellion—the various chronicle entries, government records—reveal a schizophrenic authorial voice, with writers sympathetic to the rebels' ideology but abhorrent toward their actions. At the crux of this uneasy relationship between thought and action of the rebels resides, I contend, the realisation that 'gentlemen' could engage in untoward behaviour, where the grandee once stood now resides the churl.

'Gentilesse' in the Later Middle Ages

What did it mean to be a gentleman in the later Middle Ages in England? Perhaps there is no greater word in Middle English that exemplifies the possibilities and potential of a gentleman than the word *gentilesse*, a word like so many terms in the English language concerning manners and status whose etymology is Old French, in this case *gentillece*. *Gentilesse*, a noun, can describe a person's elevated social rank, and it also defines a person who is born into nobility.[1]

In Geoffrey Chaucer's *Boece*, his translation of Boethius' *Consolation of Philosophy* (ca. 1380), the poet describes *gentilesse* as following:

> For it semeth that gentilesse be a maner preisynge that cometh of the desertes of auncestres; and yif preisyng make gentilesse, thanne mote they nedes ben gentil that been preysed. For which thing it folweth that yif thou ne have no gentilesse of thiself (*that is to seyn, prys that cometh of thy deserte*), foreyne gentilesse ne maketh the nat gentil. But certes yif ther be ony good in gentilesse, I trowe it be al only this, that it semeth as that a maner necessite be imposed to gentil men for that thei ne schulde nat owtrayen or fortlynen fro the virtus of hir noble kynrede.[2]

> [For it seems that nobility is a manner to be praised that comes from the worthiness of ancestors; and if praising makes nobility, then it must be necessary for those who are noble. For it follows that if you do not have any nobility within yourself (*that is to say, reputation from your merit*), foreign nobility will not make you noble. But certainly if there is any good in nobility, I believe it all is only this, that is seems that a necessary manner be imposed to noble men, so that they should not stray unnaturally or degenerate themselves from their noble lineage.]

Boethius' words from the sixth century certainly delighted and informed Chaucer's thinking of the word and the ways in which individuals—real and imagined—manifested certain 'noble' traits. Inherent within Chaucer's glossing and translation of Boethius is the belief that nobility and thus elevated manners and behaviour was connected to one's genealogy and thus passed down from one generation to the next. However, Boethius and Chaucer are both very much aware that just because one is born into aristocracy it does not of course mean that he or she is fallible. Chaucer's word *owtrayen* denotes one's potential (and perhaps predilection) towards straying from one's noble flock, but the word also means to travel down a path of excess, to overindulge in earthly delights and vices.

Chaucer himself had an interesting relationship with *gentilesse* and wrote about its mutable nature. After all, he was born into a well-to-do family of vintners in London, which allowed him to live a comfortable life and to interact with people from all social ranks. Around 1366, he married Philippa, who had a number of connections to the nobility, most importantly her sister, Kathrine Swynford, who became John of Gaunt's

Geoffrey Chaucer: The Father of English Poetry. (Stephen Basdeo's Personal Collection)

third wife. Chaucer himself held a number of important posts, including an esquire in the court of Edward III, an envoy to Richard II, comptroller for the London ports, and clerk of the king's works. As a social being, he had personal access to noble men and women and thus was keenly able to note their qualities, both idealised and corrupt. As such, his working relationship among members of all three of the estates of the late Middle Ages allowed him to explore how perceptions of *gentilesse* permeated the minds of medievals, especially those of the third estate, who were gradually gaining more wealth and at times political power.

Perhaps there is no such greater representation of *gentilesse* and all of its connotations in medieval England than in Chaucer's *Canterbury Tales*, a text that was written for and read by a wide audience of learned individuals who could afford manuscripts and later printed books. This audience of Chaucer's *Canterbury Tales* by the time of the poet's death in 1400 would have included people very much like the author himself and people with whom he associated: the noble-born 'gentlemen', merchants, gentry, elected and appointed officials, and yeomen. Therefore, the tales and the individual characters who populate them—especially the pilgrims in the frame narrative who tell the tales—would serve as touchstones for fifteenth-century readers, including those directly involved with the Cade Rebellion, of gentlemanly behaviour. The apex, of course, for *gentilesse* resides in Chaucer's Knight, who in the General Prologue is described as:

> a worthy man,
> That fro the tyme that he first began
> To riden out, he loved chivalrie,
> Trouthe and honour, fredom and curteisie ...
> He was a varray, parfit gentil knyght.[3]

Chaucer's Knight's nobility is born into him but it is also earned, for he fought hard and well in service of England's crown during a number of crusade battles in Asia and Africa. Of course, one could aspire to nobility through the outward display of signs that could mirror one who was born into aristocracy. As such, *gentilesse* in the late Middle Ages also characterised one who demonstrated '[n]obility of character or manners; generosity, kindness, gentleness, graciousness'.[4] Of the members of Chaucer's pilgrimage from the third estate, perhaps there is no greater representation of a person not born into nobility but who practised well its virtues than the Franklin. His house is well stocked with good food and wine, his table is always ready (to entertain but also to conduct business); in terms of his work, he presided in the past over court sessions, was a member of parliament, served as a sheriff, and audited taxes. Indeed, as Chaucer tells us, 'Was nowher swich a worthy vavasour'.[5] Of course, Chaucer loved irony, and there are several of his pilgrims who appear to possess gentility: on the outside, they seem wise, cultured, mannered, and wholesome, but on the inside their true selves reveal immoral and unethical thoughts and actions. As such, we have the 'gentil Maunciple', the Summoner who 'was a gentil harlot and a kynde', and most tellingly the 'gentil Pardoner', all figures who lie, cheat, steal, and perhaps do much worse than what we are explicitly told.[6]

Gentlemanly manners and noble comportment in England was also being codified by the middle of the fifteenth century in guidebooks, which were directed primarily at the young who lived in noble and wealthy middle class families. The *Babees' Book*, for example, was written for young pages who were in charge of their equally young masters, and focused mainly on being able to ride horses properly, speak and write expertly, and practice good table manners and social etiquette. John Russell, who composed his *Book of Nurture* around 1450, was usher in chamber and marshal in hall to Humphrey, Duke of Gloucester (1390-1447). His work, much like the *Babees' Book*, concerns manners and etiquette, but is more broadly focused on the responsibility of various posts within noble households, such as sewer, chamberlain, usher, and marshal. Of course, the guidelines within these books are wholly situational and should not be applied to all social interactions and contexts within the later Middle Ages in England. However, guidebooks served as a means toward the refinement of one's being, especially those of the third estate who worked with and served their superiors. The young and not-so-young pages, esquires, carvers, and butlers would have brought back to their own gentry, yeoman, or mercantile homes and families the 'simple conditions' expressed by Russell in his *Book of Nurture*, and thus generations of England's commons would be exposed to and engage directly with the precepts of *gentilesse*. Nevertheless, not all of them did. As with a number of Chaucer's pilgrims, many of the broad middle class of England who took part in the Cade Rebellion espoused gentlemanly ideals, but who in action were involved in atrocious actions. Indeed, many failed to adhere to one of Russell's most pointed aphorisms: 'Be not rash or reckless—that is not worth a clout'.[7]

Jack Cade the Gentleman?

The historical person and figure of Jack Cade is incomplete. What we know of him comes from the surviving chronicles of the fifteenth and sixteenth centuries, government records, and popular poems, most of which contain a fair amount of embellishment and ideological bias. We do not have a genealogical record of Cade, nor a will. Much like the earlier famous rebel Wat Tyler, Cade appeared and disappeared in the span of a few months in 1450. Indeed, his name, 'Jack Cade', may not be his true name, as he was identified and went by a number of designations, including John Cade, John Mortimer, John Aylmere, and John Amendall. The latter name suggests that Cade's role or mission to 'amend all' of the problems that the commons are facing. This entry from the fifteenth-century history *An English Chronicle, 1377-1461* presents a complex portrait of the leader of the rebellion:

> And this same year in the month of May arose those of Kent and made them a captain, an Irishman, a ribald, called John Cade, who at his start took onto himself and usurped the name of a gentleman and called himself Mortimer in order to get and have more favor of the people. And he called himself also John Amendall, for as much as then and a long time before the realm of England was out of rule and governance and ruled by untrue counsel, wherefore the common good was greatly hurt and decreased so that the common people, with great taxes and great levies and other oppressions done by lords and others, might not [be able to] live by their husbandry and handiwork, wherefore they grumbled greatly against those that had the governance of the land.[8]

From this chronicle entry, we can note how Cade's *gentilesse* was not innate but rather forged or stolen. His ability or willingness to adopt a number of names or aliases to fit within certain political or social contexts reveals a cunningness on his part. However, these names that are assigned to Cade may not have been done by his own volition. As I. M. W. comments, King Henry VI and his court believed Cade came from Ireland, the 'home of some Mortimer lands and the country in which [Richard Duke of] York [1411–1460] was then posted as the king's lieutenant'.[9] This oblique link to nobility, it seems, went both ways as some chroniclers and nobles were eager to explore and exploit the notion that Cade was not only living among York's kin but was also related to him by blood. York would prove to be a critical person who participated in the First Battle of Saint Albans on 22 May 1455 and thus a key player in the start of the Wars of the Roses. R. A. Griffiths describes how writers from the fifteenth century were willing to suggest a number of elevated social positions for Cade; for example, John Aylmere was supposedly a 'physician who had married the daughter of a Surrey squire ... [and] The royal proclamation issued on 10 June [1450] for the arrest of Cade announced that he had once served Charles VII and that he has been residing in Sussex in the household of Sir Thomas Dacre—until, that is, he killed a pregnant woman and had to flee'.[10] Official records and personal chronicles suggest that these writers were trying to attack Cade's character and origins by any means necessary. One could understand how suggestions that link him to the gentry or perhaps even lesser nobility would create a strong degree of aversion from those groups toward Cade and especially his and his group's activities and demands.

The Parliament Rolls of England, and especially the Attainder of Jack Cade from the parliament of 1453, which formally declared him a traitor, portray the rebel leader in wholly negative terms. However, the document's own language suggests that Cade was no fool and that he had a sharp intellect. As one who commanded a large host and negotiated with local and national officials, he was obviously one who excelled in the use of rhetoric and the politics of statecraft, though towards rebellious ends:

> That where the most abominable tyrant, horrible, odious, and errant false traitor, John Cade, calling and naming himself sometime Mortimer, sometime Captain of Kent, which name, fame, acts and deeds, are to be put out of every true Christian man's language and memory forever, falsely and traitorously proposing and imagining the uttermost destruction of your most royal person, and final subversion of this your noble realm, taking upon him royal power, and gathering to him your people in great number, by false, subtle, and imaginative language, and seditiously made commotion, rebellion, and insurrection under color of justice and reformation of your laws, robbing, slaying, and despoiling a great part of your true people, purposing also by diverse subtle, false, and untrue imaginations to make variances and commotion between you, our sovereign lord, and your true people.[11]

The above proclamation includes the word 'subtle' twice to describe Cade and his actions, which is a word that appears in a later chronicle to describe the rebel leader, in this instance *Hall's Chronicle* (ca. 1532):

> The subtle captain named Jack Cade, intending to bring the king farther within the compass of his net, broke up his camp and retreated back to the town of Sevenoaks in Kent, and there, expecting his prey, encamped himself and made his abode.[12]

The Middle English word *sotil* (adj) has numerous connotations. On the one hand, it can refer to a person who is refined and intellectually superior, one with a benevolent, genteel disposition: 'penetrating, ingenious, perspicacious, sophisticated, refined, articulate, persuasive'.[13] Conversely, the term can be applied to someone who uses their wits for nefarious purposes, where the devil is often described in texts as such: 'insidiously sly, treacherously cunning, deceitful'.[14]

The Rebel Host and Its Complaints

Jack Cade's heredity and origins remain uncertain, though as Griffiths argues, 'there is measure of agreement among contemporaries that Cade came from the lower ranks of society rather than from the country squirearchy or the urban patriciate'.[15] Those individuals who constitute the host, the military force that took part in the rebellion, likewise were not a homogenous unit of fifteenth-century England.

What we know of the persons who took part in the rebellion can be gleaned from the pardon issued to and accepted by the insurgents on 6 and 7 July 1450. There are roughly 3,000 individuals named on the general pardon; however, by most conservative estimates, some 20,000 took part in the rebellion. Griffiths cautions against viewing the pardon as an accurate snapshot of the entirety of the rebel force. There are individuals named who killed elected and appointed officials, at least a dozen men whom the rebels themselves saw as their enemies are pardoned, and several individuals who likely did not take place in the revolt are listed. As Griffiths remarks:

> [t]o regard those who received a pardon as active rebels to a man, deducing therefrom conclusions about their occupations and geographical origins, is thus quite unwarranted. The most that can be said of the pardon-list is that it undoubtedly contains the names of many rebels—but also many loyalists and others who took no part at all in the incidents of 1450.[16]

In studying the geographical distribution of the 3,000 or so persons named, Harvey concludes that 65% came from Kent, 14% were from eastern and mid-Sussex, 12% derived from eastern Surrey (especially the northeastern corner closest to London), and 12% were from eastern Surrey (especially the north-eastern corner nearest London).[17]

JACK CADE *in Henry VI Reign* *declaring himself* LORD *of the* CITY *of* LONDON, *1450.*

In addition to names and locations, the pardon list also includes the professions of those included in the document. Griffiths discerns that the list 'represents, in brief, a cross-section of society in the south-east of England, but little more'.[18] Nonetheless, when we study the occupations of those named on the pardon list, we begin to see the wide range of professions that are included. The two largest groups represented on the list are yeomen and husbandmen. The former is a catch-all term in the late Middle Ages that describes a free man, who is allowed to own land, and who could be an attendant in a royal

Jack Cade declaring himself the ruler of London (Eighteenth-century illustration). (Stephen Basdeo's Personal Collection)

household (below the rank of a squire), a labourer, or a subordinate officer.[19] The latter can refer to the head of a household, a farmer, a steward, or a husband.[20] There are close to 100 different professions represented on the pardon list, and they represent the professional working class of England in the southeast. There are plumbers, thatchers, tilemakers, and millers. There are some who may have been members of a guild: mercers, goldsmiths, grocers, drapers, and weavers. Lastly, there are those named who held elevated positions within English society: gentlemen (seventy-four named), esquires, bailiffs, burgesses, one mayor, and many constables.

In *Gregory's Chronicle*, the host is described as a 'multitude of riff-raff', yet the pardon roll presents, indeed, a cross-section of middle and lower middle class England.[21] Significantly, M. A. Bohna's research on the composition of the armed force—and specifically the presence of constables in the pardon and their role in the rebellion—reveals the presence of men of the middle class who helped to lead the revolt. Bohna asserts that the primary force of the rebels that fought in Kent and in London was derived from the Kentish militia, armed and on guard to ward off any potential incursion from France:

> The fall of Rouen and subsequently of the Norman channel ports in the spring of 1450 caused the English government to pay serious attention to the defence of its southern counties, now vulnerable to French raiding. On 14 April 1450, for the first time in seven years, the government issued a commission of array for Kent, headed by the royal officer and recent shire-knight Sir John Cheyne.[22]

While Griffiths and to some extent Harvey dissuade us from reading the pardon list as wholly accurate of the armed force, Bertram Wolffe astutely argues that

> the most striking aspect of all is the way their 3,000 or more ultimate pardons were grouped together in their hundreds of origin, under constables. Fifty-three constables from thirty-one of the sixty-eight hundreds of Kent headed their named contingents, sometimes followed by the note "and all others of the said hundred." In addition there were constables and their contingents from fourteen Sussex hundreds, three from Surrey, one from Middlesex and four from Surrey towns.[23]

The conventional wisdom of the chroniclers of the fifteenth and sixteenth centuries was that the commons rallied around Cade and followed his lead as a singular mass. For example, in the Middle English Prose *Brut* chronicle, a typical opening remark on the rebellion reads thus: 'This year was a great assembly and gathering together of the commons of Kent in great number, and they ordained themselves a captain called John Cade'.[24] What is missing with the chronicle entries is the organisational structure of the rebellion, specifically those individuals who served as commanders on the ground. Bohna asserts that since the militia in Kent was at the ready, with constables already in command of their units, '[i]t is inherently probable Cade and his lieutenants would choose to utilize a structure familiar and ready to hand rather than to create their own from scratch'.[25] The inclusion of fifty-three constables on the general pardon highlights the participation of 'gentlemen' within the rebellion and illuminates the reasons for the uprising and what the insurgents wished to amend.

Kent was on edge since the death of the Duke of Suffolk, William de la Pole, Henry VI's chief counsellor who is often blamed for the crown's losses in France (especially Normandy and Rouen). Suffolk is exiled from England, and on 1 May his ship is intercepted by another, the *Nicholas of the Tower*, where he is given a mock trial. On another vessel, on 2 May, he is beheaded on Dover Road; his head is placed on a pole and his body is left on Dover Beach.[26] Almost all contemporary chronicle accounts of the rebellion begin with this incident, for it serves as a precursor to the revolt. Who took part in Suffolk's murder remains a mystery, though the crown is quick to assign blame on all of Kent, with rumours that the 'King intended to hold the entire county for the deed, that a hanging court would soon be sent into the county'[27] and that it would be 'turned into a wild forest, a threat believed to have been made by the king's treasurer, Lord Saye, a former sheriff of Kent'.[28] Bohna expertly assesses what those in Kent are feeling, as two potential threats loom: an invasion from France on their coast, and royal retribution:

> In short, as rebellion brewed in men's minds, the tedious machinery of the English state ground on, and from place to place across the county men were called out to stand upon village greens, their weapons in hand, their constable at their head, to await the arrival commissioners and their clerks. While the Kentishmen waited for these gentlemen to appear, they talked of their grievances against their governors, and found general agreement among themselves. Forced, in many cases for the first time in their lives, to consider themselves as the defenders of their land by the literal act of mustering, they must often have found soon after a sense of responsibility for the land's welfare. It was a short step from the muster on the village green to the London road in the spring of 1450. And, characteristically inept, the Lancastrian regime itself brought the soon-to-be rebels together under arms, charging them in the resounding language of the commission the realm against its enemies. The government had enemies across the Channel in mind, but the militiamen knew that the kingdom's enemies lay nearer at hand, just across the Thames.[29]

As the rebels amass and muster in May, by early June Cade is chosen (or he appoints himself) leader of the host. Reports in the chronicles suggest that by 11 June the rebels are gathering around Blackheath, and on 15 June, Henry VI sends a number of high-ranking officials to listen to the rebels' demands, which he rejects. Instead, the king sends a small force into Kent, including Sir Humphrey Stafford and his brother William Stafford, and both are killed in battle near Sevenoaks.

The demands of the rebel host survive in three different versions and are often referred to as the 'Complaints' or 'Petitions of the Commons of Kent'. Harvey notes that there exists a great deal of uncertainty regarding the sequence and dating of these three versions, though all surviving extant texts are from the fifteenth and sixteenth century.[30] When we examine the three versions of the rebels' complaints, a number of important elements stand out related to the composition of the host and their demands. First, these complaints are not wild rantings of the 'riff-raff' of England; conversely, they are logical, well thought through and argued, and fairly sophisticated. As Harvey contends, 'the drafters of these petitions and those acting at the centre of events were neither illiterate nor informed'.[31] Moreover, when one reads the bills of complaint, it is clear that the rebels are not engaging in radical or anarchic rhetoric; instead, these rebels are seeking to reform government in a liberal sense, working with the prevailing order and status quo to make a more equitable existence for the broad commons. Item 11 in Version II of the bills of complaint decrees that

> they ask for gentlemen's lands and goods in Kent, and call us risers and traitors and the king's enemies, but we shall be found to be true liegemen and his best of friends with the help of Jesus, to whom we cry daily and nightly, with many thousand more, that God by his righteousness shall take vengeance on the false traitors of his royal realm that have brought us into this mischief and misery.[32]

The host here and elsewhere in these bills sees Henry as the true king, though one who has been the victim of unscrupulous counsellors, and that the host's true complaints reside with corrupt sheriffs, undersheriffs, and bailiffs.

Harvey argues that the 'voice of [the Kent] county community can be heard in the rebels' bills', and their complaints and solutions are focused mostly on economic, labour, and election concerns.[33] The constables were upset as they were now called to enforce labour laws under a renewed statute of labourers, tax collectors (sheriffs, under-sheriffs, and bailiffs) were accused of skimming money, the barons of the Cinque Ports were suddenly exempt from tax collecting; moreover, the selling of

Jack Cade strikes the London stone. From an illustration included in *The Complete Works of William Shakespeare* (1881)

the office of tax collector by knights of the shire, and the lack of free elections when choosing the knights of the shire upset the commons of Kent. With a sizeable portion of the county's population able to meet the net income threshold of 40 shillings per year to vote, the 'merchants, well-to-do artisans, and the up-and-coming yeomen who formed a group so characteristic of fifteenth century Kentish society' were rightly angry with their rights being abused, bought, and sold.[34]

The Attack on London and the End of the Rebellion

Around 18 June, Henry VI brought together some 2,000 men to attack the rebel force, but he decided to not advance his host. Instead, the king placed James Fiennes, Lord Saye and Sele, the Constable and Treasurer of England, in the Tower of London for his own protection, as the rebels saw him as one of their chief enemies. On 25 June 1450, Henry left London for Kenilworth Castle in Warwickshire, thus leaving the city of London to defend itself. The rebels saw this as an opportunity, and on 3 July, Cade and his army entered London and were in command of the scene. The rebel force now numbered upwards of 26,000, having increased its number from a large contingent from Essex.

It is this entry into London and the events that transpired inside and outside the city walls that shaped the sentiments of those living within and governing the city against the rebels. While the rebels' aims were logical and their grievances accurate, their actions now became less gentlemanly and more churlish. Foolishly, ironically, or sadistically, Cade and his lieutenants and followers mimicked the codes and customs of civil, noble, and legal society as they carried out their actions.

While Cade at one time may have been one of or one with the commons, once in London his demeanour changed. In the *Robert Bale's Chronicle*, the author notes how Cade rides on horse from Southwark to St. Paul's 'in a blue gown of velvet, with fur sables and a straw hat upon his dead and a sword drawn in his hand'. *An English Chronicle* noted that the hat now was longer made of straw but rather a 'gilded salet' and he wore 'gilded spurs' and a 'pair of brigandines'.[35] Cade and his lieutenants enjoyed the performative aspects of gentlemanly behaviour, especially those visual cues and rituals that conveyed a sense of grandeur and officialdom. Cade and his retinue's journey through London mirrored and parodied the temporal and civic ceremonial elements of the city's Midsummer Watch. The Midsummer Watch was a celebration that occurred during Whitsuntide in many cities in England, and which included a purposeful parade through the city, led by the town's oligarchy, to literally and figuratively protect the wealthy homes from robbery.[36] Next to Cade, perhaps the most noted individual of the rebel force whose behaviour embraced the formal elements of *gentilesse* along with the savage cruelty of members of the rebellion is Robert Poynings, an esquire from Twineham and Sutton, Sussex. Poynings was the most noted defector, for he was originally commissioned by Henry VI to arrest English soldiers who were returning from France who were robbing people in Edenbridge, near Sevenoaks.[37] He decided, instead, to desert his post and join Cade's forces, where he became the Captain of Kent's carver and sword-bearer. Poynings spared at least one man from execution, John Payn, a servant of the wealthy Norfolk landowner and knight Sir John Fastolf (1380–1459). Fastolf, keen to learn about the plans of the nearby rebels, sent Payn to investigate, and his employee was captured and nearly executed. Payn's letter, which is found among the important collection of letters and papers of the Paston family, details a harrowing, near-death scene, and recounts how Poynings and other important men who were in Cade's camp vouchsafed for Payn's and Fastolf's good character.[38]

One of the cruellest moments came on 4 July, when Cade ordered a commission be held in the Guildhall where trials of wrongdoers would commence. The following lengthy section from *The Great Chronicle of London* illuminates Cade's abuse of power and how, in the words of the chronicler, the rebel commander and his host went too far:

> And at London Stone he struck upon it like a conqueror. And as he was in the city he sent for Lord Saye from the Tower, and he was taken and brought into the Guildhall where he was indicted with others of treason. And upon the same morning the captain sent for Robert Horne, alderman, where with great labor of his friends he escaped with his life and was ransomed at a great sum of money, and so were others dealt with in a similar manner. And while the mayor was at the hall, the captain came again into the city and went into the hall, and from there [to find] one Crowmer, a squire who had married Lord Saye's daughter and had been sheriff of Kent and had done much extortion there as they said. In the meantime, the Lord Saye was at the Guildhall before the mayor and the king's justices, who desired him to be judged by his peers, but the Kentishman would not allow that, and by force and strength brought him to the Standard at Cheap and there smote off his head, and after set his head upon a spear and carried it about the city. And the same day before the beheading of Crowmer the captain with a certain number of persons with him went into Philip Malpas' house and robbed him of many goods. And from there he went to one Gest's house beside Tower Street and dined there and robbed him in the same manner. And it is to be remembered that when Crowmer was beheaded at the same time a man who was called Bailey was also beheaded, and after they brought the heads of the Lord Saye and Crowmer upon two stakes or polls, and in many places in the city put them together causing one to kiss the other. And when the citizens saw that he had robbed Philip Malpas and Gest, those who were wealthy believed very strongly that afterward he would rob them in the same way, and they withdrew their hearts and love from him, for if he had not been tempted by robbery it is believed that he might have gone far in the land, for the king and all the lords were departed, except the Lord Scales who kept the Tower.[39]

Extrajudicial trials and executions, desecration and abuse of corpses, pillage and robbery: not gentlemanly behaviour at all. Indeed, as the anonymous chronicler pointedly asserted, it was the robbing of notable persons of London that turned favour against him. Philip

Malpas was an important figure, for he was a notable member of the Drapers Guild as well as sheriff and alderman of London. We know little of Gest, but *A Chronicle of London* describes how Cade robbed Malpas' house and then 'went into one Gest's house, beside Tower Street, and there dines, and in the like manner robbed him'.[40] There was thus, with Gest, the double humiliation, of not only Cade robbing him, but also firstly of dining in his victim's house, perhaps with Gest as his own guest and witness. The gentry, yeomen, and constables who first sided and mustered with Cade, and who wrote and stood behind the bills of complaint, must have now reconsidered their involvement with the rebellion, for the aims of it had changed from reform to despoil. The treasury and exchequer of England recovered some of the property and money stolen, including some of Malpas'. All told, £114, 9 shillings, and 4 pence from the Draper were found along with many valuable household goods made of gold and silver.[41]

The following evening, 5 July 1450, the armed civilians of London had enough of the looting of their city and stopped another incursion from the rebels who had temporarily left the city's wall. At night, a battle ensued on London Bridge, beginning around 10 p.m. and lasting into the next morning, ending around 8 a.m. or 9 a.m. The bridge caught fire, and some forty Londoners perished along with around 200 Kentish men. The rebel force fled and dispersed back to their home counties, and Cade escaped. A reward of 1,000 marks was placed on his head, alive or dead. Cade was apprehended on 12 July by the newly appointed sheriff of Kent, Alexander Iden. Cade presumably died as a result of injuries sustained in his capture, and the closing remarks on this event by the author of *The Great Chronicle of London* describe the extended form of punishment that was dealt to those involved in the rebellion:

> [B]ut in the taking the said captain was slain, and so brought to Southwark so that all men might see him and that night left [him] in the King's Bench. And from there he was drawn to Newgate and then beheaded and quartered and his head set upon London Bridge. And his four quarters were sent to four separate towns in Kent. And soon after the king rode into Kent and commanded his justices to sit at Canterbury to inquire who were the accessories and causers of this insurrection. And then there were seven men judged to death on one day and in other places more. And from there the king rode into Sussex, and from there to the west country, where a short time before the Bishop of Salisbury was slain. And this year there were so many judged to death that twenty-three heads stood upon London Bridge, upon whose souls and all Christians, God, to his pleasure, have mercy. Amen.[42]

After Cade's death and the end of the rebellion, a number of minor rebellions continued in the 1450s in southeastern England, including Parmynter's Rising, which lasted from August to September 1450, Hasilden's Rising of April 1451, Wilkyn's Rising of May 1452, and Percy's Rising of April 1456. As Harvey observes, these rebellions 'were all connected by a common outcry that Cade's sought-after reforms should be implemented'.[43]

The Jack Cade Rebellion of 1450 was just one of many popular rebellions in England's history that sought to reform the country for the betterment of the commons. Initially, the leaders sought to engage with the concerns that would appeal to the more established, landed classes, the 'gentlemen' of the third estate. The language and rhetoric of the rebellion were literate and polished, yet the leaders of the revolt quickly fell into rough-arm tactics and gluttonous and greedy appetites. The 'golden mean' of Aristotle was fast tossed aside, and the country would have to engage in both the Wars of the Roses and the English Civil War before another member of the gentry, and perhaps an even more controversial figure than Cade, Oliver Cromwell, would argue for reform, though in more radical ways and with even greater lasting effects.

Notes

1. *Middle English Dictionary*, *s.v.* "ğentĭlesse," (n.), 1.(a).
2. Geoffrey Chaucer, *The Riverside Chaucer*, gen. ed. Larry D. Benson. 3rd ed. (Boston: Houghton Mifflin, 1987), 427.38-51. Translation is my own.
3. Ibid., 24.43-46, 24.72.
4. *Middle English Dictionary*, *s.v.* "ğentĭlesse," (n.), 2.(a).
5. Chaucer, *Riverside*, 29.360.
6. Ibid., 32.567, 33.647, and 34.669.
7. *The Babees' Book: Medieval Manners for the Young: Done into Modern English from Dr. Furnivall's Text*, trans. Edith Rickert and L. J. Naylor (London: Chatto and Windus, 1908), 57.
8. Alexander L. Kaufman, ed., *The Jack Cade Rebellion of 1450: A Sourcebook* (Lanham, MD: Lexington Books, 2020), 29. For the Middle English edition of this passage see William Marx, ed. *An English Chronicle, 1377-1461: A New Edition*. Medieval Chronicles 3 (Woodbridge: The Boydell Press, 2003), 67.
9. I. M. W. Harvey, *Jack Cade's Rebellion of 1450* (Oxford: Clarendon Press, 1991), 78.
10. R. A. Griffiths, *The Reign of King Henry VI* (Phoenix Mill: Sutton, 1998), 617.
11. Kaufman, *Jack Cade Rebellion*, 187.
12. Ibid., 83. See also Edward Hall, *Hall's Chronicle*, ed. Henry Ellis (London: J. Johnson, et al., 1809), 220.
13. *Middle English Dictionary*, *s.v.* "sotil" (adj), 1.(a).
14. Ibid., "sotil," (adj.), 2b.(a).
15. Griffiths, *Henry VI*, 617.
16. Ibid., 621.
17. Harvey, *Jack Cade's Rebellion*, 192.
18. Griffiths, *Henry VI*, 621.
19. *Middle English Dictionary*, *s.v.* "yēman," (n.), 1-3.
20. Ibid., *s.v.* "hus-bŏnd-man," (n.), 1.
21. Kaufman, *The Jack Cade Rebellion*, 43. For the Middle English edition of the chronicle, see Gairdner, James Gairdner, ed. *The Historical Collections of A London*

Citizen of the Fifteenth Century. Camden Society, ns 17 (Westminster: Nichols and Sons, 1876), 191.

22. Montgomery Bohna, "Armed Force and Civic Legitimacy in Jack Cade's Revolt, 1450," *The English Historical Review* 118, no. 477 (2003): 563-82 (573).

23. Bertram Wolffe, *Henry VI* (New Haven and London: Yale University Press, 2001), 233.

24. Kaufman, *Jack Cade Rebellion*, 54. For the Middle English edition, see Friedrich W. D. Brie, ed. *The Brut or The Chronicles of England*. Part II. EETS, os 136 (London: Oxford University Press, 1908), 517.

25. Bohna, "Armed Force and Civic Legitimacy," 572.

26. Harvey, *Jack Cade's Rebellion*, 73.

27. Bohna, "Armed Force and Civic Legitimacy," 574.

28. Harvey, *Jack Cade's Rebellion*, 73.

29. Bohna, "Armed Force and Civic Legitimacy," 574.

30. Harvey, *Jack Cade's Rebellion*, 186. Harvey produces transcriptions of the three Middle English versions on 186-91. For present-day English translations of them, see Kaufman, *The Jack Cade Rebellion*, 113-21.

31. Harvey, *Jack Cade's Rebellion*, 105.

32. Kaufman, *The Jack Cade Rebellion*, 118.

33. Harvey, *Jack Cade's Rebellion*, 105.

34. Ibid.

35. Kaufman, *The Jack Cade Rebellion*, 14, 30. For the Middle English edition of *Robert Bale's Chronicle*, see Ralph Flenley, ed. *Six Town Chronicles of England* (Oxford: Clarendon Press, 1911), 133.

36. Alexander L. Kaufman, *The Historical Literature of the Jack Cade Rebellion* (Farnham: Ashgate, 2009), 93-130.

37. For parliament's petition against Poynings, see Kaufman, *The Jack Cade Rebellion*, 190-2.

38. For a translation of this letter, see Kaufman, *Jack Cade's rebellion*, 193-9.

39. Kaufman, *The Jack Cade Rebellion*, 69. For the Middle English edition of the chronicle, see A. H. Thomas and I. D. Thornley, ed. *The Great Chronicle of London* (London: The Sign of the Dolphin, 1939; repr., Gloucester: Alan Sutton, 1983), 184.

40. Kaufman, *The Jack Cade Rebellion*, 62. This chronicle of London is from British Library MS Cotton Vitellius A.XVI, and the Middle English edition can be found in Charles Lethbridge Kingsford, ed. *Chronicles of London* (Oxford: Clarendon Press, 1905), 161.

41. For an inventory of Malpas' money and goods recovered, as well as what was recovered from a few other individuals, see Kaufman, *The Jack Cade Rebellion*, 181-3. All persons whose goods were recovered and who wanted them returned were required to buy them back from the exchequer at a reduced rate.

42. Kaufman, *The Jack Cade Rebellion*, 70.

43. Harvey, *Jack Cade's Rebellion*, 174.

Section Two

The English Revolution

Oliver Cromwell and John Lilburne

Sheldon Goldfarb

What is Oliver Cromwell doing in this book? Was he a radical? If radicalism means opposition to tyranny and defending the rights of the people, did he do that? Don't ask the Irish. But the Irish aside, there are other issues. For one thing, Cromwell took power and served as Lord Protector of England for nearly five years. Can you still be a radical once you're in power? Perhaps it depends on what sort of things you do with your power. Cromwell certainly was interested in making a radical transformation of England, mostly in the religious sphere: does that count?

Or perhaps what matters is results more than intentions. Cromwell is sometimes credited with having (temporarily) abolished the monarchy and the House of Lords. This is actually not true; he was appalled by the abolition of the House of Lords and only reluctantly went along with the trial and execution of Charles I. In the absence of a traditional king, he eventually became a new sort of ruler, more beholden to parliament and his Council of State, a model for future constitutional monarchs perhaps, or as Blair Worden puts it, an inadvertent Whig.[1] But was that radical? And what about John Lilburne? Known as a turbulent and vexatious spirit in his lifetime, he was always in opposition (and often in prison). He saw tyranny everywhere and was constantly challenging authority. Perhaps that is more what we mean by radicalism. And he fought for things that in the long run transformed a traditional hierarchical society with few guarantees of civil rights into a liberal democracy with universal suffrage and protections for citizens.

And what about Cromwell and Lilburne together? They started out as friends and allies, Cromwell being something of a mentor or even hero to the younger Lilburne in the early days of the fight against Charles I. But by the end, Lilburne was denouncing Cromwell as a tyrant, and was languishing in prison while Cromwell ruled the land. 'I had once as great a power as he had,' Lilburne said, 'and greater too, and am as good a Gentleman, and of as good a family.'[2] But their endings were quite different. Their beginnings, on the other hand, were fairly similar. They both came from the lower echelons of the landed gentry. Cromwell came from an established family in Huntingdonshire, but was the son of a younger son, so his inheritance was limited, and in any case, the whole Cromwell family was in decline. Lilburne came from an even older landed family, in the north near Newcastle, but as a second son found himself apprenticed to a clothier in London. Cromwell never sank that low, though he did at

Oliver Cromwell and John Lilburne

Oliver Cromwell. (Stephen Basdeo's Personal Collection)

one point find himself without any lands of his own, having to become a tenant farmer. As Antonia Fraser puts it, it's enough to make you believe in the discredited thesis that the English Revolution was made by members of the declining gentry.[3]

However, Cromwell's fortunes had revived by the time of the Civil War, and he had returned to the ranks of the gentry and been elected to parliament as one of the two members for Cambridge, probably as the result of the work of the godly party in that constituency, radical puritans who sought a representative who would speak out against the 'popish' drift of English politics.[4] Once in parliament he became known as a presenter of petitions, and it is in this capacity that his path first crossed with Lilburne's because Lilburne by that time was already a languisher in prisons who was in need of help to get released. A petition on his behalf was presented by Cromwell to the newly assembled Long Parliament in November 1640. Cromwell was said to have done so in a passionate way, 'his eloquence full of fervour',[5] and the result was that Lilburne was released and his conviction by the notorious Star Chamber was reversed. He was even promised reparations for the injustice done to him under the old regime, though he had a difficult time collecting them.

At this point, Lilburne was probably a more celebrated figure than Cromwell. He had been arrested in 1637 at a time when Charles I's Archbishop of Canterbury, William Laud, was pushing religious practices in a direction that some thought was too ritualistic, even Catholic, prompting protests from Puritan writers such as William Prynne, John Bastwick, and Henry Burton. Lilburne at the time had become part of a Puritan network by way of his master Thomas Hewson and met Bastwick, whose books he decided to help circulate. To do this he first headed to Amsterdam to get them printed, but on his return, he was arrested and brought before Star Chamber.

Here began Lilburne's radical career. Rather than submit meekly to the standard Star Chamber interrogation, he refused to answer, demanded to see the charges against him, questioned the legitimacy of the proceedings, and in general sought the protections now taken for granted in courts of law. At the time, however, such objections were unheard of, though Lilburne had learned of earlier puritans who had made similar objections in another venue, the Court of High Commission. This had never been done in Star Chamber, however, and the presiding authorities were appalled, finding Lilburne in contempt in addition to convicting him of circulating seditious materials. The result was that on 18 April 1638, Lilburne was ordered to be flogged through the streets of London and made to stand in the pillory at New Palace Yard. The sun was hot and he suffered 500 lashes, but he remained undaunted, and was supported by crowds of onlookers, whom he proceeded to entertain with denunciations of the Laudian Church similar to those found in the pamphlets he was accused of circulating.

This led to his being gagged while he stood in the pillory, but he then proceeded to hand out copies of the pamphlets, which he had in his pockets. Star Chamber was outraged: this was the very thing he was being punished for in the first place, and he was doing it again while being punished. He was sent back to the Fleet Prison and kept in chains and in solitary confinement, and yet somehow he was able to begin a career of publishing pamphlets of his own from prison (he issued dozens), including *The Christian Man's Trial, A Work of the Beast,* and *Come out of her my people.* In 1639, he even managed to smuggle out a pamphlet calling on the apprentices of London to rise up against Archbishop Laud. This pamphlet, *A Cry for Justice,* followed the usual formula of Lilburne's pamphlets: he began by describing his own suffering and then made larger points about the evils of his time, in the early pamphlets usually the evils caused by the system of bishops, though later he moved on to more secular topics.

And the apprentices did gather and demonstrate outside Laud's palace. The Star Chamber meanwhile ordered a change in its procedures to prevent prisoners from handing out pamphlets: their pockets were to be searched and their hands were to be tied. But Star Chamber was about to be abolished, and reforms began moving the country in a different direction. There was even a temporary suspension of censorship, but it was reintroduced under the rule of the Presbyterians in the mid-1640s, causing more problems for John Lilburne.

Lilburne thus was an agitator from the beginning. Cromwell was very different. He did, it is true, get held in custody at one point, in late 1630 after a local dispute in Huntingdon, where he was apparently a leading figure in the community. He had served as an MP for the area the year before, but now after a disagreement over filling seats on the town council in which he lost his temper, he was summoned before the Privy Council in London and held for six days before being ordered to make a public apology. Now, if this had happened to Lilburne, one can imagine the result: he would have refused to apologise. He might have refused to appear before the Privy Council in the first place. He would have denounced the proceedings if he had. He would have ended up in prison for months or years and would have begun issuing pamphlets detailing his suffering and denouncing his oppressors. Cromwell did none of this. He seems to have made the apology (the sources are unclear), then perhaps feeling embarrassed or out of favour, left his home town of Huntingdon, moving first to St Ives and then to Ely, where he remained for the rest of the decade before being elected to both the Short Parliament and the Long Parliament in 1640.

During the decade before 1640, he seems to have had a religious conversion and was probably part of a Puritan group, perhaps even preaching at separatist 'conventicles' outside the established Church (which would have been illegal). There is thus a similar beginning to both his career and Lilburne's, in that they both started among the radical puritans, but their temperaments seem to have been much different. Although he had a temper, Cromwell, unlike Lilburne, was one to follow orders. Much later, as a commander of the parliamentary forces, he would let orders from London restrain him from an attack on the Royalists. He did what he was told. John Lilburne never did what he was told. So much the more radical he, if radicalism is a question of temperament and oppositionalism.

Cromwell, of course, became a leader of the opposition to Charles I, but he did it very much as part of the parliamentary party and in accordance with the norms of parliament. Besides presenting petitions, he sat on committees, made speeches in the House of Commons, and carried messages from the Commons to the House of Lords. He did take the lead to a certain extent, pushing his fellow parliamentarians to make more active preparations for the defence of the kingdom against Charles, when war seemed to be in the offing. And he did not even wait for the war to officially start before heading up to Cambridge to seize gold plate that the University was intending to send to the king.

Cromwell also got busy recruiting men and horses for a cavalry troop and was soon taking part in early skirmishes as part of the Eastern Association, the parliamentary army in the eastern section of the country. Still, he seemed more the loyal soldier than a rebel, though of course it could be said that he was on the side of the rebels, the parliamentarians fighting the king, seeking a redress of grievances and eventually a restructuring of the constitution. This seems very different from Lilburne's one-man show of defiance which led eventually to the creation of a party or movement centred upon him (the Levellers); it is hard to imagine Lilburne being merely a loyal follower even of a rebellious party.

And yet it is true that when the Civil War broke out, he signed up as a captain (the same rank Cromwell had to begin with) and served with the parliamentary forces against the king at Edgehill in 1642. Cromwell eventually recruited him into the Eastern Association, but of course he couldn't just serve; he ended up in opposition, first to a Colonel King over both military matters and religion, and then to the Earl of Manchester over whether to capture Tickhill Castle in 1644. Manchester, commander of the Eastern Association, said no, but Lilburne went ahead and captured it anyway (of course). Cromwell had his differences

John Lilburne, from an illustration by Theodorus Varax in 1649. (British Civil Wars Project—Public domain work licenced under Wikimedia Commons)

with Manchester too, whom he felt was too lukewarm in the fight against Charles. This led to charges and counter-charges heard before a parliamentary committee (but not to Cromwell just going ahead with a military manoeuvre against Manchester's orders, Manchester being his commanding officer too). What Cromwell did was to out-manoeuvre Manchester politically. Or perhaps the manoeuvring was done by forces sympathetic to Cromwell, the so-called Independents in their fight against the more moderate Presbyterian party. Cromwell often seemed to benefit from actions that he did not have a hand in himself, at least not overtly. Not for him the noisy Lilburnian show. More the working behind the scenes. Or letting others work behind the scenes while he communed with God over what to do next.

Cromwell was very devout. This explains how he chose sides in the first place. He was a strong Puritan, or member of the godly party, seeking above all a godly reformation, a moral regeneration. And in day-to-day affairs, he was constantly looking for the hand of Providence – and finding it, though it did make him delay and delay, and sometimes just be conveniently somewhere else when, for instance, Colonel Pride made his purge of parliament. In any case, the result of the struggle with Manchester led to a Self-Denying Ordinance under which members of parliament had to give up their military commands. This meant Manchester had to go. It would also have meant Cromwell giving up his military commands, but by this time, after his victory in 1644 at Marston Moor, it was clear that Cromwell was the best parliamentary commander in the field, so parliament kept making temporary exemptions so he could retain his command. And he went on to stunning victories at Naseby and Preston in the first and second civil wars against Charles I and then at Dunbar and Worcester against Charles's son and the Scots in what is sometimes referred to as the Third Civil War.

Perhaps one way that Cromwell was a radical was in his soldiering, perhaps because he had no military experience to restrain him and keep him conventional. He was known for being close to his men, yet keeping them disciplined both on and off the field, and he was celebrated for his daring and creativity, being able to out-manoeuvre enemy armies and defeat forces much larger than his own. He was especially fond of cavalry charges and pitched battles rather than sieges. But it was sieges that he was engaged in when he went to subdue Ireland in 1649, two in particular, Drogheda and Wexford, that have blackened his reputation because they ended in massacres. And besides the massacres, Cromwell in Ireland is also associated with mass resettlement of the Catholic Irish to make way for Protestant settlers from England. Cromwell himself had invested money in the Irish expedition, with the promise of receiving lands for himself afterwards. He seems to have received some eventually,[6] but he was constantly giving away money for such causes, and it seems that what motivated him most was religion: in the early days of the Long Parliament, the Irish rose in rebellion and word reached England of massacres of Protestants. Eight years later, these events were still on Cromwell's mind. In general, he was no friend of Catholicism; though he fought for liberty of conscience and opposed the sectarianism that broke out among Protestants during the Civil Wars, he did not include Catholics among those to whom he would grant religious liberty, though to be fair he said he could not know what people thought; they could believe what they liked in religion, but he would not allow the performance of the Mass.

Some have argued that this was a security issue for Cromwell; he wanted to preserve order, so would not allow Catholic activities. And he feared Catholic forces invading England. At Drogheda and Wexford, he also found his forces repulsed at first, and he never took kindly to reverses. It has also been argued that the Wexford massacre was the result of his men running amok rather than any plan from Cromwell himself. No such defence has been made of the events at Drogheda, though a general defence has been put forward that what happened in the Irish fighting was not much different from fighting elsewhere in the seventeenth century. Still, Cromwell prided himself on restraining his troops and acting in a humanitarian way towards defeated adversaries – but that's not what happened in Ireland, and his name remains anathema to the Irish.

Meanwhile back in England, before the Irish expedition, Cromwell eventually became supreme in the field, thanks to the Self-Denying Ordinance and the creation in its wake of the New Model Army, modelled largely on Cromwell's own troop structures. The New Model did its work, assisted by the Scottish Presbyterians who, as the price of alliance, demanded that the English sign on to the Solemn League and Covenant, which called for Presbyterian church government once the fight against Charles I had been won. Cromwell, though no Presbyterian, signed the Covenant. Though not happy with the Presbyterian tendency to impose their views on other Protestants, and though he kept reporting that among his troops, the details of his soldiers' beliefs were not important and everyone got along, whether they were Presbyterian, Independent, or Baptist, he agreed to the Covenant, because it was made a condition for continuing to serve in the army. Lilburne did not sign the Covenant. He held to his principles and left the army. How might things have been different otherwise, but this marks the beginning of his divergence from Cromwell. He returned to pamphleteering and when he found himself running afoul of the new instruments of censorship brought in by the Presbyterian-controlled parliament, he began to shift his focus from religious arguments to the more secular issue of civil liberties, or the rights of freeborn Englishmen.

Lilburne began by quarrelling with two of his former mentors, William Prynne and John Bastwick, and a pamphlet war ensued, leading to Lilburne being called before parliament's new Committee of Examinations. He proceeded to treat this parliamentary committee the way he had treated Star Chamber, questioning its procedures and citing Magna Carta. He also cited the common law of England as interpreted by Sir Edward Coke, and he eventually began to refer to natural law and reason, perhaps influenced by some of his new associates, Richard Overton and William Walwyn.[7] With Lilburne, Overton and Walwyn formed the core of a new movement which its opponents called the Levellers, trying to bring them into disrepute by suggesting that they wanted to level estates, in other words, make everyone equal socially and economically. Lilburne and the others vigorously rebutted this charge, made by Cromwell among others, saying their aim was to have everyone treated equally (for instance before the law) while still preserving property. They were not the ancestors of socialists but of liberal democrats.

The democratic part of their program began to develop now, leading to the creation of the *Agreement of the People*. Before this, the focus, when not on Lilburne's personal sufferings and Church government, had been on individual liberties such as free speech and freedom of the press; also the right to a free trial, including the right not to incriminate oneself. Now the focus was larger: it was time to set the whole government on a different basis. The English Civil War had begun as a contest between the rights of the king and the rights of parliament. Lilburne had been very much on the side of parliament, and gone even further, saying that it was the House of Commons alone that was the source of supreme power. But now the Levellers went further still, perhaps because they were disillusioned with the House of Commons, which kept arresting them. They began to see the House of Commons more as trustees than a source. Power did not emanate from the Commons; it was entrusted in them by the people. Only with the consent of the people could the House of Commons rule. Hence the *Agreement*, a constitution, something new for England, under which the people would give their consent.

How much Lilburne was involved in drawing up the first version of the *Agreement* (it went through several revisions) is unclear, but he certainly became involved in promoting it and working on later versions. He was the centre of a movement now, a somewhat complicated movement because it had both a civilian wing (Lilburne, Walwyn, Overton, etc. in London) and another set of radicals in the New Model Army, known as Agitators. The Agitators, who were the elected representatives of the rank and file, arose in part to demand payment of arrears, but also to make political demands, becoming supporters of the *Agreement*.

Meanwhile, the senior officers of the army, known as the Grandees and including Cromwell, tried to exercise a moderating influence. Cromwell tried to mediate between the army and parliament (he was a member of both) and also between the officers and the men. He did not want the army to march on London and use force against parliament, 'for that which you have as force I look upon it as nothing'.[8] Meanwhile, he told parliament that the soldiers should be paid their arrears, and if that happened, then parliament could disband the army, as it wanted to do. But the army radicals wanted more than back pay, as they made clear at a set of debates held at Putney in the fall of 1647 between the Agitators and the Grandees. *The Agreement of the People* was discussed, along with a more moderate proposed constitution from the officers called the *Heads of Proposals*. There was talk of annual or biennial elections to parliament and debate about extending the suffrage, making it universal or almost universal: excluding women, of course, and others such as servants and beggars, but still extending it dramatically. Cromwell presided. Lilburne, being in prison, was not present. Cromwell had visited him there and told him that if he promised to refrain from 'hurley-burleys', he could be released. But he declined.[9]

Then the king escaped, provoking the Second Civil War, leading ultimately to Pride's Purge when the Presbyterians in parliament persisted in seeking negotiations with the twice-defeated Charles to try to come to some mutually acceptable arrangement. Meanwhile, Cromwell was up north conducting a siege of the last Royalist stronghold in Pontefract and arrived in London just after the Purge, which created a House of Commons much more intent on executing Charles and creating a republic, or Commonwealth. Cromwell only reluctantly went along with this, and was especially dismayed by the abolition of the House of Lords, but in the end, he became one of the judges of the defeated king and was one of those who signed the death warrant.

The arrest of King Charles I. (Stephen Basdeo's Personal Collection)

Lilburne, who had been released from prison just a few months before, was also asked to be a judge, but declined, saying he found the proceedings irregular. Lilburne's attitude was that the important thing was the rights of the people, and these could be guaranteed under a monarchy as well as in a republic, and he saw Purge, Trial, and Execution as just one set of oligarchs replacing another. Cromwell had earlier said something similar, calling the forms of government mere 'dross and dung' compared to the essential thing, which was liberty of conscience in religious matters. He also noted that the ancient Hebrews, a model for Cromwell and other puritans, had moved through various forms of government, including judges and kings.[10] It is interesting to note that Cromwell and Lilburne were essentially in agreement in not caring too much about the form of government, but Cromwell went along with rule by the Purged Parliament (or Rump), whereas Lilburne continually denounced its rule as illegitimate. Still, they both were actually more interested in larger ends: Lilburne in civil liberties and popular sovereignty, Cromwell in godly reformation. Cromwell was the one with the power to push for his larger end, and when he found the Rump Parliament not making progress on liberty of conscience or other godly matters, nor on other reforms he favoured, such as improvements in the legal system, he stepped in and dissolved it. This was one of the few times he took direct action himself, going to the parliament with his troops and ordering it to depart after calling its members drunkards and whoremasters.[11] He was angry, perhaps because he felt that members of the Rump had misled him about their intentions. He later said that he was concerned that the Rump was trying to extend its life indefinitely, but his real concern, as explained by Blair Worden,[12] may have been almost the opposite: that it was going to dissolve itself at last and allow free elections. Cromwell seems to have feared that such elections were premature: he was hoping for a godly nation, but feared that it was still less than godly and might elect Presbyterians or even old Royalists.

What followed was an attempt at a godly parliament, the so-called Barebone's Parliament, made up of pious men nominated by Cromwell and his Council who it was hoped would lead the nation into godly paths. Unfortunately for Cromwell, what it did instead was dissolve into factional disputation and in less than a year, it was gone, paving the way for the Protectorate at the end of 1653, at which point Cromwell became head of state and took on the trappings of royalty (there was even a quasi-coronation in 1657), but did not accept the crown. He was to be addressed as Your Highness and took up residence in royal palaces, but in practice deferred to his Council of State, for instance on the issue of readmitting Jews to England (Cromwell was favourable, but his Council said no, so officially Jews remained banned, though unofficially they began to return). Barebone's was 'a story of my own weakness and folly', Cromwell said later,[13] and returned to elected parliaments during the Protectorate under a new constitution called the Instrument of Government. But he dissolved this parliament after a mere five months, frustrated with its focus on revising the constitution. What he wanted was godliness, and to that end, he issued ordinances creating a system of Triers and Ejectors to rid the nation of 'scandalous' ministers and ensure that new ones were pious and moral. He pushed harder for this when he created the system of Major-Generals. Dividing the country up into districts, he installed a Major-General in charge of each one, in part to look after security but also to aim for a reformation of manners by shutting down alehouses, restricting May Day festivities, and instilling good morals. The people would have none of it. They even wanted their old prayer book back, the Book of Common Prayer that the puritans had banned.

Cromwell's aim was to do what was good for the people whether they wanted it or not: he would act 'for the people's good, not what pleases them'.[14] Lilburne's approach was more to let the people do what they wanted, opposing monopolies, restrictions on trade, restrictions on speech, and arbitrary authority in general. Cromwell's godly reformation failed; Lilburne's approach bore long-term fruit in liberal democracies that enshrined civil liberties in their written or unwritten constitutions and gave the people some recourse against arbitrary rule. In the short term, though, Lilburne mostly languished in jail, though he did have some spectacular triumphs, as when he convinced a jury that they had the power to judge the law as well as the facts of a case, leading them to acquit him of treason in 1649, a decision that prompted much popular celebration. However, in 1651, the Rump seized him again and exiled him from England for writing pamphlets they deemed slanderous. He went to Amsterdam and then Bruges, still writing pamphlets. He called Cromwell a tyrant and called for his impeachment. He returned home in violation of his banishment order and was put on trial again, once again calling on the jury to judge the law as well as the facts, and once again he was acquitted, to much cheering. But the government wouldn't release him despite the acquittal. Instead, it investigated the jury and sent Lilburne off to the island of Jersey, later moving him to Dover. He fell ill, became tired, and on being exposed to some Quaker teachings converted. He would not lift up the 'temporal sword' anymore, he said.[15] His wife petitioned for his release. There were demands that he sign a statement promising not to raise a rebellion against the government, as the Quaker leader George Fox had done, but he refused. George Fox is a good man, he said, but the rules he follows are not binding on John Lilburne. He was John Lilburne to the end. He died on 29 August 1657, while out on day parole from his Dover prison. His birth date is uncertain, but he was only in his early forties. Cromwell outlived him by little more than a year, dying in 1658 at the age of fifty-nine on 3 September, a date important to him as being the anniversary of his victories at both Dunbar and Worcester.

The Cromwellian Protectorate survived for less than two years after that, a Stuart king was put back on the throne, and the old Established Church was re-established, as was the House of Lords. As for godliness, the Restoration period was marked by as complete a reaction as possible against that Puritanical agenda. And yet King Charles II was not as his father, and the powers of the monarchy would never be the same. Perhaps that is owed in part to Cromwell, who though he kept dissolving parliaments, also kept bringing them back. The Established Church was not the same either. Nonconformists were allowed to attend their own chapels. Perhaps that owed something to Cromwell too and his fight for liberty of conscience, however limited it may have been. And the Jews were officially readmitted soon as well.

The legacy of Oliver Cromwell has been much fought over. Was he a revolutionary or a military dictator and ethnic cleanser? Was he a revolutionary who betrayed the revolution? Or was he simply a surprisingly skilled general who was called on to lead the country after its upheavals and who failed to instil the godliness he was most attached to, his most radical belief, but who helped maintain stability and order, leading to the constitutional monarchy of later centuries? Perhaps as Christopher Hill once said he was George Washington to John Lilburne's Tom Paine.[16]

And what of Lilburne? He has been claimed as a Christian democrat, a social democrat, and a libertarian. Some have tried to see him as a socialist, but that label probably belongs more to Gerrard Winstanley and the Diggers. His Leveller movement faded away in the 1650s, as did the parallel radical movement of the Agitators in the army after Cromwell crushed their mutinies. And yet modern liberal democracies owe much to his fight for civil liberties and popular sovereignty. Regular elections, extended suffrage, freedom of the press, and (somewhat ironically) the right to remain silent owe a good deal to the man whose courtroom antics perhaps prefigured the antics of Sixties radicals. Who else but John Lilburne would have demanded a chamber pot in the middle of a treason trial? And who else, having spent so much time in the Tower of London, would have named one of his children Tower? Cromwell still has his bloody legacy in Ireland to live down, but he and Lilburne, though often at odds, somehow between them helped usher in the world of constitutional rule and civil rights. It is no small accomplishment, radical or not.

Notes

1. Blair Worden, "Oliver Cromwell and the Cause of Civil and Religious Liberty," in *England's Wars of Religion, Revisited*, ed. Charles W.A. Prior and Glenn Burgess (Farnham, Surrey and Burlington, VT: Ashgate, 2011), 232.
2. Cit. Pauline Gregg, *Free-Born John: The Biography of John Lilburne* (London: Phoenix, 2000 [originally published in 1961]), 316.
3. Antonia Fraser, *Cromwell, Our Chief of Men* ([London: Phoenix, 2011, originally published in 1973]), chap. 1, Kindle.

4. For more details on this, see Andrew Barclay, *Electing Cromwell: The Making of a Politician* (London and New York: Routledge, 2011).

5. Cit. Ian Gentles, *Oliver Cromwell: God's Warrior and the English Revolution* (Basingstoke: Palgrave Macmillan, 2011), 12.

6. Patrick Little, "Cromwell and Ireland before 1649," in *Oliver Cromwell: New Perspectives*, ed. Patrick Little (Basingstoke: Palgrave Macmillan, 2009), 118.

7. For more on the different views among the Levellers, see Rachel Foxley, *The Levellers: Radical Political Thought in the English Revolution* (Manchester and New York: Manchester University Press, 2013).

8. Fraser, *Cromwell*, chap. 8.

9. Gregg, *Free-Born John*, 194.

10. Fraser, *Cromwell*, chap. 9.

11. Fraser, *Cromwell*, chap. 15.

12. Blair Worden, *The Rump Parliament, 1648-1653* (Cambridge: Cambridge University Press, 1974), chap. 16.

13. Cit. Peter Gaunt, *Oliver Cromwell* (Cambridge, MA: Blackwell, 1996), 150.

14. Cit. John Morrill, *Oliver Cromwell and the English Revolution* (London and New York: Longman, 1990), 8.

15. Michael Braddick, *The Common Freedom of the People: John Lilburne & the English Revolution* (Oxford: Oxford University Press, 2018), 266.

16. Christopher Hill, "Oliver Cromwell" (1958), in *The Collected Essays of Christopher Hill*, vol. 3: *People and Ideas in Seventeenth-Century England* (Amherst: University of Massachusetts Press, 1986), 91.

The Levellers

Joseph Saunders

The seventeenth century saw social and political upheaval where the very notions of England and Englishness were challenged. It was 'a world turned upside-down', an era of Civil War and Revolution where her people 'reached a stature, moral and intellectual, which dwarfed their normal selves'.[1] In 1642, part of parliament and the people of London revolted against an unpopular king and his detested policies. A divided country then fought a bloody war in which a larger proportion of Englishmen died than in any conflict before or since. By 1649, a small group of politicians, lawyers and generals who had been radicalised by this conflict emerged holding power and put on trial a defeated king for committing treason against his own people.

For the first time in English history, a king was executed by his subjects. This period was briefly but intensely one of English Revolution. It was driven by thinkers and activists who propagated ideas, protested on the streets and joined armies in the name of legal and religious freedoms which they felt were under threat. Increasingly the clamour was to advocate for fundamental political and social changes and while some were soon enacted (though later reversed) such as republicanism, the abolition of the House of Lords and a degree of religious tolerance previously unseen; other changes like free trade, equality under the law and universal male suffrage would take centuries to secure.

While many radical groups emerged, the Levellers were *the* radical movement of the Civil Wars in England. We can argue over the degree of their radicalism, their effectiveness or the very nature of the 'Levellers' as a distinct entity but a broad movement pejoratively called by their enemies 'Levellers' had undoubtedly emerged by at least 1647 with a brief influence over events before their suppression in 1649. In a world of kaleidoscopic cross-currents of ideologies, they were able to draw together at certain points radical strands at the vanguard of a wave that knocked a hole through the bastions of the old authorities, Church and State. In the surge of the English Revolution, the Levellers were not the most radical group but were most disciplined and convincing and had influence across society from the London mob to the common solider to generals and MPs. Moreover, they were a movement for their time, combining radical religious ideology and church organising with the new print media and techniques such newsbooks and petitioning. They were of and for the groups which made the success of the Parliamentary causes, the puritan middling sorts, from tradesmen and apprentices to New Model Army soldiers. Their demands challenged the status quo but importantly developed out of a tradition of opposition and reform, sitting within popular culture and thought in such a way as to make them widely influential.

The Levellers were essentially polemicists and pamphleteers drawn from a broad opposition that emerged first to the Crown and a more radical core that came to resist aspects of the Parliamentary government. During the fragmented distillation of radicalism through these two prisms, the Levellers as a distinct but loose movement came to espouse freedom from the abuses of government and the law in all its forms. At times they pushed against opposition and at others, they drove forward elites who may otherwise have taken a more neutral and uncertain path. Any doubts we have in the present looking back at what they achieved can be assuaged by how much influence they had over the course of 1647–9 when the Parliamentary coalition was transformed from a movement defending tradition to a force that introduced wide-ranging change. If England had indeed adopted a true democratic government in 1649 as it came close to doing so, the Levellers would have been a significant reason for it.

Part I: Origins

The Levellers were a logical but far from inevitable result of long-standing conditions, sparked by a series of short-term crises. The circumstances which gave rise to this movement were that inseparable and heady mix of religion in all aspects of life through politics and war across Europe. In over a century of Reformation and Counter-Reformation, a theoretical war over the very ideology and ideas that underlay the whole of European society raged, regularly erupting into bloody and violent conflict. During this process, some very modern concepts and technologies emerged, from standing armies to nations, to the public sphere. In the 1620s and 30s, the brutal Thirty Years' War set the scene of bitter civil wars across the continent. Dissent and conflict simmered on the surface of English society with the Puritan movement of the 1580s and fear of Catholics stoked by the Spanish Armada in 1588 and the Gunpowder Plot of 1605. By the 1630s, the English looked across to the bloody wars being fought in central Europe, advertised to them in an increasingly prominent print culture and was faced with the prospect of its own divisions being disrupted still further by a king determined to pursue government and Church policy in a direction that alienated his own people to revolt against him.

The Long English Reformation

The Reformation in England was a haphazard affair. It stopped and started, pushed and pulled in various directions as different versions of the 'true' Christian religion were enforced from above by successive monarchs, followed by varying levels of enthusiasm from below. The Elizabethan Church Settlement of 1559 in theory put an end to this and set the official religion of England in stone, assisted by her long and stable reign. This pragmatic solution settled upon a sort of moderate Protestantism, with the added English peculiarity that the monarch was Head of the Church. For the vast majority, this arrangement suited them well, and they continued to live their lives with religion and faith as merely a ubiquitous fact of life. There were, however, fervent dissenters who would feel at odds with the position of the official Church; Catholics who would become recusants (non-Church goers) even to the point of exile and death, and puritans, the 'hotter sort of Protestants', who pushed for further reformation within the Church.

During the middle of Elizabeth's reign tensions grew between Catholic and Protestant powers in Europe and within nations themselves. The resurgence of the Protestant Dutch Revolt against Spanish Habsburg authority and the French Wars of Religion fought between adherents of the two faiths drew in England as Europe's main Protestant nation. There was growing competition with Spain such as the English pirating of New World shipping and in 1588, the attempted invasion by the Spanish Armada. At home, general anti-Catholic and anti-puritan sentiment were major aspects of public and political life. In the 1580s, unsatisfied with the perceived stagnation of the Reformation these 'puritans' as they became known advocated reforms peacefully and within the Church. Alongside this, puritan writers were enthusiastic in their use of print media to denounce the perceived wrongs of the established Church, such as in the illegally printed rude and satirical tracts of 'Martin Marprelate'. While still accessible only for a minority of the population, print was by 1600 a fact of life in European society, an important conduit of information and ideas and an influence on culture and politics. Even at the lowest levels of society, if you could not read or afford to buy a book, a pamphlet, or a newspaper at the very least you would hear the ideas around you. The crackdown on the puritan movement was strict, but puritanism lived on as a vociferous undercurrent within the Church as a 'puritan underground' and with a continued presence in print. A second and then a third generation of puritans emerged, some became writers and thinkers, some (perhaps as many as 30,000) emigrated to the American colonies. By the 1630s, an undefined minority within the English population were sympathetic to the push for further reformation and were certainly unwilling to countenance what they saw as reversals. This puritan tradition was more than an ideological background to the radicalism of the Civil Wars. The culture of such movements also had great influence, where it was normal

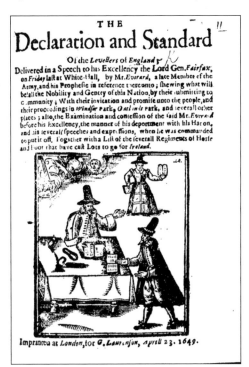

The Declaration and Standard of the Levellers of England. (Wikimedia Commons)

for all members of a congregation to speak, to question or interrupt the speaker and generally such meetings and movements required organisational abilities which by the 1640s had been honed over generations.

From 1618, the confessional struggle between Reformation and Counter-Reformation in Europe entered its final but most destructive phase. The onset of the Thirty Years' War drew in every European nation in some way or another. While the British kingdoms of the Stuarts were not formally involved, there were many who sought to come to the aid of their religious brethren. Soldiers with strong beliefs enlisted with one or another of the great powers. Across the continent, print media went into overdrive to report on the war, following the movements of the armies, political intrigues and massacres with grim but insatiable fascination. In England, the appetite for information also led to a further increase in print volume and types, especially as the ban on domestic news enabled reporting of the war as (an often thinly disguised) commentary on affairs closer to home. It also reflected a wide disaffection that King Charles and then his son James refused to throw English weight outright behind the Protestant cause.

The Personal Rule

To this tinderbox of generational and inter-confessional division was added the spark which caused the descent into civil war. King Charles I in 1625 inherited a country riven by internal division over politics and religion, balanced precariously in the edge of a pan-European conflict that threatened to engulf it. Unfortunately, Charles possessed as little tact as humanly possible. Believing absolutely in the Divine Right of Kings that his rule was ordained from God he pursued government and Church policy as he saw fit, alienating many of his nobles and large swathes of his other subjects. He was also prone to favouritism firstly of the Duke of Buckingham and secondly Thomas Wentworth who he made Earl of Strafford. Both were widely unpopular and blamed for the king's failings and as a result, Buckingham was unceremoniously murdered and Strafford (very) ceremoniously tried. In response to parliament's questioning of his absolute authority, Charles simply decided not to call it in what became known as the Personal Rule (1629-1640). While at this time a parliament was an event to be called at will rather than a regular feature of life, to actively decide to rule without it was an affront to many. Social custom dictated that the king listen to the advice of his subjects, even if he did not take it. Parliament was also the only body that could agree to new taxes. For both these reasons his predecessors had called them at intervals of a few years, even if they did not like doing so. To circumvent the lack of taxes, Charles introduced a series of measures that he either resurrected from the distant past or stretched to their limits. Probably the most hated was Ship Money which had been traditionally paid by coastal counties in times of emergency toward the upkeep of the navy. By making this a regular levy and extending it to inland areas, Charles alienated many otherwise loyal subjects.

Given the divisions within the country, the most unpopular aspects of the Personal Rule were unsurprisingly regarding religion. Charles' 'Arminian' policies were seen as attempts to reverse the Reformation by introducing aspects of worship closer to traditional Catholic forms. The fear of Catholics again played an important factor here, especially as Queen Henrietta Maria was a Catholic herself and the king controversially allowed her to practice her religion. Charles upset many ordinary worshippers as well as the fiercer puritans by his attempt to introduce an English Book of Prayer in Scotland which led to two wars where the Scots took up arms against him. One of Charles' favourites and the leading proponent of his Church policy was William Laud, Archbishop of Canterbury. As well as pursuing Charles' reforms, Laud was a vociferous opponent of puritanism and came to enforce a crackdown similar to that of the 1580s. A culture war ensued leading to the very public condemnation of puritan authors Henry Burton, John Bastwick and William Prynne who were turned into martyrs after charges of sedition and libel led to lengthy imprisonment and the public 'cropping' of their ears.

It was in this climate of heightened tension that a pamphlet war in London ensued, fed by various strands of reformist thinking arrayed against the king and his policies. This included disaffected nobles and many in the middling and lower sorts across the city who aligned themselves against the king. Within this wave of popular opinion and in the thick of the print debate emerged a loose opposition party from Lords to apprentices who would soon take up the fight for the rights of parliament. Men like John Lilburne, whose life and career has been discussed by Sheldon Goldfarb in-depth, was a young apprentice from a gentry family who had become a supporter of the three puritan martyrs, visiting them in prison and taking up his pen to advocate for his view of the world in troubled times. He in turn was pilloried and imprisoned for his pains, famously refusing to plead in court before he had heard the charges against himself, setting a precedent against perjury still used today. Lilburne was ably assisted by his wife Elizabeth and together they belonged to the puritan underground which was at the heart of the civil discord now raging. While there were many other Leveller leaders and organisers, many of whom were drawn from this same milieu, Lilburne in these early years established himself as a talisman for a wider radical movement through his words and actions, presenting himself as a martyr of the law, though inspired by religion.[2]

Part II: Civil War

The tortuous progress of the English Reformation and the antagonistic Personal Rule of Charles I together caused cultural and political divisions within Charles's kingdoms which slowly descended into civil war. By 1640, this had led to a stand-off between a king unwilling to relinquish supreme power but increasingly unable to rule and parts of the ruling classes, supported by a vocal print media and the London mob, who were increasingly minded that he had hoarded power for too long and eroded English customs and liberties. The events may briefly be retold here as the fires of war were critical to the emergence of the Levellers.

King and Parliament

The Scottish revolt against Charles's Church impositions ended with their occupation of the north of England. It was in a state of desperation that the king was finally forced to call a parliament to help him raise money to fend off the Scots. Parliament however refused and instead pressed their issues. The king speedily prorogued it, thus earning it the epithet, the Short Parliament. It would be the last time he would do so. Facing the same difficulties with the additional prospect of rebellion in Ireland the next year, he called a parliament once again, known to history as the Long Parliament as it sat in some form or another for the next twenty years. A party of MPs led by the enigmatic puritan John Pym were by now determined to resist Charles until they could secure his acknowledgement to rule upon the established convention of 'King, Lords and Commons'. These men became a thorn in his side though a by now desperate Charles felt unable to dissolve parliament and so in January 1642, attempted the infamous arrest of the five most troublesome MPs. He stormed into the House of Commons with an armed guard, in contravention of all the customs of the land but found the members had fled and their colleagues refused to give them up. Coupled with a fresh wave of street protests, Charles no longer felt safe in the capital and fled with his family. During the tense spring, Royalist and Parliamentary sides began to coalesce before the king finally raised his standard in Nottingham, declaring war against his rebellious English subjects.

The subsequent conflict was one of the most destructive events ever to occur on English soil. Armies passed across the countryside, landscapes were marked forever and lives were ruined. The death toll of soldiers to the overall population was proportionally higher than the English soldiers who died in the First World War. Parliament from the outset controlled the richest parts of the country around London and had quickly taken the navy, major ports and arsenals. Royalist forces had broad swathes of popular support, not just from fierce supporters of the king but also many who had been his enemies previously but had sided with him out of a sense of duty or fear of the unknowns that parliament offered. The Royalists arguably had the best of the fighting in the first two years and parliament was hamstrung by both their lack of energetic commanders and a (justifiable) question over their authority to wage such a war. Appreciating the situation before them was slowly developing into a stalemate parliament sought to make a decisive move to win and established England's first standing army, the 'New Model Army'. This force was put under the command of Sir Thomas Fairfax, a successful and well-respected general. By 1645, the New Model had won a series of victories and had begun to turn the tide in parliament's favour.

Presbyterians, Independents and Levellers

It is here, as the war closed that the debate over just what the country had shed its blood for began. During the conflict, there had emerged several factions within the Parliamentary alliance but while the fight against the king was underway, they battled collectively for success. As the war entered its final stage they now began to divide sharply. On one hand emerged broadly a conservative faction who sought a peace settlement with Charles and the restoration of law and order based broadly on the pre-war consensus. Most importantly, this party dominated parliament and had sought to impose a Church settlement following the Presbyterian Scottish model which they believed was a sensible middle-ground between Charles' Arminianism and the sectarianism on their other side.

The other main faction was the 'Independents' who opposed the desire for a peace settlement with the king and thought he had to be fully defeated in order to bring him to the table on Parliamentarian terms. The support for Independency was particularly strong in the New Model Army with leading men such as Cromwell and his right-hand man and son-in-law, Henry Ireton, as well as radical MPs such as the Republican, Henry Marten. The rank-and-file soldiery was particularly concerned with what they had fought for and the other main position of the Independents was that they had been fighting for religious toleration in the form of allowance for independent meetings and gatherings. On this radical wing and beyond were several sects and factions who pushed the boundaries even of mainstream Independent thinking and would later break off more distinctly, leading to groups such as the Quakers and Diggers.

From 1645, the most prominent radical strand on the Independent fringe begun to coalesce in opposition to the Presbyterian party who were then in the ascendancy. While they had no coherent platform, or ever arguably emerged into a distinct 'party' from this time there developed a cohesion between a few key activists, polemicists, and printers. Most came from the puritan underground and had cut their teeth in the heady days of the 1630s in opposition to Charles. Several had been acquainted at that time including Richard Overton who had printed some of Lilburne's works. Many future Levellers had served in the militia which had been the chief source of Parliamentary support in 1640-2 or the army, which in turn proved to be a hotbed for radical support, the logical result of enlisting ideologically driven men to fight and die for the cause. While there was a large body of secondary leadership across London and into the country, three leaders had emerged by 1646 sharing similar ideas about religious toleration and freedoms under the law and referred readers of their works to the others, even if they did not yet constitute an organised movement.

Arguably the chief of these was John Lilburne who had joined the army at the outbreak of war, fighting bravely at Edgehill and Brentford where he was captured. Taken as a prisoner of war to Oxford, he was tried for treason but refused to plea asserting his right that as a soldier he was protected under the conventions of war. Determined to press ahead, the Royalists sentenced Lilburne to death and were only stopped when parliament threatened to begin executing prisoners in retaliation. Even then the execution was only prevented when the Parliamentary decree was ridden through army lines by a heavily pregnant Elizabeth Lilburne. John continued to serve, this time in the Eastern Association Army, where he struck up a brief friendship with Oliver Cromwell and joined in his growing feud with the Earl of Manchester. Having refused a commission in the New Model because of his increasing disillusion with the Parliamentary cause Lilburne, by now a Lieutenant-Colonel, returned to London and took some of his grievances with the army to court. He also began to lobby for reparations for his imprisonment in the 1630s which he was eventually granted. However, he was imprisoned once again. Through his own publicisation and of those sympathetic Lilburne became a figurehead for the struggle of the Independents against the Presbyterians as he went through trials and imprisonment. The most famous Leveller, though he would often decry the name, he was in many ways far bigger than the movement itself. Lilburne became a figurehead during the late 1640s as he became a voice for those who having rebelled against their king, now asked what they had done so for, if the ruling Presbyterians were only going to keep much of the status quo.

Often described as Lilburne's lieutenant, though he was far more, was Richard Overton, the printer and polemicist, whose work has been lauded for its wit and satirical quality. He came to be imprisoned almost as much as Lilburne. His writing was often more refined and likely edited many of Lilburne's works. In July 1646, it is likely he who penned the electric anti-monarchical *A remonstrance of many thousand citizens* which blasted those who sought a quick and lenient settlement with the king and asserted the supremacy of the House of Commons. The third leader to emerge was William Walwyn who wrote measured prose first against the bishops and then the Presbyterians in favour of freedom of conscience. He became an implacable enemy of Thomas Edwards, the Presbyterian propagandist, a sign of how feared Walwyn's mind was in the minds of the opposition. In January 1646, Walwyn had produced one of the first tracts of the developing Leveller movement, *Toleration justified and persecution condemned*, where he made a forceful case for religious tolerance. Along with these were organisers, printers and preachers of a secondary rank such as Katherine and Samuel Chidley, Thomas Prince, William Larner and Thomas Lambe who organised mass protests and petitions and spread Leveller thought through print and speech. Beneath them were innumerable organisers and sympathisers across the country, though most were concentrated in London.

The New Model Army and the Agitators

As well as the various factions emerging within the Parliamentary camp, the New Model Army was an entity unto itself which was divided but generally more supportive of the Independents and the radicals, especially amongst the common soldiery. These men had been drawn from the most committed of those who had been fighting passionately for several years in a bloody and traumatic civil war. They had been recruited based on Cromwell's maxim that he would have a 'plain russet-coated' captain who knew what he fought for than a gentleman who was nothing else. While there had been some conscription, this was largely a volunteer army, especially among the cavalry regiments, and the typical soldier seems to have been of middling social rank with a strong puritan streak. Many were returning New Worlders and often their puritanical beliefs could border on militancy, their zealousness and fervour causing them to have a reputation for iconoclasm and dissent. The army was itself a hotbed of preaching and a melting pot of people from across the country with all manner of ideas and it soon became known for two things, as an effective fighting force and for its radicalism.

While many in the army had been inspired by the writings of the 'Levellers', as they were becoming derisively known by their enemies, they had also come from the same background and had believed in the cause against the king for similar reasons. In the crucible of war and its immediate aftermath, it is impossible to say what ideas came first as the Leveller polemicists were increasingly in favour of the grievances of the army, probably out of genuine desire though it was also politically convenient to align with this powerful force. In early 1647, the army, restless and worried at what their futures would hold, came to take several steps which would change the face of the peace, just as they had changed the face of the war. In parliament, the Presbyterian party had gained the upper hand. As well as negotiating with the king for a peace settlement which was widely unpopular they were refusing to announce indemnities for acts committed during the war (requisitioning a horse for example was in peacetime theft and punishable by death), had failed to deliver significant arrears, and were threatening to disband the most of the army, sending a few remaining regiments to fight in Ireland. At the same time, the army set up a printing press under Leveller John Harris and was making its own demands, including the freedom of imprisoned Levellers such as John Lilburne. A key figure was Edward Sexby who worked with Harris and organised the distribution of pamphlets and petitioning campaigns and became arguably the leading Leveller in the army. This alliance developed throughout 1647 and came to the fore with the appointment of the Agitators. These Agitators (or Agents) from each regiment would represent the soldiers in their discussions with the generals as the army agreed a position and sought redress. At the same time, the soldiers agreed not to disband until their demands were met. They began to call on Fairfax to order a general rendezvous and he appointed representatives of the Agitators to the General Council of the Army, a revolutionary concession.

Working in tandem, the Agitators and their civilian allies increasingly represented the radical wing of the Independent party. It is in this sense that the Levellers must be viewed as part of the wider revolutionary current. While many have tried to claim them as a distinct 'party', they were much more a group of intellectual collaborators and activists whose words and actions came to inspire popular opinion, particularly in the New Model. The degree to which the Levellers ever had any control over events, or indeed any distinct plan to take or run the army or government is uncertain, other than to promote a programme which was increasingly a dual ambition of providing redress for grievances and a radical peace settlement in opposition to the Presbyterian drive for a return near to the pre-war status quo.

During the first part of 1647, the debate within the Parliamentary camp between Presbyterian and Independent factions was settled when the army did what each side respectively had not been able to do during four long years of war, to capture London and King Charles. In 1647, members of the New Model, probably with the knowledge of Cromwell, if not under his orders caused a coup when they seized the king from his keepers at Holmby House in Northamptonshire, greatly strengthening their hand in the peace settlement debate. At the same time, the Presbyterians in parliament moved to consolidate their position and for a moment they appeared to have snuffed out Independency. However, Cromwell and Commissary-General, Henry Ireton, fled London to re-join the army which then marched on the capital taking it apparently without bloodshed. It was through the power of the New Model that Independent control of the Parliamentary cause was established.

Taking the king and London confirmed the army in its view that it held immense power. Even Charles acknowledged this and began to negotiate with it directly, as well as with parliament, thinking he could play one against the other. He was right. The divisions within the Independent coalition was divided between its power bases in the army, parliament and London and along ideological lines. While there was a broad spectrum of opinion across the different areas of support, it became clear over the course of the summer that the New Model and the Levellers were far more radical than the Independent leadership in parliament.

Part III: Revolution

By 1647, a group had emerged in opposition to Presbyterianism including the by now cooperating Leveller leaders Overton, Lilburne and Walwyn, the army printer, John Harris, and chief Agitator, Edward Sexby, as well as sympathetic officers such as Captains Bray and Eyre and Colonel Rainsborough, the New Model's siege expert. Once Cromwell and Ireton had put their faith in the New Model as a counter to Presbyterianism, a considerable Independent movement had emerged which encompassed the military forces of parliament and the most radical thinkers and activists. In the first part of the year, the Levellers in the New Model and in London had enabled Independent victory over the Presbyterians but by the autumn the army's grievances remained unmet and the future of the country still uncertain.

The Case of the Army and An Agreement of the People

It is in the context of continuing uncertainty that a broad Leveller 'programme' emerged from the radical wing of the Independent party. The ideas that came to be espoused were advertised in proclamations and tracts aimed often ostensibly to the Independent leadership but with appeal amongst the common people. Of the most important of such claims were the calls for the release of political prisoners (such as Lilburne), back pay for soldiers and indemnity for crimes committed during the war using the assertions of natural and historic rights and liberties. However, the ambitions of this movement extended into the very heart of what the war had been fought for. From defensive demands over their rights, the argument was increasingly that the Parliamentary cause and particularly those who had shed their blood for it had done so for the 'safety of the people' and that the soldiery should accept nothing which could jeopardise this. For some radicals, including many within the Leveller movement, the rebellion against the king had been an act of rejection with the past and not only were ancient rights and liberties to be restored but new innovations were required to protect them.

In September 1647, the Agitators and Levellers drew up a document called *The Case of the Army truly stated* and presented it to Commander-in-chief Fairfax. In it, they called for the redress of their grievances, the dissolution of parliament within the year and changes made so that the election of future parliaments were to be regulated by set conditions. They followed this with another tract, which became the most famous of these calls due to its succinctness. *An Agreement of the People* was in many ways a proto constitution, probably penned by the young lawyer, John Wildman. It had four clauses that outlined the core of Leveller beliefs:

I) That Members of Parliament were to be elected in proportion to the population of their constituencies.

II) That the existing Parliament should be dissolved within a year.

III) Future Parliaments to be elected biennially and sit every other year from April to September.

IV) That this biennial Parliament (a single elected House) should be the supreme authority with powers to make or repeal laws, appoint officials and conduct domestic and foreign policy.

The last of these was arguably the most radical though all were relatively unheard of demands at this point. Along with these clauses was however the call for a series of regulations on how parliament should conduct itself which could never be altered. Parliament was not to interfere with freedom of religion or impress men to serve in the armed forces, soldiers were to be given indemnity for the past war, all were to be equal in the eyes of the law and all new laws passed should be for the common good. The programme expressed here was based firmly in natural and civil law, supposed precedent with the history of England and overwhelmingly a sense of fairness. These last conditions came to stand as some of the most radical concepts in an age when each of these things had not even been countenanced before the war.

Putney and Corkbush

During 1647, a series of army rendezvous and councils had met to discuss what the New Model's position should be, with an increasing number of the rank-and-file supportive of the Leveller programme. In the spring, the election of the Agitators caused such a stir that the Council of the Army had been forced to include their representatives and to agree to meetings and a rendezvous at Newmarket. Even Ireton, who was at heart a radical Independent, was sympathetic to some of the demands. The issue came to a head in the later summer of 1647 after several months of polemicising and increasing uncertainty as talks with the king dragged on and the demands of the Agitators had not been met. In this frustration was published the *Case of the Army* and in some regiments, new Agitators were elected who were thought to be more radical still. The Council of the Army had from August met at the church at Putney and the concerned Council invited the Agitators including Sexby to meet and discuss the document at the end of October. They were joined by civilian Levellers including Wildman. So, although this was essentially an army debate it was in fact much more, reflecting the fact decisions made by the Council had importance across the country because of the power of the New Model.

Unbeknownst to the Council, the Agitators arrived with the *Agreement of the People* which had only just been printed and declared they debate the contents of that document instead. A far more concise manifesto now in front of them, the surprised Grandees readily agreed. The *Agreement* however pushed the debate past army grievances and the peace settlement onto one regarding the fundamental principles of democracy which the Agitators and their supporters came to argue forcefully. Ireton spoke for the Grandees while Cromwell sat in the chair, Fairfax having called in sick. The opposition found a range of voices but most powerfully Wildman, Sexby and Rainsborough. Over the course of a week in Putney Church and a house nearby Council, Levellers and Agitators debated the points in the *Agreement* particularly over the extent of the franchise. Should all men over twenty-one be eligible, only those born in England, or who met a certain property threshold? Should servants be disbarred because they could be influenced by their master? It was here that Rainsborough set out his belief that:

> I think that the poorest he that is in England hath a life to live, as the greatest he; and therefore truly, Sir, I think it's clear, that every man that is to live under a government ought first by his own consent to put himself under that government.

Had the Agitators won the argument and convinced the Council, it is possible that the army could have advocated for the imposition of democracy similar to that not won until the nineteenth century; near-universal male suffrage, the abolition of pocket boroughs and the practical supremacy of the House of Commons. However, Cromwell and Ireton remained unconvinced, were able to counterattack and the Council was adjourned for a fortnight with the promise of another general rendezvous which was later replaced by three separate meetings.

A few days later, the news broke that the king had escaped captivity, possibly encouraged by the Grandees who had been worried that radicals would seize him. Parliamentarians rushed to restore unity in the face of renewed war. Promises for arrears of pay were given and some vague commitments to political reforms. The respected Fairfax who had remained above the fray even threatened to resign if these concessions were not agreed to. Despite these efforts, at the first partial rendezvous at Corkbush field near Ware, there was a skirmish when two regiments tried to attend despite orders not to. The men wore copies of the *Agreement* in their hats and it looked like full-scale mutiny was about to break out. In no mood for dissent, Cromwell arrived and rode along the ranks plucking out the papers from the soldier's hats. In the restoration of order, several men were sentenced to death and a Private Richard Arnold was shot on the field to serve as a warning to the rest. At the next partial rendezvous at Kingston, the regiments there were unsurprisingly compliant.

The Second Civil War

The fallout from the mutiny at Corkbush was relatively minor, tempered by the prospect of imminent war and with popular resentment stoked at both the horrors of war and disillusionment at the lack of real change in Church and State. Attentions were once again focussed on to the defence of the broad Parliamentary cause against Charles. Cromwell was dispatched to Wales to deal with an uprising there while Rainsborough was sent to take command of the navy in Kent. He had been earmarked for the admiralty before Putney, but in revealing his colours as a Leveller sympathiser, he had fallen from grace. Given the situation and with some apologetic sounds, his career was given a reprieve. However, shortly after his arrival, he lost most of the force to a Royalist mutiny which feared his radicalism as well as the imposition of the New Model's influence. Rainsborough instead joined Fairfax who drove the rebels across the Thames into Essex where the Royalists of both counties were corralled into the town of Colchester.

Given their unsuccessful attempts to influence army command, the movement shifted its focus back to the print war. They began petitioning campaigns that stretched via a network of sympathisers from London into the shires to gather signatures. From mid-April, the Levellers also had their own weekly newsbook, *The Moderate*, which proved to be a mouthpiece for the movement in these later stages. While its political thought was far from original, it appears to have developed a strong readership. The revolutionary aspect of *The Moderate* was however that it did not just report news but actively sought to influence events by engaging with issues, questions and reprinting petitions and in this way was drawn directly from the now-established Leveller methods of protest and dissent.

In early 1648, another prominent Leveller ally, the MP Henry Marten left for his county of Berkshire to raise a regiment to fight the Royalists threatening to mass in the West Country. He was joined by his neighbour William Eyre, a Leveller and Agitator recently released from prison after his part at Corkbush. Together they raised a regiment but did so by requisitioning supplies, including horses from local landowners causing fury and consternation. Despite repeated calls from parliament to desist, Marten refused to return. His regiment soon became known for its radicalism and was eventually merged into the New Model rather than risk disbanding its soldiers. In 1648, Leveller influence if anything appeared to be on the rise. There still appears to have been demand for their ideas in the army, perhaps reinvigorated with the threat posed by a resurgent Royalism. Not only was Marten able to recruit a radical unit but the rehabilitation of Levellers Eyre and Rainsborough was quick. Throughout 1648, there was continued unrest in the army, with two further Leveller-inspired mutinies; a plot in January to seize Gloucester and a second in April at St Albans where new Agitators were appointed. Both like Corkbush were non-starters but show the continuing Leveller influence. The Levellers commanded broad civilian and army support but it seems that this was not enough to influence events beyond the now-familiar putting of words in print, signatures on a petition and their bodies on the line in the name of dissent. In August, John Lilburne was released from the Tower and in the following few months was the period of closest cooperation between the Levellers and Independents as they sought each other's support.

Rainsborough, the *Remonstrance* and Pride's Purge

With the ending of the Second Civil War in sight, only the key stronghold Pontefract Castle remained in Royalist hands and Rainsborough, who had just cemented his reputation as the New Model's siege master at Colchester, was dispatched north. Part of the reason the siege had gone on so long however was that the Parliamentary commander had been lax in allowing foraging parties to slip out of the castle. Before he could take command, Rainsborough was murdered by a party of Royalist soldiers who had been allowed through the lines. His life had one final act to play out and as his funeral procession wound through London, there was a huge outpouring of popular sympathy for a man who had come to embody both Parliamentary success and the radical ideals which had driven many to support the cause. It was in print after his death that the first real calls for the execution of the king were made, sometimes with explicit reference to revenge and justice for Rainsborough's murder. It was here where his family colour of sea-green was worn, becoming an emblem for the Leveller movement. The funeral itself became a rallying point for the radical wing of the Revolution and brought into sharp relief just how precarious their position was.

The petitioning of parliament now increased. A popular method of lobbying ever since the 'Root and Branch' petitions against Charles's Church policies, these documents were circulated usually at county or regiment level for signatures. They had been used often by the Levellers especially for the release of their own from prison but now their *Large Petition* came forth amidst a tidal wave of petitioning and even inspired many subsequent ones which borrowed some of its demands and phrasing. The murder of Rainsborough at the end of a brief but bloody Second Civil War appears to have swung many Independent MPs and commanders behind the idea that Charles continued to pose a threat and their supporters, particularly amongst the London crowd and the New Model, would brook no more toleration of him.

The funeral of Rainsborough and the petition war was followed by a brief period of alignment between the Levellers and the radical Independents and common ground was found in a series of meetings in Whitehall to discuss Ireton's proposed peace settlement, the *Remonstrance*. While Lilburne saw an attempt to silence the Levellers by buying them off, rather than a real attempt to compromise, there appears to have been a serious discussion. Arguably it was Ireton, who had opposed the Levellers at Putney but had a strong radical bent himself, who moved his position most. He appears to have been genuinely supportive of the final document. These meetings were the successful conclusion of the debates began the year before, only that it had taken the fire of a Second Civil War for both sides to reach an agreement. It is unlikely that without the support of the Levellers who were known to command influence over the soldiers and the London crowd and who had consistently been the anti-Charles party (though many had reservations about his execution and the abolition of the monarchy) that Ireton would have been able to push enough officers and MPs into finally breaking with the king.

At this point, the irrevocable shattering of the Revolution occurred. The Independent MPs in parliament refused to dissolve to make way for new elections and instead the House of Commons was reduced to only members who had previously agreed to break ties with the king. Colonel Pride, with an armed guard, turned away the ejected members at the door. The remainder, the 'Rump' left a veneer of respectability masking the emerging de facto rule by the army and it was they who pushed for the trial of King Charles in January 1649 at which he was found guilty of treason against his people and executed. The subsequent tightening of power by the army and a small group of Parliamentarians fractured the Leveller movement. Many were angered that despite their agreement with Ireton that the Rump had been installed and the democratic rights they thought they had won had been abandoned. Others were wary of the execution of the king. Lilburne put forward the excoriating pamphlet *England's new chains discovered* attacking the government. Many of their supporters were placated however by the regime's support of independent worship. The radical elements in the army were still dissatisfied and a series of mutinies occurred throughout 1649 at Bishopsgate, Burford and Oxford which each required loyal troops to put down and led to clashes, deaths and recriminations through executions. Several leaders including Lilburne, Overton, Walwyn and Prince were imprisoned. Lilburne was put on trial for his life for publications stirring the army to mutiny though he was acquitted despite clear evidence against him, a sign of his continued influence and popularity. By the end of 1649, the Levellers in the army and the civilian population had been crushed or placated and while some pamphleteers and activists would continue to harry the regime, there would be no more concerted effort from them as a movement.

Part IV: Legacy

The Levellers were a significant influence on the direction of the Parliamentarian cause from 1647-9 and though they never held power many of their beliefs did come to fruition such as the abolition of the House of Lords, the removal of the king (army printer and Leveller John Harris was a guard on Charles' scaffold), fair terms for soldiers and a certain degree of religious toleration. In addition, John Lilburne's defiance of the legal system, from refusing to perjure himself, for a fair trial before the law and even the need for the comfort of the defendant (i.e. the ability to go to the toilet) were all things that became received wisdom afterwards. The Levellers as a bloc of organised radicalism had influence in the army and London crowd and at various points swung behind the radical Independent party to help them win them the battle for control or push them to a more radical position. The Levellers inspired less organised groups such as the Ranters, Quakers, and Fifth Monarchists. Also inspired by but contrasted to them were the 'True Levellers' or Diggers who sought redistribution of land and wealth that the Levellers were regularly but erroneously accused of desiring.

The Levellers were radical, but they were bounded by a sense of fairness and reason and were a product of their time espousing supposed natural rights and accountable government.[3] They were able to draw on a broad swathe of public opinion based on the London middling sorts but had appeal across society and into the country. Their entreaties to natural law, historical precedent and what was 'just' were simple but understandable to people who would have seen these ideas as an expression of things they knew to be right and felt to be true. Their emphasis on the rights of property was an important aspect of this, as was their acceptance of a state Church (as long as it did not compel people to attend) and their desire to vest power in the House of Commons. Generally, they proposed radical ideas but through a programme of change and reform taking things such as the justice system, fair pay for the army and widening the franchise and arguing for them to be improved in the interests of fairness and for the 'safety' of the people.

They used various tactics to achieve this including writing polemical tracts, petitioning, calling for mass protest and attempting to influence army. Arguably, they were moderately successful at all these things. These techniques were all new and of their time and before the later days of Charles' rule, it would have been unthinkable for there to have been a standing army in England, mass protests in the street, freedom to print the things the Levellers did and a petitioning culture which had simply not existed. Print was central to the creation of the Leveller movement, they expertly promoted their programme using these new methods and in this heady situation, better than any other radical group and often better than the government of the day.

It is hard for us with the distance of time and hindsight to fully understand how revolutionary the Levellers were. By seeking a written constitution based on inalienable rights such as equality under the law, freedom of conscience, limits on government power and an extension of voting rights to unpropertied men they were not just looking to re-establish lost rights or import them from elsewhere but create those which had never existed and were not to come into existence for over three centuries.[4] Truly radically they developed a sense that that the true power of the country lay with the 'free-born' people of England for who they desired fairness and justice. The adoption of so many of their demands in the short and long-term may be considered a success. Their resonance was such that their ideas were still being expressed at the end of the century when the Bill of Rights was drawn up and they have long been touted as inspiration for the American and French Revolutions. Arguably, the 'most important political principle' of modern times is the right to live in a participatory democracy as laid out in the Universal Declaration of Human Rights.[5] Arguably, these principles are the inheritance not of the slave-owning societies of Athens and Rome, or the French estates and ideals of the general will but from 'buff-coated and blood-stained English soldiers and tradesmen'.[6] It was the Levellers who were their loudest voice and who came closest to making the English Revolution a democratic one.

Notes

1. H. N. Brailsford, *The Levellers and the English Revolution*, ed. Christopher Hill (Nottingham: Spokesman, 1983), 19. I would like to thank Kathleen Moran for reading early drafts of this paper.
2. Michael Braddick, *The Common Freedom of the People, John Lilburne and the English Revolution.* (Oxford: Oxford University Press, 2018), 26.
3. Andrew Bradstock, *Radical Religion in Cromwell's England.* (London: I.B. Tauris, 2011), 50.
4. David Wooton, 'Leveller Democracy and the Puritan Revolution' in *The Cambridge History of Political Thought,* ed. J. H. Burns with Mark Goldie (Cambridge: Cambridge University Press 1991), 412-3.
5. Geoffrey Robertson, *The Levellers: The Putney Debates.* (London: Verso, 2018), vii-viii.
6. Ibid.

Appendix

[Richard Overton with William Walwyn], *A Remonstrance Of Many Thousand Citizens, and other Free-born People of England, To their own House of Commons.* **London, Printed in the Yeer, 1646.**

WEE are well assured, yet cannot forget, that the cause of our choosing you to be *Parliament-men*, was to deliver us from all kind of Bondage, and to preserve the Common-wealth in Peace and Happinesse: For effecting whereof, we possessed you with the same Power that was in our selves, to have done the same; For wee might justly have done it our selves without you, if we had thought it convenient; choosing you [as Persons whom wee thought fitly quallified, and Faithfull,] for avoiding some inconveniences.

But ye are to remember, this was only of us but a Power of trust, [which is ever revokable, and cannot be otherwise,] and to be imployed to no other end, then our owne well-being: Nor did wee choose you to continue our Trust's longer, then the knowne established constitution of this Commonly-wealth will justly permit, and that could be but for one yeere at the most: for by our Law, a Parliament is to be called once every yeere, and oftner (if need be,) as ye well know. Wee are your Principalls, and you our Agents; it is a Truthe, Yhe you cannot but acknowledge: For if you or any other shall assume, or exercise any Power, that is noe derived from our Trust and choice thereunto, that Power is no lesse then usurpation and an Oppression, from which wee expect to be freed, in whomsoever we finde it; it being altogether inconsistent with the nature of *just Freedome*, which yee also very well understand.

The History of our Fore-fathers since they were Conquered by the *Normans*, doth manifest that this Nation hath been held in bondage all along ever since by the policies and force of the Officers of Trust in the Common-wealth, amongst whom, wee always esteemed Kings the chiefest: and what (in much of the former-time) was done by warre, and by impoverishing of the People, to make them slaves, and to hold them in bondage, our latter Princes have endeavoured to effect, by giving ease and wealth unto the People, but withall, corrupting their understanding, by infusing false Principles concerning Kings, and Government, and Parliaments, and Freedoms; and also using all meanes to corrupt and vitiate the manners of the youth, and strongest prop and support of the People, the Gentry.

It is wonderfull, that the failings of former Kings, to bring our Fore-fathers into bondage, together with the trouble and danger that some of them drew upon themselves and their Posterity, by those their unjust endevours, had not wrought in our latter Kings a resolution to rely on, and trust only to justice and square dealing with the People, especially considering the unaptnesse of the Nation to beare much, especially from those that pretend to love them, and unto whom they expressed so much hearty affection, (as any People in the world ever did,) as in the quiet admission of King *James* from *Scotland*, sufficient, (if any Obligation would worke Kings to Reason,) to have endeared both him and his sonne King *Charles*, to an inviolable love, and hearty affection to the *English Nation*; but it would not doe.

They choose rather to trust unto their Policies and Court Arts, to King-waste, and delusion, then to Justice and plaine dealing; and did effect many things tending to our enslaving (as in your First *Remonstrance*; you shew skill enough to manifest the same to all the World:) and this Nation having been by their delusive Arts, and a long continued Peace, much softened and debased in judgement and Spirit, did beare far beyond its usuall temper, or any example of our Fore-Fathers, which (to our shame,) wee acknowledge.

But in conclusion, longer they would not beare, and then yee were chosen to worke our deliverance, and to Estate us in naturall and just libertie agreeable to *Reason* and common *equitie*; for whatever our Fore-fathers were; or whatever they did or suffered, or were enforced to yeeld unto; we are the men of the present age, and ought to be absolutely free from all kindes of exorbitancies, molestations or *Arbitrary Power*, and you wee choose to free us from all without exception or limitation, either in respect of Persons, Officers, Degrees, or things; and we were full of confidence, that ye also would have dealt impartially on our behalf, and made us the most absolute free People in the world.

[Several hands but chiefly John Wildman], *An Agreement Of The People For A firm and present Peace, upon grounds of common-right and free-dome.* **Printed** *Anno Dom.* **1647.**

Having by our late labours and hazards made it appeare to the world at how high a rate wee value our just freedom, and God having so far owned our cause, as to deliver the Enemies thereof into our hands: We do now hold our selves bound in mutual duty to each other, to take the best care we can for the future, to avoid both the danger of returning into a slavish condition, and the chargeable remedy of another war: for as it cannot be imagined that so many of our Country-men would have opposed us in this quarrel, if they had understood their owne good; so may we safely promise to our selves, that when our Common Rights and liberties shall be cleared, their endeavours, will be disappointed, that seek to make themselves our Masters: since therefore our former oppressions, and scarce yet ended troubles have beene occasioned, either by want of frequent Nationall meetings in Councell, or by rendring those meetings ineffectuall; We are fully agreed and resolved, to provide that hereafter our Representatives be neither left to an uncertainty for the time, nor made useless to the ends for which they are intended: In order whereunto we declare,

Appendix

1. That the People of England being at this day very unequally distributed by Counties, Cities, & Borroughs, for the election of their Deputies in Parliament, ought to be more indifferently proportioned, according to the number of the Inhabitants: the circumstances whereof, for number, place, and manner, are to be set down before the end of this present Parliament.
2. That to prevent the many inconveniences apparently arising from the long continuance of the same persons in authority, this present Parliament be dissolved upon the last day of September, which shall be in the year of our Lord, 1648.
3. That the People do of course chuse themselves a Parliament once in two yeares, viz. upon the first Thursday in every second March, after the manner as shall be prescribed before the end of this Parliament, to begin to sit upon the first Thursday in Aprill following at Westminster, or such other place as shall bee appointed from time to time by the preceding Representatives; and to continue till the last day of September, then next ensuing, and no longer.
4. That the power of this, and all future Representatives of this Nation, is inferiour only to theirs who chuse them, and doth extend, without the consent or concurrence of any other person or persons; to the enacting, altering, and repealing of Lawes; to the erecting and abolishing of Offices and Courts; to the appointing, removing, and calling to account Magistrates, and Officers of all degrees; to the making War and peace, to the treating with forraigne States: And generally, to whatsoever is not expressly, or implyedly reserved by the represented to themselves.

Which are as followeth,

1. That matters of Religion, and the wayes of Gods Worship, are not at all intrusted by us to any humane power, because therein wee cannot remit or exceed a tittle of what our Consciences dictate to be the mind of God, without wilful sinne: neverthelesse the publike way of instructing the Nation (so it be not compulsive) is referred to their discretion.
2. That the matter of impresting and constraining any of us to serve in the warres, is against our freedome; and therefore we do not allow it in our Representatives; the rather, because money (the sinews of war) being alwayes at their disposall, they can never want numbers of men, apt enough to engage in any just cause.
3. That after the dissolution of this present Parliament, no person be at any time questioned for anything said or done, in reference to the late publike differences, otherwise then in execution of the Judgments of the present Representatives, or House of Commons.
4. That in all Laws made, or to be made, every person may be bound alike, and that no Tenure, Estate, Charter, Degree, Birth, or place, do confer any exemption from the ordinary Course of Legall proceedings, whereunto others are subjected.
5. That as the Laws ought to be equall, so they must be good and not evidently destructive to the safety and well-being of the people.

These things we declare to be our native Rights, *and therefore are agreed and resolved to maintain them with our utmost possibilities, against all opposition whatsoever, being compelled thereunto, not only by the examples of our Ancestors, whose bloud was often spent in vain for the recovery of their Freedomes, suffering themselves*, through fraudulent accommodations, *to be still deluded of the fruit of their Victories, but also by our own woful experience, who having long expected, & dearly earned the establishment of these certain rules of Government are yet made to depend for the settlement of our Peace and Freedom, upon him that intended our bondage, and brought a cruell Warre upon us…*

[Anon. but likely John Lilburne with William Walwyn and Richard Overton], *To The Right Honourable The Commons of England; in Parliament assembled. The humble Petition of Thousands wel-affected persons inhabiting the City of London Westminster, the Borough of Southwark, Hamblets, and places adjacent.* **[11ᵗʰ September 1648]**

Sheweth,

That although we are as earnestly desirous of a safe and well-grounded Peace, and that a final end were put to all the troubles and miseries of the Common-wealth, as any sort of men whatsoever: Yet considering upon what grounds we engaged on your Part in the late and present Wars, and how far (by our so doing) we apprehend our selves concerned, Give us leave (before you conclude as by the Treaty in hand) to acquaint you first with the ground and reason which induced us to aid you against the King and his Adherents. Secondly, What our Apprehensions are of this Treaty. Thirdly, What we expected from you, and do still most earnestly desire.

Be pleased therefore to understand, that we had not engaged on your part, but that we judged this honourable House to be the supreme Authority of England, as chosen by, and representing the People; and entrusted with absolute power for redress of Grievances, and provision for Safety: and that the -King was but at the most the chief publike Officer of this Kingdom, and accomptable to this House (the Representative of the People, from whom all just Authority is, or ought to be derived) for discharge of his Office: And if we had not bin confident hereof, we had bin desperately mad to have taken up Armes or to have bin aiding and assisting in maintaining a *War against Him*; The Laws of the Land making it expresly a crime no less than Treason for any to raise War against the King.

But when we considered the manifold oppressions brought upon the Nation by the King, His Lords and Bishops; and that this Honourable House declared their deep sense thereof; and that (for continuance of that power which had so opprest us) it was evident the King intended to raise Forces, and make War; and that if he did set up His Standard, it tended to the dissolution of the Government: upon this, knowing the safety of the People to be above Law, and that to judge thereof appertained to the Supreme Authority, and not to the supreme Magistrate, and being satisfied in our Consciences, that the publike safety and freedom was in imminent danger, we concluded we had not only a just cause to maintain; but the Supreme Authority of the Nation, to justify, defend, and indempnifie us in time to come, in what we should perform by direction thereof; though against the known Law of the Land, or any inferiour Authority, though the highest.

And as this our understanding was begotten in us by principles of right reason, so were we confirmed therein by your own proceedings, as by your condemning those Judges who in the case of Ship-money had declared the King to be Judge of Safety; and by your denying Him to have a Negative voice in the making of Laws; where you wholy exclude the King from having any share in the Supreme Authority: Then by your casting the Bishops out of the House of Lords, who by tradition also had been accounted an essential part of the Supreme Authority; And by your declaring to the Lords, that if they would not joyn with You in settling the Militia, (which they long refused) you would settle it without them, which you could not justly have done, had they had any real share in the supreme *Authority.*

These things we took for real Demonstrations, that you undoubtedly knew your selves to be the supreme Authority; ever weighing down in us all other your indulgent *Expressions concerning the King or Lords.* It being indeed impossible for us to believe that it can consist either with the safety or freedom of the Nation, to be governed either by three or two Supremes, especially where experience hath proved them so apt to differ in their Judgments concerning Freedom or safety, that the one hath bin known to punish what the other hath judged worthy of reward; when not only the freedom of the people is directly opposite to the Prerogatives of the King and Lords, but the open enemies of the one, have bin declared friends by the other, as the Scots were by the House of Lords.

And when as most of the oppressions of the Common-wealth have in all times been brought upon the people by the King and Lords, who nevertheless would be so equal in the supreme Authority, as that there could be no redress of Grievances, no provision for safety, but at their pleasure:. For our parts, we profess our selves to be so far from judging this to be consistent with Freedom or Safety, that we know no greater cause. Wherefore we assisted you in the late Wars, but in hope to be delivered by you from so intollerable, so destructive a bondage, so soon as you should (through Gods blessing upon the Armies raised by you) be enabled.

But to our exceeding grief, we have observed that no sooner God vouchsafed you victory, and blesseth you with success, and thereby enableth you to put us and the whole Nation into an absolute condition of Freedom and Safety: but according as ye have bin accustomed, passing by the ruine of the Nation, and all the bloud that hath been spilt by the King and his Party, ye betake your selves to a Treaty with him, thereby putting him that is but one single person, and a publike Officer of the Common-wealth, in competition with the whole Body of the People, whom ye represent; not considering that it is impossible for you to erect any Authority equal to your selves; and declared to all the world that you will not alter the Ancient Government, from that of King, Lords, and Commons: not once mentioning (in case of difference) which of them is supreme, but leaving that point (which was the chiefest cause of all our publike differences, disturbances, wars, and miseries,) as uncertain as ever.

In so much as we who upon these grounds have laid out our selves every way to the uttermost of our abilities: and all others throughout the land, Souldiers and others who have done the like in defence of your supreme Authoritie and in opposition to the King, cannot but deem our selves in the most dangerous condition of all others, left without all plea of indempnitie for what we have done; as already many have found by losse of their lives and liberties, either for things done or said against the King; the law of the land frequently taking place, and precedencie against and before your Authoritie, which we esteemed supreme, and against which no law ought to be pleaded. Nor can we possibly conceive how any that have any waies assisted you can be exempt from the guilt of murderers and robbers, by the present laws in force if you persist to disclaim the supreme authoritie, though their own consciences do acquit them, as having opposed none but manifest Tyrants, Oppressors, and their adherents.

And whereas a Personal Treaty, or any Treaty with the King, hath been long time held forth as the only means of a safe and wel-grounded Peace; it is well known to have been cryed up principally by such as have been alwaies dis-affected unto you; and though you have not contradicted it: yet it is beleeved that you much fear the issue thereof; as you have cause sufficient, except you see greater alteration in the King and his party then is generally observed, there having never yet been any Treaty with him, but was accompanied with some underhand-dealing; and whilst the present force upon him (though seeming liberty) will in time to come be certainly pleaded against, all that shall or can be agreed upon: Nay, what can you confide in if you consider, how he hath been provoked; and what former Kings upon lesse provocations have done, after Oaths, Laws, Charters, Bonds, Excommunications, and all tyes of Reconcilliations, to the destruction of all those that had provoked and opposed them: yea, when your selves so soon as he had signed those bills, in the beginning of this Parliament, saw cause to tell him, *That even in or about the time of passing those bills, some design or other was on fact, which if it had taken effect would not only have rendred those bills fruitless, but have reduced you to a worse condition of confusion than wherein the Parliament found you.* And if you consider what new wars, Risings, Revolting invasions, and Plottings have been since this last Cry for a Personall Treaty, you will not blame us if we wonder at your hasty proceedings thereunto: especially considering the wonderfull Victories which God hath blessed the Army withall.

We professe we cannot chuse but stand amazed to consider the inevitable danger we shall be in, though all things in the Propositions were agreed unto; the resolutions of the King and his party have been so perpetually violently and implacably prosecuted and manifested against us; and that with such scorn and indignation, that it must be more than such ordinary bonds that must hold them. And it is no lesse a wonder to us that you can place your own security therein, or that you can ever imagin to see a free Parliament any more in England.

The truth is (and we see we must either now speak it, or for ever be silent,) We have long expected things of an other nature from you, and such as we are confident would have given satisfaction to all serious people of all Parties…

Sects and Dissenters of the English Revolution

Joseph Saunders

During the civil wars, a deluge of ideas emerged espousing what was best for England and her people. Anything felt possible as new waves of print information broke through censorship and absolute monarchy gave way to a republic. A passionate minority believed that they were owed for the sacrifices made, for the innumerable dead and injured. Some felt they had earned a better world, usually one which involved new freedoms to think, say and do. Many had the powerful certainty that parliament's victory was a sign of divine favour. Others had simply lost faith in the previously unassailable institutions of Church and State to protect their bodies and souls. This was understandable given that so much had crumbled or been torn down. Many of the old certainties were no longer certain. There was a 'sense of living in the shadow of the Apocalypse'.[1] At a simpler level many people would have desired 'a future world freed from the insecurity of the seventeenth century' with its famine, confusion and taxes.[2] Just as the army and parliament were reshaping England a few radicals saw the opportunity to remake the country as they saw fit. Even if these ideas might stretch the bounds of the possible, they were only conceivable in a world where so much had already changed, where there was felt to be a need and at least some hope of success.

We should not overestimate the revolutionary mood, however. Most people would have desired a return to normality and to be left to their lives. Continuity beneath the tumult of print and politics was the norm and radicals generally existed on the fringes of society.[3] Even the Levellers, whose radicalism led them to be quashed, distanced themselves from the 'True Levellers'. Historians have studied the dissenters of the civil wars precisely because of this precarious position, almost unbelieving that such thoughts could exist in the undercurrent of society. The dissenting movements were however deeply rooted in the radical wing of Protestantism and developed in the turbulence of the civil wars. The Levellers were a critical step in this process as the most coherent voice for radical change until 1649. In the vanguard of dissent, they opened up discussion and began to seriously question the conditions of society down to its very foundations.

Following the defeat of the Levellers, a further wave of dissenting radicalism emerged under the relative toleration of the new government. Some movements took the form of sects while others were more like societies or were even just broad labels.

They all sought in some way to shape a new world, some for all England and others just for their small part or within their own consciences. They ranged from Diggers who sought to inspire a new version of society through a form of agrarian communism to Fifth Monarchists who mostly looked to the Second Coming of Christ. Some like the Baptists and Muggletonians believed in the equality of an elite elect, others like the Quakers and Diggers sought to challenge social hierarchies and create a much more egalitarian world. Many of these movements bordered on zealousness in their beliefs and only ever gained a small following, with little influence at the very edge of society. Many inspired fear in their fellows and the Ranters and Muggletonians even embraced the effects of the terror they instilled.

Given this complexity, it is understandable that there are often issues defining these movements. Between their own propaganda and that aimed against them, it is impossible and even undesirable to consider them as anything but a broad wave of dissent, with identifiable strands within. While they shared a common heritage of radical puritanism which had come to fruition with the Baptists and Levellers in the 1640s, these movements took many paths. They were also divided amongst themselves, constantly changing and evolving. Many historians rightly focus on the role of individual movements but despite their differences at heart these groups often had more in common to one another than they would have liked to admit. Often members and even leaders would move from one to another. There was confusion within sects, and within individuals themselves. There were even common directions of travel, many graduated from the Baptists to greater radicalism and from other forms of dissent to Quakerism. Quakers recruiting in the 1650s even took lists of known dissenters with them when they visited an area so they could contact the most likely converts.

The dissenters of the 1640s and 50s were inherently paradoxical at the time and have similarly confounded historians. They were and are considered powerful radical forces, but their voices were disproportionate to their size and influence within society. They have been revered for pushing the English Revolution to its furthest points but also dismissed as ineffectual failures. They have been lauded as the forerunners of modern radical religion and politics but somehow are constantly being forgotten and remembered. Just as their contemporaries had to come to their own conclusions, the modern reader must also make up their own minds about them.

Part I: Reformation

The dissenting movements of the mid-seventeenth century were the latest in a line of Christian movements which pushed the boundaries of established orthodoxies. While we should not be tempted to claim direct descent from one to the other, it is possible to follow a common theme through the history of opposition and free-thinking, often in the name of becoming closer to God and his ideal of the world. The ideas of past radical religious movements, especially those within recent history were incorporated into popular culture from which inspiration could be taken. In a world where religion was all-encompassing faith underlay the entire moral and political world. The necessity of ensuring that you were following the 'true' faith, was therefore of utmost importance. Many in Christian history were lured by the promise of a new system that brought them nearer to God, often proposing a measure of equality before his eyes, and to cut out perceived injustices, inaccuracies and inefficiencies. The persecution of such movements was often a severe attempt to restore order to society. The Reformation obliterated this hegemonic system, fracturing Christendom so that the accepted faith could vary across borders and with a change of ruler. As with all revolutionary movements, this was soon thought by some to have not gone far enough. Almost from the outset, there appeared the drive for further reformation across Europe of which England's puritans were a potent variant.

Heretics and Anabaptists

Dissent in the medieval Catholic Church often meant death. Pitted against the monolithic power of Christendom the conviction of having found the 'true' faith still drove many men and women to act upon their own consciences. The control of such deviations was a regular fact of life but from the Cathars to the Hussites there were heresies that took hold deeply, causing whole communities to rebel even over generations. In England, the Lollards, under their founder John Wycliffe, emerged in the late 1300s as a small but committed heretical movement. Wycliffe sought to bring the people closer to God and made what was probably the first translation of the Bible into English. They were anti-clerical and critical of the hierarchical structure of Church authority, emphasising instead personal piety, humility and simplicity in their relationship to God. Their influence was so great that there may have still been Lollards in England two centuries after their apparent destruction.

The last and greatest heretic of medieval Christendom was Martin Luther, a German monk and professor, who from 1517 caused the Church to break irrevocably. Over the coming years, Luther gathered sympathisers as he preached a reformed faith. Perhaps most importantly of all, he translated the Bible into German and used the new technology of print to spread it and his other writings so that they could be understood by ordinary people. The movement spread like wildfire across Europe.

Almost from the outset, Luther found he no longer had control over his reformation. His teachings were electric and as well as his radical theological re-interpretations, ordinary people took his revolution to be a social one. Across Germany, men and women educated themselves in this new faith and sought to break the social and political bounds of the time. The ensuing pillage and destruction of the Peasants' War were coupled with real attempts to create a new world order. This included many radical reformers who rejected all Church authority and organisation, including the Anabaptists who shunned infant baptism and were persecuted brutally for this heresy. Some forms of this belief were millenarian, obsessed that creation of heaven on earth was imminent. In 1535, in the German town of Münster, a group of Anabaptists seized the town and instituted a brutal theocracy. Despite a year-long siege and a crackdown, some Anabaptist ideas lived on in small pacifist communities, particularly in the Netherlands. The bloody legacy of Münster would however haunt future separatist movements across Europe for generations.

The Puritan Reformation

In England, despite King Henry VIII's loud break with Rome, the Reformation took a generation to take hold. Official policy twisted and turned during the reigns of the changeable Henry and his children to the point that it must have been difficult for the ordinary person to know what faith they were meant to have held. However, some fervent believers, Catholic and Protestant alike, were willing to die for their cause. During the reign of Queen Mary, several hundred Protestants were burned at the stake as heretics. The martyrdom of these men and women and their subsequent use as propaganda helped to secure the Reformation in England and in 1559, Queen Elizabeth I determined a Protestant Church Settlement upon the nation.

The Protestantism of Elizabeth's reign had however been forged under Mary where believers had been forced to become sectarians or semi-sectarians at home and abroad. Some within the mainstream Church grew dissatisfied with the progress of the Reformation. They saw the Settlement of 1559 not as a final achievement but as a step toward further reform of worship and Church practice. This group became known by their enemies as 'puritans' and advocated for the stripping of any vestiges of Catholicism, promoting plain forms of speech, worship and churches believing that this would help to bring them closer to God. Their beliefs followed those of the French reformer, Jean Calvin, who had adopted the principle of predestination which judged that God had already determined who would go to Heaven or Hell, regardless of how anyone lived their lives. Those who followed his teachings had to hope they were amongst the Godly 'elect' which could cause them great doubt, as well as utter surety in their convictions.

From the 1560s, puritans were an increasingly prominent voice within the Church but their efforts for further reformation were increasingly frustrated. By the 1570s, there had developed a network of ministers who preached and held meetings outside of the official Church structure in what became known as the 'Conference Movement'. Puritans also used print to spread their beliefs. Prominent among these texts were conversion narratives, stories where non-believers were 'converted' by faithful puritans. Some like Arthur Dent's *The plain man's path-way to heaven* remained bestsellers for decades. A group of puritans also published the 'Marprelate Tracts', a series of illegally printed satires on the state of the Church. The threat was deemed so great that a restriction was ordered and puritan thoughts, meetings and literature were suppressed. By the 1590s, Elizabeth's authority had prevailed and puritanism had been silenced through exile and execution. Far from eradicating the movement, it was simply driven underground. Meetings were more secret, print became the most important way of sharing ideas and many thousands emigrated to the American colonies and established their religion there.

One of the groups which emerged within the puritan movement was the Brownists, named after Robert Browne, a lecturer who had preached against the doctrines of the Church. Going even further than other puritans, Browne sought separation from, rather than reform of the Church. In 1581, he had become the leader of a movement in Norwich which attempted to set up an independent congregation. After his arrest, this group moved to the Netherlands where he wrote several influential tracts. By the late 1580s, the group had split and Browne returned to England, renouncing his earlier separatism. Yet his ideas lived on and in the following decades, there were several revivals of the Brownist movement.

Another group established in England at this time were the Family of Love or Familists, a mystical sect inspired by the Anabaptists who claimed that all things were ruled by nature and not God. They also rejected infant baptism, that no man should be put to death for his opinions and opposed the taking of oaths and carrying of arms. They seem to have existed within established Churches, preferring not to spread their message too wide and risk persecution for heresy. As well as a certain level of respect for authority, they believed in the need for love, tenderness and sympathy to fulfil their spiritual needs. It has been said that this group had members in Elizabeth's court, and even perhaps Elizabeth herself.

Part III: Independency

For a generation, there was an underground community within the Church of England that desired further reformation but were forced to operate as a semi-separate entity with their own networks, values and culture. Some even made the extreme decision to make a definitive break. There was a tradition of religious discussion in the household, dissecting the day's sermons and of larger conventicles where believers came together to enhance their religious experience. Their opponents within society and the government mocked and feared these puritans. In the 1630s, they were vehemently set against King Charles I who sought to follow an 'Arminian' policy and re-introduce some aspects of ceremony to worship, which puritans saw as a step back toward Catholicism. This was a main cause of tension between Charles and his subjects which led, in 1642, to the outbreak of civil war. Against the king, a coalition under parliament emerged between all those who opposed Charles. Though they could agree on what they did not want, this coalition disagreed greatly over what the alternative should be. By the end of the war, the cracks between them had widened into chasms. The Parliamentarian cause was taken over by the 'Independent party' who sought a settlement that included an element of freedom of worship and the reduced power of the king. By 1648, radical Independents, supported by the New Model Army had taken power and installed what was in effect a military regime.

Baptists

Though most puritans remained at least nominally within the Church of England on its radical wing were established a series of illegal congregations totally split from the Church. They followed the inspiration of John Smyth, a Brownist who had begun meeting with a group of separatists. Persecution led Smyth and others from his congregation to flee to Amsterdam in 1609. Smyth, supported by his lay friend Thomas

Helwys, stood out from other separatist groups as they adopted the radical belief that only adult believers should be baptised. This followed a short period of association with Dutch Mennonites who traced their descent to the Anabaptists. Around 1612, Helwys led part of the group back to England and established a congregation in London. By 1624, there were five Baptist churches in the city. To these 'General Baptists' were added the 'Particular Baptists' who adopted adult believers' baptism under the leadership of Henry Jacob but held to the Calvinist belief that only a predestined elect were saved. In contrast, General Baptists believed that all could find salvation. The two sides were opposed to the point of even considering one another heretics.

Like many of the dissenting movements to come, the Baptists called for the abolition of tithes and had an antipathy for clergy. These visions for society were radical enough without considering their illegal separatism. Their distinguishing quality was however adult baptism and many were 're-baptised' into the new faith. The entire concept of adult baptism was incendiary to most of the population who saw it as an offence to God and a condemnation of innocent children. To its opponents, it became derisively known as 'dipping'. The hostility to such practices often led to baptism by night in rivers and ponds and so spawned further accusations of lewd Baptists taking young men and women out naked into the night. A regular claim was that people died subsequently from the cold.

Baptists had gained a good following by the 1630s and during the civil wars, their support soared, especially in London, the West Country and the Midlands. There was considerable enthusiasm for gatherings led by lay 'tub-preachers' such as Thomas Lambe and William Kiffin. At their height, it is estimated that the sect could be measured in the tens of thousands, making them the largest radical movement until the Quakers. However, their appeal was not universal, and support seems to have peaked during the 1640s when for a time they were the foremost example of dissent. They were quite detached from the customs of mainstream society and people feared them because of the association with the Anabaptist atrocities at Münster. The Baptists offered a religious and organisational education in the practice of dissent and offered the example of an alternative social model. By the late 1640s, many radicals however felt that the Baptists had not gone far enough and moved onto more radical positions. While their own radicalism was soon overshadowed, they were in many respects the originators of all the dissenting movements of this period.

The Triumph of the Independents

For all puritans, the prospect of the Reformation's reversal under King Charles in the 1630s was too much to bear. Some joined the Baptists but many more sailed to the New World and looked there to establish their own forms of religion. The vast majority remained but were increasingly certain that their salvation could not be secured through the attendance of a false Church. They became an important element in a growing culture war fought out in print and politics as society divided between those for and against the king's policies. In 1642, this erupted into civil wars which in many ways were England's wars of religion.

Puritans from across society formed the core of the opposition to Charles, including leading politicians right down to many of the rank-and-file soldiers. It was the godly puritan who came to represent the popular image of the Parliamentarian, from John Pym, the early leader of the cause, to Oliver Cromwell, who rose to become a prominent general. Puritanism marked the common soldiery in particular, with their faith being an influence on many to fight and the armies of parliament soon became known for their zealousness and even radicalism. This was not a radicalism of words alone but there are innumerable stories (though often exaggerated by Royalist propaganda) of puritan soldiers stripping churches of their decorations, breaking stained glass windows and stabling horses in them.

In the tense climate of war and the uncertain times in which they lived, ordinary men and women increasingly turned to stronger versions of their faith and many felt able to associate openly for the first time as members of separatist congregations. These separatists on the fringe of society from the outset recognised the king as their clear enemy. Many also hoped that their support for parliament could secure them religious toleration. Baptists enthusiastically joined the army and formed a popular base from which the Leveller movement drew much of its support. Many leading Levellers were Baptists and their congregations were used to mobilise support for their petitions and marches.

The Parliamentarians had been united against what they did not want, the king and his Church policies, but during the course of the war, they moved even further apart on what settlement they wanted. Two broad camps emerged in the Parliamentary coalition. The Presbyterians sought a strong national church settlement on the Scottish model and to reach terms with the king through negotiation. The Independents believed that the king had to be brought to terms with his ultimate defeat in the field and that any settlement had to contain checks on his power and an element of toleration for the separatists. A sign of this division can be seen in the Westminster Assembly, a national meeting convened by parliament to decide on the form of the post-war Church. It was a divisive convention riven with debate and for several years, it agonised over the nature of the Church, including the emotive issue of allowing separatist congregations. In the mid-1640s, fearful Presbyterian writers like Thomas Edwards published accounts of the heresies, sects and schisms said to have proliferated in England during the war. Ironically, in the absence of a decision by the Westminster Assembly for parliament to enforce, the number of sects and dissenters continued to grow.

At the end of the war, the Independents found themselves with support across the increasingly powerful New Model Army, which, like all of parliament's armies, was a hotbed of religious and political radicalism. Attention shifted to peace negotiations with the king who was being held in captivity. In response to a tightening of power by the Presbyterians, the Independents and the army seized the king and the capital. However, the stalemate continued, and no peace agreement could be found. In this vacuum, the Levellers, a movement born of puritanism, the Baptists and the conflict of the civil wars advocated for a democratic settlement based on principles of justice and freedom. It was partly through the influence of the Levellers that a radical wing of the Independent party felt emboldened to seize power in late 1648 in what essentially amounted to a military coup. The junta which was subsequently established saw no way to broker a settlement with the implacable Charles. They put him on trial for treason for which he was found guilty and executed.

Part III: A New World

In 1649, a country that had already been racked by years of upheaval was in the midst of a revolution. Ordinary people had been critical in directing the course of world-changing events, they had marched, signed petitions and fought in battle for their beliefs. They read all manner of news and opinion through a flourishing print culture, much of it aimed at the masses. As the world was remade all manner of ideas proliferated. Many notions which could never have been countenanced before the wars were now part of mainstream politics. This included a level of toleration for Baptists and other separatist congregations outside of the official Church. It seems that while many Baptists believed in equality, it was the equality of the godly, not of all Englishmen as the Levellers had pronounced. The Baptist break with the Levellers was arguably an important factor in their subsequent fall and the collapse of their movement and the integration of the Baptists into the new constitutional settlement left a vacuum for radicalism. New movements emerged and while the spirit of remaking the world was shared between them their methods and aims were quite distinct. This included those who sought to simply wait for the world to be remade by God to others who took to labour with their own hands to create the world anew. However, they shared origins in the puritan tradition and the same radicalism and brutality of the civil wars which had also shaped the Baptists and the Levellers. Ideas and people moved between movements as individuals and groups evolved. Together they contributed to a flood of dissent which opposed in varying degrees the established order and offered competing radical visions of how society should be rebuilt.

Digging, the True Levellers

The approaches to this newfound sense of possibility were diverse. The first and most distinct dissenting movement sought to physically create a new world on earth. The Diggers were a brief experiment in what we would now describe as agrarian communism. For a year, they took to cultivating and building on wasteland to form egalitarian communities. The main settlement was at St George's Hill in Surrey and later in the nearby parish of Cobham. They claimed that the earth was a 'Common Treasury', disdained private property as sinful and believed that a better world was within their grasp, if only they were to reach out and build it. This truly revolutionary movement acquired some fervent supporters, but those who took action can probably be counted in scores rather than hundreds. There were at least two more communes in Nottinghamshire and Buckinghamshire and perhaps as many as half a dozen more. They were begun by Gerrard Winstanley in 1649 as the 'True Levellers' but became known as Diggers due to their activities. Winstanley wrote several tracts during his lifetime expounding his ideas and seems to have been the driving force behind the Diggers. Their original name was taken from their belief in economic equality which they believed had been ordained in the Bible and they strongly objected to the Levellers who did not promote egalitarianism. The Levellers in return made repeated attempts to distance themselves while their enemies deliberately conflated the two groups.

The actions of the Diggers in 1649-50 would have been truly shocking to much of society. Indeed, it was the neighbours of the Diggers who often gave them the most opposition, fearing their ideas and that they would spread onto their land. It was the violent opposition of ordinary people and landlords which ended the Digger project, not the intervention of the regime. This is an important point with the dissenting sects, that they truly terrified people. In later years, many dissenters would embrace this and would build shock into their practice deliberately such as the free swearing of Abiezer Coppe, the cursing of their enemies by the Muggletonians and the Bible burning of some Quakers. Though they were only one of the dissenting groups that emerged at this time, the Diggers were an important forerunner of dissent. Their example served to influence other groups but while some elements of Digger belief such as egalitarianism and refusing the practice of 'hatting' continued to inspire no other group challenged the economic status quo in the same way they had. After the successive defeats of the Levellers and Diggers in 1649-50 with violence, it is no wonder that new outlets for the creation of the new world were sought, directing the drive for reform to within.

Ranting and the Fifth Monarchists

One of the most studied dissenting groups were the Ranters who embraced the same shock factor which had ruined the Diggers. Of all the movements in this period, it was the Ranters who came closest to outright heresy in their questioning of established beliefs. Though tiny and unorganised, they came to have a disproportionate impact. Operating from 1649, they were essentially pantheistic, believing that God was everywhere and denied the authority of any Church. Ranters, like Familists in the previous century, rejected sin and believed in their own perfectibility. Because they believed that God was present in all living creatures, the Ranters rejected all obedience. This was often taken to extremes such as by Abiezer Coppe who would use colourful profanities and Lawrence Clarkson, a prolific adulterer. Many stories of the Ranters describe their free smoking, drinking and sex. For the average Englishman and woman, these beliefs and their actions were truly terrifying and it is almost as if the Ranters were a connection of the worst fears of the mainstream. Indeed, it has even been suggested that they were invented as propaganda. It is much more likely however that they were simply the name given by the established order to an unconnected body of extreme dissenters. However, some Ranters did publish writings including Coppe who encapsulated many of his ideas in vivid prose.

A quieter approach was to be found within the more long-lived sects. This was particularly strong in the millenarian groups who believed in the Second Coming of Christ and the imminent establishment of the kingdom of heaven on earth. Instead of changing the earthy estate, which was proving futile, they thought it better to focus efforts on what was to come. This tendency seems to have become particularly strong during the early 1650s when the new government under Cromwell was seen as the saviour of England by many within the puritan tradition. Millenarianism influenced all manner of dissenters from Diggers to Quakers. Given the destruction of so many bastions of order, it was understandable that many could believe that they were witnessing the upheavals which heralded the world's transformation. The Fifth Monarchists were the most prominent millenarian group and were active from 1649 through to 1661 and their support likely numbered in the tens of thousands, making them one of the largest sects. They took their name from a prophecy in the Book of Daniel that four ancient monarchies would proceed Christ's return. They also believed that the year 1666 and its relationship to the biblical Number of the Beast marked the end of earthly rule by human beings. Many even saw Oliver Cromwell as their deliverer and one of their most influential members was one of his Major-Generals, Thomas Harrison. One of the most famous Fifth Monarchists was Anna Trapnell who claimed to be a prophet and shared her prophecies in print. Some shared concerns for the reform of earthly life too including the desire to have annual elections and the election of army officers.

Seeking and Prophets

The Ranters and Fifth Monarchists booth looked away from the earthly estate, inwards and up to God as they looked for the new world. The same desires can also be seen in the Seekers. Like the Ranters, they were not a distinct sect but were more akin to a religious position. Seekers considered all churches and denominations to be in error and that only a new church established by Christ upon his return could possess his grace. Seekers were millenarians as they believed what they were seeking was nigh, that the revelation of the true church was imminent. They anticipated this event by holding meetings as opposed to religious services and had no clergy or hierarchy. During these meetings, they would wait in silence and speak only when they felt God had moved them to do so. Seekers also denied the effectiveness of external forms of religion such as the sacraments, baptism and even the scriptures as a means of salvation. They have been used as a useful category in which to place those radical puritans who defy definition including Cromwell, the Leveller William Walwyn and maybe even Winstanley. However, there were vast numbers of people across the country who withdrew from formal churches with nowhere to go, many who did not feel pulled by an allegiance. While an indistinct and vague category, it may be that 'seeking' was a very popular position to hold. From this movement later grew the Quakers who very quickly gained huge support. Perhaps many of those seeking perhaps later found the 'true' church in Quakerism.

The Muggletonians also grew out of the Ranters though they were a small, dedicated sect and developed their ideas in opposition to Seekers. The movement began in 1651 when two London tailors announced they were the Last Witnesses, prophets foretold in the Book of Revelation. Their beliefs included hostility to philosophical reason, a scriptural understanding of the universe and that God had appeared directly on earth as Jesus. They also believed that God took no notice of everyday events on earth and would not intervene in the world until it came to an end. Named after their leader Lodowicke Muggleton, the sect avoided all forms of worship or preaching and met only for discussion amongst members. The movement was egalitarian, apolitical, and pacifist. Muggletonians attained a degree of public notoriety however by cursing those who reviled their faith, a trait inherited from the profanities of Ranterism. As a defence mechanism during persecuting times, they decreed that someone had to enquire about their faith before they discussed it with them. This also meant that although the Muggletonians had an evolved philosophy and a faithful core of adherents they did not go out and spread the word like other dissenting movements. It is also this which enabled them to be one of the only groups to survive past 1660, though their practice of cursing people was abandoned in the mid-nineteenth century shortly before their sect was believed to have died out.

The Parliament of Saints

Between 1649 and 1653, England changed significantly. In the four years from the first Digging experiment on St George's Hill, all manner of dissenting movements had emerged, evolved and in some cases receded again. The government had largely honoured their promise of toleration through the rewriting of the Blasphemy Act and the decriminalisation of non-church attendance in 1650. For the first time in English history, some degree of acceptance was established and you could be absent from church without the fear of fines or imprisonment, though you may still have received a large measure of social judgement.

Amid this outpouring of radical dissent, the Baptists had survived. They had lost the impetus of being the main radical sect and were welcomed, albeit hesitantly, into the mainstream of society. Their support for the Protectorate appears to have varied greatly from resignation to enthusiasm. As time drew on, Baptists created structures of control similar to those they had rejected in the old Church and their generous system of charity was refined to include only those they felt deserving. They became a sect that represented some of the better-offs in society rather than the London crowd as they had been. While this gained them new adherents, many of their members moved onto new movements and would continue to do so in the coming years.

In 1653, an attempt was made to begin to create a real state settlement beyond that which had been put hastily together by the army and the radical Independent MPs. The Parliament of Saints was established in July 1653, the last effort of the English Commonwealth to form a stable government. It was however an assembly nominated by Cromwell and the Army Council who chose members guided, they claimed, by God's providence. Major-General Harrison, drawing on his Fifth Monarchist beliefs was a chief supporter of this idea and proposed a council of seventy, based on the ancient assemblies of the Israelites, though this number was doubled to 140. It seems though there was widespread dislike for the idea, many sects welcomed this decision. The Council accepted nominations from congregations across the country from whom

MPs were chosen. Five army officers, including Cromwell and Harrison, were also included as members. The member for the City of London, Praise-God Barebone, a Fifth Monarchist preacher was soon to give his name to the assembly which became known mockingly as Barebone's Parliament. Though MPs were largely drawn from the most prosperous parts of society and represented the ruling elite of England, it soon gained a reputation for radicalism and around a third of members can be considered radicals, including about a dozen Fifth Monarchists.[4]

The Parliament of Saints was in many ways the high-water mark of radical dissenting in the civil wars as the point at which a sweeping programme of social and religious reform came closest to being carried out.[5] Particularly prominent in their debates was the abolition of tithes which all dissenting groups opposed. The parliament also debated significant reforms of the legal system and the incendiary trial of John Lilburne for treason. These contentious issues, however, caused divisions and infighting. In December, the assembly broke down when moderates criticised radical members for causing disagreement and the speaker, with around forty members, walked out. Soon after Cromwell and the army forced any remaining members to leave.

Quaking, the Society of Friends

The collapse of the Parliament of Saints at the end of 1653 marked a shift in the consolidation of the regime and a change in the nature of the English Revolution. In December, Cromwell was offered the position of Lord Protector, effectively becoming king in all but name and in the coming years, he would be offered the crown itself. A new attempt to create normality after a decade of civil war ensued. People across society were increasingly tired of wars, famines and a proliferation of ideas that could be diverse and exciting but confusing and terrifying also. The defeat of the main thrust of revolutionary activity in the late 1640s had left people with few places to give their support, either to the regime which seemed increasingly reactionary, or to a fringe of radical sects. Throughout the 1650s, the influence of the Fifth Monarchists and Ranters continued but never reached the heights promised in their early days and their support declined in favour of new directions as it had with the Baptists before them. Many Fifth Monarchists turned against the regime they had once championed and from 1654, a propaganda campaign against the Protectorate was underway. Fifth Monarchist leaders conspired secretly with other disaffected parties including some Baptists and former Levellers but to no avail. In 1657, a frustrated Fifth Monarchist, Thomas Venner, led an abortive uprising of artisans and labourers in London.

The last, and arguably greatest, upswell of dissent came during the tense latter part of the 1650s. The Quakers, unlike their later reputation for pacifism, meekness and soberness were from the outset a protest movement. The Quakers were a loosely knit group who were the inheritors of Seekers, emerging firstly in the north of England. Their proper title was the Society of Friends and George Fox, one of their early leaders, said that their alternative name was from a judge who called them Quakers because of their physical trembling, supposedly a sign of the inward waking of God. The Quaker message was one of 'The Light Within' that all could be saved, an utter rejection of the traditional puritan belief in predestination. They were spiritual millenarians and believed that attaining this inner Jerusalem was the true salvation. Quakers taught that it was even possible for a person who had achieved a state of grace to become sinless, reminiscent of Ranter teaching. They drew in many of the humanistic and democratic beliefs of the previous sects, and while radical in their religion, were able through the sheer force of will, leadership and popularity to survive. However, until the 1670s, they had little defined theology other than in negatives. In practical terms, their ideas were truly radical. They believed in a ministry of ordinary men, and even women, who should preach. One of their early leaders was the preacher Margaret Fell and many women held prominent positions in the movement. They used the informal terms of address 'thee' and 'thou' to all including their social superiors, they refused to bow and like the Diggers rejected the doffing of hats. Like the Familists, Quakers came to oppose the taking of oaths and carrying of arms, though they were drawn strongly from the army and navy and continued to serve into 1660.

The incendiary ideas of the Quakers took hold quickly and they rapidly gained a huge following. Within a few years, they were one of the largest denominations in England. Uniquely compared to any other dissenting groups, they directly addressed agrarian concerns and though they had support in cities such as London and Bristol, they were mainly a rural movement. It seems that their appeal drew back on the radical tradition of egalitarianism established in the late 1640s. It is perhaps fitting that John Lilburne and Gerald Winstanley both converted to Quakerism. Indeed, it is with the Quakers that much of the legacy of this period rests, as the group was able to take many of these radical dissenting ideas beyond the Restoration. General Monck compared them to Levellers for their refusal to obey or be obeyed. A strong part of their attempt to make more equal the world was the Quaker's fierce opposition to tithes which they petitioned against and incited the refusal to pay amongst ordinary people.

The radicalism of the Quakers coupled with their genuine appeal and rapid growth caused concern to the government who increasingly sought to curtail them. Despite theoretical toleration, many local magistrates removed Quaker preachers from their towns and cities, sometimes violently. In 1656, the early Quaker leader, James Nayler, took what was seen by the authorities as a step too far when he entered Bristol on a donkey, greeted by fawning crowds in imitation of Jesus's entry into Jerusalem. Rumours had also been abounding that he had the power to resurrect people. In his subsequent trial, he was made an example of and though he narrowly avoided the death penalty, he was punished brutally by being branded, having his tongue bored and being placed in solitary confinement indefinitely. Generally, the government now sought to reduce some of the toleration extended over the previous years, partly out of fear for the Quakers. The crackdown continued and when in 1657 attending a Church service was again made compulsory, Quaker meetings were deemed one of the only unacceptable forms of worship. Generals Henry Cromwell and Monck actively purged their forces of Quakers.

Part IV: Aftermath

With the death of Lord Protector Oliver Cromwell, the army and parliament faced a crisis to secure a new settlement. Across the channel, the exiled Charles Stuart, son of the late king reached for the throne. Quakers supported the army and parliament and were vociferous in doing so. They raised petitions, asked for deprived Quakers to be returned to their positions and suggested lists of Friends to become JPs. This strident upturn in Quaker activity appears however to have ended up alarming people and may have pushed some to support the Restoration. This was especially so of the Presbyterians who were far from enthusiastic about the return of a king but came to see it as a necessary step to counter the feared dissenters and sects. Many across the country would have shared a similar view and desired some return to stability after decades of uncertainty. Even the General and Particular Baptists came together in an unprecedented move in 1659 to jointly declare neutrality. The flood of dissent was therefore ended partly because of the strength of these radical ideas and movements as the prevailing mood of the country turned from toleration to fear. 'So long as the end of the world seemed imminent, psychological tension could be maintained, and intense moral pressure was tolerable', but not in ordinary times.[6] After the Restoration, there continued to be dissent but it once again went underground. The Quakers were forced to adopt pacifism to survive. The only real attempt at violent resistance was another Fifth Monarchist uprising led by Thomas Venner.

The cause of their fate was largely due to the dissenters themselves. They rejected leadership and organisation and the leaders they did have were often styled as prophets rather than political thinkers. Christopher Hill recognised the difficult task, achieved best by George Fox, of creating a disciplined sect made up of those 'new to the idea of thinking for themselves about religion'.[7] Where they did change, as the Baptists did, they saw their support dwindling. Neither could the dissenters sustain their momentum or endure their continued fracturing. Not only were they feared and hated by most of society, they were riven by division between, and within, sects themselves. Even hugely popular movements such as the Quakers failed to win widespread support and active dissenters in this period probably never numbered more than one per cent of the population.

Their complexity means that there is still an open debate over the role of the dissenters and sects of the civil wars, their size, impact and radicalism. It is difficult to compare to the other behemothic forces of this period which moved slowly against one another like tectonic plates, the king, Cromwell, parliament and the army. Instead, they burned strongly and brightly as flashes in the pan. We must understand that while they existed on the edge of popular culture in these sects, we see a distillation of all the radicalism of the period. They were also expressions of the English people and culture and were rooted within the customs, beliefs and desires of society.[8]

Establishing the long-term impact of the dissenters is probably simpler than gauging their immediate effect. Most notably, they helped to establish a place in English society for the oppositional free-thinking which had emerged throughout the wars. It was 'the very fact they questioned' which was important.[9] Their legacy is one of challenge, a 'refusal to accept the received order of things' and as a result 'the world in which they lived would never quite be the same again'.[10] For centuries afterwards, dissension was carried through English society, often in radical religion. Baptists and Quakers adapted their radicalism as simultaneously their ideas permeated throughout society to make them more tolerable, and they survived. The inspiration of the civil war dissenters can clearly be seen in the non-conformist tradition in Britain, particularly the Methodist phenomenon of the eighteenth century. In turn, dissent and non-conformism came to play a significant role in shaping the ideals and practical organisation of the nascent trade union and labour movements. A non-conformist education was the hallmark of many early British socialists such as the Tolpuddle martyrs and Keir Hardie. There is more than a little truth in Harold Wilson's statement that the Labour Party owed more to Methodism than to Marxism.

Sometimes history is closer than we realize. The relevance of the civil war dissenters to the modern world was thrown sharply into focus in 1974 when the historians E. P. Thompson and Christopher Hill published a series of articles in the *Times Literary Supplement*. To their surprise, a reader wrote to tell them he knew a Muggletonian. The authors were put in touch with the Kent farmer, Philip Noakes. He had kept his faith a relative secret, even from his close family, never talking about it unless asked. When he died in 1979, he may not have been the last Muggletonian.

Notes

1. Bernard Capp, "The Fifth Monarchists and Popular Millenarianism," in *Radical Religion in the English Revolution,* eds. J. F. McGregor and B. Reay (Oxford: Oxford University Press, 1986), 165.
2. Ibid, 189.
3. John Morrill, "The Church in England, 1642-9," in *Reactions to the English Civil War*, ed. John Morrill (London: Palgrave, 1982), 104-7.
4. Austin Woolrych, *Commonwealth to Protectorate.* (Oxford: Clarendon Press, 1982), 193, 232.
5. B. Reay, "Radicalism and Religion in the English Revolution: an Introduction," in *Radical Religion in the English Revolution,* eds. J. F. McGregor and B. Reay (Oxford: Oxford University Press, 1986), 20.
6. Christopher Hill, *The World Turned Upside Down: Radical Ideas During the English Revolution.* (Harmondsworth: Penguin, 1975), 375.
7. Ibid, 373.
8. Andrew Bradstock, *Radical Religion in Cromwell's England.* (London: I.B. Tauris, 2011), 160-61.
9. Reay, "Radicalism and Religion in the English Revolution," 21.
10. R. J. Acheson, *Radical Puritans in England 1550-1660.* (London: Longman, 1993), 77.

Appendix

Thomas Edwards, *The first and second part of Gangrœna, or, A catalogue and discovery of many of the errors, heresies, blasphemies and pernicious practices of the sectaries of this time.* **London, 1646.**

There is one *Samuel Oats* a Weaver... who being of *Lams* Church, was sent out as a Dipper and Emissary into the Countreyes: Last summer I heard he went his progresse into *Surrey* and *Sussex,* but now this yeare he is sent out into *Essex* three of foure months ago, and for many weeks together went up and downe from place to place, and Towne to Towne, about *Bochen, Braintry, Tarling,* and those parts, preaching his erroneous Doctrines, and dipping many in rivers; this is a young lusty fellow, and hath traded chiefly with young women and young maids, dipping many of them, though all is fish that comes to his net, and this he did with all boldness end without all control for a matter of two months: A godly Minister of Essex coming out of those parts related, hee hath baptized a great number of women, and that they were call'd out of their beds to go a dipping in rivers, dipping manie of them in the night, so that their Husbands and Masters could not keep them in their houses, and 'tis commonly reported that this *Oates* had for his pains ten shillings apeece for dipping the richer, and two shillings six pence for the poorer; he came verie bare and meane into *Essex,* but before hee had done his work, was well lined, and growne pursie. In the cold weather in *March,* hee dipped a young woman, one *Ann Martin* (as her name is given in to me) whom he held so long in the water, that she fell presently sicke, and her belly sweld with the abundance of water she took in, and within a fortnight or three weeks died, and upon her death-bed expressed her dipping to the cause of her death...

[Gerrard Winstanley], *A Declaration from the Poor oppressed People of England, Directed To all that call themselves, or are called Lords of Manors, through this Nation.* **[London,] Printed in the Yeer, 1649.**

WE whose names are subscribed, do in the name of all the poor oppressed people in *England*, declare unto you, that call your selves Lords of Manors, and Lords of the Land, That in regard the King of Righteousness, our Maker, hath inlightened our hearts so far, as to see, That the earth was not made purposely for you, to be Lords of it, and we to be your Slaves, Servants, and Beggers; but it was made to be a common Livelihood to all, without respect of persons: And that your buying and selling of Land, and the

Fruits of it, one to another, is *The cursed thing,* and was brought in by War; which hath, and still does establish murder, and theft, in the hands of some branches of Mankinde over others, which is the greatest outward burden, and unrighteous power, that the Creation groans under: For the power of inclosing Land, and owning Propriety, was brought into the Creation by your Ancestors by the Sword; which first did murther their fellow Creatures, Men, and after plunder or steal away their Land, and left this Land successively to you, their Children. And therefore, though you did not kill or theeve, yet you hold that cursed thing in your hand, by the power of the Sword; and so you justifie the wicked deeds of your Fathers; and that sin of your Fathers, shall be visited upon the Head of you, and your Children, to the third and fourth Generation, and longer too, till your bloody and theeving power be rooted out of the Land.

And further, in regard the King of Righteousness hath made us sensible of our burthens, and the cryes and groanings of our hearts are come before him: We take it as a testimony of love from him, That our hearts begin to be freed from slavish fear of men, such as you are; and that we finde Resolucions in us, grounded upon the inward law of Love, one towards another, To Dig and Plough up the Commons, and waste Lands through *England;* and that our conversation shall be so unblameable, That your Laws shall not reach to oppress us any longer, unless you by your Laws will shed the innocent blood that runs in our veins.

For though you and your Ancestors got your Propriety by murther and theft, and you keep it by the same power from us, that have an equal right to the Land with you, by the righteous Law of Creation, yet we shall have no occasion of quarrelling (as you do) about that disturbing devil, called *Particular propriety*: For the Earth, with all her Fruits of Corn, Cattle, and such like, was made to be a common Store-house of Livelihood to all Mankinde, friend, and foe, without exception.

And to prevent all your scrupulous Objections, know this, That we must neither buy nor sell; Money must not any longer (after our work of the Earths community is advanced) be the great god, that hedges in some, and hedges out others; for Money is but part of the Earth: And surely, the Righteous Creator, who is King, did never ordain, That unless some of Mankinde, do bring that Mineral (Silver and Gold) in their hands, to others of their own kinde, that they should neither be fed, nor be clothed; no surely, For this was the project of Tyrant-flesh (which Land-lords are branches of) to set his Image upon Money. And they make this unrighteous Law, That none should buy or sell, eat, or be clothed, or have any comfortable Livelihood among men, unless they did bring his Image stamped upon Gold or Silver in their hands...

For after our work of the Earthly community is advanced, we must make use of Gold and Silver, as we do of other metals, but not to buy and sell withal; for buying and selling is the great cheat, that robs and steals the Earth one from another: It is that which makes some Lords, others Beggers, some Rulers, others to be ruled; and makes great Murderers and Theeves to be imprisoners, and hangers of little ones, or of sincere-hearted men.

And while we are made to labor the Earth together, with one consent and willing minde; and while we are made free, that every one, friend and foe, shall enjoy the benefit of their Creation, that is, To have food and rayment from the Earth, their Mother; and every one subiect to give accompt of his thoughts, words, and actions to none. but to the one onely righteous Judg, and Prince of Peace; the Spirit of Righteousness that dwells, and that is now rising up to rule in every Creature, and in the whole Globe. We say, while we are made to hinder no man of his Priviledges given him in his Creation, equal to one, as to another; what Law then can you make, to take hold upon us, but Laws of Oppression and Tyranny, that shall enslave or spill the blood of the Innocent? And so your Selves, your Judges, Lawyers, and Justices, shall be found to be the greatest Transgressors, in, and over Mankinde.

But to draw neerer to declare our meaning, what we would have, and what we shall endevor to the uttermost to obtain, as moderate and righteous Reason directs us; seeing we are made to see our Priviledges, given us in our Creation, which have hitherto been denied to us, and our Fathers, since the power of the Sword began to rule, And the secrets of the Creation have been locked up under the traditional, Parrat-like speaking, from the Universities, and Colledges for Scholars, And since the power of the murdering, and theeving Sword, formerly, as well as now of late yeers, hath set up a Government, and maintains that Government; for what are prisons, and putting others to death, but the power of the Sword to enforce people to that Government which was got by Conquest and Sword, and cannot stand of it self, but by the same murdering power? That Government that is got over people by the Sword and kept by the Sword, is not set up by the King of Righteousness to be his Law, but by Covetousness, the great god of the world; who hath been permitted to raign for a time, times, and dividing of time and his government draws to the period of the last term of his allotted time; and then the Nations shall see the glory of that Government that shall rule in Righteousness, without either Sword or Spear,

And seeing further, the power of Righteousness in our hearts, seeking the livelihood of others as well as our selves, hath drawn forth our bodies to begin to dig, and plough, in the Commons and waste Land, for the reasons already declared,

And seeing and finding ourselves poor, wanting Food to feed upon, while we labor the Earth to cast in Seed, and to wait till the first Crop comes up; and wanting Ploughs, Carts, Corn, and such materials to plant the Commons withal, we are willing to declare our condition to you, and to all, that have the Treasury of the Earth, locked up in your Bags, Chests, and Barns, and will offer up nothing to this publike Treasury; but will rather see your fellow Creatures starve for want of Bread, that have an equal right to it with your selves, by the Law of Creation: But this by the way we onely declare to you, and to all that follow the subtle art of buying and selling the Earth with her Fruits, meerly to get the Treasury thereof into their hands, to lock it up from them, to whom it belongs; that so, such covetous, proud, unrighteous, selfish flesh, may be left without excuse in the day of Judgment.

And therefore, the main thing we aym at, and for which we declare our Resolutions to go forth, and act, is this, To lay hold upon, and as we stand in need, to cut and fell, and make the best advantage we can of the Woods and Trees, that grow upon the Commons, To be a stock for our selves, and our poor Brethren, through the land of *England*, to plant the Commons withal; and to provide us bread to eat, till the Fruit of our labors in the Earth bring forth increase; and we shall meddle with none of your Proprieties (but what is called Commonage) till the Spirit in you, make you cast up your Lands and Goods, which were got, and still is kept in your hands by murder, and theft; and then we shall take it from the Spirit, that hath conquered you, and not from our Swords, which is an abominable, and unrighteous power, and a destroyer of the Creation: But the Son of man comes not to destroy, but to save.

And we are moved to send forth this Declaration abroad, to give notice to every one whom it concerns, in regard we hear and see, that some of you, that have been Lords of Manors, do cause the Trees and Woods that grow upon the Commons, which you pretend a Royalty unto, to be cut down and sold, for your own private use, Thereby the Common Land, which your own mouths doe say belongs to the poor, is impoverished, and the poor oppressed people robbed of their Rights, while you give them cheating words, by telling some of our poor oppressed Brethren, That those of us that have begun to Dig and Plough up the Commons, will hinder the poor; and so blinde their eyes, that they see not their Priviledge, while you, and the rich Free-holders make the most profit of the Commons, by your over-stocking of them with Sheep and Cattle; and the poor that have the name to own the Commons, have the least share therein; nay, they are checked by you, if they cut Wood, Heath, Turf, or Furseys, in places about the Common, where you disallow.

Therefore we are resolved to be cheated no longer, nor be held under the slavish fear of you no longer, seing the Earth was made for us, as well as for you: And if the Common Land belongs to us who are the poor oppressed, surely the woods that grow upon the Commons belong to us likewise: therefore we are resolved to try the uttermost in the light of reason, to know whether we shall be free men, or slaves. If we lie still, and let you steale away our Birthrights, we perish; and if we Petition we perish also, though we have paid taxes, given free quarter, and ventured our lives to preserve the Nations freedom as much as you, and therefore by the law of contract with you, freedom in the land is our portion as well as yours, equal with you: And if we strive for freedom, and your murdering, governing Laws destroy us, we can but perish…

[Abiezer Coppe], *A Fiery Flying Roll: A Word from the Lord to all the Great Ones of the Earth, whom this may concerne: Being the last WARNING PIECE at the dreadfull day of JUDGEMENT.* Imprinted at London, 1649.

An inlet into the Land of Promise; the new *Jerusalem*; and a gate into the ensuing Discourse, worthy of serious consideration.

> MY Deare One.
> All or None.
> Every one under the Sunne.
> Mine own.

My most Excellent Majesty (in me) hath strangely and variously transformed this forme.

And behold, by mine owne Almightinesse (In me) I have been changed in a moment, in the twinkling of an eye, at the sound of the Trump.

And now the Lord is descended from Heaven, with a shout, with the voyce of the Arch-angell, and with the Trump of God.

And the sea, the earth, yea all things are now giving up their dead. And all things that ever were, are, or shall be visible—are the Grave wherein the King of Glory (the eternall, invisible Almightinesse, hath lain as it were) dead and buried.

But behold, behold, he is now risen with a witnesse, to save *Zion* with vengeance, or to confound and plague all things into himself; who by his mighty Angell is proclaiming (with a loud voyce) That Sin and Transgression is finished and ended; and everlasting righteousnesse brought in; and the everlasting Gospell preaching; Which everlasting Gospell is brought in with most terrible earth-quakes, and heaven-quakes, and with signes and wonders following. *Amen*

And it hath pleased my most Excellent Majesty, (who is universall love, and whose service is perfect freedome) to set this forme (the Writer of this Roll) as no small signe and wonder in fleshly Israel; as you may partly see to the ensuing Discourse.

And now (my deare ones!) every one under the Sun, I will onely point at the gate, thorow which I was led into that new City, new *Hierusalem*, and to the Spirits of just men, made perfect, and to God the Judge of all.

First, all my strength, my forces were utterly routed, my house I dwelt in fired, my father and mother forsook me, the wife of my bosome loathed me, mine old name was rotted, perished; and I was utterly plagued, consumed, damned, rammed, and sunke into nothing, into the bowels of the still Eternity (my mothers wombe) out of which I came naked, and whetherto I returned again naked, And lying a while there, rapt up in silence, at length (the body or outward forme being awake all this while) I heard with my outward eare (to my apprehension) a most terrible thunder-clap, and after that a second. And upon the second thunder-clap, which was exceeding terrible, I saw a great body of light, like the light of the Sun, and red as fire, in the forme of a drum (as it were) whereupon with exceeding trembling and amazement on the flesh, and with joy unspeakable in the spirit, I clapt my hands, and cryed out, *Amen, Halelujah, Halelujah, Amen.* And so lay trembling, sweating, and smoaking (for the space of half an houre) at length with a loud voyce (I inwardly) cryed out, Lord, what wilt thou do with me; my most excellent majesty and eternall glory (in me) answered & sayd, Fear not, I will take thee up into mine everlasting Kingdom. But thou shalt (first) drink a bitter cup, a bitter cup, a bitter cup; wherupon (being filled with exceeding amazement) I was throwne into the belly of hell (and take what you can of it in these expressions, though the matter is beyond expression) I was among all the Devils in hell, even in their most hideous how.

And under all this terrour, and amazement, there was a little spark of transcendent, transplendent, unspeakable glory, which survived, and sustained it self, triumphing, exulting, and exalting it self above all the Fiends. And confounding the very blacknesse of darknesse (you must take it in these tearmes, for it is infinitely beyond expression.) Vpon this the life was taken out of the body (for a season) and it was thus resembled, as if a man with a great brush dipt in whiting, should with one stroke wipe out, or sweep off a picture upon a wall, &c. after a while, breath and life was recurred into the form againe; whereupon I saw various streames of light (in the night) which appeared to the outward eye; and immediately I saw three hearts (or three appearances) in the form of hearts, of exceeding brightnesse; and immediately an innumerable company of hearts, filling each corner of the room where I was. And me thoughts there was variety and distinction, as if there had been severall hearts, and yet most strangely and unexpressibly complicated or folded up in unity. I clearly saw distinction, diversity, variety, and as clearly saw all swallowed up into unity. And it hath been my song many times since, within and without, unity, universality, universality, unity, Eternall Majesty, &c. And at this vision, a most strong, glorious voyce uttered these words, *The spirits of just men made perfect* the spirits &c, with whom I had as absolut, cleare, full communion, and in a two fold more familiar way, then ever I had outwardly with my dearest friends, and nearest relations. The visions and revelations of God, and the strong hand of eternall invisible almightinesse, was stretched out upon me, within me, for the space of foure dayes and nights, without intermission.

The time would faile if I would tell you all, but it is not the good will and pleasure of my most excellent Majesty in me, to declare any more (as yet) then thus much further: That amongst those various voyces that were then uttered within, these were some, *Blood, blood, Where, where? upon the hypocriticall holy heart, &c. Another thus, Vengeance, vengeance, vengeance, Plagues, plagues, upon the Inhabitants of the earth; Fire, fire, fire, Sword, sword, &c. upon all that bow not down to eternall Majesty, universall love; I'le recover, recover, my wooll, my flax, my money. Declare, declare, feare thou not the faces of any; I am (in thee) a munition of Rocks, &c.*

Go up to *London*, It not being shewen to me, what I should do, more then preach and print something, &c. very little expecting I should be so strangely acted, as to (my exceeding joy and delight) I have been, though to the utter cracking of my credit, and to the rotting of my old name which is damned, and cast out (as a toad to the dunghill) that I might have a new name, with me, upon me, within me, which is, I am to *London*, that great City, write, write, write. And behold I writ, and lo a hand was sent to me, and a roll of a book was therein, which this fleshly hand would have put wings to, before the time. Whereupon it was snatcht out of my hand, & the Roll thrust into my mouth; and I eat it up, and filled my bowels with it, (*Eze.* 2. 8. &c. *cha.* 3. 1, 2, 3.) where it was as bitter as worm-wood; and it lay broiling, and burning in my stomack, till I brought it forth in this forme.

And now I send it flying to thee, with my heart, And all
Per AUXILIUM PATRIS…

George Fox, For the Parliament of England and their Army, So-Called. [London] 11th *month*, 1659.

YOUR day into darknesse is turned; the Sun is gone down over you; ye have had a large day, and power given unto you; to have done the will of God; But you have abused the power; and sleighted your day; and you have Refused to doe the Lords worke and have sought to serve your selves; and not the Lord; Therefore in Justice and Righteousnesse is the day wherein you might have wrought for God; taken from you; and the thick dark night of Confusion is Come upon you; wherein you are groping and stumbling, and cannot worke, the decree is gone out, and sealed against you; and it Cannot be Recalled; you are not the men (as ye stand) in whome God will appeare to worke deliverance for his People, and Creatures; (and yet deliverance shall Come, but not according to mans Exspectation) But as for you, yee have Rejected the Councell of the Lord; and greeved his spirit, and he hath long borne you; yea; you are departed from the Lord, and his presence is departed from you; Indeed he hath hewed with you (and if you had been faithfull to the End, he would have honoured and prospered you, and have been your sufficient Reward) yee were his Ax, but you have bosted your selves against him; therefore as you have beaten, and hewed, and broken others, Even so must you be beaten, hewed and broken, for you have greevously provoked the Lord, and if he should now suffer that tree, which yee have Cut, to fall upon you; and to break part of you, it were Just.

Oh ye Trecherous, willfull, proud, selfe-seeking people, who have despised the Counsell of the Lord, and would not take warning though he hath sent his prophets and servants Early and Late among you, some of whome you have Imprisoned, and despitfully used; what will yee doe now, whom will you now flee unto for help; seeing yee are departed from the Lord, and are now Rending and tearing, biting and devouring one another, for proud ambissious selfe Ends; (Mark) if yee would now build againe, the thing that you once destroyed; that shall not be able to hide, or shelter you from the wrath of the Lambe that way whereby you think to strengthen your selves, thereby shall you make your selves much weaker, and help forward your own destruction; you are now, but a Rod, Remember your End, which hastens greatly; And now Breach upon Breach, Insurrection upon Insurrection, Overturning upon Overturning, Heaps upon Heaps, Division upon Division shall there be; untill he Come to Raigne, whose Right it is; and all Nations must bow before him; Else he will break them with his Iron Rod.

They that trust in, or leane upon you, for help; it is as if they leaned upon a broken Reed which is not able to help it selfe; nor others; indeed you have been made to doe many good things; but you would not goe through with the worke, which God will have accomplished; and therefore are these things come upon you; Therefore tremble and dread before the Lord, yee who have been as strong Oakes, and tall Sedars; for now shall your strength faile you and you shall be weake, even as the weakest of men, but if you would yet beleive in the light; and truely submit to Gods righteous judgements, many of you might come to witnesse your soules saved, in the day of the Lord; though many of your bodyes are to be thrown by (because of your greivous backslidings) as not counted worthy to be the Lords workmen.

There is a small remnant yet among you (for whom my soule breaths) who may be winnowed out; and if they will owne the judgements of the Lord, and truly and throughly deny themselves, and follow his leadings, he will heale their backslidings; and purge them; that so they nay be instruments in his hand: But they that will continue with you; in your sins; shall partake with you; of your judgements.

11th month (59)

From one, who am made willing both to suffer, and to raigne with Christ; even to follow him whether soever he goeth.

George Fox the younger.

The Rod of the wicked, shall not alwayes rest upon the back of the righteous; yet even as gould is tryed; so shall they be; that they may be white, and without spot, before the Lambe: But God will avenge their cause; and woe then will be to their oppressors and then shall the majesty, and glory of the Lord, fill his people (who have long been troden under) and they shall be the dread of all Nations, the zeale of the Lord of Hosts shall performe it.

Section Three

The Eighteenth Century

Thomas Paine

Frances Chiu

On 29 October 1805, a cantankerous John Adams wrote to Benjamin Waterhouse:

> I know not whether any man in the world has had more influence on its
> inhabitants or affairs or the last thirty years than Tom Paine ... For such a
> mongrel between pig and puppy, begotten by a wild boar on a bitch wolf,
> never before in any age of the world was suffered by the poltroonery of
> mankind, to run through such a career of mischief. Call it then the Age
> of Paine.[1]

This 'Tom Paine', of course, was none other than the author of the three bestsellers of
the eighteenth century: *Common Sense, Rights of Man*, and *Age of Reason*. Who was
this man—a modern Prometheus who seemed to offend the powers that be across two
continents? A man whose works they desperately tried to censor? But a man who also
came to inspire the diverse likes of the Duke of Richmond—as discussed in the next
chapter—William Blake, Percy Bysshe Shelley, Andrew Jackson, Abraham Lincoln,
Ronald Reagan, Glenn Beck, and Occupy Wall Street?

Life and Social Context

Born on 29 January 1737 O.S., to a Quaker corset maker, Joseph Pain (Thomas added
the 'e' in America) and his Anglican wife, Frances Cocke, in Thetford, England,
Thomas Paine was an only child who grew up in a cottage within sight of the town
gallows. Details regarding his youth are sparse, with little correspondence on him by
either his parents or relations—apart from the fact that he may have attended Quaker
and Anglican churches. It was then that he may have begun to question the foundations
of Christianity while gleaning from the Quakers an empathy 'for the hard condition of
others' as he noted in a letter to the town of Lewes.[2]

Enrolled in the 'declining' Thetford Grammar School despite his parents' inability
'to give me a shilling beyond what they gave me in education',[3] Paine displayed a talent
for mathematics and poetry. Certainly, a 'raw and adventurous mood' was driven into
his psyche by a teacher's account of life aboard a man-of-war, thereby fuelling a desire

to journey abroad. But whatever talents or interests Paine possessed, he was pulled out of school at thirteen to become his father's apprentice in corset making. That he must have been bored by his prospective career is nowhere more apparent than in his decision to board a privateer, *The Terrible*. Paine was saved from early death as his father was able to drag him back home just as the sixteen-year-old boy was signing the roster: had he remained, he would have perished with the crew of 150 after a battle with a French privateer. Paine's plans for joining a privateer, however, would come to fruition not long after his arrival in London four years later.

Thomas Paine. (Wellcome Collection)

After nearly eight months at sea, he returned to Covent Garden, London, where he attended lectures of Benjamin Martin, James Ferguson, and John Bevis, of the Royal Society. As his funds dwindled, he made his way to Sandwich, where he returned to his former vocation as corset maker while possibly preaching on the side as an independent or Methodist. Marrying a servant two years his junior, Mary Lambert, he lost her in little over a year when she and her infant died in childbirth. Perhaps inspired by his father-in-law's experiences in the Excise, Paine decided to enter its service in 1764. His first stint at Alford was cut short when he was dismissed for allegedly 'stamping' his book (e.g., not examining goods or accepting bribes): that this termination was later discovered to be unjustified allowed him to be reinstated a year later after a few months of teaching in London. Moving to Lewes, Paine befriended his landlord, Samuel Ollive, before espousing his daughter, Elizabeth. It was during his years in this town, with its rich Dissenting republican history, that Paine grew increasingly engrossed by politics, winning debates held by the Headstrong Club at the White Hart Inn. His abilities as the renowned 'General of the Headstrong War' led his fellow Excise officers to send him to London in order to petition parliament for a raise. The two years in London, however, came to nought as his pamphlet, *Case of the Officers of the Excise*, failed to sway parliament despite winning the praise of Oliver Goldsmith. More trouble ensued upon his return to Lewes, when he was discharged for his prolonged leave of absence: a problem which was compounded by the failure of the grocery shop that he managed with his wife. Bankrupt and facing a demand for separation from his wife, Paine decided to sail for America after seeking the advice of a London acquaintance: Benjamin Franklin.

After falling ill aboard and landing in a stretcher two months later, the 'ingenious, worthy young man'—as Franklin referred to him—found a job in late January 1775 as an editor of the monthly *Pennsylvania Magazine*. His liberal leanings were already on ample show in his selection of articles for the magazine: for instance, an essay on women's rights translated from French, another which mocked aristocratic titles, and still others which criticised slavery, wars of conquest, and British conduct in India. Despite the significant rise in readership during Paine's tenure, the publisher, Robert Aitken, was reluctant to offer him a contract. As hostilities between Britain and the American colonies escalated, Paine commenced work on *Common Sense*, which outsold virtually every other work published in the colonies. His strong belief in the cause of independence was affirmed not only by his refusal of the copyright, but also his donation of the profits to the struggling Continental army.

Growing steadily committed to the revolutionary cause, Paine would also enlist with a Pennsylvanian 'flying' camp before accompanying General Nathaniel Greene as an aide-de-camp. It was after Washington's upsets in New York that Paine began to write the *American Crisis* papers. If Paine was a rather timid fighter, 'always' keeping 'out of danger', according to a fellow soldier, Paine was less fearful of political controversy. In 1778, he exposed Silas Deane's war profiteering, namely, the selling of French arms to the Americans even though they were intended as gifts. Although Paine was vindicated, his allegations against Deane came at a heavy price, including resignation from office, calumny, and a public beating.

Over the following decade, Paine continued to put effort into shaping the new republic, such as calling for a stronger union between the colonies. Shortly after being rewarded with a confiscated Loyalist farm and 300 acres of land in New Rochelle, New York for his wartime efforts, he began to pursue his hobbies, including the design of a durable single-span iron bridge: a singularity in an era of wooden bridges. Failing to procure funding for his bridge, he sailed to France in May 1787. But as his plans for the bridge stalled in England as well as in France, Paine gradually began to shift his attention to the early signs of revolution in France. At the same time, his fame as the author of *Common Sense* led Paine into some of the most distinguished political and literary circles. In Paris, he was the constant guest of Marquis de Lafayette, Brissot, and Condorcet, while in England, he befriended not only the former MP, Edmund Burke, a supporter of the American colonies, but also the radical publisher, Joseph Johnson, and his young guests: the poet William Blake, Mary Wollstonecraft, the future author of *The Vindication of the Rights of Woman*, and her husband-to-be, William Godwin, the future author of *An Enquiry concerning Political Justice* and *Caleb Williams*.

When Edmund Burke published his *Reflections on the Revolution in France* in 1790, a lengthy work critical of the French revolution, he shocked many who assumed he was a friend to liberal causes. Along with Wollstonecraft, Joseph Priestley, and others, Paine defended the revolution with Part 1 of *Rights of Man* in March 1791. Outselling all of the other replies to Burke, not to mention Burke's *Reflections* itself, *Rights* did not yet alarm the government in spite of its controversial passages since it was priced at a somewhat costly three shillings: which meant there was little access for the masses. Instead, Prime Minister William Pitt the Younger would save his ire for the modestly priced Part 2, published a year later. As Part 2 outsold Part 1, Pitt grew alarmed at its potential for revolution in Britain. Issuing a proclamation against 'wicked and seditious writings', on 18 May 1792, the government lost no time in encouraging conservative populist rebuttals to *Rights of Man* such as Hannah More's *Village Politics* (1792) and commissioning hostile biographies of Paine. At the same time, Paine's effigies were burned across Britain with the tacit backing of local magistrates and gentry. Finally, after being informed by William Blake of a warrant for his arrest by Pitt, Paine would escape to France where he had just been elected to the National Convention as a representative of Pas-de-Calais to the National Convention.

As Paine resided on the outskirts of Paris, he socialised with American and English expats as well as the Girondins, the more moderate supporters of the revolution. Elected to the committee to draft a new constitution, despite his inability to speak French, he conferred with the Marquis de Condorcet and Emmanuel-Joseph Sieyès. Here, however, Paine faced new problems during Louis XVI's trial for treason in 1793, after the latter not only tried to flee the nation with his family, but also to derail the revolution. Although Paine agreed that Louis XVI was guilty of treason, he stood in opposition to Robespierre, Marat, and Danton who demanded the execution of the king. Within hours of the completion of Part 1 of *The Age of Reason*, Paine was dragged to the Luxembourg prison in December 1793. Falling ill and comatose, Paine narrowly escaped the guillotine by a mere accident: although an X had been marked right on the inside of the door to his cell as a sign that he was to be executed the following day, the door was shut by chance as another turnkey made his rounds to notate the persons to be sent to the guillotine. After being released from prison with the assistance of Thomas Jefferson, Paine was invited to recuperate at the residence of the recently appointed ambassador to France, James Monroe. In less than a year, Paine would fire off an angry public letter to the president, George Washington, accusing him of turning a blind eye to his pleas for release from the Luxembourg, as well as Part 2 of *The Age of Reason*: publications which came to destroy his reputation in light of Washington's popularity and the emergence of the Second Great Awakening.

After residing with the family of a radical journalist, Nicholas Bonneville, for seven years, Paine returned to America in 1802. Here, he learned that his fame had turned to infamy as friends and acquaintances shunned him; even Jefferson, though genial, kept his distance. Indeed, over the following years, Paine would find himself despised and variously derided as a 'dangerous fiend', 'monster', and 'a compound of all that is base, disgusting, and wicked without the relief of any one quality that was great or good'.[4] Paine, according to his friend and biographer, Cleo Rickman, was 'coldly neglected … and cruelly treated'.[5] Insult was added to injury in New Rochelle as election officials questioned his citizenship, ultimately denying him the right to vote. Paine's request to be buried in a Quaker cemetery was also denied. Dying on 8 June 1809, after a bout of pneumonia, Paine was laid to rest in his backyard. Unlike the funerals of Franklin or Jefferson, Paine's was attended by a mere handful of people, including the wife and sons of Bonneville and two African-American boys. Not long after his death, a children's rhyme was circulated:

Poor Tom Paine! there he lies:
Nobody laughs and nobody cries
Where he has gone or how he fares
Nobody knows and nobody cares.[6]

In order to assess the extent of Paine's radicalism, however, it is important to understand the development of popular politics in the 1760s and 1770s. One of the most influential writers was James Murray, a Scottish-born activist in Newcastle politics and Presbyterian minister, whose popular *Sermons to Asses* (1768) opens cheekily with 'We read of the asskind preaching to mankind: and why may not men preach to asses'.[7] Complaining of taxes on basic necessities, corrupt electioneering, and disabilities faced by Protestant Dissenters, Murray would denounce the ills arising from oligarchical representation in parliament. Elections, according to Murray, were inordinately dominated by 'a few monopolizers of privileges' who were not only wealthy but wielded great power.[8] Urging voters to examine the measures supported by MPs running for office, he declared it high time for voters to take heed of their own 'natural rights and privileges'.[9] Although Murray refrained from demanding the end of hereditary government, his searing caricatures of aristocrats and Anglican prelates in subsequent writings such as *New Sermons to Asses* and *Sermons to Lord Spiritual* signalled a new frame of mind.

Populist themes were no less pronounced in James Burgh's three-volume *Political Disquisitions* (1769-1774), a work greatly esteemed on both sides of the Atlantic—with Paine himself among its admirers. Just as Jean-Jacques Rousseau underscored the 'general good' in his *Social Contract* a decade earlier, Burgh claimed that all lawful authority derived from the people. Moreover, like Murray, Burgh would criticize disproportionate taxation on the poor while recommending an expansion of suffrage. It was all too clear that their sufferings could be blamed on their lack of means for 'determining who shall be the lawgivers of their country'.[10] No less problematic for Burgh was the power of royal influence on parliament.[11]

At the same time, a heightened and more wide-ranging awareness of natural rights and equality would emerge for the first time since the civil war of the 1640s—discussed in this volume by Sheldon Goldfarb and Joseph Saunders—with the collected impact of the conflict brewing in Britain and her American colonies in addition to the campaign for the abolition of slavery in Britain. As Granville Sharp defended the escaped slaves Jonathan Strong and James Somerset in 1774, his writings offered clear evidence of this new consciousness of rights as he emphasised the concepts of 'natural rights' and 'equal rights'. Slavery, according to Sharp, was not only a violation of 'civil liberty'[12] and of the 'British constitution and liberties', but a 'gross infringement of the common and natural rights of mankind'.[13] Similarly, when arguing for parliamentary reform in *A Declaration of the People's Natural Right to a Share in the Legislature* (1774), he asserted that only were all subjects in 'Great Britain, Ireland, or the Colonies ... *equally* entitled to the same *Natural* Rights', but that it was wrong to assume that the 'more distant parts of the British Empire' did not share the same rights.[14]

The demands for greater political participation and awareness of natural rights would have failed to resonate without the gradual overturning of the traditional assumption that the common man was ill-equipped to understand government. Even though the Unitarian minister and chemist Joseph Priestley agreed that propertied elites were better suited to governing on account of their education, he would also maintain that those of 'moderate fortunes' were 'more truly *independent,* than those who are born to great opulence'.[15] Likewise, while discouraging his readers from heeding electoral advice from a 'duke or lord, knight or 'squire' with 'their drunken rabble of attendants',[16] James Murray believed it wrong to think that ordinary men 'are not competent judges, nor ought to give their opinion concerning these mysteries'.[17] Indeed, some of the lowest class of the people' can 'understand the theory of financiering as well as the First Lord of the Treasury' particularly when his wisdom could not be 'much admired'.[18] Nor is it fortuitous that this championing of the common man and woman was increasingly reinforced by references to 'common sense'. In *Crito* (1766), for instance, James Burgh touted the superiority of 'common sense … and a moderate knowledge of history' over the seemingly lofty attainments of those 'who have undertaken administration in this country'.[19] Similarly, Granville Sharp contended in *Declaration of the People's Natural Right*, that 'when the Natural rights of any of our fellow-Subjects' are under threat, everyone can draw 'plain conclusions of reason and common-sense'. [20]

All told, according to contemporary liberals, the state of Britain was a precarious one. Burgh imagined that:

> Liberty seems indeed to be bidding mankind farewell ... All Europe was once free. Now all Europe is enslaved, excepting what shadow of liberty is left in England, Holland, Switzerland, and a few republics in Italy. [21]

He declared the necessity for a 'Grand Association for Restoring the Constitution', a call that was taken up by Major John Cartwright, when he published his first of many pamphlets calling for universal male suffrage and annual elections, *Take your choice* (1776). Yet, despite the broad appeal for electoral reform in the 1760s and 70s, greater confidence in the intellectual capacities of the poor and middling orders, as well as a newly awakened sense of activism, what is equally significant is a general satisfaction with the British constitution and government. After all, reformers of the 1760s-80s were not so much the direct heirs of such post-civil war republicans as James Harrington or Algernon Sidney, but rather of John Locke, sharing the latter's overall acceptance of a monarch as well as a House of Lords and Commons. Many probably shared Priestley's preference of hereditary monarchies to elective monarchies since the latter was full of 'cabal, confusion, and misery'.[22] Even the outspoken Murray would express a preference for monarchical power rather than ministerial power since there was greater 'security to a people from the honour of a crowned head'.[23]

It is perhaps hardly surprising that this questioning of political establishments and dogma was accompanied by a questioning of Anglican and Catholic establishments, if not Christianity itself. Although it is difficult to determine exactly how and when deism materialised, many trace it back to the early seventeenth-century writings of Lord Herbert of Cherbury, particularly *Of Truth* (1624), with its theory that individuals were capable of determining religious truths for themselves. Such ideas were later reinforced by John Locke in his *Letters on Toleration* (1689-92), where he maintained that rational demonstration, rather than compulsion, served as the only valid basis for revelation. This idea would be reiterated by his disciple, John Toland, in a work titled *Christianity not Mysterious* (1696), which held that revelation should not violate the dictates of reason while highlighting 'rational proofs' and 'convincing evidence'. Explaining that the sense of 'mystery' in ancient Christianity differed substantially from the modern sense of the word, Toland stated that the original use of *mysterium* did not transcend reason. Many of these ideas would shape the trajectory of French deism even if there was already a popular native tradition of scepticism in clandestine anti-clerical writings (printed in Holland and 'imported' back to France) which expressed doubts of miracles and ridiculed superstition. Since French freethinkers were already enamoured of the relatively democratic politics of British society, they were quick to coopt the arguments of Locke and his disciples. By 1760, Voltaire felt secure enough to publish his most vocal attacks on Christianity such that Diderot would refer to him affectionately as the 'sublime, honorable and dear Antichrist'.[24] But whatever scorn Voltaire heaped on Christianity, he refused to embrace atheism, partly out of pragmatism. Belief in God helped preserve social order in kings and beggars alike.

His friend, the Baron d'Holbach (1723-1789)—also a friend of Claude-Adrien Helvetius, David Hume, Benjamin Franklin, Joseph Priestley, and Adam Smith—would disseminate markedly different views. Having translated and republished a number of sceptical writings, he penned a few of his own as well—taking care to publish them under the names of such deceased writers as John Trenchard, or in the case of *Christianity Unveiled,* Nicholas Boulanger. Educated in the natural sciences, D'Holbach sought to 'tear from [Christianity] the Veil with which it has shrouded itself',[25] explaining that many of the incidents and phenomena described in the Old Testament, itself a 'hotchpotch of sacred Hebrew books'[26] could be attributed to entirely rational causes. Indeed, it is worth examining his critique of Christianity. Despite its beginnings as a charitable 'religion of the poor', it was far from being either compassionate or altruistic. Teaching disciples to 'love and adore this god who is hostile, harsh and capricious', Christians eventually came to 'disrupt society', proving tolerant only when 'they were themselves persecuted'; indeed, it was hardly surprising that Christians could not decide between 'mercy' or 'extermination'. No less deplorable was the Christian 'war on science and the humanities' since ignorance was 'much more advantageous for religion and its ministers'.[27] Priests choose to keep the people uninformed of the 'contents of their Holy Books' because knowledge 'is the surest way of all to disabuse Christians of their respect for the Scriptures'. Here, we are not far from entertaining the Marxist notion of religion as an opiate for the masses. As such, *Christianity Unveiled* closes with a vision of new enlightenment, during which 'Reason' and 'rationality' will prevail while 'the shackles of superstition will shatter'.[28]

If deism was not as popular in Britain as in France during the latter half of the eighteenth century, there was nonetheless a similar distrust of ecclesiastical establishments accompanied by an emphasis on reason. As deists blamed the corruption of Christianity on ecclesiastical establishments, radically inclined Protestant Dissenters aimed their attacks at Roman Catholic and Anglican churches without criticising the Bible. Anglican supremacy was viewed as a refinement upon Roman Catholic bigotry and persecution while the Book of Common Prayer, according to Joseph Priestley, harboured 'The traces and remains of popery [sic]'. Anglican and Catholic ceremonies represented a privileging of style over substance. For Joseph Priestley, the 'punctual observance of certain rites, ceremonies, and modes of worship' frequently went hand-in-hand with 'the most horrid and shameful violation of the plainest natural duties'.[29] By contrast, Dissenters posited themselves as rational and enlightened practitioners of religion in a Britain where 'light and knowledge prevail, and from hence the arts and sciences diffuse their influence'.[30] They would also present religion as a precise and systematic methodology: just as Priestley extolled the ancient Arians for being 'men of science … addicted to geometry', James Murray elevated 'judgment', 'reasoning', and 'free enquiry' above 'divine inspiration' and 'intuition'.

The following sections will show how Thomas Paine adopted many of these ideas on democratic representation, inequality, populist rhetoric, Christianity, and science, radicalising them to a far greater extent than any of his predecessors and contemporaries.

Common Sense

The idea of American independence was hardly a novel idea by 1776, even if seldom discussed in the open. As Paine was petitioning parliament for a raise on behalf of his fellow excise men in early 1774, Major John Cartwright was in the midst of writing ten letters on American independence anonymously for a newspaper, before republishing them in pamphlet form as *American Independence the Interest and Glory of Great Britain.* Here, Cartwright defended the rights of 'a free people' to tax themselves and vindicated 'the liberty of mankind' as he proposed a confederacy between Britain and the colonies. He exhorted his readers to observe that when a people find themselves 'subject to a distant power', particularly a 'tyranny', they should 'shake off such an unjust yoke' and 'erect a free government'.[31] By claiming the king's sovereignty in the first and final letters, however, Cartwright was not quite ready to sever all links between Britain and the colonies; even as he maintained that American colonists had the right to have their laws 'enacted by their own governors', he would assert the king's sovereignty in the first and final letters. A similar reluctance is equally discernible in Thomas Jefferson's *Summary Rights of British America.* Although Jefferson argued that the colonies had long managed their own affairs since their founding and thereby did not owe any feudal fees to Britain, he would nonetheless conclude his text with a declaration that he wished to preserve 'that harmony which alone can continue both to Great Britain and America' for 'it is neither our wish, nor our interest, to separate from her'. He was also inclined to 'sacrifice every thing' for 'the restoration of that tranquillity for which all must wish'.

It is difficult to determine Paine's familiarity with either work. Instead, what is more interesting are the ways in which Paine supersedes their arguments. The difference in this first American bestseller is already conspicuous from the opening paragraphs where Paine pictures the beginnings of society in a manner that harks back to the second and eighth chapters of John Locke's *Second Treatise of Government*, yet diverges dramatically:

> But as the Colony encreases, the public concerns will encrease likewise, and the distance at which the members may be separated, will render it too inconvenient for all of them to meet on every occasion as at first … This will point out the convenience of their consenting to leave the legislative part to be managed by a select number chosen from the whole

body, who are supposed to have the same concerns at stake which those have who appointed them, and who will act in the same manner as the whole body would act were they present.[32]

Paine proceeds to emphasise the importance of the elected, never assuming 'an interest separate from the electors' while underscoring the importance of frequent elections. It is here, however, that he goes beyond contemporary British reformers: if writers like Murray and Burgh stressed the importance of enfranchisement, Paine immediately launches into the disadvantages of monarchies, shrewdly observing that it is 'the republican and not the monarchical part of the constitution of England which Englishmen glory in, viz. the liberty of choosing an house of commons'.[33]

Moreover, unlike many English and American writers, Paine rejects customary assumptions on the shared British culture of Britons and Americans by aiming to debunk the alleged superiority of the British government: a blatant example of 'national pride and prejudice'. For Paine, the rationale behind the branches of government 'reciprocally checking each other' was 'farcical',' one a distrust between the king and his people. No less problematic was the element of unpredictability inherent to monarchies: did the king's successors possess an innate ability to govern anyway? It was a problem aggravated by the sense of self-entitlement inculcated in the monarch from an early age. Not unlike a James Burgh or James Murray who censured aristocratic arrogance, Paine warned that 'Men who look upon themselves born to reign, and others to obey, soon grow insolent'. More to the point, since their world 'differs so materially from the world at large', they wind up becoming 'the most ignorant and unfit'.[34] At the same time, Paine would make his arguments all the more effective by his use of populist references. Knowing that American colonists were well-versed in the Bible, for instance, he alluded to Gideon and Samuel. Similarly, knowing how Americans harboured British prejudices, he would also refer to William the Conqueror as a 'French bastard' when pointing out that he stood at the fount of the British monarchy.

But if section 2 on the monarchy offered a resurrection of republicanism barely witnessed since Cromwell's Protectorate, sections 3 and 4 are yet more daring as Paine delivers his final blow, draping it in the folds of 'common sense'. His proposal for Americans to declare independence opens innocuously enough when he promises to offer no more than 'simple facts, plain arguments, and common sense'.[35] When examined 'on the principles of nature and common sense', there were, in fact, few benefits in a sustained relationship of dependency between Britain and America. Here, he would reject the notion that America was a prodigal child spurning Mother England, denying that England had ever conducted herself like a parent. Indeed, if she were a parent, her conduct was shameful for 'even brutes do not devour their young'.[36] Nor did he hesitate to refute the erroneous idea that America was largely of British origin since 'not one third of the inhabitants … are of English descent'.

Even more convincing are the everyday issues overlooked by other writers. It was not just the fact of clashing differences between Britain and America or that colonial America would be dragged into Britain's wars. The sheer distance between the island and continent constituted 'strong and natural proof, that the authority of the one, over the other was never the design of Heaven'—to say nothing of the fact that there was

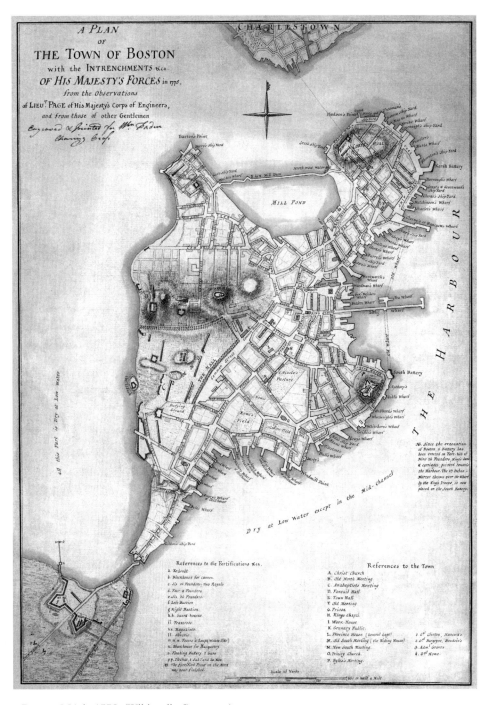

Boston, MA in 1775. (Wikimedia Commons)

'something very absurd in supposing a continent to be perpetually governed by an island'.[37] The references to God and the relatively new science of astronomy not only help Paine appeal to devout readers of the Bible as well as science enthusiasts, but also reinforce the prevailing impression of a 'common sense' that is shared by all.

Certainly, his appeal to the passions is strong—considerably more so than either Cartwright's *Letters* or Jefferson's *Summary Rights*. Bypassing the Stamp Act, the Townshend Acts, and the Intolerable Acts altogether, Paine zeroes in on the physical violence enacted by the British with a stream of indignant questions:

> Hath your house been burnt? Hath your property been destroyed before your face? Are your wife and children destitute of a bed to lie on, or bread to live on?[38]

Comparing Britain to a 'ravisher', Paine justifies a desire for retaliation by explaining that 'The Almighty hath implanted in us an outrage over injustice'; instead, he argues, anger is a human instinct which 'distinguishes us from the herd of common animals'.[39] As such, war against Britain was fully warranted.

No less tangible is Paine's command of colloquial speech. As Jefferson aptly noted, 'No writer has exceeded Paine in ease and familiarity of style, in perspecuity of expression, happiness of elucidation, and in simple and unassuming language'. In contrast to the prolix phrases preferred by his educated contemporaries, Paine's sentences are relatively succinct. If Paine, like Murray and Burgh, harbours few doubts in the abilities of 'the vulgar', he makes greater efforts to accommodate them. Take, for instance, the uncluttered parallel structure of these lines: 'And however our eyes may be dazzled with show, or our ears deceived by sound; however prejudice may warp our wills, or interest darken our understanding, the simple voice of nature and reason will say, 'tis right'. No less striking is this much-quoted passage:

> The Sun never shined on a cause of greater worth. 'Tis not the affair of a City, a County, a Province, or a Kingdom; but of a Continent—of at least one eighth part of the habitable Globe. 'Tis not the concern of a day, a year, or an age; posterity are virtually involved in the contest, and will be more or less affected even to the end of time, by the proceedings now.

Together, the two near-parallel sentences create a sense of impression of magnitude, as 'city' stretches out to 'continent' and 'day' to 'age'. Not least does Paine rely on visual cues in the form of italics and capitals, as if instructing his readers how to read aloud to listeners.

The American Crisis

With a series of defeats dealt by the British army and their Hessian mercenaries, the Continental army appeared to have reached their nadir in late December 1776 as they retreated from Long Island and White Plains after the destruction of Forts Lee and Washington. As service contracts for the soldiers were due to expire on 31 December,

Paine knew that a boosting of morale was needed. It was as such that he reportedly sat at a drumhead in General George Washington's camp at McKonkey's Ferry on the Delaware, scribbling the first in a series of sixteen *Crisis* papers published between 1776 and 1783. The opening words are among the most distinctive lines of prose:

> These are the times that try men's souls. The summer soldier and the sunshine patriot will, in this crisis, shrink from the service of their country; but he that stands by it now, deserves the love and thanks of man and woman. Tyranny, like hell, is not easily conquered; yet we have this consolation with us, that the harder the conflict, the more glorious the triumph. What we obtain too cheap, we esteem too lightly: it is dearness only that gives every thing its value.[40]

All too aware of the extraordinary challenges to be surmounted by the Continental army over the summer and fall, Paine fires up stark contrasts. Here, he opens with a terse, declaratory, eight-word sentence followed by three longer ones, each composed of antithetical clauses that pair a brief vision of loss coupled with a longer one of rewarding victory against the odds. With recourse to anaphora and concluding repetitions, Paine suggests he is absolutely convinced of their truth.

The remainder of the pamphlet seeks to alleviate the anxieties of his readers by extolling Washington and his troops for their pragmatism and foresight while chiding General Howe for his foolishness and the Tories for cowardice: tactics which Paine would rely upon throughout the *Crisis* papers, including that of 12 September 1777, after the American defeat at Brandywine, Pennsylvania. Knowing that American colonists were almost equally divided on the subject of American independence, Paine argues that, if anything, independence should have been called for earlier with military operations taking place the previous winter. Nonetheless, he quickly adds, there are still more chances for victory as he proceeds to diminish Howe's successes, referring to them as a 'ravage' rather than a 'conquest'. As Paine maintains that Howe could have been easily trounced by the 'spirit of the Jerseys, a year ago', we cannot help but wonder if this rousing optimism and confidence in the army's abilities did not in fact help Washington crush the Hessians on 26 December and the British on 3 January—or ultimately for the Americans to declare victory in 1783 with the final number triumphantly echoing the opening words of the series, 'These are times that tried men's souls, and they are over—and the greatest and completest revolution the world ever knew, gloriously and happily accomplished' (19 April 1783). This assurance in the might of the army is bolstered by Paine's invocation of a divine mandate, as he trusts that 'God Almighty will not give up a people to military destruction' or protect George III who was little more than 'a common murderer, a highwayman, or a house-breaker'.[41] (These jibes would, of course, also help deflate a king who was still widely venerated by colonists.) It is no wonder that Joel Barlow would aptly attest that 'Without the pen of Paine, Washington's sword would have been wielded in vain'.

From there, Paine presents the defeats of the previous months in a more positive context. Again, Washington is made to appear canny in his ability to make sound decisions amidst the confusion; by contrast, Howe is a fool who fails to seize opportune moments. By squandering a chance to capture the Continental army's stores at Brunswick and intercept their march through Pennsylvania, he has lost greatly—a failure which was interpreted by Paine as an instance of 'providential control'.[42] At the same time, Paine creates a sense of phenomenal strength that defies the odds. If nothing else, he claims, the troops handle their burdens 'with a manly and martial spirit' in defiance of a lack of 'rest, covering, or provision'.[43] He then turns to admire Washington for 'a natural firmness in some minds' and 'fortitude'.[44] (It is worth pointing out that Paine would revoke his praise for Washington some twenty years later in a public letter out of his belief that the general-turned-president turned a blind eye to his pleas to be rescued from the Luxembourg prison in Paris.) Not least does Paine castigate the Tories for their cowardice in a manner calculated either to shame them or to prevent Howe from recruiting them. Knowing that the Tories were notoriously hesitant to take military action in their tacit support of the British, Paine scolds them by declaring that 'Howe is as much deceived by you as the American cause is injured by you' for 'Your opinions are of no use to him, unless you support him personally, for 'tis soldiers, and not Tories, that he wants'.[45] His censure of the Tories is reinforced in the following paragraph where he vindicates the revolutionary war by implying that it is more pragmatic for the present generation to declare independence, thereby securing peace for their children:

> I once felt all that kind of anger, which a man ought to feel, against the mean principles that are held by the Tories: a noted one...was standing at his door, with as pretty a child in his hand, about eight or nine years old, as I ever saw, and after speaking his mind as freely as he thought was prudent, finished with this unfatherly expression, 'Well! give me peace in my day'... a generous parent should have said, 'If there must be trouble, let it be in my day, that my child may have peace ...'[46]

Paine proceeds to observe that the errors made thus far did not result from a lack of willpower, but rather a 'proper application of that force' because 'Wisdom is not the purchase of a day'.

Finally, Paine exhorts his readers to stay the course with a series of diametric contrasts between apparent dejection and hope, persistence and weakness, not unlike the opening paragraph:

> Let it be told to the future world, that in the depth of winter, when nothing but hope and virtue could survive, that the city and the country, alarmed at one common danger, came forth to meet and to repulse it ... I love the man that can smile in trouble, that can gather strength from distress, and grow brave by reflection. 'Tis the business of little minds to shrink; but he whose heart is firm, and whose conscience approves his conduct, will pursue his principles unto death'.[47]

That they have not lost their effect more than two and a quarter centuries later is proven by Barack Obama's quotation of the passage 'Let it be told ...' during his inaugural speech of 2009. As if brushing aside the shrinking number of soldiers, Paine projects zeal, anticipating that 'Once more we are again collected and collecting; our new army at both ends of the continent is recruiting fast, and we shall be able to open the next campaign with sixty thousand men, well armed and clothed'.

With so much riding on their courage and determination, Paine presses his point with the use of anaphora to emphasize stark oppositions in outcome while hinting at dire scenarios of loss with sputtering dashes:

> By perseverance and fortitude we have the prospect of a glorious issue; by cowardice and submission, the sad choice of a variety of evils—a ravaged country—a depopulated city — habitations without safety, and slavery without hope—our homes turned into barracks and bawdy-houses for Hessians, and a future race to provide for, whose fathers we shall doubt of.[48]

Victory must be attained.

The second *Crisis*, published on 13 January 1777, only two weeks after the victories at Trenton and Princeton may be read as a puff piece in paradoxes—one again designed to validate the American cause. Things are not what they might seem: Americans are more valiant and honourable than supposed, just as the British are weaker and more venal than commonly imagined. Here, Paine opens this public letter to Lord Howe by claiming that the Republic of Letters is not only at least as ancient as any monarchy but also more democratic; indeed, those who resist tyranny have 'a better title to "Defender of the Faith", than George the Third'. As a matter of fact, the present *Crisis* paper ranks above Howe's recent proclamation of 1776 (which demanded all to surrender their arms for a pardon); Paine taunts him, observing that 'your lordship's performance, I see, has already fallen many degrees from its first place'.[50] Predicting that The UNITED STATES of AMERICA, will sound as pompously in the world or in history, as the kingdom of Great Britain', he wagers that 'the character of General Washington will fill a page with as much lustre as that of Lord Howe'.[51] Britain, on the other hand, is anything but civilised, having torn through America 'with as much barbarism as if you had openly professed yourself the prince of ruffians'. Paine would appear to invoke Granville Sharp's criticisms of slavery, doing so even more forcefully as he denounces British brutality in Africa and Asia:

> Britain, as a nation, is, in my inmost belief, the greatest and most ungrateful offender against God on the face of the whole earth. Blessed with all the commerce she could wish for, and furnished, by a vast extension of dominion, with the means of civilizing both the eastern and western world, she has made no other use of both than proudly to idolize her own "thunder," and rip up the bowels of whole countries for what she could get. Like Alexander, she has made war her sport, and inflicted misery for prodigality's sake. The blood of India is not yet repaid, nor the wretchedness of Africa yet requited. Of late she has enlarged her

list of national cruelties by her butcherly destruction of the Caribbs of St. Vincent's, and returning an answer by the sword to the meek prayer for "Peace, liberty and safety."[52]

That Paine felt quite passionately about this issue is evident when he reiterates these excoriations of imperialism and slavery in the *Crisis* Papers of 21 March 1778 and 21 November 1778.

The second *Crisis* also dismantles other prevalent preconceptions of British power. First of all, Howe himself has miscalculated his military strategy in New York and New Jersey:

> By what means, may I ask, do you expect to conquer America? If you could not effect it in the summer, when our army was less than yours, nor in the winter, when we had none, how are you to do it? In point of generalship you have been outwitted, and in point of fortitude outdone; your advantages turn out to your loss, and show us that it is in our power to ruin you by gifts.[53]

Asserting that 'It has been the folly of Britain to suppose herself more powerful than she really is' in her inability to 'carry on a war without foreign assistance', he adds that Britain is the poorest nation in Europe. In short, the unstated message is that of an inevitable American victory.[54]

Although the *Crisis* papers were mostly intended as propaganda—to rally the troops, support the cause of independence, belittle British authorities, and occasionally ponder upon the means of building a stronger federal union, there are also glimpses of important humanitarian themes. Note, for instance, the following criticism of the practice of war and the idea of natural enemies from the *Crisis* paper of 20 October 1778 which anticipates the discussion of war in *Rights of Man*, part 2:

> In the close of the paragraph which I last quoted, France is styled the "natural enemy" of England, and by way of lugging us into some strange idea, she is styled "the late mutual and natural enemy" of both countries. I deny that she ever was the natural enemy of either; and that there does not exist in nature such a principle. The expression is an unmeaning barbarism, and wholly unphilosophical … But man with man cannot arrange in the same opposition. Their quarrels are accidental and equivocally created. They become friends or enemies as the change of temper, or the cast of interest inclines them. The Creator of man did not constitute them the natural enemy of each other.[55]

Other insightful assessments of war and the recognition of its burdens on the people are likewise present in the *Crisis* paper of 21 November 1778. Seduced by the 'sound of victory' and 'frenzy of arms', Britons are rarely cognizant of 'the cost or the consequences'.[56] A British victory over America would only enrich 'favorites at court' rather than ordinary Britons. After all, despite the 'many conquests' resulting from the Seven Years' War, taxes had barely tapered. Where were the rewards for the people at large?

Moreover, Paine raises questions on the British constitution, the purpose of government, and the purported value of a monarchy that looks forward to *Rights of Man*, namely:

> 2d, Whether the prerogative does not belong to the people?
> 3d, Whether there is any such thing as the English constitution?
> 4th, Of what use is the crown to the people?
> 5th, Whether he who invented a crown was not an enemy to mankind?
> 6th, Whether it is not a shame for a man to spend a million a year and do no good for it, and whether the money might not be better applied?[57]

That Paine believed that Britain was ready for a revolution well before his publication of *Rights of Man* is not only apparent here, but in his initial plans to travel back to Britain incognito for the purposes of launching one there. Not least, we find Paine scoffing at the veneration of the ancients while applauding the notion of American innovation—thereby reversing the widely received preconception of Greek, Roman, and British political and cultural superiority.

> The wisdom, civil governments, and sense of honor of the states of Greece and Rome, are frequently held up as objects of excellence and imitation. Mankind have lived to very little purpose, if, at this period of the world, they must go two or three thousand years back for lessons and examples ... America has surmounted a greater variety and combination of difficulties, than, I believe, ever fell to the share of any one people, in the same space of time ... Had it not been for America, there had been no such thing as freedom left throughout the whole universe. England has lost hers in a long chain of right reasoning from wrong principles ... The Grecians and Romans were strongly possessed of the spirit of liberty but not the principle, for at the time that they were determined not to be slaves themselves, they employed their power to enslave the rest of mankind.

Ironically, however, Paine does not mention the fact of American slavery, despite his opposition to the practice.

The Rights of Man

When the erstwhile Whiggish liberal Edmund Burke lashed out against the French Revolution in *Reflections on the Revolution in France* (1790), many responded to him, including the likes of Mary Wollstonecraft, discussed in this volume by Rebecca Nesvet,

Joseph Priestley, Sir Brooke Boothby, and James Mackintosh. However, it was Paine's *Rights of Man*, Parts 1 and 2 which quickly outsold all other responses to Burke. If the affordably priced second part went on to surpass the first instalment in sales, both would nonetheless be translated in a variety of languages, including French, German, Polish, and Turkish. In order to understand the significance of *Rights of Man*, it is necessary to briefly explore Burke's *Reflections on the Revolution in France*.

A lengthy volume that was penned as a public response to a letter from the French nobleman, Charles Jean Francois Depont, *Reflections* was most likely intended as a reply to Richard Price and his fellow reformers. Where Price had celebrated the French Revolution in *A Sermon on the Love of our Country,* opining that Britain had much farther to go in terms of enlightenment and modernity, Burke took issue by criticising the concept of 'rights of men' as vague and metaphysical. He would also defend the 'establishments' of church, aristocracy, and monarchy as well as tradition, remarking that it was 'neither unnatural, nor unjust, nor impolitic' for 'some decent, regulated preeminence, some preference to birth and pedigree' and that, as such, the aristocracy was hardly mistaken in being 'too tenacious of those privileges'.[58] Moreover, by virtue of their education, aristocrats were the 'Corinthian capital of polished society'[59] and thus better qualified to govern than the 'swinish multitude'. No less worthy of retention was a state-sanctioned church that had essentially gone unchanged since the fourteenth or fifteenth century, thereby proving that a political pragmatism accumulated through the centuries was the best. Not least, he would mourn the passing of the age of chivalry with its 'generous loyalty to rank and sex, that proud submission, that dignified obedience'.[60] Despite Burke's various nods towards 'improvement', he mocked 'innovations', claiming that 'People will not look forward to posterity, who never look backward to their ancestors'. Overall, the predominant impression of *Reflections on the Revolution in France* was one of conservatism.

As if responding to Burke's undisguised contempt for 'the rights of men', it is not coincidental that Paine not only titled his rebuttal *Rights of Man* but opened his text with that very subject. Just as Burke censured Price for stating that the Glorious Revolution of 1688 upheld the right of Britons to choose their own governors, cashier them for misconduct, and frame a new government for themselves, Paine, in turn, excoriated Burke for his conceptualisation of a permanent constitutional settlement which deprived future generations of Britons of the right to alter their government. Since circumstances were always changing[61] and 'Man has no property in man', it was no less true that no generation had 'a property in the generations which are to follow'.[62] He would one-up Burke with the latter's claims to history by arguing that Burke 'did not go back far enough into antiquity'. After all, the only generation that could logistically dictate any mode of government was 'the first generation that existed': namely, the time when 'man came from the hand of his Maker'. Since 'every history of the creation ... all agree in establishing one point by which 'all men are born equal, and with equal natural right', why should there be any political or social preeminence on account of birth or lineage?[63]

Thus would Paine question the premises of hereditary government. The fact that hereditary government was itself a vestige of an 'uncivilised' conquest, not to mention 'the base idea of men having property in man, and governing him by personal right', nullified its purpose in an age of progress. Not unlike Mary Wollstonecraft in her *Vindication of the Rights of Men* (the first reply to Burke), Paine would also criticise primogeniture, another privilege derived from an accident of birth. There was no justification for a first-born heir to enjoy preferential treatment at the expense of his younger siblings, who were 'begotten to be devoured'. Indeed, the fact that heirs and their younger male relations frequently occupied both Houses of Parliament, could be regarded as an extension of arbitrary privileges on a broader scale particularly when they generally held themselves 'accountable to nobody'. As such, the unnecessary offices and places in governments and courts' created for these relations and maintained 'at the expense of the public' were patently wrong.[64]

Similarly, Paine would also counter Burke's endorsement of a State-Church establishment. In anticipation of *The Age of Reason*, Paine denied the right of government to regulate private spiritual matters:

> Who then art thou, vain dust and ashes! by whatever name thou art called, whether a King, a Bishop, a Church, or a State, a Parliament, or anything else, that obtrudest thine insignificance between the soul of man and its Maker? Mind thine own concerns.[65]

The history of government interference in ecclesiastical and theological matters was one that ironically subverted the very foundation of religion itself. If 'all religions are in their nature kind and benign, and united with principles of morality' they were marred by acts of persecution: whether it be the mild form of disabilities suffered by Roman Catholics and Protestant Dissenters in Anglican Britain or the more violent form of the Inquisition in Catholic Spain. Neither could be said to 'proceed from the religion originally professed' but 'from this mule-animal, engendered between the church and the state'.[66]

If the first part of *The Rights of Man* raised a few eyebrows, it was Part 2 that aroused intense anxieties among the propertied classes. Even though Paine's arguments on the advantages of republics and disadvantages of monarchies did not diverge much from those he presented in *Common Sense* or those articulated by James Harrington and Algernon Sidney

Edmund Burke. (Wellcome Collection)

113

more than a century earlier, they were now perceived in a more ominous light since they were aimed at a contemporary British audience. Here, he would maintain more vigorously that monarchy was the result of 'bands of robbers' parcelling out the world and transmogrifying this usurped power into an inheritance. Thus would monarchies establish the blueprint of a warmongering government—an argument that expands upon the observations made in the *Crisis* paper of 20 October 1778:

> From such beginning of governments, what could be expected but a continued system of war and extortion? It has established itself into a trade … What inducement has the farmer, while following the plough, to lay aside his peaceful pursuit, and go to war with the farmer of another country? or what inducement has the manufacturer? What is dominion to them, or to any class of men in a nation? … Are not conquest and defeat each of the same price, and taxes the never-failing consequence? … War is the Faro-table of governments, and nations the dupes of the game. [67]

By contrast, according to Paine, republics were less prone to wars over kinship and descent: a view that stood at odds with those held by other contemporary advocates for republicanism such as Alexander Hamilton.

Perhaps more controversially, Paine would assert that the role of monarch could be easily filled by 'any child or idiot' while observing that wisdom and the ability to govern cannot be guaranteed in any one family. If he had observed pithily in Part 1 that 'the idea of hereditary legislators' is as inconsistent as that of hereditary judges, mathematicians, or poet laureates, he would declare in Part 2 that:

> Whatever is the rule by which she, apparently to us, scatters them among mankind, that rule remains a secret to man. It would be as ridiculous to attempt to fix the hereditaryship of human beauty, as of wisdom. Whatever wisdom constituently is, it is like a seedless plant; it may be reared when it appears, but it cannot be voluntarily produced. There is always a sufficiency somewhere in the general mass of society for all purposes; but with respect to the parts of society, it is continually changing its place … As this is in the order of nature, the order of government must necessarily follow it, or government will, as we see it does, degenerate into ignorance. The hereditary system, therefore, is as repugnant to human wisdom as to human rights; and is as absurd as it is unjust. [68]

Reiterating from *Common Sense* that 'the more perfect civilization is, the less occasion has it for government', Paine also drew attention to the disparate burdens of taxation.

Even though the claim that the vast majority of Britons (rather than propertied elites) bore the brunt of taxation was not entirely new, as we have seen with Murray and Burgh, Paine takes this argument a few steps further by attributing social discontents and riots to the pressures caused by economic hardship, suggesting that the poor only 'become tumultuous' when their interests are neglected. As such, Paine undermines Burke's argument that the French Revolution was purely the result of a scheming intelligentsia.

After delving into the flaws of hereditary governments, Paine proceeds to address the advantages of republican governments. Here, he explained that the term 'republican' was not limited solely to its representative aspects or confined to 'any particular form of government'—but was instead rooted in its fundamental purpose, namely:

> the public affairs, or the public good; or, literally translated, the public thing … Republican government is no other than government established and conducted for the interest of the public, as well individually as collectively. It is not necessarily connected with any particular form, but it most naturally associates with the representative form, as being best calculated to secure the end for which a nation is at the expense of supporting it. [69]

The superiority of republican governments was already evident in America where general national expenditures were significantly less than in England—especially when the sum involved in English 'quarter sessions, juries, and assizes' were already less costly than in America. Reiterating his remarks from the *Crisis* paper of 21 November 1778, he would find it 'inhuman' to defend governments where 'a million sterling a year' was 'paid out of taxes of any country' to support a monarch while the majority of the population were starving. More horrendous still was the fact that even the poor were forced to pay duty on almost all life's necessities which ate away at their meagre earnings. Here, Paine would highlight like no other writer the irony of vast inequality of wealth in civilised nations. The sad truth was that England was a supposedly 'civilised' nation whose outward appearance seemed to indicate that everyone was happy but was hardly so: instead, what 'lies hidden from the eye of common observation' is 'a mass of wretchedness'.[70] Too often, the aged were consigned to workhouses and youths sent to the gallows while the nation's wealth was squandered on the monarchy and aristocracy.[71] Only with a thorough reform of government—rather than a cosmetic change in ministry or party—could real change be accomplished.

Stating that 'civil government does not exist in executions, but in making such provision for the instruction of youth and the support of age', Paine arrived at a solution that would look forward to Franklin Delano Roosevelt's Social Security in 1932 as part of the 'New Deal'. Paine wanted the use of taxes to be redirected to the people, including sums for young married couples, destitute families, widows, and the elderly. There would be funds for couples with newborns and those willing to send their children to school. Employment centres would provide work, food, and housing to as many as six thousand. Only then would crime— particularly urban theft committed by unemployed young men—distress, and poverty decline. Moreover, the elderly would receive annual sums rather than work themselves to death. All told:

> When it shall be said in any country in the world, my poor are happy; neither ignorance nor distress is to be found among them; my jails are

empty of prisoners, my streets of beggars; the aged are not in want, the taxes are not oppressive … when these things can be said, then may that country boast its constitution and its government. [72]

It is a testament to Paine that these concerns have remained as relevant as ever into the twenty-first century, even if they still remain imperfectly addressed by governments.

No consideration of *Rights of Man* would be complete without a consideration of its style, one that guided working-class political discourse and class identity over the following century. Like *Common Sense*, it was written for a broad range of readers, including the least literate. Pithy and unpretentious, there are few prolix and multiple clauses or Latin quotations such as found in other writings of the period. Take, for instance, this passage with its clear images and easy-to-follow parallel sentences:

> Toleration is not the opposite of Intolerance, but is the counterfeit of it. Both are despotisms. The one assumes to itself the right of withholding Liberty of Conscience, and the other of granting it. The one is the Pope armed with fire and faggot, and the other is the Pope selling or granting indulgences. The former is church and state, and the latter is church and traffic.[73]

It is also worth noting Paine's concrete handling of religious toleration here: instead of providing a belaboured explanation of the contradictions inherent in toleration, he draws upon popular knowledge of Inquisitions and indulgences.

No less appealing was Paine's use of colloquialisms and references to ordinary working-class experiences—for instance, 'Ride and tie' and 'swabbing the deck'. Or take this comical reference to the 'necessary house' (i.e., toilet) in his discussion of useless posts in the king's court:

> It is easy to conceive that a band of interested men, such as placemen, pensioners, Lords of the bed chamber, Lords of the kitchen, Lords of the necessary house, and the Lord knows what besides can find as many reasons for monarchy.[74]

But equally striking—and perhaps more worrisome to Pitt and his government—was Paine's pointed recrimination of the 'establishments'. If derisive observations such as 'This is the general character of aristocracy, or what are called Nobles or Nobility, or rather No-ability, in all countries' could be easily laughed away, other comments may have appeared more belligerent to an elite audience accustomed to deference. Note how Paine scolds the various monarchs and rulers across Europe and Asia in his remarks on the exorbitance of taxes expended upon them:

> Is it, then, better that the lives of one hundred and forty thousand aged persons be rendered comfortable, or that a million a year of public money be expended on any one individual, and him often of the most worthless or insignificant character? Let reason and justice, let honour and humanity, let

even hypocrisy, sycophancy and Mr. Burke, let George, let Louis, Leopold, Frederic, Catherine, Cornwallis, or Tippoo Saib, answer the question. [75]

The fact that Part 2 of *Rights of Man* was affordably priced for the poor and quickly turning into the bestselling work of the century led both local and state governments to persecute and prosecute Paine. Yet it is equally ironic that while censoring *Rights* and exiling Paine, Pitt would later implement some of the ideas contained in *Rights of Man* by introducing progressive taxation.

The Age of Reason

If *Rights of Man* upset the ruling classes, *The Age of Reason* was to prove an even more controversial work. Although Paine's avowed purpose was to strike back against the rise of atheism in France, with his declaration that he believed 'in one God and no more', he nonetheless proceeded to repudiate organised religion, including 'the creed professed by the Jewish church, by the Roman church, by the Greek church, by the Turkish church, by the Protestant church, nor by any church that I know of' because 'All national institutions of churches … appear to me no other than human inventions, set up to terrify and enslave mankind, and monopolize power and profit'.[76] Simply put, 'My own mind is my own church'. Infidelity did not consist in believing, or in disbelieving, but rather in 'professing to believe what he does not believe'.

Questioning the premises of the Bible, Paine rejected the conjoined ideas of mystery, miracles, and revelation for 'truth never envelops itself in mystery', explaining:

> But the resurrection of a dead person from the grave, and his ascension through the air, is a thing very different as to the evidence it admits of, to the invisible conception of a child in the womb ... A thing which everybody is required to believe, requires that the proof and evidence of it should be equal to all, and universal … Instead of this, a small number of persons, not more than eight or nine, are introduced as proxies for the whole world, to say they saw it, and all the rest of the world are called upon to believe it. But it appears that Thomas did not believe the resurrection, and, as they say, would not believe without having ocular and manual demonstration himself. So neither will I, and the reason is equally as good for me, and for every other person, as for Thomas.[77]

How can anyone trust mere hearsay--however long it's been around? So even as he described Jesus, 'the reformist and revolutionary' as 'a virtuous and an amiable man', lauding his morality as 'the most benevolent' without being 'exceeded by any', readers took offence at his claim that 'not a line of what is called the New Testament is of his own writing'. [78]

No less appalling was Paine's disavowal of redemption—an idea that he found abominable from an early age, which seemed to make 'God Almighty act like a passionate man, that killed his son when he could not revenge himself in any other way'. After all, when someone commits a crime, 'moral Justice still cannot take the innocent for the guilty, even if the innocent would offer itself'. For Paine, such irrationality showed the doctrine of redemption to be 'founded on a mere pecuniary idea corresponding to that of a debt which another person might pay'. Instead, the true word of God is 'THE CREATION WE BEHOLD': in nature, in the various planets, and other universes. [79]

Particularly disturbing to Paine's critics was his meticulous deconstruction of the Bible in Part 2, not to mention his irreverent tone, as he explored contradictions, teasing out inconsistencies: was there in fact 'sufficient authority for believing the Bible to be the Word of God?' Far from it. Proceeding further than d'Holbach who regarded the Bible as a 'hotchpotch', Paine would deny authenticity to 'every book in the Bible, from Genesis to Judges'. [80] If the authorship of the Book of Moses was unlikely to be Moses himself, in addition to being composed several hundred years later no less, the same could be said of the Book of Joshua; after all, 'in the name of common sense, can it be Joshua that relates what people had done after he was dead?'[81] Paine would also pronounce the Book of Isaiah as 'one of the most wild and disorderly compositions ever put together', forming only 'one continued incoherent, bombastical rant, full of extravagant metaphor, without application, and destitute of meaning'. [82] Nor did he perceive the Book of Jeremiah as anything more than a 'medley of detached, unauthenticated anecdotes put together by some stupid bookmaker'.[83] Similarly, the Book of Judges 'has not so much as a nominal voucher' but 'is altogether fatherless'.[84] As for the Book of Job, it was one of the better sections, but most likely not of Hebrew origin (given its scientific bent) and probably did not belong to the Bible either, while the Psalms of David were obviously drafted by various writers.

Like d'Holbach and other writers, Paine would also express outrage and disgust at Biblical depictions of violence. In Part 1, he had already fumed that 'Whenever we read the obscene stories, the voluptuous debaucheries, the cruel and torturous executions … with which more than half the Bible is filled, it would be more consistent that we called it the word of a demon, than the word of God'. In addition, 'there are matters in that book, said to be done by the express command of God, that are as shocking … as anything done by Robespierre, by Carrier … by the English government in the East Indies'. [85] No less abhorrent was Moses, one of most 'detestable villains than in any period of the world have disgraced the name of man'. [86] Equally offensive were the accounts of sexual license—most notably, the circumstances involved in the birth of Jesus. 'Blasphemously obscene', the story 'gives an account of a young woman engaged to be married' only to be 'debauched by a ghost … Notwithstanding which, Joseph afterward marries her, cohabits with her as his wife, and in his turn rivals the ghost'. In short, it is a tale where 'there is not a priest but must be ashamed to own it'. [87]

In all, only one dire conclusion could be drawn from Christianity: that of all religions, there were 'none more derogatory to the Almighty, more unedifying to man, more repugnant to reason, and more contradictory in itself, than this thing called Christianity'. It was an 'engine of power' that yielded only 'atheists and fanatics'. Flatly denying any value to theology, Paine slammed it repeatedly as 'nothing':

> The study of theology as it stands in Christian churches, is the study of nothing; it is founded on nothing; it rests on no principles; it proceeds

by no authorities; it has no data; it can demonstrate nothing; and admits of no conclusion. Not any thing can be studied as a science without our being in possession of the principles upon which it is founded; and as this is not the case with Christian theology, it is therefore the study of nothing. [88]

What was the alternative to the study of this 'nothing'? Certainly not the dead languages as taught by traditional universities where the 'philosopher is lost in the linguist', but the sciences. Just as Murray, Priestley, and others praised the sciences, Paine would defend it as the true 'Bible of creation', because one could 'know God only through his works' and by 'the order and manner in which it acts'. It is science that fully reveals the sublimity of God's creation:

> But it is not to us, the inhabitants of this globe, only, that the benefits arising from a plurality of worlds are limited. The inhabitants of each of the worlds of which our system is composed enjoy the same opportunities of knowledge as we do … Neither does the knowledge stop here. The system of worlds next to us exhibits, in its revolutions, the same principles and school of science to the inhabitants of their system, as our system does to us, and in like manner throughout the immensity of space.
> Our ideas, not only of the almightiness of the Creator, but of his wisdom and his beneficence, become enlarged in proportion as we contemplate the extent and the structure of the universe … We see our own earth filled with abundance, but we forget to consider how much of that abundance is owing to the scientific knowledge the vast machinery of the universe has unfolded. [89]

Here, God is no longer a lowly trickster but rather the 'great mechanic of the creation, the first philosopher and original teacher of all science'.

Not unlike *Rights of Man, Age of Reason* was prosecuted by the government for blasphemy. But unlike *Rights of Man,* few chose to defend it as Part 2 proved to be too extreme for any to embrace. There were others, however, who defended, if not applauded this highly controversial text. William Blake was to argue that Paine was a better Christian than the Bishop of Llandaff, the author of a rebuttal to *Age of Reason*. In 1818, Richard Carlile would unequivocally agree to be sentenced for six years in prison for printing it, rejecting any legal conditions on a one-year term—after cheekily reading aloud *Age of Reason* from beginning to end at his trial.

Conclusion

When Paine expired on 8 June 1809, his remains would be seemingly confined to a grave in his backyard. But just as in life, Paine's corpse would meet an unexpected fate as William Cobbett, an erstwhile Tory who once abhorred Paine, came to admire him, believing that the latter was downright accurate on inequality and government waste. Crossing the Atlantic ten years later with his son to dig up Paine's corpse, Cobbett had lofty plans for the latter, including a processional ceremony and reinternment which he believed would magically 'effect the reformation of church and state' in England. But after being denied permission by the British government since *Rights of Man* and *Age of Reason* were still censored, Cobbett stuck the corpse in his attic, inscribed his initials on the bones, and forgot about the literal skeleton in his closet when he ran for parliament. It is said that after his son faced bankruptcy twenty years later and auctioned off the family estate, with the auctioneer refusing to traffic in bodily parts—that the bones somehow became scattered, appropriately enough, like the relics of Jesus, 'the reformist and revolutionary' with a skull allegedly turning up in Australia and the brain stem winding up back in New Rochelle. The posthumous fate of Thomas Paine—his body and his ideas—has been summed up famously by biographer Moncure Conway: 'As to his bones, no man knows the place of their rest to this day. His principles rest not. His thoughts, untraceable like his dust, are blown about the world which he held in his heart'. Perhaps it is fitting that Paine has inspired numerous activists and causes through the past two centuries around the world, from Irish and Uruguayan independence, to the principles of the Tea Party, Arab uprising, and Occupy Wall Street.

Notes

1. Quoted in Gregory Claeys, *Thomas Paine: Social and Political Thought* (London: Unwin Hyman,1989), 1.
2. Quoted in Tom Keane, *Tom Paine: A Political Life* (London: Bloomsbury, 1994), 24.
3. Quoted in Keane, *Tom Paine: A Political Life,* 25.
4. John S. Harford, *Some Account of the Life, Death, and Principles of Thomas Paine* (Bristol: J.M. Gutch, 1819), 69.
5. Cleo Rickman, *The Life of Thomas Paine* (London: 1819), 11.
6. Jack Fruchtman, *Thomas Paine: Apostle of Freedom* (New York: Basic Books, 1996), 441.
7. James Murray, *Sermons to Asses* (London: J. Johnson, 1768), 1.
8. Ibid, 27.
9. Ibid, 42.
10. James Burgh, *Political Disquisitions*, vol. 1 (London: E. and C. Dilly, 1774-5), 37.
11. Ibid, vol. 1, 110.
12. Granville Sharp, *Representation of the Injustice of Slavery* (London: B. White and R. Horsfield, 1769), 40.
13. Ibid, 40.
14. Granville Sharp, *A Declaration of the People's Natural Right to a Share in the Legislature* (London: B. White, 1774), 8.
15. Joseph Priestley, *Essay on the First Principles of Government* (1768) in *Political Writings,* ed. Peter N. Miller (Cambridge: Cambridge University Press, 1992), 1-13, 15.
16. Murray, *Sermons to Asses*, 23.
17. James Murray, *Sermons to Ministers of State* (Newcastle: T. Robson,1781), 33.
18. Murray, *Sermons to Ministers*, 57.
19. James Burgh, *Crito*, vol. 1 (London: Dodsley, 1766-77), i.
20. Sharp, *Declaration*, 1–2.
21. Burgh, *Political Disquisitions*, vol. 3, 416.
22. Priestley, *Essay on the First Principles of Government*, 15.
23. James Murray, *Freeman's Magazine* (Newcastle: T. Angus, 1778), 157.
24. Quoted in Peter Gay, *The Enlightenment: The Rise of Modern Paganism* (New York: W.W. Norton, 1966), 391.
25. Baron Paul Henri Thiry d'Holbach, *Christianity Unveiled,* trans. and ed. David Holohan (Surrey: Hodgson Press, 2008), 19.
26. Ibid, 79.
27. Ibid, 27, 29, 92, 134.
28. d'Holbach, *Christianity Unveiled*, 160.
29. Joseph Priestley, *History of the Corruptions of Christianity*, vol. 2 (London:J. Johnson,1782), 197.
30. Richard Price, *Britain's Happiness, and the Proper Improvement of It,* in *Political Writings,* ed. D.O. Thomas (Cambridge University Press, 1993), 1-13, 5.

31. John Cartwright, *American Independence, the Interest and Glory of Great Britain* (London: H.S. Woodfall, 1775), 15.
32. Thomas Paine, *Common Sense,* in *Rights of Man, Common Sense, and other Political Writings ,* ed. Mark Philp (Oxford: Oxford University Press, 1995), 7. All quotations from *Common Sense* are drawn from this edition.
33. Ibid, 17.
34. Ibid, 17.
35. Ibid, 19.
36. Ibid, 22.
37. Ibid, 24, 27.
38. Ibid, 26.
39. Ibid, 35.
40. Thomas Paine, *American Crisis #1,* in *Complete Writings of Thomas Paine*, ed. Philip Foner, vol. 1 (New York: Citadel Press, 1945, Reprint, 1969) 50.
41. Ibid, 51.
42. Ibid, 52.
43. Ibid, 53.
44. Ibid.
45. Ibid.
46. Ibid, 54.
47. Ibid, 55.
48. Ibid, 57.
49. Ibid, 58.
50. Ibid, 59.
51. Ibid, 59–60.
52. Ibid, 66.
53. Ibid.
54. Ibid, 69–70.
55. Ibid, 136.
56. Paine, *American Crisis*, 150.
57. Ibid, 152.
58. Edmund Burke, *Reflections on the Revolution in France* (London: Dodsley), 187.
59. Ibid.188.
60. Ibid, 127.
61. Thomas Paine, *Rights of Man*, ed. by Claire Grogan (Peterborough, Canada: Broadview Press, 2011), 77. Quotations from *Rights* are drawn from this edition.
62. Ibid, 74.
63. Ibid, 98–99.
64. Ibid, 114–16.
65. Ibid. 118.
66. Ibid.,119–20.
67. Ibid, 199.
68. Ibid, 205.
69. Ibid, 207–08.

70. Ibid, 244.
71. Ibid.
72. Ibid, 288.
73. Ibid, 118.
74. Ibid, 159.
75. Ibid. 269.
76. Thomas Paine, *The Age of Reason*, in *Complete Writings of Thomas Paine, Vols. I-II*, ed. Philip Foner (New York: Citadel House, 1945), I, 464.
77. Ibid, 467.
78. Ibid, 467.
79. Ibid, 481–82.
80. Ibid, 535.
81. Ibid. 532.
82. Ibid, 552.
83. Ibid, 559.
84. Ibid, 534.
85. Ibid, 518.
86. Ibid, 528.
87. Ibid, 571.
88. Ibid, 601.
89. Ibid, 503.

Eighteenth Century Radicalism, Riot, and Rebellion

Stephen Basdeo

Thomas Paine is obviously one of the most famous radical voices from the late eighteenth century, but he was by no means the *only* voice during the whole century. And there have always been people who, if not 'radical', certainly were vocal in criticising members of the establishment. The author and travel writer Daniel Defoe, to take one example, was placed in the pillory in 1703 for publishing a satire entitled *The Shortest Way with Dissenters*. Being a dissenter—that is to say, he was not a member of the Church of England—his pamphlet mocked the Anglican establishment's intolerance of other denominations. So enraged was the government that Defoe was briefly imprisoned in Newgate gaol, tried for seditious libel, and put into the pillory. The pillory was usually used to punish cheats, homosexuals, rioters, and other petty criminals. While shackled here, they would be liable to be pelted with all manner of revolting articles like dead animals, rotten fruit and vegetables, excrement. In extreme cases, some of those sentenced to the pillory had stones, bricks or saucepans thrown at them. Many people were maimed for life. Yet Defoe was luckier. The public, in a show of support, only pelted flowers at him, while Defoe's friends sold copies of his tracts by the pillory.

The Jacobites

The biggest threat to the establishment in the early part of the century was, of course, Jacobitism. In 1715, the newly-united kingdom of Great Britain had a new monarch: George I of Hanover. He had inherited the throne the year before because Queen Anne's closest Protestant relation (there were several people in line to the throne before him, but none of them was Protestant and therefore they couldn't inherit the throne). The new monarch could barely speak English, however, and seemed to be uninterested in the business of government—so much so that it fell to his favourite minister, Robert Walpole, to assume many of the king's functions, and Walpole became the United Kingdom's first *de facto* Prime Minister (his official title being First Lord of the Treasury) partially because of George's disinterest in politics.

In some ways George was the perfect king; not only was he a Protestant but, although he had the right to, he largely refrained from interfering in politics, unless he had to, and largely accepted parliament's supremacy. Yet some in the country were unhappy; many people in various parts of the country still recognised the legitimacy of James Francis Edward Stuart's claim to the British throne. James Stuart, or, 'the Old Pretender', was the son of James II, the last Catholic monarch of England and Scotland, who had been ousted from the throne during the Glorious Revolution of 1688. With the accession of George I to the British throne, the Earl of Mar who was a supporter of the Pretender (who was then living in exile in France), decided it would be a good idea to raise the standard of James III and reclaim the 'true' monarch's stolen kingdom. The Earl of Mar and his initially small army were successful in capturing many towns in the north of Scotland and England, before being defeated by the Duke of Cumberland. The British government responded to the rebellion by suspending habeas corpus. In August 1715 also, the Act for Preventing Tumults and Riotous Assemblies, and for the more speedy and effectual Punishing the Rioters, or, 'the Riot Act', first came into force.[1]

Of course, the Jacobites were hardly radical, even if they were a threat to the establishment. In fact, the only motive underlying the Earl of Mar's rebellion was simply a desire to restore the Stuart monarchy, so we might even say they were reactionary in some sense. A further Jacobite rebellion occurred in 1745. This time it was led by a good-looking, gallant young prince named Charles Edward Stuart, nicknamed 'Bonnie' Prince Charlie. It is true that the heir to the Stuarts enjoyed what might be termed 'sentimental' support among both Catholic and Protestant subjects of George II. It was the custom in some families, particularly in the north of England and Scotland, to toast 'the King over the Water' at dinner parties with like-minded friends. Yet this sentimental support rarely translated into actual, material support. Indeed, when Charles landed on Eriskay Island, Scotland in July 1745, he was leading the revolt with the sole aim of regaining 'his' lost kingdom and ruling as an absolute monarch according to divine right, thereby disregarding the principles laid down during the Glorious Revolution of 1688. Apart from that, they had no manifesto; it was unclear to many people how their lives would be improved if there were a Stuart restoration. Had the Jacobites been savvier, they would have sought to ride the wave of popular discontent over 'union economics'.[2] Several parts of the 1707 Act of Union were

PRINCE CHARLES STUART (THE YOUNG PRETENDER). FROM AN AUTHENTIC PORTRAIT.

Bonnie Prince Charlie. (British Library)

economically favourable to Scottish landowners but the Scottish poor—as well as the poor from the north of England—failed to see any improvement in their own situation and enclosures still continued apace. But the Jacobites did not harness this popular discontent with the Hanoverian regime. Jacobitism was finally crushed by the Duke of Cumberland at the Battle of Culloden.

John Wilkes

As the threat of Jacobitism receded, new voices emerged which began to question *how* Britain was governed. Before Thomas Paine began writing his ground-breaking works, one prominent radical voice was the MP and journalist John Wilkes. He made a name for himself in 1763 when he published an article in his newspaper *The North Briton*—founded as a response to the Earl of Bute's pro-government paper *The Briton*—in which he attacked George III's speech on the conclusion of the Treaty of Paris which was negotiated after the Seven Years' War (1756–63).

This was an era in which most people accepted that the king had an undisputed right to choose his prime minister and his government, and Wilkes had an issue with this. This manner of operating was deficient, argued Wilkes, because it meant that parliament was often unable to voice opposition to the edicts of the prime minister lest any opposition be marked out as seditious, which is why Wilkes felt compelled to voice his views in the press—the concept of 'a loyal opposition' not having yet been fully formed:

> The parliament, which is the constitutional guardian of the liberties of the people, has in this case no opportunity of remonstrating, or of impeaching any wicked servant of the crown … A despotic minister will always endeavour to dazzle his prince with high-flown ideas of the prerogative and honour of the crown, which the minister will make a parade of firmly maintaining. I wish as much as any man in the kingdom to see the honour of the crown maintained in a manner truly becoming royalty. I lament to see it sunk even to prostitution.[3]

Although the king's speech had been written by the Prime Minister, the Earl of Bute, the king felt so insulted that he issued what is called a general warrant—which gave wide-ranging powers to magistrates and bailiffs to seize a number of persons—for the arrest of people associated with *The North Briton*. Over forty people were arrested but at his trial, Wilkes claimed that parliamentary privilege protected him from prosecution—the Lord Chief Justice agreed, much to the chagrin of the government.

Further scandals followed. Wilkes published, along with Thomas Potter, a satirical poem in honour of Fanny Murray, the mistress of the Earl of Sandwich. A flavour of the poem is given below:

> When pleasure's standard is erected high,
> Would grasp the treasure, and let virtue die.

In lazy apathy let others reign,
Whose blood's congeal'd like ice in every vein;
Fill with coy virtue, all the spacious breast
Kissing I love, and hate insipid rest;
The rising —— —— charms the female soul,
Eager we guide it to the mystic hole:
Where nature's treasure lie conceal'd from view.[4]

The government was seriously unimpressed and the House of Lords declared the poem to be pornographic, obscene, and blasphemous. Wilkes fled to France because the Lords took the step of, what was by the eighteenth century, a rather antiquated way of declaring Wilkes to be an outlaw—a sentence which had been hardly used since the Middle Ages. Court proceedings were then initiated against Wilkes. The Lords pressed ahead with the prosecution anyway and convicted him of obscene and seditious libel *in absentia*.

Eventually Wilkes returned to England to face the music and stood as an MP again. He was elected as the member for Middlesex and then surrendered himself to the courts. In 1768, he was fined £100 and sentenced to two years' imprisonment. Yet at his sentencing, on 10 May, a crowd of almost 15,000 people gathered in London to protest against the sentence, and they were chanting various slogans such as 'Wilkes and Liberty', 'No Liberty, No King', and 'Damn the King! Damn the Government! Damn the Justices!' Troops opened fire on the protestors, killing seven people and injuring many more—an event now known as the St George's Day Massacre. The Wilkites responded to this by rioting outside the Drury Lane Theatre while a pro-government play was being staged. Wilkes was still imprisoned but it was evident that he enjoyed popular support. Indeed, although the government expelled Wilkes from parliament, on the grounds that he was an outlaw when he won the Middlesex election, Wilkes simply responded by standing for election again—and he won.

John Wilkes addressing the Court of the King's Bench, from the *Gentleman's Magazine* (1768).

Although he was in gaol, Wilkes founded one of the first extra-parliamentary pressure groups: The Society of Gentlemen Supporters of the Bill of Rights. It numbered among its ranks one John Horne Tooke, who would become famous during 'Pitt's Terror' in the 1790s. The group was concerned with keeping an eye on government activity, and promoting freedom of the press and civil liberties. If they felt these were being infringed, they made sure to print articles highlighting those abuses.

After his release from prison in 1770, Wilkes assumed several appointments in local and national government. He was instrumental in securing the right of the press to publish parliamentary proceedings; he spoke in favour of the colonists during the American War of Independence; and he brought the first-ever motion for parliamentary reform into the House of Commons. Other radicals were becoming more vocal in the press during the 1770s. Frances Chiu, it will be recalled, drew attention to the writings of Major John Cartwright.[5] Thomas Spence, to take another example, published *Property in Land Every One's Right* (1775) which argued for:

1. The end of aristocracy and landlordism.
2. All land should be publicly owned by self-governing 'democratic parishes'.
3. Parish land rents to be distributed equally among parishioners.
4. Universal suffrage (including female suffrage) at both parish level and through a system of deputies elected to represent parishes at a national level.
5. A 'social guarantee' which would provide income for those unable to work;
6. The 'rights of infants' to be free from abuse and poverty.

Charles Lennox, Duke of Richmond

However, let us backtrack somewhat from the period related above and highlight the life and career of another radical voice: On 22 February 1735, Charles Lennox, the Duke of Richmond, and his wife, Sarah Cadogan, welcomed into the world a son, whom they named Charles, after the father. The young Charles received the upbringing that was typical to many of the aristocracy's sons at the time; educated at Westminster School— alongside Warren Hastings and Roman Empire historian Edward Gibbon—he was then sent on a Grand Tour of the Continent, before enrolling as a student at Leiden University in the Netherlands. For most noble youths the Grand Tour was a rite of passage and Lennox applied himself to his studies in art, history, and philosophy.[6]

It was while he was at university that news came to him, in 1750, of his father's death. He decided therefore to return to England and take up his seat as the 3rd Duke of Richmond and Aubigny. The social structure of aristocratic domains, in one sense, was thoroughly medieval; as a lord of the manor in times gone by might have, Richmond found himself in charge of a vast estate, with tenant farmers, or peasants, who worked small holdings of land for their lord. Yet Lennox was not a tyrant; he sponsored several building works in his local area, treated his tenants well, provided them with free beer, and bailed his tenants out of debtors' prisons on several occasions.[7]

A career in the army awaited the young man; at the time, it was fairly easy for an aristocrat to rise through the ranks because rich families often purchased military appointments for the sons. It was a means by which the sons of aristocratic families might make a name for themselves in the world. Lennox received his commission during the Seven Years' War (1756–63) and, by all accounts, distinguished himself with bravery at the Battle of Cherbourg. After the war, Lennox returned home and began seeking a career in politics. Through the connection of fellow friends in the Lords, Lennox was invited to become Secretary of State in May 1766 in the Duke of Rockingham's ministry. At the time, the electorate voted for MPs but ministries were appointed by the king, who could 'hire or fire' governments at will, although he did have to take account of who held the most power in the Commons. What 'parties' existed were often grouped around prominent individuals; Lennox was a member of the Rockingham Whigs; some attached themselves to the Duke of Newcastle; others declared loyalty to the Earl of Chatham—cabinet members like Lennox could come from either the Commons or the Lords.

It was during this early phase of his political career that Lennox began to express reservations about the role of the king in the constitution. Lennox had witnessed the formation of three ministries in three years due to the various manoeuvrings of the king. Very few people at this period doubted George III's right to hire and fire his ministers, but all the same, Lennox reasoned, ministers should be allowed to govern with little interference from the king and should not be forced to resign simply because they had brought in legislation which the king disliked. As Richmond said: 'They [the administration] are never changed but when they are getting strong enough to do the country some real service'.[8] Lennox—who had always disliked George III on a personal level (the feeling was mutual)—began to form in his own mind even more objections to this state of constitutional affairs. How could it be right that the government, once elected, can be disposed of by the king, and the ministers be sacked when their appointments had been the will of the electors? In Lennox's view, it was ministers who should dictate terms to the king, not the other way around.[9]

By the 1770s, Lennox was out of government but took a keen interest in the affairs of state from the Lords. He disagreed with the Declaratory Act, passed back in 1766, which granted the UK parliament the right to legislate for the colonies and made private suggestions to Rockingham that someone in government ought to repeal it.[10] He watched with horror the government's treatment of the American colonists whose demands for the repeal of certain taxes and the hated quartering acts (where British troops were stationed in American homes) spilt over into outright rebellion in 1775.

Lennox stopped short, however, of criticising the government openly. This was probably wise; public opinion in England at the time of the American war was almost wholly with the government. When news reached England of the colonists' defeat at Long Island in 1776, people in Leeds, Manchester, Bristol, York, and Halifax celebrated in the streets and burnt effigies of George Washington, John Adams, John Hancock, and Arthur Lee. At most, as the war began to go badly for the British, Lennox simply urged the government to recognise the American colonies' independence.[11]

Meantime, Lennox began corresponding with Major John Cartwright and he also began reading the works of Thomas Paine. When Lennox began reading Paine and Cartwright's works, very few people could vote in general elections. The franchise was awarded to you only if you owned property that was worth over 40 shillings, and all voting was public (the franchise was not uniform throughout the country, however, and in some boroughs, universal male suffrage existed). Lennox thought this was wrong and he came to sympathise with the goals of many of the political reform societies, such as the Yorkshire Association, which campaigned for universal male suffrage and annual elections. Yet these groups, although they were prolific publishers, had very few friends in high places. It was probably his exposure to Cartwright's and Paine's radical ideas, and his sympathies with the Yorkshire Association, that moved him, in 1780, to present a bill to the House of Lords. The preamble declared:

1. That the Government of this Realm, and the making of laws for the same, ought to be lodged in the hands of King, Lords of Parliament, and Representatives of the whole Body of the Freemen of this Realm.
2. That EVERY MAN of the commonalty (excepting infants, insane persons and criminals) is of common right, and by the laws of God, a FREE MAN, and entitled to the full enjoyment of liberty.
3. That Liberty or Freedom consists in having an actual share in the appointing those who frame the Laws, and who are to be the guardians of every man's life, property, and peace. For, the all of one man is as dear to him as the all of another; and the POOR man has an equal right, but more need, to have Representatives in the legislature, than the rich one.[12]

This was the draft of a constitution for the British people. Given that all men should have a right to have a say in the government, the Bill further proposed:

1. A vote for all people over twenty-one years old
2. Annual elections
3. The creation of 558 constituencies containing an equal number of electors.

Three of these aims would later be incorporated into the People's Charter during the Victorian era, as related in this book by Rebecca Nesvet. Lennox's emphasis on people, rather than simply men, must give us pause for thought here. Women could in fact already vote in the eighteenth century, contrary to popular belief, for the franchise was based upon property value and not sex. It was in 1832 when the law specifically granted voting rights to men that women were denied the right to vote. It can be inferred that Lennox included women in this projected scheme and with the exception of the preamble, the terminology used throughout the bill is largely gender-neutral. Richmond refers to 'The Right of Every Commoner' or the

'Rights of the Commons'. Indeed, when the bill simply spoke about the people who would not be able to vote, all we read is the following:

> *Who shall not vote,*
> AND be it enacted, that no person who has been or shall be duly convicted in a court of law within this realm of the crimes of high treason, treason, murder, felony, perjury, forgery, grand or petty larceny, or any of them, shall be capable of being elected, or of voting for the election of a Member of Parliament in or for any borough within this kingdom.[13]

Cartwright had in fact reviewed the bill privately and offered suggestions on several points, so this was probably his suggestion. The major was an early advocate of true *universal* suffrage, which included the granting of the right to vote for women as well, and he disagreed with those who only sought universal male suffrage.[14]

The Gordon Riots

Lennox's bill was a far-reaching and progressive one which, unfortunately, Lennox's fellow aristocrats were not quite ready to endorse. Indeed, circumstances were conspiring against Lennox's bill and it would never get a fair hearing. Unfortunately for Lennox, the very day that his bill was presented to the Lords on 3 June 1780, there was a commotion outside of parliament. The commotion was occasioned by the recent passage of the Catholic Relief Act (1778). The government in London had thought it prudent to extend to Catholics certain rights. Meantime, Catholics had been 'bending over backwards' to prove their loyalty to the Hanoverian regime and by the late 1770s, there was a good 'rapport' between the king and his Catholic subjects. The Act required Catholics to swear loyalty to George III and renounce any loyalty to the deposed Stuart dynasty.[15] If Catholics took the oath then they would be allowed to purchase freehold and leasehold land, live in London, found their own schools, and they would be permitted to join the British army. The act passed through all stages of parliament without a dissenting voice.[16]

But what was going on outside the Houses of Parliament? A man was leading a crowd of 60,000 people. The leader was Lord George Gordon, a bigoted anti-Catholic nobleman from Scotland who was leader of the Protestant Association. He and the crowd were there to deliver a petition calling on the government to repeal the Papists' Act. He had been ignored by the king and the cabinet for two whole years, now he turned up to parliament in a show of strength. The crowd was getting restless; they attacked the carriages of several Lords' members as they turned up—the very people who would be called upon to debate and vote upon Lennox's bill. The crowd got angry and began attacking several embassies and the riots descended into a week-long period of carnage, when the protestors attacked all symbols of government authority, until the army was called in to quell the rebellion. No wonder, then, that on 3 June, the Lords rejected Lennox's bill.

A reproduction of John Seymour Lucas's painting *The Gordon Riots*, completed in 1879 and published in Joseph Clayton's *The Rise of Democracy* (1911)

One eye-witness, an attorney named Joseph Ritson, who would later become a radical, wrote to his family back in Stockton and described the events:

> Grays Inn, 7th June, 1780
> Dear Mother,
> I am very well and am much grieved to find that you should continue otherwise, but hope to God you will soon get better of your complaint ... the confusion which reigns here would have prevented me from writing sooner. A general spirit of discontent has long been increasing among the people: it has at last broken out among the lower class in London.[17]

By the fourth day of the riots, the cause had evolved: it was no longer anti-Catholic but was a chance for settling scores with the rich, whatever their religion. As Ritson went on to explain:

> Five of the mob having been committed to Newgate, and the keeper refusing to set them free, their comrades yesternight, burnt it to the ground, and set not only their own people, but all of the debtors and felons at liberty, three or four of whom were to be executed within these few days ... Sir John Fielding's house was also plundered of everything, and the furniture, &c. burnt in the street ... Lord Mansfield's house,

in Bloomsbury Square, was burnt this morning … Lord Mansfield's country seat, about four miles from town, is said to be now in flames … destruction has been vowed against the houses and persons of several noblemen, bishops, and gentry.[18]

Neither John Fielding nor Lord Mansfield was Catholic. There was looting. What little law and order there was—London at this point did not have a professional police force—had completely broken down. After Ritson wrote his letter the army had to be called in to quell the riots, which they did, but the total cost of damages amounted to over £300,000. It was unlikely that Lennox's bill would have ever passed, but the Gordon Riots killed any sympathy it might have received. One radical, who had previously been admired by the populace—the aforementioned John Wilks—lost his credentials as a 'man of the people' because he helped to defend the Bank of England from rioters during that tumultuous week.

As for Lennox, he remained quiet about his radical politics after 1780. He took various roles in the government until the end of his life. He was Master of the Ordnance in William Pitt the Younger's first ministry, and remained closely allied with the 'Pittite' Tories until the 1790s. Further events across the channel cooled Lennox's enthusiasm for reform even further. When the French Revolution initially broke out, many people in the British establishment welcomed it. The kingdom of France seemed to finally be moving away from absolute monarchy towards a constitutional monarchy on similar lines to that which the British enjoyed. *The English Chronicle; or Universal Evening Post* declared that 'the hand of JUSTICE has been brought upon France' in her 'great and glorious REVOLUTION'. *The London Chronicle* reported that 'in every province of this great kingdom [France] the flame of liberty has burst forth'.[19]

Radicals and reformers in Britain thought that this was also the perfect time to further the cause of political reform and extension of voting rights to all men. Some people, whom we might call 'independent radicals', took up the pen to write words in favour of political reform. Among these were the Romantic poets William Wordsworth, Samuel Taylor Coleridge, and Robert Southey, the latter of whom wrote a poem about Wat Tyler in 1794—discussed briefly in the first chapter—in which the eponymous rebel appears as a member of the medieval sans-culottes. The aforementioned Joseph Ritson, in *Robin Hood: A Collection of All the Ancient Poems, Songs, and Ballads* (1795), likewise used another medieval legend, that of Robin Hood, and portrayed him as a medieval Thomas Paine.

The London Corresponding Society

Other radicals got organised. Inspired by the Society for Constitutional Information—founded by Major Cartwright in 1780—the London Corresponding Society (LCS) was formed in January 1792 by Thomas Hardy. Its modest name obscures its aim somewhat, but this society was committed to securing the by now familiar radicals' demands of universal male suffrage and equally-sized constituencies. Only nine people attended

English Rebels and Revolutionaries

the society's first meeting but membership soon grew, with some members making some, perhaps exaggerated, claims of the society having between 29,000 and 80,000 members.[20] It eventually numbered among its members some famous names including John Baxter, Francis Place, Edward Marcus Despard, and former slave and anti-slavery activist, Olaudah Equiano. LCS members were also very unforgiving about the 'apostasy' of Lennox and his old friend, William Pitt the Younger, who had originally been sympathetic to the cause of reform but, being now prime minister, had turned his back on the subject. As a broadside entitled *To the Affrighted Nobles* (1792) makes clear:

> You have fled to the standard of corruption, for fear of losing your titles and estates, by which you have exposed the former to general contempt, and the latter to danger. You have, all on a sudden, deserted the cause of the people; and, instead of becoming their leaders on the day of trial, have, as it were, declared against the Liberties of Mankind.[21]

Harsh words indeed towards Richmond, though they were not untrue. Richmond and Pitt were now supporters of 'the Old Corruption'. It was a term levelled by reformers against a seemingly oligarchical political system, with MPs elected in 'Rotten Boroughs', and in which very few people could vote (voters were usually paid or bribed by a prospective MP into voting for them anyway), and in which the government patronised its friends by offering certain people sinecures and pensions—all of which were paid for from the public purse. Meanwhile, the true voice of the people went unheard. This was the system that needed reforming.

The LCS was dedicated to educating people. It held debates, public meetings, and also printed books, and the London-based organisation soon became national in its scope when provincial organisations in Manchester, Sheffield, and Norwich were established. It was also cheap to become a member; the subscription cost of 1d meant that many of the 'lower orders' could participate in the debates. Although the members held their own personal political beliefs, the ideology of the LCS might, broadly speaking, be called pro-Declaration of the Rights of Man—a charter which the French Revolutionaries adopted—and pro-Paineite. They wanted universal male suffrage and a progressive system of taxation.

But the French Revolution turned violent: the Committee of Public Safety in France began, with the execution of Louis XVI in 1792, to execute supposed 'enemies of the revolution'. Revolutionary France then declared war on Britain in 1793. The war would last until 1815. It was, to all intents and purposes, a world war. Fighting occurred on every continent; Europe, Africa, the Americas, and the Indian subcontinent were all touched by the war in some way. The entire resources of the British nation were channelled into defeating, first the Revolutionary French government, and later, Napoleon. By 1794, the British government, led by William Pitt the Younger, grew increasingly paranoid of anything which smacked of revolutionary activity and groups like the LCS found themselves being watched. So-called 'Church and King' gangs intimidated members as they went to their meetings while the government hired spies

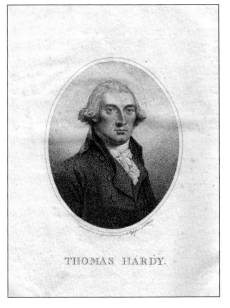

THOMAS HARDY.

JOHN HORNE TOOKE.
(From an old Print.)

John Horne Tooke and John Thelwall (British Library)

to join the organisation and keep an eye on the proceedings. Oftentimes the evidence of the subversive activities that the spies relayed back to the authorities was highly exaggerated. So the LCS decided to begin holding their meetings in secret. Now they really did look like a dangerous and secret revolutionary society.

The government decided to issue warrants of arrest for the crime of high treason against LCS members in London. Thirty people were arrested in total, among whom were Thomas Hardy, secretary of the LCS; Horne Tooke; the novelist Thomas Holcroft; Jeremiah Joyce; John Thelwall; Thomas Spence; and John Baxter. The Attorney General attempted to portray these men and their society as a dangerous organisation which, in league with other like-minded societies, was seeking to completely overthrow the government. The details were recorded in *The Newgate Calendar*:

> The Attorney General here went into a very full and very able detail of the correspondence of these two societies, and of the many other societies in different parts of the country, with whom they corresponded, remarking that though until late they had concealed their real designs,—under the veil of parliamentary reform, yet he would endeavour to prove that those societies wished to overturn the whole constitution and government of this country. This he shewed, among other things, from voting their thanks to Thomas Paine, for certain parts of his works, in which he described himself to be an enemy to hereditary monarchy, and in which he compared the subjects of kings to cattle and sheep. It was therefore

clear, that while they thanked him for these works, and wished to see the doctrines therein contained spread over the globe, it was wishing, in truth, for the destruction of the British constitution, which they affected to be anxious to purify and reform.[22]

The fact that the Duke of Richmond had proposed the very same measures in the House of Lords in 1780 was used to the defendants' advantage. Richmond's bill was alluded to several times during the men's trials, as their counsel stated to the jury:

> When the Corresponding Society first instituted its proceedings their objects were avowed and expressed to be those of Richmond ... there is no statute of limitation upon treason, this might equally be brought forward many years hence as now, this that was published by the Duke of Richmond ... was not considered by the officers of the crown as a libel, for if it is, it is not too late, if the Attorney General thinks such a proceeding would be decent, to call to account [Richmond] who published it.[23]

A clever argument indeed: if the Attorney General was going to prosecute Horne Took and his comrades, then he must prosecute Lennox as well. All three men were acquitted in quick succession, the juries in each man's case were evidently able to see that the charges were completely without foundation.

The government had been embarrassed. Not only had the defendants' counsel pointed to the Duke of Richmond's former radical sympathies, they had also drawn attention to the fact that Pitt, the Prime Minister himself, had also favoured parliamentary reform in his younger days. The government responded to this embarrassment by passing new laws designed to suppress freedom of speech and assembly, and suspending *habeas corpus*—supported by both the Duke of Richmond and that 'Saint', the anti-slavery activist William Wilberforce. Now radicals could be locked up without a trial indefinitely. The government's paranoia of all things even remotely 'reformist' lasted until even after the war, and would have fatal consequences in 1819 during the Peterloo Massacre.

Thus far, however, the world of eighteenth century radical thought and action has appeared as a man's world. In the next chapter, Rebecca Nesvet, therefore, introduces us to Mary Wollstonecraft, the author of *A Vindication of the Rights of Woman* (1791).

Notes

1. An Act for Preventing Tumults and Riotous Assemblies, and for the more speedy and effectual Punishing the Rioters, 1 Geo.1 St.2 c.5 (London, 1715).
2. Anon. [online], 'Jacobites and the Union', *BBC History*, September 19, 2014, accessed April 29, 2020. Available at: www.bbc.co.uk.
3. John Wilkes, 'No. 45', *The North Briton*, April 23, 1763, 250–57.
4. John Wilkes, *An Essay on Women* (Aberdeen: James Hay, 1888), 12.

5. Part of this chapter originally appeared as a short article: Stephen Basdeo [online], "The Noble Radical: Charles Lennox, 3rd Duke of Richmond," *Here Begynneth a Lytell Geste of Robin Hood* March 16, 2020. Accessed May 30, 2020. Available at: www.gesteofrobinhood.com.
6. M.M. Reese, *Goodwood's Oak: The Life and Times of the Third Duke of Richmond, Lennox, and Aubigny* (London: Threshold Books, 1987), p. 51.
7. Alison Olson, *The Radical Duke: The Career and Correspondence of Charles Lennox, Third Duke of Richmond* (Oxford: Oxford University Press, 1961), p. 10.
8. Richmond to Newcastle, 20 July 1766, Add. MS. 32,990, f.322.
9. Richmond to Rockingham, 12 February 1771, Fitzwilliam MS R158–44.
10. Richmond to Rockingham, 2 November 1777, Fitzwilliam MS RI-968-1.
11. Richmond to Rockingham, 15 March 1778, Fitzwilliam MS RI-983.
12. Charles Lennox, *The Bill of the Late Duke of Richmond for Universal Suffrage and Annual Parliaments* (London: William Hone, 1817), p. 1.
13. *Ibid.*, p. 15.
14. Rachael Eckersley, 'Of Radical Design: John Cartwright and the Redesign of the Reform Campaign, c.1800–1811', *History*, 89: 296 (2004), 560–80 (p. 561).
15. Stephen Basdeo, *Discovering Robin Hood: The Life of Joseph Ritson—Gentleman, Scholar, Revolutionary* (Barnsley: Pen and Sword, 2021) [Forthcoming].
16. Robert E. Burns, 'The Catholic Relief Act in Ireland, 1778', *Church History*, 32: 2 (1963), 181-206 (p. 183).
17. Joseph Ritson, 'Letter VI', in *The Letters of Joseph Ritson*, ed. by Joseph Frank, 2 vols (London: William Pickering, 1833), I, pp. 14–15.
18. Ibid., 16.
19. Quoted in Basdeo, *Discovering Robin Hood*, 104.
20. Michael T. Davis, "The London Corresponding Society," The Oxford Dictionary of National Biography, accessed May 30, 2020. Available at: www.oxforddnb.com.
21. *To the Affrighted Nobles of the Land* (London: [n.pub.], 1792). MS Home Office Papers and Records: Part One: HO 42, Boxes 1-23, 1782-1792 Box 21. The National Archives (Kew, United Kingdom).
22. *The Newgate Calendar; or, Villainy Displayed in all its Branches*, 6 vols (London: Alex Hogg, 1794), VI, pp. 294–95.
23. *Proceedings at Large on the Trial of John Horne Tooke for High Treason*, 2 vols (London: J.S. Jordan, 1795), I, p. 391.

Mary Wollstonecraft

Rebecca Nesvet

On 11 December 1792, a man emerged, heavily guarded, from the Temple Prison in Paris. He was thirty-eight years older, but seemed older, wore a brown coat, and had not shaved for several days.[1] His name was Louis Capet. At least, that is the name by which the men who came to the Temple to fetch him had addressed him. He informed them that he did not prefer that name.[2] For most of his lifetime, M. Capet was known as Louis XVI, King of France, a title that the government had abolished. He was helped into a coach, which was escorted by throngs of guards. He was going to his indictment for crimes against the people of France. The National Convention wanted him conveyed securely, for justice must be seen to be done.[3] Fifteen days later, he repeated the journey from the Temple to the Convention, this time to attend his trial.

On that day, 26 December, among the people who watched the bulletproof carriage proceed slowly down the boulevards was an extraordinary Englishwoman. Age thirty-two, Mary Wollstonecraft had come to Paris about a month earlier, eager to perform field research. Like many English radicals, she was intrigued by the French Revolution. Since its commencement on 14 July 1789, this cataclysm was hysterically reviled by the British establishment. Wollstonecraft wanted to see firsthand if the revolution would produce a genuinely rational, egalitarian, and just society. A frequent contributor to the press of the London radical publisher Joseph Johnson, Wollstonecraft planned to document France's grand experiment for English radical readers. Back in 1789, she told Johnson, she had greeted the news of the Revolution by looking forward to an 'epoch, when, in the course of improvement, men would labour to become virtuous, without being goaded on by misery'.[4] This era, she then believed, might prove a true 'golden age'.[5] Once embedded in Paris, however, she was no longer so certain of France's utopian potential, but as she watched the deposed king pass through an eerily silent city, she changed her mind. Erroneously believing that Louis was being escorted to his execution, she praised her fellow onlookers. 'The inhabitants of Paris flocked to their windows, but the casements were all shut, not a voice was heard, nor did I see any thing like an insulting gesture,' she reported to Johnson,[6] 'For the first time since I entered France, I bowed to the majesty of the people, and respected the propriety of behavior so perfectly in union with my own feelings'.[7] As for Louis, while she underhandedly approved of his 'dignity' ('more ... than I expected of his character'), she saw him not as an individual but a time-spanning tyrannical institution justly brought down to earth.

138

In her imagination, the man in the carriage melted away.[8] He was transformed into his ancestor Louis XIV, the absolutist Sun King, 'with all his pomp' witnessing at last 'the sunshine of his prosperity overshadowed by ... sublime gloom'.[9]

Wollstonecraft, whose family hailed from Spitalfields, must have known Louis XIV as the demagogue whose suppression of religious liberty turned Huguenot (French Protestant) silk-weavers into refugees. Many weavers of Spitalfields were those refugees' descendants.[10] Even so, Wollstonecraft did not see the Bourbon kings merely as embodiments of spiritual tyranny, monarchic arbitrariness, and class oppression. They also stood for patriarchy. First in France and then in England, would Wollstonecraft's lifetime see all these institutions abolished or severely altered? Could she herself contribute significantly to the advent of such a golden age? She intended to pursue these goals.

Early Life

Since the dawning of her consciousness, Wollstonecraft's antipathy to absolutism was always to some degree personal. She was born in 1759 to Edward Wollstonecraft and his wife Elizabeth (neé Dickson). Edward, the son of a Spitalfields weaver made good, declared himself a gentleman and moved his family away from that working-class outpost of London. He invested his ambition and hope in his own eldest son and namesake, Edward Bland Wollstonecraft. For as long as Wollstonecraft had been aware, her father treated 'Ned' very much like a Sun King. The rest of the Wollstonecraft family followed suit. Ned received more parental attention and praise than his siblings, including his younger brothers. His grandfather willed him property, investments, and a painting of himself, intended to be the first in a dynastic succession of portraits that would someday distinguish Ned's home.[11] He was even his mother's favourite. 'The family injustice' of Ned's preferment 'would embitter and fuel Mary's life', observes her biographer and editor, Janet Todd.[12]

A more frightening figure was their father. Edward Wollstonecraft Senior's desire to live as a gentleman farmer compelled him to drag his family across England, from Essex to Yorkshire and then back to the London metropolitan area and later to Wales. In each new location, he established a family farm and saw it quickly and expensively fail. He turned his frustration on his children, always excepting Ned. Physically violent to Mary and some of her siblings her father was, in biographer Lyndall Gordon's estimation, 'a common kind of bully, the failure who picks on the vulnerable'. So too, perhaps, was Louis XVI, the failed, fugitive king of a starving nation whose attempts to draw foreign armies down upon that nation led to his arrest and imprisonment in the Temple.

Families do not inherently create love, Mary Wollstonecraft learned early on, but the opposite could be true. By choice, she loved her younger brother Charles and her two sisters, the beautiful, heroine-like Eliza and romantically named Everina. To two other brothers, she was indifferent and her feelings for her mother were complicated, infused with both frustration and pathos. Pitying her mother, Wollstonecraft decided that her salvation from this household would not be marriage. Instead, she decided to go into education. Books supported her. A Yorkshire friend, Jane Arden, took Wollstonecraft home and showed her how a family could operate in security and love, but what really impressed Wollstonecraft about the Ardens was their library, which consisted of the serious literature that, as Gordon explains, increasingly marked out the country's 'professional middle class'.[13] Wollstonecraft's late eighteenth century youth saw the development of what critic William St. Clair has called 'the English reading nation', a critical minority of the increasingly industrialised nation and its Irish and American colonial populations that read widely and for pleasure and viewed themselves as a community of readers.[14] The teenage Wollstonecraft's education in reading was continued by a kind neighbour, the eccentric, reclusive Reverend Clare of Hoxton, east of Islington. Mr Clare introduced the inquisitive teenager to the magic of poetry and also, Gordon speculates, taught her the beginnings of how to teach; specifically, how to teach children to become rational, empathetic participants in civil society.[15] As an adult, Wollstonecraft saw pedagogy as the most effective tool of peaceful change. Clare instilled that idea in her.

He also treated his wife well, in great contrast to her parents' relations. In 1775, Mrs Clare took Wollstonecraft under her wing and introduced her to the woman who would have more impact upon her adult life than any other, and nearly than any other person, Frances 'Fanny' Blood. Eighteen years old to Wollstonecraft's sixteen, Fanny was the eldest child of seven. Ancestrally Anglo-Irish and upper class in derivation, the Blood family lived in genteel poverty in Newington Butts, South London, constantly dodging the alcoholic Mr Blood's many creditors. Fanny cared for her siblings and read widely. 'Until she met Fanny', Gordon says of Wollstonecraft, 'she had not thought of writing as an art'; Fanny encouraged her to see literature in this new way.[16]

She also opened Wollstonecraft's eyes to the educational potential of visual art. A talented, meticulous artist, Fanny supplemented her father's income by scientific illustration. She provided illustrations to a botanical encyclopedia, *Flora Londinensis, or, Plates and Descriptions of such Plants as Grow Wild in the Environs of London* (1777), by the botanist William Curtis, who instructed the Company of Apothecaries in the medicinal uses of plants.[17] The *Flora Londiniensis* was a handsome work. It contains some colour plates and parallel English and Latin texts for each entry. There is also a glossary of all the scientific names for the plant species. During the Romantic era, middle-class London writers and artists began to express a unique metropolitan cultural identity, 'Cockneyism'. Critic Gregory Dart dates this phenomenon slightly later than Wollstonecraft's residence in Hoxton, finding it at its height c. 1810-50, but claims it was 'all about fanciful imaginings in restricted settings' and the establishment of London and its outskirts as a subject worthy of contemplation, writing, art, and poetry.[18] Arguably, Fanny's documentation for vernacular readers of the flowers that forced their way up from between the metropolitan cobblestones was a Cockney endeavour. The volume as a whole suggests that observations of urban life might be worthy of recording and publication.

Wollstonecraft needed more than a role model for metropolitan intellectual activity. She also sought love. She soon began to cherish Fanny as 'a friend, whom I love better than all the world beside, a friend to whom I am bound by every tie of gratitude and inclination'.[19] Wollstonecraft sometimes lived with Fanny's family. Eventually, she envisioned Fanny as her future domestic partner. 'To live with this friend is the height of my ambition,' she declared. Although her stated reason for this aspiration was Fanny's intelligent 'conversation', she was also clearly attracted to Fanny in a far more intense way.[20] In the final years of her life, Wollstonecraft would remember her 'fervent' attachment to Fanny as 'the ruling passion of my mind'.[21] She might have understood the sexual nature of this passion. In 1778, when Wollstonecraft was nineteen years old, two Irish gentlewomen, Lady Eleanor Butler and Sarah Ponsonby, eloped, accompanied by Ponsonby's devoted domestic servant Mary Carryll, to the secluded Vale of Llangollen in North Wales. There, they set up a home, Plas Newydd ('New Place'), that they maintained for decades. Butler and Ponsonby declared their love for each other, wore men's hats, and seemed, in effect, an indisseverable unit. Renowned as the 'Ladies of Llangollen', they cultivated a library that Wollstonecraft would have envied, and which they occupied on a daily basis.[22] In the words of scholar Nicole Reynolds, Butler, Ponsonby, and Carryll lived out 'a complex performance of bourgeois domestic life, one that both mirrored and inverted the imperatives of the heterosexual family unit'.[23] In spite of the Plas Newydd household's subversion of patriarchal norms, the Ladies of Llangollen won the admiration of tourists and, in 1785, sent a 'plan' of Plas Newydd's architectural innovations to Queen Charlotte. She disapproved only of the musk-based perfume with which the Ladies had scented the parcel.[24] By that year, Caryll had begun regularly giving tours of Plas Newydd. Later, the Ladies impressed visiting literati such as the Romantic poets William Wordsworth, Samuel Taylor Coleridge, and Lord Byron and *Black Beauty* author, Anna Seward.[25] They accomplished their risky social balancing act in part by publicly fashioning themselves as an 'exemplar of the tradition of romantic friendship', not sexual love, creating a 'socially sanctioned narrative of their life together'.[26] With such celebrity, the Ladies may well have been known to Wollstonecraft during her pursuit of romantic friendship and domestic tranquillity with Fanny Blood.

Maintenance of a household is impossible without money, as Wollstonecraft knew. Unwilling to consider heterosexual marriage as a means of subsistence, she sought other kinds of careers. In 1779-80, she worked as a companion to an ornery upper-class woman, Mrs Dawson, in Bath, the southern spa city that Jane Austen's novels represent as the capital of the Romantic-era marriage market. The arrangement was uncongenial to both Wollstonecraft and Dawson. Within eighteen months, it was over. Fanny Blood proposed that she, Wollstonecraft, and Wollstonecraft's sister, Eliza Bishop, whom Wollstonecraft had extricated from a youthful, impetuous marriage, should live by the proceeds of visual art and sewing. Instead, Wollstonecraft decided that the three should operate a school for girls. Initially, they founded their school in Islington, but, in 1784, they attracted an angel donor, Hannah Burgh, widow of the philosopher and pedagogue, Dr James Burgh. Mrs Burgh lived further north, in Newington Green. At her request, Wollstonecraft, Eliza, and Fanny relocated their school to that village.

It was a wise decision, and not just for the school's viability. Located between Islington and Hackney, Newington Green was a vibrant centre for Dissenting culture.

Its main gathering place was the Newington Green Unitarian Church, founded in 1708. In Wollstonecraft's day, the Church's minister was Dr Richard Price, a Welshman and a friend of philosophers David Hume and Adam Smith, zealous reformer of social injustice, and critic of arbitrary government. Price became Wollstonecraft's beloved mentor, occupying the role in her life that Mr Clare had done. Price preached that humans were by Creation intended for freedom and equality, ideas that quickly captivated Wollstonecraft.[27] When the American Revolution broke out, he supported it wholeheartedly. Despite the American founding fathers' failure to liberate the enslaved contingent of the population of the thirteen colonies, Price celebrated the colonies' independence from the yoke of monarchy as a sign of political progress that English radicals would do well to emulate.[28] Moreover, Price made the basic human rights championed by Enlightenment philosophy central to his theology. 'He preached liberty as part of a programme of moral perfection', Gordon explains, 'a religious utopianism stressing the divine image implanted in our nature'.[29] In essence, Price schooled the Dissenters of Newington Green, people who considered other people either hereditarily entitled or hereditarily inferior, who acted against God's intentions for humanity. In Wollstonecraft's quarrel with society, Price's God was on her side.

At Newington Green, Wollstonecraft blossomed as an intellectual. She met some of the major philosophical and literary figures of her day. These included not just Price but also Dr Samuel Johnson, magisterial author of the Dictionary, who died a year after Wollstonecraft met him, and the poet Samuel Rogers. He was considered one of the most prominent of London poets. In her correspondence, Wollstonecraft calls him 'the Poet' (note the capitalisation).[30] She conversed with all these individuals in a culture in which conversation was an art form and a powerful medium for political debate and personal and communal self-improvement. In the 1760s-80s, critic Jon Mee has found, conversation as a medium for learning, growing, and consolidating community 'multipled across the new spaces' of greater London's 'urban renaissance'.[31] The American scientist and revolutionary Benjamin Franklin noted on his visit to London the intense, sophisticated conversation of what he called the 'Club of Honest Whigs' and described as 'friends of liberty and science'.[32] This loosely defined coffee-house conversational society included Price, James Burgh, and others whom Wollstonecraft would later come to know, or to know about, during her sojourn in Newington Green.[33] As she practised conversation with the luminaries of Newington Green, she gained political consciousness. For many participants in the coffee-house conversation scene, Mee demonstrates, 'the desire for a dialogue that transcended the everyday world was often related to an explicitly democratic desire to critique hierarchy'.[34] Wollstonecraft, having been for quite some time engaged in critique, needed an intellectual community with whom to share it. In Newington Green, with the school to provide her with subsistence, Fanny with love, and the Newington Green literati with intellectual challenge and fulfilment, Wollstonecraft seemed to have found herself a genuine oasis.

Unfortunately, it was not to last. Fanny contracted tuberculosis (or 'consumption', as it was then known). Meanwhile, Fanny's brother George Blood, whom Wollstonecraft liked, fled to Ireland, accused—wrongly, Wollstonecraft thought—of fathering the child of his employer's maidservant. This scandal negatively impacted the reputation of his sister's school. Fanny had long been courted by a peripatetic wine merchant, Hugh Skeys. She finally married him and let him take her to Lisbon, Portugal in a desperate bid to improve her health. There, her tuberculosis was complicated by pregnancy. Wollstonecraft sailed to Lisbon to nurse her and the expected child, only to watch a difficult birth helplessly and see the newborn die. On 29 November 1785, Fanny Skeys, too, passed away. Devastated, Wollstonecraft lingered in Lisbon for a month, convincing herself that she was helpful to Fanny's widower. Then she returned to Newington Green. 'Life seems a burthen almost too heavy to be indured', she wrote in February 1786.[35] The school was foundering. She had lost her kindred spirit of a decade. How was she to subsist, and for what purpose?

The Beginning of a Writing Career

Wollstonecraft found answers to both these questions as a professional writer. Through her Newington Green intellectual network, she met the radical publisher Joseph Johnson. For his press, she composed a pedagogical treatise, *Thoughts on the Education of Daughters* (1787). This was the first of her radical prose publications. In it, she combined the freethought and social justice of the Newington Green Dissenters with her practice-based knowledge of teaching girls to survive in a world set thoroughly against them. Denouncing the 'unfortunate situation of females, fashionably educated, and left without a fortune', she goes well beyond the problem of what to teach middle-class British girls and how to teach it, but why.[36] For what were these girls to be prepared? What ought to be their learning objectives? Not to be married as soon as possible, she insists. 'Early marriages are … a stop to improvement', she theorizes.[37] A woman married too young, like Wollstonecraft thought her sister Eliza was, stops learning, growing, and discovering herself and the world. Women are too often (mis-) educated, and then required, to focus all their efforts on the domestic sphere. They 'too often confine their love and charity to their own families', denying any more expansive 'moral obligation'.[38] Ultimately, the pedagogy gives way to ontology. What is a woman, or, given the class background of her target audience, a lady? What is her ultimate potential and moral purpose? 'In the fine Lady how few traits do we observe of those affections which dignify human nature? … though she lives many years she is still a child and of so little use to society that her death would scarcely be observed'.[39] Wollstonecraft's outrage at the misogyny of her society is tinged with outrage at the class system.

With this view of 'fine ladies', it might seem surprising that, having wound up the school, Wollstonecraft took a position as a governess to the three daughters of a fine lady, but she had to do something to support herself financially. She travelled to Ireland to teach the children of Lord and Lady Kingsborough at their estate of Mitchelstown Castle in County Cork. This went as badly as her employment as Dawson's companion. Lady Kingsborough nagged Wollstonecraft about her appearance, as she refused to spend money on finery and, told she was unpresentable, exiled herself from the Mitchelstown Castle parlour. Other disagreements led to the termination of her employment. However, she had a lasting impact. One Kingsborough daughter, Margaret, later Lady Mount Cashell, followed Wollstonecraft's teachings to embark upon 'her own experimental course that would allow her to develop a medical practice', leave her aristocratic marriage for an Irish agronomist, George Tighe, befriend Wollestonecraft's adult daughter Mary Shelley, and raise two daughters as rational beings.[40]

At Mitchelstown Castle, Wollstonecraft had been productive in other ways than the pedagogical. In 1788, she published her first and only completed novel, *Mary, a Fiction*. Begun at Mitchelstown, it follows the fortunes of a woman who is pointedly *not* a heroine in the tradition of the novels of Samuel Richardson or, looking forward, Jane Austen. In *Mary,* the marriage plot is no resolution to the problems of being a rational woman in an irrational society. It was published by Johnson, of course, who also allowed Wollstonecraft to live as his lodger in his home above the printshop in Ludgate Hill, in the shadow of St Paul's Cathedral. There, at Johnson's conversational dinners, she met prominent radicals, including Johnson's most controversial author, Thomas Paine, a key intellectual architect of American independence. She also communed with artists in Johnson's community. The eccentric, visionary poet and artist, William Blake, illustrated another of her Johnson publications, the didactic children's book *Original Stories from Real Life* (1791), while John Opie painted her portrait in about 1790-1. In Opie's composition, Wollstonecraft holds a writing book and quill pen and stares intently out of the frame. The portrait emphatically defines her as a writer.

Another artist whom Wollstonecraft met via Johnson was the Swiss painter Henry Fuseli (née Heinrich Füssli). He is most famous for painting Gothic nightmares. His most enduring work is the bizarre, erotically charged *The Nightmare* (1789). He also created scenes from Shakespeare and Milton's works and pornographic sketches that embarrassed his wife Sophia, who, after his death, burned many of them in her kitchen

stove. Fuseli shared Johnson and Paine's ideas about liberty and political justice. One of his more obscure but visually powerful compositions is *The Oath on the Rütli*, completed c. 1779-81. This picture, monumental in size and commissioned for the state house at Zurich, dramatizes an iconic moment in Swiss history: the first swearing of the *rütlischwur* (German: 'Oath on the Rütli') by which representatives of Switzerland's three cantons bound those bodies together and committed themselves to the dream of a Swiss Republic, independent of both foreign

John Opie. *Mary Wollstonecraft.*
c. 1790-1. Tate Britain.[41]

government and monarchy. Supposedly, the first *rütlischwur* was sworn on the banks of the River Rütli in 1307, but Fuseli's minimally costumed, muscular figures belong not to history but to mythic time. Above their heads, their hands and a short sword trace out a quadrangle to which the viewer's eye is immediately drawn. It looks like a picture frame, but at its centre is open air, which parts surrounding dark clouds. This composition invites the viewer to see the Swiss Republic in its founders' imagination as a space of infinite possibility.

Just as radical is Fuseli's painting *Blind Milton Dictates to his Daughters* (1793). Painted after Fuseli met Wollstonecraft, for a series of Milton-themed images conceived in 1790 for publication by Johnson, this canvas foregrounds a woman writing. Bright light illuminates her page. Tall and imposing, she appears in sharp contrast to her sister, who sits in the lower lefthand corner, eyes on her sewing, and even to Milton, who sits in darkness. The bluish complexion of his face weirdly suggests that he is already dead. Could his ideas about political liberty liberate his daughters? Could those daughters, remembered by some of his eighteenth century biographers as his amanuenses, have written something of significance themselves, whether or not it has survived? Fuseli's small, square tableau, a genre-crossing mix of the domestic and epic, invites those questions.

No wonder, then, that Wollstonecraft fell in love with him. He was married but also a radical and a rebel. Moreover, they witnessed together the outbreak, on 14 July 1789, of the French Revolution. Fed up with arbitrary monarchy,

Henry Fuseli. *The Oath on the Rütli*. The Rathaus, Zurich.[42]

Henry Fuseli. *Blind Milton Dictates to his Daughters*. The Museum of the Art Institute of Chicago.[43]

aristocratic tyranny, and starvation, the people of Paris brought down the walls of the Bastille. Other, less concrete walls could come down too, even in London. However, Wollstonecraft was a woman of reason, a 'bluestocking', in the parlance of her day, whose lack of finery had infuriated Lady Kingsborough. The women in Fuseli's erotic paintings had impossibly elaborate hairstyles, and he himself had married one of his artist's models.

Todd claims that it is 'impossible to know when Wollstonecraft realised the significance of the Bastille's fall', but that her friends at Newington Green and Ludgate Hill sympathised with the revolutionaries of France. In November 1790, they were outraged by the Conservative MP, Edmund Burke's newly published polemic *Reflections on the Revolution in France.* She already disliked Burke on account of the primacy of weakness and softness in his definition of female beauty, explained in his masterpiece of aesthetics, 'On the Sublime and the Beautiful' (1757). In *Reflections,* Burke attacks not only the Parisian revolutionaries, whom he painted as sacrilegious attackers of the beautiful and therefore sympathetic Marie Antoinette, Queen of France, but someone much closer to home for Wollstonecraft: the revolutionary-sympathising, Reverend Price.

Wollstonecraft fired back in her anonymous pamphlet *A Vindication of the Rights of Men,* which rolled off Johnson's press slightly less than a month after Burke's *Reflections* appeared.[44] While defending the French Revolution and Price, *A Vindication of the Rights of Men* also develops the main idea of *Thoughts on the Education of Daughters*: that woman is born a rational creature, as much so as man, and therefore should enjoy the rights and responsibilities that society grants to men. Speaking supposedly of the French aristocracy, Wollstonecraft deplores the 'barbarous feudal institution, that enables the elder son to overpower talents and depress virtue'.[45] Obviously, she was also inspired by the phantasmagorical image of her estranged brother Ned. 'In what respect are we superior to the brute creation'—animals, she asks, 'if intellect is not allowed to be the guide of passion?'[46] Reason would prevail if 'the *native* unalienable rights of men were recognised in their full force?' (emphasis Wollstonecraft's).[47] 'I reverence the rights of men,' she declares, and attacks Burke for suggesting that 'one half of the human species, at least, have not souls' and outright insisting that 'Nature … never designed' that women 'should exercise their reason', making Wollstonecraft 'tremble for the soul of women' and for that of 'the good natured man' whose actions are warped by thinking women inferior.[48] As for the lawlessness of the Bastille's destruction and the arrest of Marie Antoinette, '[w]hat were the outrages of a day to' the 'continual miseries' of primogeniture, classism, and misogyny?[49]

A Vindication of the Rights of Men struck a chord with radicals and conservatives alike. The British sympathisers with the Revolution and their anti-adversaries read and discussed Wollstonecraft's pamphlet. Most assumed it was written by a man. Its impact was deep. Paine's *The Rights of Man,* perhaps radical England's most inspiring and dangerous book, appeared a few months later, evidently informed to some degree by Wollstonecraft's similarly-titled work.[50] Meanwhile, Wollstonecraft let Price know that she had written the *Vindication.* He praised it and thanked her for her defence from his deathbed.[51]

This proved a watershed moment in Wollstonecraft's life. As Todd explains, the polemic 'formally associated Wollstonecraft with radicals, especially Paine'.[52] She was accepted as a radical thinker in her conversational network and far beyond. This fame emboldened her to assert herself a voice worth hearing. On 13 November 1791, William Godwin dined at Johnson's. A former Dissenting minister from one of the poorest areas in the country, Godwin had come to London in 1782, where he became an anarchist philosopher. Godwin wished to speak with Paine, but Wollstonecraft monopolised Paine. In Godwin's opinion, she talked too much. Others shared this opinion. As Mee points out, many of Johnson's associates attributed to Wollstonecraft a 'combative flair for talk'.[53]

Wollstonecraft's next publication was more combative than her conversation and is today generally considered her most significant contribution to philosophical thought and Western culture. In *A Vindication of the Rights of Woman* (1792), Wollstonecraft seized the revolutionary moment to pursue the goal of female liberty for which she had striven since childhood. Marriage as women's only life goal makes 'animals' of them, she claims.[54] The major problem, however, is that 'women are not allowed to have sufficient strength of mind to acquire what really deserves the name of virtue': not chastity, but ethical action and civic goodness.[55] Women seem senseless because they 'receive only a disorderly kind of education', calculated to make them amenable to libertines and to keep them in line.[56] If they were properly, rationally educated, they could pursue subsistence and purpose in occupations other than marriage, 'which might save many from common and legal prostitution'; that is, from sex-work and marriage.[57] 'Make women free,' she concludes, 'and they will quickly become wise and virtuous', for woman 'must grow more perfect when emancipated'.[58] This is precisely the destiny that her radical community desired and prayed for the people of France.

Critical reactions to the *Rights of Woman* were considerably more mixed than the reactions to the *Rights of Men.* A fellow bluestocking, Mary Hays, loved *Rights of Woman,* begged to meet its author, and considered her and mentor and friend, Anna Seward called it a 'wonderful book', and virtually everyone read it, but many women and men were horrified.[59] A respectable mother—or, at least, an author claiming to be one—wrote to a women's periodical to complain that Wollstonecraft's ideas had driven her daughters to wild, mad, and unmarriageable enthusiasms; a dangerous accusation in an era when female 'enthusiasm' of any kind was often interpreted as mental derangement.[60] Playwright Hannah Cowley turned against it, and the Neoplatonist philosopher and translator, Thomas Taylor, satirised Wollstonecraft and Paine's ideas in a mock *Vindication of the Rights of Brutes,* effectively portraying French plebeians and English women as animals who mistakenly think themselves human.[61] The Cornish minister Richard Polwhele is now notorious for his verse rant 'The Unsex'd Females' (1800). Deploring the 'Gallic freaks'—sympathy with the French Revolution—of the bluestockings, Polwhele lambasts 'Wollstonecraft, whom no decorum checks' / 'the intrepid champion of her sex', who 'o'er humbled man assert[s] the sovereign claim, / And slight[s] the timid blush of virgin fame'.[62] She would hardly be the first feminist to be accused of wanting women to dominate men or to be shamed for her sexual activity.

In 1792, Wollstonecraft was concerned about other struggles, primarily the one then unfolding in France. King Louis XVI and Marie Antoinette had attempted to flee the country with their children, all disguised as plebeians. At an inn in Varennes, they were recognised, captured, and hauled back to Paris. In the Temple prison, Louis awaited his fate. Wollstonecraft and her friends at Johnson's dinner table buzzed with conversation about this epic moment. Would the Revolution fail, as England's own regicidal and Republican experiment in the 1640s-50s had failed? Would it succeed and provide an example for English radicals to follow, ideally more gradually and peacefully than the original? How could one know without seeing the events in Paris unfold in full colour and at close range—without observing history in the making scientifically? Wollstonecraft decided to go to Paris, find out, and report back. In December 1792, she sailed. She must have noted, on her voyage across the Channel, that the last time she had taken this journey, en route to Lisbon in 1785, the object of her intense passion had given birth to a terminally afflicted child and then died. Would the newborn Republic and its mass of parents have a better chance to survive and succeed?

This is the question that Wollstonecraft pursued in several writings of this period, including the letters to Johnson quoted at the beginning of this chapter and her treatise *An Historical and Moral View of the Origin and Progress of the French Revolution* (1793). In this work, written at the height of the Reign of Terror, Wollstonecraft confronted by the problem of the guillotine is horrified but hopeful. 'Men become vicious' because of 'ignorance', she argues, but mass ignorance may be only temporary.[63] 'A new spirit has gone forth' from France 'to organize the body-politic' and is 'now enthroned in the hearts of half the inhabitants of the globe'.[64] Whatever has happened in France, the spirit of the revolution will inspire other nations to rise up; other populations to liberate themselves, perhaps by better means than France employed.

In Paris, Wollstonecraft pursued a kind of liberation of her own. Finished with Fuseli, she encountered an exotic suitor, Gilbert Imlay. An American from New Jersey and a veteran of the Revolutionary War, Imlay was forty-one, handsome, and a self-fashioned frontiersman. A First Lieutenant in the Continental army, he claimed to be a Captain, and, an ocean away from the battlefield, no one was likely to contradict him. A kind of Hawkeye a generation before James Fenimore Cooper invented that character, Imlay published *A Topographical Description of the Western Territory of North America* in London in 1792. He had pretensions to literary fame, especially if it could be combined with patriotism and profit. In 1793, he published a novel, *The Emigrants,* a fanciful potboiler involving an English heroine who ends up settling in the American wilderness outside Pittsburgh, Pennsylvania. Imlay was in France to represent the interests of an Ohio-based land company and, rather more surreptitiously, to profit from the transfer of American Revolutionary arms to France. Wollstonecraft saw him as a free spirit and he pursued her love. Both remained averse to marriage, though Wollstonecraft called herself 'Mrs. Imlay' socially and his protection saved her from the banishment or worse imposed on many English people who remained in France during the Terror. She must have been grateful, for she had seen brilliant, moral people whom she knew personally taken to the guillotine or hounded to death: Madame and Monsieur Roland, the scientist-philosopher Condorcet, and her fellow proto-feminist Olympe de Gouges. On 10 May 1794, Wollstonecraft gave birth to a girl, whom she named after her own lost love, nine years' dead. With Imlay's surname applied for respectability, Wollstonecraft's daughter was christened Frances 'Fanny' Imlay.

By this point, the frontiersman was looking for new frontiers. Wollstonecraft's relationship with Imlay deteriorated. Business kept him from Paris, but he was also tired of her. She wrote him desperate letters, begged for constancy, and attempted suicide by ingesting laudanum, a tincture of opium readily available at pharmacies. Then, Imlay gave her what seemed an opportunity to prove her love and to earn the renewal of his. Ever the speculator, he had obtained a ship to run guns and silver to and from France, evading the British naval blockade. The ship was named the *Maria and Margaretha,* evidently after Wollstonecraft and her French maid, Marguerite. Loaded with silver, it left for Scandinavia, piloted by a Norwegian captain who promptly vanished with it. Imlay was informed the ship had foundered but refused to believe it. His silver was probably stolen, and he wanted it located or reimbursed. He had useful contacts in Scandinavia but little way to reach them. In such a delicate situation, a personal touch was necessary. In 1796, Wollstonecraft agreed to go make inquiries. Accompanied only by Marguerite and two-year-old Fanny, she headed north into the icy sea. While seeking the ship or news of its fate, she wrote many letters to Imlay. In these letters, she begs for Imlay's love, but it was not only the American whose absence she felt. She also mourns 'a dear friend, the friend of my youth'—Fanny Blood—feeling that 'still she is present', somehow.[65]

In Scandinavia, Wollstonecraft never found the silver ship, nor did she productively intercede on Imlay's behalf. Compounding these disappointments, upon her return to England, she found that Imlay had taken up lodgings with a new mistress. She again attempted suicide. This time, she threw herself into the Thames with wet, heavy clothing, but was rescued by strangers and resuscitated. Having decided to live, she published her missives to Imlay as *Letters Written During a Short Residence in Sweden, Norway, and Denmark* (1796). Of course, she redacted any reference to the illegal silver ship and made it seem as if her voyage was one of pure self-discovery, without a practical purpose. In this version of her Scandinavian adventures, she finds the independence that she had always craved. For instance, near Gothenburg, Sweden:

> Rocks were piled upon rocks, forming a suitable bulwark to the ocean.
> "Come no further," they emphatically said ... I gazed round with
> rapture ... delighted by the rude beauties of the scene.[66]

She also paints baby Fanny as an adventuress in her own right. In a field of wild strawberries, 'the gaiety of my babe was unmixed'.[67] Fanny, Wollstonecraft claims, preferred the bright wild fruits to toys.[68] Perhaps this made her take after Fanny Blood, illustrator of London's wild vegetation.

Upon publication, *Letters* achieved quick fame and genuinely entertained its audience. If Wollstonecraft the revolutionary was unpalatable to many, Wollstonecraft the adventuress was an eccentric worth tolerating for the vicarious pleasures of extreme armchair travel. One of the original readers most captivated by Wollstonecraft's *Letters* was William Godwin, the anarchist dinner guest of Johnson who in 1791 had been frustrated with Wollstonecraft's loquaciousness. Fifteen years later, he found her travel narrative 'a book calculated to make a man [fall] in love with its author'.[69]

WILLIAM GODWIN.

William Godwin. (British Library)

These are strong words for a writer whose own *magnum opus,* the treatise *Inquiry Concerning Political Justice,* offers to explain the workings of human society but, as his biographer St Clair observes, does not contain a single instance of the word 'love'.[70]

Still, Godwin was far from heartless. In fact, to many radicals of Wollstonecraft's acquaintance, Godwin was nothing less than a hero. In 1794, the British elite feared that domestic radicals would foment a revolution like that of France, terminating the monarchy and inaugurating a reign of terror. The government cracked down on dissent in all its manifestations, from print, sermons, theatrical performances, and public and private gatherings of all varieties. Several prominent radicals were arrested for treason. They included Godwin's friend Thomas Holcroft. A playwright and translator of French drama; notably, Beaumarchais's radical, politically prophetic *The Marriage of Figaro* (1781, trans. 1784), Holcroft also belonged to the radical London Corresponding Society and supported the publication of Paine's *Rights of Man.*[71] Godwin responded to the arrests by publishing a polemic arguing that the authorities had not correctly interpreted the English law that they levied against the supposed traitors. *Cursory Strictures on the Charge Delivered by the Lord Chief Justice Eyre to the Grand Jury* (1794) was widely read and anonymously attacked by a reactionary polemic, *An Answer to Cursory Strictures,* to which Godwin wrote back in print, extending what had quickly become a pamphlet war.

Godwin further risked his life by attending the Treason Trials in person. It was a well-calculated risk, for, on account of the *Cursory Strictures* phenomenon, they ended with the acquittal of all defendants. When Holcroft was acquitted, he and Godwin remained in the courtroom. They sat together in the gallery, watching the final trial, that of orator John Thelwall. This moment is powerfully captured in a sketch that shows both Holcroft's relief and Godwin's taut, concerned face as he paid rapt attention to the arguments. This sketch and its context reveal Godwin as a quiet, attentive hero and a man as devoted to his friend as Wollstonecraft had been to the dying Fanny Skeys. Only, when Godwin came to the assistance of Holcroft and the other suspected traitors, did he succeed in vanquishing injustice and death.

He was also not unattractive. In the Treason Trials sketch, Godwin's unpowdered hair is relatively long but neat, at once romantic and Spartan. At forty-one, he was the same age Gilbert Imlay had been when Wollstonecraft met him, but, peering through fine wire-rimmed spectacles, he was opposite in type to the self-fashioned frontier-

150

settler. Godwin immediately captivated Wollstonecraft just as her *Letters* had captivated him. Still, he may have seemed odd. Imlay had turned out a seasoned serial *roué*, Godwin in 1795 had probably never experienced a sexual or romantic relationship. The disproportionate risks that women took in relationships with men must have seemed even more evident to him when he saw Wollstonecraft with her fatherless, toddling daughter in tow, but political and philosophical conversation brought them together, eventually at home and alone. They became lovers. As documented by William St Clair and other biographers, theirs was one of the great love affairs of intellectual history. Wollstonecraft confided in him how she had treasured Fanny Blood and mourned her loss. In him, she found a friend who could requite her love as neither Fanny, Fuseli, nor Imlay ever did.

Their relationship constituted a microcosmic social revolution. They kept separate houses and literary vocations. As Godwin's diary indicates, they tried to practice birth control. When it failed, they married, but only in the simplest possible ceremony, the fact of which they shared with very few of their acquaintances. They intended it only to legitimise their child, particularly in the event that it should prove male. Wollstonecraft, no longer 'Mrs. Imlay', also did not call herself Mrs Godwin. On 30 August 1797, when she went into labour, Wollstonecraft expected to be up and working the next day.

That did not happen, though. The birth was difficult and although she delivered a living daughter, the placenta refused to emerge. Godwin, panicking, called in several physicians, one of whom extracted parts of the placenta with his unsterilised hands. Wollstonecraft contracted puerperal fever and passed away on 10 September 1797. As Godwin would write in the first biography of her, *Memoir of the Author of Vindication of the Rights of Woman* (1798), she was memorable for that achievement and as a proponent in the radical ideas that education could reveal the inherent equality of all human beings and that arbitrary custom should not dictate sexuality, domestic organisation, or intellectual communion.

Twenty-one years later, their daughter Mary Shelley saw the publication of her own enduring novel *Frankenstein, or, the Modern Prometheus* (1818). At the centre of this novel's concentric frames of metafictional narration is a woman named Safie. Born in Turkey, Safie travels to Geneva, on horseback and nearly alone, in order to find freedom and experience love. More remarkable than Safie, however, is her late mother. Safie 'spoke in high and enthusiastic terms of her mother, who, born in freedom, spurned … bondage'. This woman 'taught her' daughter 'to aspire to higher powers of intellect and an independence of spirit'. These 'lessons were indelibly impressed on the mind of Safie, who sickened at the prospect of … being immured within the walls of a harem, allowed only to occupy herself with infantile amusements, ill-suited to the temper of her soul, now accustomed to grand ideas and a noble emulation for virtue'. She yearns to inhabit 'a country where women [a]re allowed to take a rank in society'.[72] This sounds very much like Mary Wollstonecraft's hopes of December 1792, when she embarked for revolutionary France. Despite the Orientalist trappings of Shelley's story, Safie's mother is Shelley's idea of the mother she knew only from her writings and Godwin's recollection. Shelley apparently named Safie after a heroine from an interior tale of the *Arabian Nights,* but critics have observed that the name functions as a pun for

'Sophie', which is both the name of the infantilised heroine of Jean-Jacques Rousseau's pedagogical treatise *Emile* (1763) and the Greek word for wisdom, as in the root of the word 'philosophy'.[73] This anecdote—brief, strange, but the kernel at the very centre of *Frankenstein*'s meta-narratival box puzzle—is a most apt memorial to Mary Wollstonecraft.

Notes

1. Alison Johnson, *Louis XVI and the French Revolution* (Jefferson, NC: McFarland, 2013), 184.
2. Ibid.
3. Ibid.
4. Mary Wollstonecraft, "Letter on the Present Character of the French Nation," *A Wollstonecraft Anthology,* edited by Janet Todd (New York: Columbia University Press, 1990), 121-4, 123.
5. Ibid.
6. Wollstonecraft, "Letter to Joseph Johnson," *A Wollstonecraft Anthology,* 120-2, 120.
7. Ibid.
8. Wollstonecraft, "Letter to Joseph Johnson," 121.
9. Ibid.
10. Lyndall Gordon, *Vindication: A Life of Mary Wollstonecraft* (New York: HarperCollins, 2005), 6.
11. Janet Todd, *Mary Wollstonecraft: A Revolutionary Life* (New York: Columbia University Press, 2000), 3.
12. Todd, *Mary Wollstonecraft: A Revolutionary Life,* 4.
13. Gordon, *Vindication.* 13.
14. William St. Clair, *The Reading Nation in the Romantic Period* (Cambridge: Cambridge University Press, 2004).
15. Gordon, *Vindication,* 15.
16. Gordon, *vindication,* 17.
17. Gordon, *Vindication,* 16-17; William Curtis, *Flora Londinensis* (London: William Curtis, 1777), 2 vols.
18. Gregory Dart, *Metropolitan Art and Literature, 1810-1840: Cockney Adventures* (Cambridge: Cambridge University Press, 2012), 26.
19. Quoted in Todd, *Mary Wollstonecraft: a Revolutionary Life,* 23.
20. Ibid.
21. Ibid.
22. Nicole Reynolds, "Cottage Industry: The Ladies of Llangollen and the Symbolic Capital of the Cottage Ornée," *The Eighteenth Century* 51, no.1 and 2 (2010): 211-227, 219.
23. Reynolds, "Cottage Industry," 212.
24. Ibid, 219.

25. Ibid, 211.
26. Ibid, 213.
27. Gordon, *Vindication,* 42.
28. Ibid, 53.
29. Ibid, 48.
30. *Mary Wollstonecraft and Newington Green: An Anthology,* curated by E.J. Clery with contributions by Miriam Al Jamil, Anna Birch, Hannah Dawson, Charlotte May, Bee Rowlatt, and Barbara Gold Taylor. Newington Green Meeting House, 27 April 2020. https://www.ngmh.org.uk/wp-content/uploads/2020/04/W-NG-Anthology-draft-with-images-1.pdf . Shared with permission.
31. Jon Mee, *Conversable Worlds: Literature, Contention, and Community 1762-1830* (Oxford: Oxford University Press, 2011), 81.
32. Ibid.
33. Ibid.
34. Mee, *Conversable Worlds,* 31.
35. Quoted in Gordon, *Vindication,* 70.
36. Wollstonecraft, *Thoughts on the Education of Daughters*, *Anthology,* 27-40, 32.
37. Ibid, 35.
38. Ibid, 38.
39. Ibid, 39.
40. Gordon, *Vindication,* 94; Emily W. Sunstein, *Mary Shelley: Romance and Reality* (Baltimore: Johns Hopkins University Press, 1991), 187.
41. *Wikimedia Commons.* Image created under a Creative Commons Licence.
42. *Wikimedia Commons.* Image created under a Creative Commons Licence.
43. *Wikimedia Commons.* Image created under a Creative Commons Licence.
44. Todd, *Mary Wollstonecraft: A Revolutionary Life,* 164.
45. Wollstonecraft, *A Vindication of the Rights of Men, Anthology,* 64-83, 71.
46. Wollstonecraft, *Rights of Men,* 74.
47. Ibid.
48. Wollstonecraft, *Rights of Men,* 75-7.
49. Wollstonecraft, *Rights of Men,* 82.
50. Todd, *Mary Wollstonecraft: A Revolutionary Life,* 164.
51. Ibid, 166.
52. Ibid, 168.
53. Mee, *Conversable Worlds,* 141.
54. Wollstonecraft, *A Vindication of the Rights of Woman, Anthology,* 84-113, 86.
55. Ibid.
56. Ibid.
57. Wollstonecraft, *A Vindication of the Rights of Woman,* 102-3.
58. Ibid, 109-114.
59. Todd, *Mary Wollstonecraft: A Revolutionary Life,* 184.
60. Todd, *Mary Wollstonecraft: A Revolutionary Life,* 184-5; Kathleen Béres Rogers, *Creating Romantic Obsession: Scorpions in the Mind* (Cham, Switzerland: Palgrave, 2019), 56-7.

61. Todd, *Mary Wollstonecraft: A Revolutionary Life,* 185.
62. Richard Polwhele, *The Unsex'd Females* (Shrewsbury, Massachusetts: Garland, 1974), 13.
63. Wollstonecraft, "An Historical and Moral View of ... the French Revolution," *Anthology,* 125-142, 128.
64. Ibid.
65. Wollstonecraft, *Letters Written During a Short Residence in Sweden, Norway, and Denmark* (London: Cassell, 1889), 18.
66. Ibid.
67. Mary Wollstonecraft, *Letters Written During a Short Residence in Sweden, Norway, and Denmark* (London: Cassell, 1889), 18.
68. Ibid.
69. Quoted in William St. Clair, *The Godwins and the Shelleys: A Biography of a Family* (New York: W.W. Norton, 1989), 161.
70. St. Clair, *The Godwins and the Shelleys,* 140.
71. Mark Philp, *Reforming Ideas in Britain: Politics and Language in the Shadow of the French Revolution, 1789-1815* (Cambridge: Cambridge University Press, 2013), 216.
72. Mary Shelley, *Frankenstein, or, the Modern Prometheus (1818),* edited by D.L. Macdonald and Kathleen Scherf, 3rd. ed. (Peterborough, Ontario: Broadview, 2012), 139.
73. This critical trend is summarised in Jerrold E. Hogle, "Romantic Contexts," *The Cambridge Companion to Mary Shelley,* edited by Esther Schor (Cambridge: Cambridge University Press, 2003), 41-55, 47.

Section Four

The Nineteenth Century

The Peterloo Massacre

Sam Quill

"To love, and bear; to hope till Hope creates
From its own wreck the thing it contemplates."
Percy B. Shelley, 'Prometheus Unbound' (1819)

"We are a physical representation."
John Boyega, 'Black Lives Matter' protest,
Hyde Park, 3 June 2020

In the heat of an August afternoon in 1817, between 60,000 and 80,000 people met in St Peter's Field in Manchester to agitate in the cause of electoral reform. Soon at least fifteen were dead and some 600 more were gravely injured; some of those would die of their wounds in the weeks to come. They were killed by the British state, specifically by the sabres of the Manchester and Salford Yeomanry and the 15th Hussars (and under the hooves of their horses) who charged on the crowd, slashing and crushing their way to the raised wooden hustings at its centre. These are the facts as we have them. Soon afterwards the Manchester Observer wrote of the 'Peterloo Massacre'. The name stuck. What follows not only sets out, as plainly as possibly, the events of 16 August 1817 and their various causes and consequences, but seeks also to understand how Peterloo shapes the continuing mythos of English Radicalism.

The first part shows how the march to St Peter's Field drew on Lancashire custom and civic performance, and that, as such, events were turned towards mythmaking long before the first sword was raised. The second attempts to articulate the day's violence in reductive and material terms, shorn as far as possible of the liberalising rhetoric that too often mediates accounts of the massacre; I will show that violence does not express argument, but that argument reduces to violence. In the third part, I examine the slaughter's contested afterlife, and how to this day it shapes the way British culture imagines political resistance.

The March

There emerged, in the wake of the massacre, two very different accounts of the march to St Peter's Field. Both cannot be true and each was fashioned under the pressures of legal argument in pursuit of some desired outcome at the trial of those charged with sedition in Peterloo's aftermath. To the state, the marchers were a pseudo-militarised block, armed and so providing ample justification for the violence with which it met them. At the trial of Henry 'Orator' Hunt and eight others,[1] at the York Assizes in March 1820, the Crown's case was that they conspired:

> unlawfully, maliciously and seditiously to meet […] in a formidable and menacing manner and in military procession and array with Clubs, Sticks and other offensive Weapons and instruments and with diverse Seditious and inflammatory inscriptions and devices to the great alarm and terror of the peaceably disposed subjects of […] the King.[2]

One of the accused, Samuel Bamford, called as a witness one James Dyson. Dyson was his neighbour from Middleton, a village outside of Manchester, from which one of the main contingents of marchers came. He recalled things differently:

> The wives of several of the party accompanied their husbands. There were several hundred of women with our party and the Rochdale party. I saw many of them at Manchester […] the women who accompanied us were relatives of the men who marched in the procession. It is customary at our wakes and rush-carts in Lancashire to have banners and music; the rush-carts are held on a Saturday, and on the following Monday the men walk in procession, but they do not keep the step.[3]

A 'rush-cart', as Bamford clarified to the court, is 'a cart in which rushes are neatly placed; this cart is drawn by young men decorated with ribbons, and preceded by young women, music, etc'.[4] Such carts were a part of Lancashire tradition; they would appear annually during the 'wakes week' festivities, when new rushes were brought in to replace the old on church floors. Dyson's vision of Merrie England, so at odds with the claims of the state, is echoed in at least one source that wasn't part of a criminal defence. Jeremiah Garnett, a reporter for the loyalist *Manchester Courier*, remarked that '[a] number of women, boys, and even children were in the procession, which had from this circumstance, more the appearance of a large village party going to a merry-making than that of a body of people advancing to overthrow the government of their country'.[5] *The Courier* suppressed the report. Garnett wrote also of 'flags and music' and that the people 'came in a sort of marching order'. He added an evocative detail: '[they] were covered with dust, having as I learnt come from some town at a distance'.[6] Imagine how strange, how almost otherworldly, such a procession would look among Manchester's mills and factories. We can readily feel how it might have been intimidating, how it might even have struck the Yeomanry as a threat, who were, for the most part, the well-heeled sons of local industrialists. Perhaps its strangeness was the point.

Most of the marchers had come from out of town. Sometimes from industrialised places, like Oldham and Stockport, sometimes from more rural ones, such as

Saddleworth or, as was the case with Bamford, Middleton. 16 August fell on a Monday that year. Workers in the factories would have been prevented from leaving their machines, and so for that reason were excluded. The marchers, on the other hand, were largely drawn from the hand-loom industry, which was then still a cottage industry – they worked from home. The working week for those in factories ran from Monday to Saturday. The hand-loom weavers, however, were not yet tied so strictly to a factory clock. They kept to an older way of time, traditionally marking what was called a Saint Monday, whereby they worked from Tuesday till Saturday, and then took two days off. Since payday was on Saturday, the press of industry was not yet felt keenly on Monday mornings. So on Monday, 16 August, they were free to march, along with their families, to the rally on St Peter's Field. The incursion into Manchester that morning was then not only an incursion of people who were in some degree already strangers, it also was an incursion of one way of life on another, in which the former structured its labour in a fashion which was a challenge to the twin hegemonies of capital and wool. This was an incursion of the edges upon the centre; of the parish upon the town; of the past upon the present. These dynamics of subversion were inscribed on the spatiotemporal facts of events, regardless of the demeanour of the marchers. It is important to remember this before taking the accounts of their jollity at face value. Under the right circumstances, even a rush-cart procession can be a howl of anger and pain.

The marchers had passed the weeks leading up to 18 August in mending and cleaning their best clothes. The men wore shirts bleached dazzlingly white. Such an aesthetic looks, from one angle, like Sunday Best, and from another like military uniform. For some weeks in July and August, on the moors behind the villages, there had been drilling and marching practice in the middle of the night. What the drilling meant to those doing it is lost to memory. Samuel Bamford would suggest much later that the purpose was solely to keep the marchers in good order, and so to avoid offering any pretext on which the state could offer violence. Recounting a version of the speech that he gave to the Middleton contingent before they set off, he noted, 'I requested they would not leave their ranks, nor shew carelessness, not inattention to the orders of their leaders; but that they would walk comfortably and agreeably together'.[7] But Bamford's *Passages in the Life of a Radical* (1840-1844), for all its genuine value as an account of the conditions of the working class after the Napoleonic Wars, was composed years after Peterloo, and was to some extent an attempt not only to mind the reputation of the by-then older man, but to launder events such that they both cohered with and propagandised for the gradualist, reformist agenda of Chartism in the 1840s. The spectre of the wars with France overhangs Peterloo, and not only in its name, coined in mocking reference to the Battle of Waterloo, then still a recent memory. Many who marched to St Peter's Field had fought in those wars. Military life and the memory of its traditions had, on the return of the soldiers to Lancashire, enmeshed with the local ways. Robert Poole gives an account their mixing, in particular reference to music:

> Musicians, too, were familiar in village life: the bassoonist who played
> for the march to St Peter's Field also played in the parish church band;
> the drum belonged to a farmer, and was occasionally used in oratorios at

the church; the fifer and drummer would have had military experience, probably as volunteers, and would thus have played both for local manoeuvres and for the rush carts and Morris dancers. The military fife and drum was becoming a folk tradition.[8]

The songs they played were often patriotic or religious pieces. If the march was a demonstration of anti-establishment feeling, it was one that marshalled the resources of establishment culture to turn the state's mythopoetic weaponry back on itself. A veteran of Waterloo who is proud of his war record has all the more reason to abjure a state that refuses to acknowledge his place in its body politic. Bamford's suggestion that the military aspects of the march are misunderstood strikes me as post-hoc. I want to draw us away from the dichotomy that the legal exigencies of the trial have forced on historical memory, in which the marchers are either safe or dangerous and nothing in between, and to try to recall us to the moment of Peterloo in its strangeness and historical specificity.

The iconography of the march might help in this aspect. The marchers carried banners, or 'colours' as they called them (a military term), decoratively emblazoned with slogans and demands. Bamford mentions, 'a blue one of silk, with inscriptions in gold letters, 'Unity and Strength.' 'Liberty and Fraternity.' A green one of silk, with golden letters, 'Parliaments Annual', 'Suffrage Universal'.[9] What Bamford chooses to mention is, again, revealing. From the perspective of the 1840s, the demands appear perfectly consistent with constitutionalist Chartism. To many they would have seemed uncontroversial – at least, not radical – and would have served to establish Peterloo as a kind of venerable ancestor of progressive reformism. This is even more true when we look from the twenty-first century. The account is an early instance of the curation of Peterloo's myth, in which it is presented as part of an inevitable sequence of events that nudge each other, domino-like, towards the instantiation of liberal democracy. This reading deploys a whiggish teleology of human progress, in which the demands of Peterloo are considered so eminently reasonable that they were, in due time (and without violence or much struggle) acceded. The problem with this argument is that the demand for universal suffrage was, in 1817, radical. There was huge resistance to the expansion of the vote from powerful and wealthy interests; participatory democracy was not the hallmark of liberal virtue in a state that it has since become in much of the developed West. More significant is the context of such a demand, and the political company that those making it would implicitly have kept.

In 1792, France extended suffrage to all males over the age of twenty-one. Male suffrage is, of course, not 'universal', and an argument can be made that the banner carried at Peterloo demands something more radical than what was granted in France. Suffrage was included in the 1793 Robespierrist Constitution, and repealed in the Constitution of 1795. Its repeal serves only further to radicalise the demand, and by 1819, it would have been seen as a radical and Republican cause for which to advocate, and Republicanism was, in the minds of those who weren't Republicans, inextricably linked to the Terror. This is the geopolitical and imaginative context of the demands made at Peterloo: the expansion of suffrage was still a 'Jacobin' concern. That alone was perhaps not enough to trouble those who held power, but combine it with the cry of 'Liberty and Fraternity' – echoing the French Republican motto, 'Liberté, égalité, fraternité' – and the presence among the marchers of Caps of Liberty, and the political aesthetics signal something quite other than what Bamford and those who follow him describe.

The Cap of Liberty, or Phrygian Cap, was a potent political symbol. In Ancient Rome, it was the sign of a manumitted slave. It had, more recently, adopted a sanguine scarlet colour and been worn in France as a symbol of revolution. The Cap, a pointed soft hat of velvet, was carried by some of the marchers on long poles, in a similar fashion to the banners. Bamford notes that after the banners in the Middleton contingent came, 'on a staff, a handsome cap of crimson velvet, with a tuft of laurel, and the cap tastefully braided with the word, Libertas, in front'.[10] Bamford 'tastefully' tries just a little too hard to obscure what the Cap would have meant to the person carrying it. It was a statement of tacit support for the Jacobin cause. Not everybody on the march was a Jacobin sympathiser, much less did they all seek to ferment a new English Revolution, but the prominence and potency of the symbol should not be downplayed. This is clear when we remember that Bamford's own downplaying occurs in the very specific contexts of his ongoing fight, either to retain his own liberty, or to advocate for an expanded suffrage in the later context of the constitutionalist tactics of Chartism.

Finally, in order to understand what brought them to St Peter's Field, we might look at where the people had come from, not geographically so much as in the emotional and material circumstances of their lives. After the wars with France had ended with the Battle of Waterloo and Napoleon's second exile, soldiers returned home and expected change. The public had paid dearly to finance the European campaign, not only through taxation but through the increased cost of living that had followed as a consequence of an embargo on the importation of French goods and the disruption of trade with the continent. This was felt most keenly in relation to the cost of bread. During the war, since only domestic farms were able to supply the domestic appetite, prices had risen because of a decreased supply. This made domestic landowners very rich. When the war was over and trade opened up, they were not happy to lose their increased profits. They lobbied parliament (indeed, many were MPs) to introduce laws that would fix the price of grain higher than the market would otherwise have set it, and so to make up for the money they would otherwise have lost. These were called the Corn Laws. Of course, keeping the price of bread artificially high, while it kept the landowners happy, made life harder for the working people. Not only was the postwar recession a strain on their finances, it was also being made worse by laws that plainly served to benefit those who already had very much, while others went hungry.

Under these circumstances, what modes of redress were open to the Peterloo marchers? They could hardly advocate for their own cause in parliament. In 1819, there were two members of parliament for the whole county of Lancashire, and the town of Manchester itself had no specific representation. Of the near-million people in the county only 17,000 could vote and these were all landowning men.[11] More broadly, the idea that even under a limited suffrage there was meaningful democratic representation was laughable. Before the Reform Act of 1832, the country was riddled with 'rotten boroughs'. These were constituencies which had, at one time, been populous and so justified MPs, but which had, for whatever reason, declined in population to such an extent that a member might now represent only a tiny number of people.

A particularly fantastic example is Dunwich in Suffolk, which had once been a thriving medieval port. At the time of the Norman Conquest, the population numbered about 3,000. The Suffolk coast, being very frangible, the town has, over the centuries, gradually disappeared beneath the North Sea waves, where much of it remains to this day. In 1817, it had a single voter and two members of parliament. Such egregious examples are rare, but not so rare as to be of no use in illustrating both why democratic reform was necessary, and the uselessness of the existing system in serving those who sought reform by constitutional means.

To compound these frustrations, political agitating was, wherever it appeared, suppressed with urgency and enthusiasm. The government, through its spymaster, Viscount Sidmouth, operated a vast network of domestic surveillance. Though Napoleon was defeated, the spirit of radical politics that had shaken the globe in the latter part of the eighteenth century – not only in France, but also in the young United States of America, in Ireland, in Haiti, and in Venezuela among others – was still very much in the air. The government, and its allies in Europe's *ancien régime*, could not rest content with Napoleon exiled on St Helena. They were always alert for new stirrings of revolution at home. Among the better-known recipients of the attention of the Georgian state's intelligence community is the poet Percy Bysshe Shelley, whose activities, at least before he left for Italy in March 1818, and especially in his earlier years when he travelled to Ireland in vociferous support of Catholic Emancipation, were monitored by Sidmouth's spies. We will return to Shelley later. The climate of oppression was felt by Britain's working people in the prohibition on trade unions, which were not legal until 1824. As with the parlous state of democratic representation in Westminster, such a grip on political organising served only to make the physical presence of people on St Peter's Field, with the implied strength in numbers and everything that entailed, all the more necessary in being one of the few avenues for political articulation which remained open the people who gathered there.

Peterloo shows us that sometimes political arguments are articulated with bodies, not words, and that when they are it is not always the decision of those making the arguments. It is precisely their position outside of democratic means that made the marchers at Peterloo so particular, and which still makes the march so unlike what we often think of as a protest today. As Poole writes, 'Neither predemocratic mob nor post-democratic demonstration, the reformers played out the role of unenfranchised citizens, presenting the government with the unanswerable physical presence of vast bodies of freeborn Englishmen and women assembled to proclaim their lost rights'.[12] We can say more. The force of the march seems to have been not only in its mobilisation of a physical presence of people, but also in its instantiation of mythic and symbolic elements to counter the emergent ideological forms of industrial capital. They fought not only by means of flesh and words, but with, and within, the space between words and flesh. We will return to this ambiguity, this slippage between words and flesh, and between argument and violence, later in the chapter. For now, it is important to remember the anger, the hunger and the seriousness of the people who marched, and not to run with the story written for the ears of the courts, that Peterloo was a carnival gone wrong.

The Massacre

In his poem 'Sixteen Dead Men', about Ireland's Easter Rising, W. B. Yeats asks, 'And is their logic to outweigh | MacDonagh's bony thumb ?' (11-12).[13] Thomas MacDonagh was a leader in the movement which took over Dublin's General Post Office and other key buildings in Dublin during Easter of 1916, as part of an attempt by Republicans to end the British occupation of Ireland, and was among the leaders executed by Britain in retaliation for his part. Yeats's question asks us to consider the relationship between the realm of ideas and that of things in the context of political struggle. Its implicit answer is, perhaps, 'no', that logic and bony thumbs exist in two wholly incommensurable scales. It is not just that we cannot translate between them, but that to conceive of a point where they make contact with each other is an imaginative impossibility. It is as good as to ask 'What colour is Tuesday?' or 'How tall is time?' The ethical consequences of that incommensurability bear heavily on any account of the Peterloo Massacre. The question of what actually occurred that afternoon is predictably vexed. Accounts in the aftermath differed and were, of course, not neutral. There were reporters present, notably John Tyas from *The Times* in London, who at first condemned the slain as rioters; their accounts must be read sceptically. It is likewise with witnesses giving statements after the fact: memories fade and are apt to be changed with time. Physical evidence is more reliable, and of that, sadly, there was plenty. We can survey the damage, then reverse-engineer an idea of what must have happened for that damage to be done. We can count the dead and examine the wounds and know the kind of violence that occurred. Any retelling of that day must rest, ultimately, on tangible facts.

E. P. Thompson's seminal account of Peterloo diverges from my own in that he emphasises the helplessness of the marchers.[14] It is certainly true that Hunt in particular took pains to urge calm in the week before the event; this does not diminish the radicalism of the demand, nor the radical ambiguity of the march's aesthetics. Thompson's claim seems concerned mostly to emphasise the fact that, once the violence began, there was no fair fight. On that, we agree. He draws attention to 'the actual bloody violence of the day', how, 'It really was a massacre'.[15] Thompson gives the following harrowing summation of the aftermath. His estimation of the number of dead is lower than that now generally agreed upon, and the number of injuries 'authenticated' by the Peterloo Relief Committee (in order to qualify the injured person for financial aid) is not the same as the total number injured. Here are some tangible facts:

> Eleven were killed or died from their wounds. That evening, on every road out of Manchester the injured were to be seen. The Peterloo Relief Committee had, by the end of 1819, authenticated 421 claims for relief for injuries received on the field (a further 150 cases still

awaited investigation). Of these, 161 cases were of sabre wounds, the remainder were injuries sustained while lying beneath the crowd or beneath the horses' hooves. More than 100 of the injured were women or girls.[16]

Having seen these facts we can ask how it came to that. What kinds of blunders and which wilful acts of aggression led to that death toll and those injuries? By the time the marchers were gathered on St Peter's Field, they were accompanied in significant numbers by the authorities. There were no police in the modern sense, but 300 to 400 volunteer special constables had been hastily recruited. On top of them, the Manchester and Salford Yeomanry, and the 15th Hussars were called in. The latter were professional soldiers. The former, as I have said, was a ragtag brigade, not well trained, and consisting, in Thompson's words, 'of the Manchester manufacturers, merchants, publicans, and shopkeepers on horseback'.[17] Hunt published a list of the occupations of the Yeomanry who were present that day: they included several sons of publicans and manufacturers, a wine merchant, commission agent, dancing-master, cheese-monger, and butcher.[18] These were not working class people and the class context is crucial. Again, Thompson puts it best: 'There is no other term for this but class war'.[19] He emphasises the vindictiveness of the fight. If representative forces of labour and capital were pitted against each other that day, they were embodied in the flesh and spilt blood of the people involved; we turn again to bodies and bony thumbs. The Yeomanry were 'the men who pursued the banners, knew the speakers by name and sought to pay off old scores, and who mustered and cheered at the end of their triumph'.[20] There is something grotesque in that last detail; the cheer, as a reaffirmation of the social bond among those men, is possible only on the back of and in conclusion to the violence they have jointly committed, as a ruling class against that part of the body politic to which they entirely owe their wealth and status. They had sharpened their swords in preparation.

They were not, however, acting alone. Overlooking the field, both judicially and literally, were the local magistrates. While the soldiers were under the command of Lieutenant Colonel L'Estrange and Lieutenant Colonel Leighton Dalrymple, the magistrates had direct control of the Yeomanry. They met earlier that day at the Star Inn on Deansgate, and from there moved to a house on Mount Street, owned by a Mr Buxton, which had large front windows offering a vantage point from which to monitor the field below. Looking down the length of the streets they could watch the marchers approaching; they could see shops boarded up by nervous shopkeepers, and the raised wooden hustings from which Hunt and the others would speak. The numbers swelled throughout the late morning, until more than sixty thousand people were crammed into St Peter's Field. The magnitude of that number is felt when we consider that the populations of Manchester and Salford, in 1805, were estimated at a combined one hundred thousand people. At around a quarter past one, 'Orator' Hunt's carriage entered the field. A band struck up Handel's 'See The Conquering Hero Comes'. Hunt's arrival was greeted by what Bamford described later as a 'universal shout'.[21] The cry was heard in the room where the magistrates watched.

The order of the events that followed is not certain. We know that Hunt was able to begin his speech:

> Friends and fellow-countrymen, I must beg your indulgence for a short time, and beg that you will keep silence. I hope that you will exercise the all-powerful right of the people in an orderly manner.[22]

His plea is consistent with the placating tone of organisers in the week preceding. That it was heard by all present is doubtful. And it was not, anyway, enough to assuage the magistrates. At some point after that 'universal shout', before or just after Hunt began to speak, they called for the cavalry reinforcements who had mustered nearby, and set about issuing a warrant for Hunt's arrest, along with that of Joseph Johnson, John Knight and James Moorhouse, who had been with Hunt in the carriage. What caused the magistrates' actions remains uncertain. It seems likely that they were spooked by the volume of people and their sudden display of unity, and moreover that they desired to shield private property from the possibility of damage in civil unrest.

There was also, it was later attested, paranoia among them regarding the scale of events. They feared that the meeting at St Peter's Field might be part of a wider mobilisation in the country, even that they were witnessing the first stirrings of revolt. William Hulton, an owner of land and coal mines, Chairman of the Lancashire and Cheshire Magistrates, and he who summoned the Yeomanry to the field that day, later claimed that when he called for the horses he, 'took it for granted that the meeting in Manchester was part of a great scheme in the district, of the existence of which they had received the most undoubted information some time before'.[23] There was no great scheme but in any case, the cavalry came, sabres drawn. It was supposed that the presence of the horses would allow Joseph Nadin, the leading special constable, to make his way through the crowd to the hustings, where he would make arrests.

At some point after the drawing up of the arrest warrant, and before the arrival of the horses, the Riot Act was apparently read. Charles Ethelston, one of the magistrates, read the act in full, first from ground level and then, being unsatisfied with that, from the upstairs window of Mr Buxton's house. He could not be heard. There is some dispute in the records over whether it was read at all. The act provided for the clearance of a gathering by soldiers if crowds did not disperse peacefully within an hour of its being read. In the event, it is at least certain that warning was not adequately given, and that people in the field had no idea what was about to happen.

The Reverend Edward Stanley, who watched from Mr Buxton's house, conjures the first moments of carnage hauntingly.[24] He describes how a group, mainly women, who were standing on raised ground behind the hustings, along Windmill Street, suddenly turned to flee. They had seen the horses approaching. Others were stood with their backs to the advance, unaware of what was coming towards them. By the time they arrived at the rally, the Yeomanry had already mown down William Fildes; he was two years old, and would die of his injuries. When the cavalry first appeared they were riding at a gallop, which meant that they would continue to gallop until an order was given to stop them. They had, by some accounts, spent the morning drinking. By Bamford's account they came around a corner, sabres drawn, then 'reigned up in a line' in front of Buxton's house.[25] The panic that had begun on the higher ground was now spread throughout the crowd. Those at the edges frayed into side streets, those in the centre began to crush and heave. The horses advanced a little way into the mass. Hunt appealed for calm but to no effect. The resolve of the march had been broken by this show of incommensurate force. At the point when the people scattered the state had, in a very real sense, defeated the day's cause: it was then unable to succeed in its original aims. It could only be redeemed as myth.

Grim irony is at play when an occasion that was planned with oratory at its centre becomes remembered in history for its violence and the number of dead. In the event, the horseman charged the crowd, 'sabering right and left in all directions', as Hunt reports it, 'Sparing neither age, nor sex, nor rank'.[26] The Yeomanry pressed into the massed bodies and towards the hustings, 'riding over and sabring all that could not get out of their way'.[27] Bamford recalls that their 'sabres were plied to hew a way through naked held-up hands, and defenceless heads; and then chopped limbs, and wound-gaping skulls were seen; and groans and cries were mingled with the din of that horrid confusion'.[28] The physicality of the account is graphic; people become collections of body parts – hands, heads, limbs – that have been, or are about to become, separated. Poole writes that 'The response of the outmanoeuvred authorities at St Peter's Field certainly went beyond the rhetorical. They cut the Gordian knot using the only political weapon which the reformers had not successfully appropriated to their cause: military force. It was a closure with casualties'.[29] Bamford's almost gothic focus on the physicality of wounds, as he recalls the massacre some years later, is telling. In responding to the state's replacement of rhetoric with violence, violence itself becomes the rhetorical energy. He redeems his political arguments through building the myth of Peterloo as a slaughter of the innocents.

Contemporary illustration of the Peterloo Massacre. (Wikimedia Commons)

The Myth

If the slaughter on St Peter's Field were the end of an argument in violence, then the afterlife of the massacre has seen its recuperation into political rhetoric. The name 'Peterloo' has a talismanic quality in radical discussion, its mere utterance a byword for a thousand assumptions that subsume the realities of August 1819 in a conquering myth. In what remains of this chapter, I will first examine the immediate aftermath of Peterloo and its consequences for radicalism in Britain, then I will turn to the broader consequences of the massacre and its memorialisation, for the way in which we speak about protest in Britain today. I have two central propositions: that the dichotomy which divides protests into either 'carnival' or 'riot' can be meaningfully traced to the necessities of legal defence in the trials following Peterloo, and that the Peterloo Massacre is most significant to British Radicalism precisely as a myth, for its talismanic magic, not for the change it affected.

To reiterate what I have said above: the British state won at Peterloo. From the moment the rally scattered it was effectively over, the magistrates having silenced politics under hoof and sabre. In terms of the freedom to organise politically and to protest, Britain was worse off after Peterloo than it was before. Between 17 November and 30 December 1819, the government passed a series of laws known as the Six Acts in direct response to the meeting and events in its wake. These laws were designed to stifle agitation for change. In addition to acts regulating firearms possession and the ability of civilians to receive military training, and an act to make it easier to imprison people and harder to bail them, there was the Seditious Meetings Act, which heavily curtailed public gatherings and banned at such gatherings the holding of banners and signs, as well as the Blasphemous and Seditious Libels Act, which, put simply, criminalised radical writing (much of what was radical at the time was also either 'blasphemous' or 'seditious'). The sixth, The Newspaper and Stamp Duties Act, might sound obscure but it had far-reaching consequences. It raised and extended taxes on publications. The act was an attack on the press, meant to make life more difficult (and costly) for radical publishers. Under the Six Acts, the meeting at St Peter's Field would have been illegal.

In the window of time between the massacre at Peterloo and the passage of the acts, there was a marked increase in radical organising. It was this, in part, which panicked the authorities into passing new laws, and which was seen by parliament as sufficient justification for more draconian measures. Joseph Cozens argues convincingly that from the earliest weeks after the massacre, various forms of radicalism and reformism, and eventually Chartism, would construct a 'political martyrology'[30] of the Peterloo dead. Meetings became mass acts of public mourning:

> Two of the largest demonstrations took place on Hunslet Moor outside Leeds and on Newcastle Town Moor. At Leeds, 40,000 working people arrived at the Moor wearing black ribbons, while at Newcastle 25,000 marched in 'divisions' carrying white rods topped with black crepe.[31]

Cozens notes that 'One flag at Newcastle was dedicated 'to the immortal memory of the reformers massacred at Manchester'.[32] After the passage of the Six Acts, since emulating Peterloo was no longer legal, the impetus to venerate the meeting and slaughter at St Peter's Field was all the stronger.

As memories of the day faded, it became easier for people to make Peterloo martyrs in their own image. Radical politics was spilt after Peterloo. On the one hand, there was the old guard of revolutionary agitators, such as the Society of Spencian Philanthropists, who were driven underground into more hardline, violent actions. These included figures such as Arthur Thistlewood, who was prominent in the Spencians and who, in 1820, was central to the Cato Street Conspiracy, which sought to assassinate the British Cabinet. There was a spy among those conspirators and the plot was discovered. Having killed a policeman as he attempted to evade arrest, Thistlewood was hanged, and for a long time, such tactics were quieted. On the other hand, there is the tradition with which we are now much more familiar, and in whose image our own 'Peterloo' is made. While the Spencians sought to meet the state's refusal to engage rhetorically with their own equally robust refusal, the emergent Chartist tradition laundered the massacre's mythology to its own rhetorical ends. Chartism was gradualist, nonviolent and as such, in the context of the day, a more 'popular' movement. It sought change by constitutionalist means.

Accounts that emphasise the peaceable, non-threatening nature of the march, such as that which we find in Bamford's legal defence of himself and in his Passages, are amplified in the process of memorialisation. As Cozens puts it, 'strands of this powerful radical memory were adopted and perpetuated by British Chartist, Liberal and socialist traditions'.[33] The meeting on St Peter's Field became a broach church, accommodating the political aspirations of many, well-differentiated sets of worshippers, whose aspirations variously became its *imago dei*, perfect and to be emulated. That does disservice to the realities on the ground, which were, by what accounts we have, more heterogeneous and combustible than the liberalised image would have it. Nonetheless, this refashioning of Peterloo has undeniably served the radical cause as a constitutive myth by which progressive politics in Britain has repeatedly articulated its desire for change and, in many valuable ways, has succeeded. In the passing of the legislation that granted Universal Suffrage in Britain, the rhetoric of Peterloo was changed into concrete, legal realities. Rhetoric upends itself and transmutes into law.

In its more recent manifestations, however, this process has had other consequences. In her impressive book on Peterloo, Jacqueline Riding speaks of the march's 'carnival atmosphere'.[34] The phrase is ubiquitous in news reportage of protest in the last decade or so. 'Carnival atmosphere at Faslane Trident protest',[35] proclaims the *Scotsman* in December 2014. The BBC furnishes the following examples, among numerous others: '"Carnival atmosphere" in Hong Kong Camp' (reporting on 'pro-democracy protests' in October 2014),[36] '"Carnival Atmosphere " in Gezi Park' (reporting on a June 2013 protest in Istanbul), 'Egypt protest: "Carnival atmosphere" among demonstrators' (in Cairo on 31 January 2011, just prior to the fall of Hosni Mubarak).[37] We also find examples of protests which identify themselves as 'carnivals' before they happen, for instance, the 'Carnival Against Capital' on Friday 18 June 1999, in the context of the G8 Summit in

Cologne, Germany. The G8 protesters were offering a preemptive form of Bamford's Peterloo defence: it was a kind of party. We see in these news articles how the phrase functions in recent discourse a byword for 'non-threatening'. The BBC's decision to hold 'carnival atmosphere' in inverted commas is particularly revealing about what kind of work the phrase is doing. The sign is a readymade, an ameliorative to a certain kind of reader, perhaps even expressing a prediction or desire about a protest's outcome. It fundamentally misunderstands the aesthetics of protest at Peterloo, and I think also in the years that have followed. The undetermined relation of familiarity to weirdness, safety to danger, was crucial to Peterloo's aesthetics, and to the aesthetics of protest considered more generally. When we seek to placate all threats, we neuter nineteenth century Radicalism of that which, ultimately, drove it: the possibility of overwhelming force turned against the state.[38]

Shelley wrote a poem about Peterloo, *The Mask of Anarchy* (1819). Its coda, which would become a radical refrain,[39] runs:

> Rise like Lions after slumber
> In unvanquishable number—
> Shake your chains to earth like dew
> Which in sleep had fallen on you—
> Ye are many—they are few (368-72).[40]

Perhaps there is something odd about Shelley's request. He seems to have forgotten that the chains that oppress are not merely metaphorical; one cannot 'shake' them to earth 'like dew'. While they may not be physical (though in the contemporaneous context of the transatlantic slave trade, they were), the ties that bind workers to their work have real consequences if they are broken: starvation, homelessness, imprisonment. Liberation is not a matter of positive thinking. In one sense, Shelley allows his ideological pacifism to blind him to the violence the Yeomanry did, and to force his hand into advocating peaceful resistance. However, in another way, such a reading is obtuse because, given sufficient numbers, chains can be made metaphorical. The disciplinary apparatus of the state is finite: 'Storm Area 51: They can't stop all of us', as a meme on the internet recently put it. Shelley's words amplify that aspect of the marches and the meeting in which they have had lasting impact. Peterloo's significance is as a point of reference for radical politics when it wishes to recall that simply showing numbers in public is a form of struggle.

In the week in which I have concluded this chapter, protests under the banner 'Black Lives Matter' (BLM) occurred across the world in response to the killing by Minneapolis police of George Floyd, who was in police custody at the time. At the protest in Hyde Park, London on 3 June 2020, actor and activist, John Boyega, said the following:

> We are a physical representation of our support for George Floyd. We are a physical representation of our support for Sandra Bland. We are a physical representation of our support for Trayvon Martin. We are a physical representation of our support for Stephen Lawrence.[41]

Boyega's words, naming victims of other racist murders, counterpose the rhetorical and the physical; they are not only the expression of a particular political argument, but a definition of protest and an elaboration of tactics. The protests, of which his speech was a part, echoed Peterloo; not least in the sight of horses running unrestrained into crowds. In understanding the earlier protest we can learn from the contemporary one. History has not yet had time to launder Black Lives Matter. We understand it both for the arguments it makes and for the ways in which it makes them; its rhetorical and physical elements stand in radical equipoise. Phenomena such as the BLM movement furnish us with the mental tools to strike vertically through centuries of rewriting, and to see Peterloo for the strange, hybrid and antagonistic piece of political work that it was in 1819.

Notes

1. The others were John Knight, Joseph Johnson, John Thacker Saxton, Samuel Bamford, Joseph Healey, James Moorhouse, Robert Jones, George Swift, and Robert Wilde. I would here like to thank Bysshe Inigo Coffey, Joshua Rigg and Sarah Fletcher, for insight and generous proofreading.
2. National Archives, London, Public Record Office, TS 11/ 1051, 'The King against Henry Hunt and Others, for a Misdemeanour'.
3. The Trial of Henry Hunt, and Others, for a Conspiracy & Riot, at Manchester, on the 16th. of August Last (Manchester: 1820), 106-7.
4. Ibid.
5. 'The report of Jeremiah Garnett', in *Peterloo Massacre: Containing a Faithful Narrative of the Events which Preceded, Accompanied and Followed the Fatal Sixteenth of August, 1819* (Manchester, 1819), 56-62.
6. Ibid.
7. Quoted Jaqueline Riding, *Peterloo: The Story of the Manchester Massacre* (London: Head of Zeus, 2019, 218. Riding's is an excellent account of the massacre, to which I am much indebted.
8. Robert Poole, 'The March to Peterloo: Politics and Festivity Late Georgian England', *Past and Present*, Number 192 (August 2006), 120.
9. Samuel Bamford, *Passages in the Life of a Radical* (New York: Cosimo Classics, 2005), 146.
10. Bamford, Passages, 146.
11. See Robert Poole, *Peterloo: The English Uprising* (Oxford: Oxford University Press, 2019), 80-84.
12. Poole, Past and Present, 112.
13. *The Collected Poems of W. B. Yeats* (London: MacMillan and Co, 1952), 205.
14. See E. P. Thompson, *The Making of the English Working Class*, 2nd edn. (Harmondsworth: Penguin, 1968), 752.
15. Thompson, 752.
16. Thompson, 754.
17. Thompson, 752.
18. See Thompson, 753 fn.
19. Thompson, 753.
20. Ibid.

21. Bamford, Passages, 205.
22. See Riding, 245.
23. J. Harrop, *A Report of the Trial, Redford Against Birley and Others for An Assault on The Sixteenth of August 1819* (Manchester: 1822), 44.
24. See Riding, 254.
25. Bamford, Passages, 206.
26. Henry Hunt, *Memoirs of Henry Hunt Esq.*, 3 vols. (London: 1820-22), III, 615.
27. Ibid.
28. Bamford, Passages, 207.
29. Poole, Past and Present, 115.
30. 'The making of the Peterloo Martyrs, 1819 to the Present', Joseph Cozens, in *Secular Martyrdom in Britain and Ireland: From Peterloo to the Present*, eds. Quentin Outram and Keith Laybourn (Palgrave Macmillan, 2018), 34.
31. Cozens, 34.
32. Ibid.
33. Cozens, 33.
34. Riding, 243.
35. 'Carnival atmosphere at Faslane Trident protest', published Monday, 1st December 2014, www.scotsman.com/news/politics/carnival-atmosphere-faslane-trident-protest-1519572.
36. "Carnival Atmosphere' in Gezi Park', published October 1, 2014, www.bbc.co.uk/news/av/world-asia-29445496/carnival-atmosphere-in-hong-kong-camp.
37. 'Egypt protest: 'Carnival atmosphere' among demonstrators', published 31 Jan 2011, www.bbc.co.uk/news/world-africa-12328506.
38. The commemoration of the massacre's bicentenary in 2019 was similarly characterised by ideological liberalisation. Peterloo was framed as part of a national journey towards liberal democracy. The Peterloo Memorial Campaign marked the occasion, to which its website refers euphemistically as 'the 200th Anniversary of the Peterloo Gathering', with an 'Illegal Picnic' (which was not, in truth, illegal). Civic performance was once again central to the day's activities but this time it occurred under the direction of Manchester City Council. There was a 'Rebel Karaoke'. There is now a memorial on the site of St. Peter's Field, designed by Jeremy Deller, which allows people to ascend a small platform, as if they were addressing an assembled crowd, and which has become mired in controversy stemming from concerns about its accessibility.
39. For instance, the title of the U.K. Labour Party's manifesto for the 2017 and 2019 elections echoed Shelley's words. It was called For the Many, Not the Few (London: Labour Party, 2016).
40. *The Poems of Shelley*, Volume 3: 1819-1820, eds. Jack Donovan, Cian Duffy, Kelvin Everest and Michael Rossington, (Abingdon: Routledge: 2014), 62.
41. 'John Boyega's BLM Hyde Park Speech Highlights The Importance Of Taking Care Of Black Women', published June 3, 2020, www.bustle.com/p/john-boyegas-blm-hyde-park-speech-highlights-the-importance-of-taking-care-of-black-women-22954788.

The 'Great' Reform Act of 1832
Stephen Basdeo

The campaign for universal male suffrage did not end at Peterloo. Its 'ringleader' Henry Hunt was indeed sentenced to two years' imprisonment but, however vain Hunt might have been, the cause continued without him. The ideas of Major Cartwright and Thomas Paine were still current, and Paine's *Rights of Man* was still being reprinted into the 1820s. The Duke of Richmond's bill which he presented to the House of Lords back in 1780 was also republished in penny papers. Radical speakers continued throughout the 1820s to hold large meetings in which their demands for universal suffrage and vote by ballot were reiterated time and again.

The Electoral System before 1832

The people in attendance at public parliamentary reform meetings were not only working class. The crowd was composed also of the middle classes too whose interests, many felt, were unrepresented in parliament. Much of this was related to the mode in which MPs were elected. There were two types of parliamentary constituencies: boroughs and counties. Since medieval times counties were entitled to elect two 'Knights of the Shire' (MPs) to parliament. Within counties, there might also be boroughs. Boroughs were ancient constituencies that had probably been important economic and political hubs in times gone by but which, by the nineteenth century, were either in decline or no longer as economically important as neighbouring towns which were not incorporated as boroughs. Thus, in the early nineteenth century Yorkshire—comprising what is now the north, south, east, and west ridings—was a single county constituency. Yet within that country constituency, there were boroughs such as Kingston-Upon-Hull which also returned two MPs. The franchise qualifications in the counties and boroughs were not uniform across the country; there was universal male suffrage in a very limited number of boroughs but in the majority of boroughs voting rights were based upon the 40 shilling freehold property qualification, which meant that the number of electors was very small.

Some of the boroughs were, in fact, described as 'rotten'. We have encountered the term 'rotten borough' in this book previously, and it makes sense to revisit the term. Rotten boroughs were constituencies where there were only a handful of voters but which returned more than one MP to parliament. The most notorious of these was Old Sarum in Wiltshire; in 1295, the place was a small town but by 1801, nobody lived there and it was nothing but a field—yet it returned two MPs to parliament. A contemporary observer described polling day at Old Sarum during the General Election of 1802:

> This election for the borough of Old Sarum was held in a temporary booth erected in a cornfield, under a tree which marked the former boundary of the old town, not a vestige of which has been standing in the memory of man, the several burgages which give the right of voting, being now without a dwelling for a human being. Mr Dean, the bailiff of the borough having read the precept for the election ... There were five electors present at this election.[1]

'Pocket boroughs' were likewise detested by reformers. These were boroughs where an aristocrat might own the majority of burgage tenements and therefore 'own' the borough. Through such means, the majority landowner was able to exercise a considerable degree of influence over whom his electors voted for. Boroughbridge in North Yorkshire was one such pocket borough that was 'owned' by the Duke of Newcastle in the eighteenth century and dictated to the town's sixty-five electors which way he wanted them to vote. The Duke of Newcastle would know how 'his' constituents voted because voting was not secret but was conducted in the open; a voter would enter the booth and declare to the onlookers who he was voting for, and his decision was then recorded in the register.

The Clamour for Reform

The campaign for universal suffrage, with its various mass meetings up and down the country, was not the only sign of unrest that the government had seen in the 1810s and 1820s. Secret plots against the government were hatched, then foiled, much as what had happened with the Cato Street Conspiracy—a plot to assassinate the whole British cabinet. There were outright rebellions in some places, although these were not always related to the cause of political reform. Luddite rebels were busy destroying machinery between 1811 and 1816. There was also the Swing Riots: based in Kent and East Anglia and led by the mythical Captain Swing, these rebels were agricultural labourers who targeted the farms and estates of farmers who had introduced threshing machines onto their land. The rebels would destroy the machines and set fire to barns. An attack was usually accompanied with an ominous note to the landowner warning them that they had been targeted for attack.

Yet the Tory government of Lord Liverpool seemed, on the face of it, impervious to demands for reform. Liverpool is, on a personal level, a complex figure. It would be too easy to cast him as an enemy of the poor and one of the villains of the Peterloo story, as the recent movie on the events would have people believe. He knew that the nation's economy was in a parlous state after the Napoleonic Wars and that unemployment was rife. To this end, his government passed the Poor Employment Act (1817) which provided people in poorer counties with employment on public works—an unprecedented intervention into the economy for a Tory government who was operating in what was then a fiscal-military state, not a welfare state.

Yet for many reformers and radicals, the solution to the nation's economic and social woes lay in achieving universal male suffrage.[2] The government and their representatives in the towns disagreed—sometimes with deadly results, as happened at Peterloo. In the wake of the Peterloo Massacre, the Liverpool government passed the so-called Six Acts which banned 'seditious meetings'; prevented unlawful drilling of unofficial militias; allowed the authorities to seize arms and ammunition; increased the speed at which offenders were processed through the courts; toughened the existing Blasphemous and Seditious Libels Act; and also imposed further taxes on newspapers and periodicals. The goal of the government was to prevent the outbreak of revolution but, in fairness to the Liverpool government, these acts were mere gestures to local magistrates who rarely saw their law enforcement powers increased—England did not as yet have a professional police force and magistrates often had to rely on paid spies and informants, whose information, even Lord Sidmouth recognised, could often be exaggerated. As John W. Derry points out: 'very few actions were taken under the legislation and one recent authority has dismissed them as an irrelevance'.[3]

Derry is correct; the quasi-military drilling of radical groups may have been outlawed but nothing stopped campaigners continuing to spread their message. The campaign for Catholic Emancipation, which was finally granted in 1829, proved to reformers that single-issue causes could be won if a national reform association was able to gather the support of the people on the one hand, and put pressure on MPs on the other. New organisations like the London Radical Reform Association, the Friends of Civil and Religious Liberty, and the National Union of the Working Classes, emerged. William Hone had made great strides in furthering the cause of press freedom.

The Whigs take Notice

Times were changing. Although eighteenth century Whig heavyweights like Charles James Fox were decidedly not in favour of extending the franchise, the Whigs came round to the idea that it might be prudent to implement a limited measure of parliamentary reform. The General Election of August 1830 saw the Tories win the election but in November the prominent Whig statesman, Earl Grey, came out publicly in support of parliamentary reform. In response, the Tory leader, the Duke of Wellington, affirmed his party's opposition to any kind of political reform. Wellington's support in the Commons was very slim and, when Lord Russell introduced a Reform Bill in March 1831, Wellington's supporters in the house killed it off. That might have been the end of the matter were it not for the fact that the public was clamouring for reform.

A general election was called in 1831, with polling taking place between April and June. The Whigs put themselves forward as champions of moderate reform—the enfranchisement of the middle classes; redistribution of seats; and the abolition of rotten boroughs—and they subsequently won a majority of 136 MPs over the Tories. They lost no time in introducing a second reform bill that passed through the House of Commons but was rejected in the House of Lords, where Wellington's Tories had a majority. Outside parliament, the atmosphere was febrile. There were riots in Derby, Nottingham, and Bristol; Henry Hunt and other members of the National Union continued their speaking tours—it seemed to some of the elites that the country was on the verge of a revolution. At first Earl Grey asked the new king, William IV, to simply flood the house with lots of new pro-reform Whig peers, but the king refused. In response, Grey and his cabinet resigned. Wellington returned to try and form a government but ultimately failed to garner enough support both inside and outside the Commons. Grey came back and the reform bill was introduced again. Wellington advised his peers in the Lords to abstain from voting on it rather than block it as they did last time. The bill passed.

The Representation of the People Act, for so the bill was called, saw the franchise extended to people who owned freehold property worth over 40s; people who owned copyhold property worth over £10;[4] and male householders who paid rent on any property worth over £50 per year. The constituency map was also redrawn: towns such as Manchester were enfranchised while some boroughs like Old Sarum lost representation. A total of 401 constituencies were created. Upwards of 650 MPs were still returned to parliament. The disparity between the number of constituencies and the number of MPs is explained by the fact that some smaller constituencies were redesigned so they only returned one MP while in larger boroughs two MPs were still returned. The 1832 Act also specified men, leading to women's *complete* disenfranchisement. As G.D.H. Cole and A.W. Wilson write: 'The House of Commons had at last been reformed. But it had not been democratised'.[5] Although the likes of Henry Hunt had favoured universal male suffrage, which would have seen working men entitled to vote, the Act of 1832 excluded them. It was the exclusion of working men from the franchise that led to the emergence of the first mass working-class political movement: Chartism.

Notes

1. Anon. "The General Election of 1802," *The Monthly Review*, March 1803, 331.
2. Anon, "The Magistrates and Inhabitants of Leeds," *The Black Dwarf* February 5, 1817, 3.
3. Derry, *Politics in the Age of George III*, 142.
4. A hangover from feudal times: this was land held by a manorial tenant which could not be passed on to a family member after a person's death but reverted back to the manorial lord.
5. G.D.H. Cole and A.W. Wilson, *British Working Class Movements: Select Documents* (London: MacMillan, 1967), 215.

The Chartists

Rebecca Nesvet

In the 2016 first season of the ITV historical-romance series *Victoria,* written by Daisy Goodwin, one of the threats to law and order with which the inexperienced young Queen Victoria must contend is 'the Chartists'.[1] In the third episode of *Victoria's* first season, a ragtag mob of men in fustian and battered hats plod down a dusty provincial road. One bears a hand-written sign that reads 'ONE MAN ONE VOTE'. Others more menacingly carry farming implements including pitchforks. Seemingly appearing out of nowhere, they stream into a gigantic crowd and shout angrily—at a detachment of soldiers who block their way. The soldiers prime their muskets; the mob explodes in anger. Shots are fired, and then, before we can see their effect, the scene abruptly ends. Later, when Prime Minister William Lamb, Duke of Melbourne, informs Victoria of this incident, he explains that there has been a riot in Newport, Wales, led by people who 'call themselves Chartists'. The queen indicates that she has never previously heard of this violent movement. As the historian F.C. Mather has put, it, it was indeed 'as a threat to public order that Chartism principally concerned the Government'.[2] However, Goodwin's television drama profoundly misrepresents the development and essential nature of Chartism. In fact, Chartism was neither spontaneous, unlettered, nor primarily physically violent. Furthermore, by the time of the Newport Rising, on 4 November 1839, Chartism was hardly obscure.

Chartism's roots are traceable at minimum to 'Peterloo', the mass political protest that took place in Manchester's St Peter's Field on 4 August 1819. Approximately sixty thousand Mancunians and residents of outlying areas came to St Peter's Field to hear Henry 'Orator' Hunt, MP, demand expansion of suffrage, among other reforms. In response, mounted guardsmen and hussars called out by the Hanoverian government arrested Hunt and rode into the crowd, killing fourteen demonstrators and the toddler child of one demonstrator. Over six hundred people were injured. The memory of 'Peterloo', kept alive in journalism, political cartoons, and poetry, informed further agitation for wider suffrage and respect for human rights. In 1832, the year of the Great Reform, parliament gave a greater swathe of the British male population the right to vote, but this right was still predicated upon property qualifications. Forty-shilling freeholders still retained the right to vote, but it was now extended also to those who owned copyhold property worth £10 per annum, as well as to occupiers who paid over £50 in rent.[3] As a result, in the wake of the Great Reform, only one-sixth of British men were eligible to vote.

This was not equity, as many working-class Britons understood. Since the dawn of mass literacy at the end of the eighteenth century, a significant minority of middle- and working-class Britons had participated in a rich intellectual tradition that employed philosophical conversation and reading to assert and justify their desire for meaningful involvement in governance. Mutual improvement societies proliferated. 'In its classic form,' observes Jonathan Rose, the mutual improvement society 'consisted of half a dozen to a hundred men from the working and lower-middle-classes who met periodically, sometimes in their own homes but commonly under the auspices of a church or chapel', to deliver papers and engage in conversation about 'politics, literature, religion, ethics' and applied knowledge of all sorts.[4] 'The aim', Rose theorizes, 'was to develop', in a purposely non-hierarchical manner, 'the verbal and intellectual skills of a people who had never been encouraged to read or think'.[5] Notably, the mutual improvement societies 'relied on working-class initiative rather than state provision or middle-class philanthropy'.[6] They benefited from widening access to books, often provided in this era by circulating libraries priced to cater to their membership. For instance, in Scotland—in which mutual improvement participation was especially strong—fifty-one libraries targeting working-class readers were founded by 1822, all of them managed by working-class people.[7] Moreover, since the 1770s at least, and more obviously during the turbulent 1790s, philosophical conversation in coffee houses, taverns, and Dissenting churches became a key mode for the disseminating of radical ideas and building of radical community. As we have seen in this book's chapter on Mary Wollstonecraft, the Unitarian congregation in Newington Green, London and the private dinner-table of publisher Joseph Johnson both functioned as platforms for radical dialogue that involved and inspired writers, changed Britain's destiny, and made history.

William Lovett (1800-77)

One vigorous participant in mutual improvement and radical conversation was one of Chartism's founders and its major intellectual architect, William Lovett. He was born in the Cornish fishing village of Newlyn, a mile outside Penzance, the son of Kezia Lovett, née Green, a hard-working, Methodist fisherman's-wife who was widowed by her husband's drowning shortly before giving birth. Her brother, a rope-maker, took her in and, together with their mother, helped to raise her child. In adulthood, Lovett fondly recalled his mother, grandmother, and especially his uncle. In his autobiography *The Life and Struggles of William Lovett in his Pursuit of Bread, Knowledge, and Freedom* (1876), Lovett recalls this uncle as a man who possessed a very few books, mainly religious in theme, and a 'well-informed mind, which he had been very assiduous in cultivating'.[8] Consequently, 'Mr Green was always held up to me as an example by my grandmother'.[9] In short, this father-like figure was Lovett's first example of a working-class autodidactic intellectual; an example that he never forgot.

Another authority that made a great impression upon the young William Lovett was the rare intrusion into Newlyn life of state-level politics in the form of the press gang.

William Lovett as depicted in *Reynolds's Political Instructor.* (Stephen Basdeo's Personal Collection)

For the first fifteen years of Lovett's life, impressment into the war against Napoleon was a threat that the adult men of his community continually faced. Unable to vote for their representatives in parliament, the fishermen of Newlyn had no say in the manner. The press gang and its guardsmen, he recollects, would appear 'with drawn cutlesses' and 'rid[e] down the poor fishermen, often through fields of standing corn where they had sought to hide themselves'.[10] The boy was impressed by those who stood up to the gang, especially a young woman, Honour Hitchens, who rescued her father from impressment by clubbing his would-captor with a spiny-scaled dogfish.[11] Emulating his rope-maker uncle, Lovett tried to establish himself in that trade, but found work scarce and exploitation abundant. He obtained an apprenticeship, but his master denied him his contracted wages, in consequence of which Lovett took him to the Penzance Magistrate's Court. Remarkably, this action succeeded. Lovett obtained his wages, and a belief in the possibility that orderly appeal to law could correct injustice, but to find further work, had to leave Cornwall.[12] He tried fishing, but got seasick, so he headed for the place where many early nineteenth century jobseekers from the south of England went: London.[13]

In the metropolis, Lovett became a cabinet-maker and discovered mutual improvement, in which he partook with great enthusiasm and what appears to be exacting activity. One of his first forays, he explains in *Bread, Knowledge, and Freedom,* involved 'a small literary association, entitled "The Liberals", which met in Gerrard Street, Newport Market ... composed chiefly of working men'.[14] Their modest dues supported a private circulating library, exclusive to the Liberals. Their main topics of conversation were 'literary, political, and metaphysical' readings and ideas, including such controversial authors as Thomas Paine, whose works Lovett devoured and appreciated.[15] Another association that he quickly joined was the Cabinet-makers' Society. His new employer, the cabinet-maker David Todd, invited him and he soon became not only a member but the society's president.[16] Meanwhile, he attended the Mechanics' Institute, a nationally organised sort of informal university of philosophy, science, and technology that, while spearheaded by elite patrons, gave many working-class London men the opportunity to obtain education and to educate each other. At the Mechanics' Institute, Lovett not only attended lectures by the Institute founder George Birkbeck, but spent meaningful time with the radical author and publisher

Sir Richard Phillips, in whose periodical *The Monthly Magazine* appeared works by key 1790s radicals such as William Godwin, Thomas Holcroft, and the self-declared Jacobin (colloquially, French Revolutionary sympathiser) and Robin Hood populariser 'Citizen' Joseph Ritson. After a Mechanics' Institute meeting, Lovett recalls, he 'got into conversation' with Phillips 'and walked with him round and round St. Paul's churchyard, Newgate-Street, and the Old Bailey for several hours' on a 'bright moonlit night', discussing philosophy and science.[17] If Lovett needed any confirmation of his acceptance as an intellectual by his peers, this sojourn was it. Anointed by men like Birkbeck and Phillips, he joined in radical conversation in venues such as Tom's Coffee House and Lunt's Coffee House.[18] Respectfully located in artisanal Holborn and impoverished Clerkenwell, these were spaces of working-class intellectual community.

Lovett also began to engage in political activism, a natural progression from his coffee-house philosophising. On 3 June 1820, he married one Mary, birth surname unknown, a lady's maid whose employer had brought her to London. Lovett promised her that he would no longer take part in the male-dominated, virtually male-only conversation clubs, but eventually she came around to his involvement in politics aimed to change the living situations and political status of their class.[19] During the 1820s and early 1830s, he helped to found the first London co-operative trading association and the British Association for Promoting Co-Operative Knowledge, funded in part by Annabella Noel, Lady Byron and dedicated to the idea of the primacy of labour over mere capital.[20] He began to write for the radical press, petitioned parliament to allow the British Museum and other mass education institutions to open on Sundays (1829), arguing that this would constitute a temperance reform because people drink out of boredom; refused to serve in the militia (1831) on the grounds that he had no stake in its activity as he had no representative in parliament, and (1831) joined the National Union of the Working Classes and Others, a group that went beyond conversation into planning political action.[21] He experimented with the utopian ideas of spiritual leader and reformer, Robert Owen, but ultimately rejected Owenitism on account of the more unconventional aspects of the communitarian way of life that Owen touted to his followers.

None of these ventures measurably improved Lovett's access to bread or freedom, but in June 1836, he embarked upon a course of action that would have national impact. In collaboration with radical publishers and printers Henry Hetherington, John Cleave, and James Watson, Lovett co-founded the London Working Men's Association (LWMA). In its own words, the LWMA aimed 'to seek by every legal means to place all classes of society in possession of their equal, political, and social rights'.[22] A key member, joining in 1836, was James Bronterre O'Brien, an Irish admirer of Henry 'Orator' Hunt and William Cobbett, who, disappointed in the compromised reform of 1832, had for some time campaigned for more significant change, especially through journalism, in Hetherington's periodicals and his own. The LWMA's official minutes indicate that they pursued five demands: 'Universal Suffrage, the protection of the Ballot, Annual Parliaments, Equal representation, and no property qualification for members'.[23] They adhered to a doctrine of 'moral force', or abstention from violence or the threat of violence, partially on the grounds that such self-restraint in the face of obvious, frequently deadly oppression demonstrates their rational, ethical nature and therefore the fitness of plebeians to govern. This entailed envisioning a new, or at least, a rarely recognisable model of working-class heroic masculinity. Lovett, Anna Clarke notes, 'stressed a notion of masculinity based on rationality and self-control'.[24] To that end, the LWMA offered membership only to men they considered to live in moral rectitude and to be likely to distinguish the movement with their conduct.[25] The LWMA, Lovett envisioned, would win universal male suffrage by exploding one of that idea's greatest obstacles in the politically enfranchised classes: the stereotype of the mob democrat or armed rebel.

In July 1837, the LWMA first announced that they would imminently publish a statement of their demands, entitled 'The People's Charter'. This document was written primarily or entirely by Lovett and completed by May 1838. Some historians have claimed that Lovett co-authored it with Francis Place, but as Malcolm Chase, preeminent modern historian of Chartism has found, all such claims ultimately trace back to Place's own assertion, which is corroborated by no contemporary witness, so it seems most likely that Lovett alone was responsible for the Charter's composition.[26] The essence of the People's Charter is comprised of the 'Six Points'. Five of them derive from the original five goals of the LWMA.[27] The Six Points are as follows: (1) universal male suffrage; (2) no property qualification (3) annual parliaments; (4) equal representation; (5) payment of Members of Parliament; and (6) vote by secret ballot. In an early draft, it also demanded suffrage for women, but Lovett was compelled to remove that demand as an impediment to the passage of the rest of the document.[28] It was called the Charter after the Magna Carta, the declaration of rights and demands famously presented by the English barons to King John on 15 June 1215, the events of which are related in the introduction to this volume. Like the 'Great Charter', the People's Charter would be a historic agreement between two entities that they would henceforth share in the responsibility and right of government. It would be not just a topical pamphlet, but a document for the ages.

The Charter was first announced in May 1838 at a public meeting in Glasgow and subsequently disseminated in the context of a wave of mass demonstrations demanding its adoption by parliament as law. These demonstrations include historic rallies across the country. On 6 August 1838, a major speaker at the Birmingham meeting was Feargus O'Connor. Formerly MP for Cork, a protégé of the Irish nationalist politician Daniel O'Connor, and publisher since 1837 of the Leeds-based newspaper *The Northern Star*, O'Connor possessed a wealth of radical experience and political talent. At the Birmingham meeting, to Lovett's chagrin, O'Connor questioned whether the Charter was achievable by peaceful means alone, a topic to which he would frequently return over the next twenty years. However, if Glasgow saw foreshadowing of division within the movement, it also was a moment of unprecedented and vital unity. At Glasgow, Chase argues, was 'established the principle of a single, mass petition in favour of the Charter' instead of many local petitions, because a unified, national one would total 'a sum greater than its parts'.[29] It was at this point that some proponents of the adoption of the Charter began to call themselves 'Chartists' and then to call the movement 'Chartism'.

In 1839, Lovett's dream of working-class political enfranchisement, nurtured in London's mutual improvement societies and coffee houses, made its way to parliament. Chartists across Britain collected signatures for a petition to accompany the Charter to parliament to be, they hoped, voted into law. Lovett claimed that the thick, heavy, tree-trunk-like roll of petition sheets was three miles long and bore over twelve hundred signatures.[30] Some of those who signed were women, which, as Malcolm Chase argues, was a sociological innovation.[31] Unequivocally, a critical mass of the metropolitan and provincial cities' population wanted the Charter to become law. On 7 May 1839, a solemn delegation of Chartists carried the petition in an elaborately decorated waggon to the home of John Fielden, MP for Oldham. There it was given to Sir Thomas Attwood, MP for Birmingham, who, as Chartism's man in parliament, had promised to present it to the House of Commons.[32] This Attwood did when parliament opened on 14 June. His fellow members mainly reacted with derision. 'No indication was given whether [they] would formally debate it,' Chase notes, 'and when Attwood' and a colleague, 'with a theatrical flourish, rolled the giant cylinder into the Commons chamber it was greeted by laughter'.[33]

This parliamentary response quickly provoked demonstrations by Chartists across the country. One such demonstration took place on 4 July in Birmingham's Bull Ring, a public, partially-covered market of over 600 vendor spaces which for some time had served as the city's space for large public meetings. The Chartists in the Bull Ring were violently dispersed by the authorities, including sixty police hastily brought in from London. These men were the 'Peelers'—members of the metropolitan police force established by the Tory Prime Minister, Sir Robert Peele. Over the next two days, Chartists nationwide formally condemned the police attack. On 6 July, Lovett was hearing and noting testimony by witnesses to the attack when he was arrested. So was Collins. Six days later, the Charter was defeated in the Commons in a landslide vote.

For Lovett, this setback ended the upward trajectory of his career as an activist. On 6 August 1839, he and Collins were tried at the Birmingham Assizes for seditious libel in connection with the Bull Ring demonstrations. Lovett defended himself and evidently believed his life at risk. In the opening moments of his defence, he requests the removal from the jury of two men who had been heard to say that they wished all Chartists hung; because he could not prove that they said this, his request was denied.[34] On several occasions during the trial, he employed his arguments in self-defence to reiterate the injustice of the official response to the meeting at the Bull Ring. For instance, on the matter of the Peelers being called in, Lovett declared that 'if the police force is to be a perambulating body to be placed at the disposal of any interested or exclusive class, the more effectually to keep back public liberty, it is very properly designated ... as an unjust and unconstitutional force'.[35] Unsurprisingly, he and Collins were both convicted.

Lovett's imprisonment in Warwick Gaol was excruciating and terrifying. After finding insects in the bucket of gruel that constituted most of his caloric allotment, Lovett refused to eat it, subsisting instead on water and small amounts of prison bread. This left him malnourished and hardly able to stand. He was hospitalised. Later, banned like most prisoners from handling razors or other potentially violent implements, he was so frightened of prison barber Jem Bradley—a man who bragged about his violence against women and would later be hanged for serial murder—that he paid Bradley to rent his razor so that he could avoid being shaved by Bradley.[36] Still, the imprisoned activist managed to keep promoting the Chartist cause, by composing the pamphlet *Chartism, a New Organization of the People, embracing a Plan for the Education and Improvement of the People, Politically and Socially,* which his long-time colleague Watson published in 1840. In this pamphlet, Lovett reaffirms his commitment to moral force Chartism and calls for a nationally organised campaign but also argues that the key to working-class liberation would be formal education, which must be allowed and encouraged. He places his hope not in politicians nor fighting men but in teachers. 'One important duty must not be neglected by the people themselves', Lovett insists:

> …*that of rewarding and honouring the teachers of their children*, as this will be the best means of perfecting the science of education, by an accession of men of genius and intelligence, who otherwise will seek rewards and honours in other pursuits.[37]

Excellent and genuinely accessible education, from infancy to adulthood, Lovett insists, will bring about a more equitable government and just society. With this idea, Lovett brings Chartism back to its roots, and his own personal ones, in the mutual improvement movement of the early nineteenth century.

Feargus O'Connor (1796-1855)

Lovett emerged from prison hoping to lead the Chartists to parliamentary victory, but the path from 1839 to 1918, when all adult British people finally won the right to vote, was to be a circuitous one. By 1840, Chartism had new complications and a new leader, O'Connor. While Lovett excelled in situations that required writing ability and tact, O'Connor followed in the footsteps of Peterloo's hero Hunt, who had died, deeply discouraged by the inadequacy of the 1832 Great Reform, in 1835. Friedrich Engels, who heard O'Connor's public oratory, praised him for 'a lucidity which cannot escape even the most obtuse mind'.[38]

Meanwhile, well before 1840, O'Connor's newspaper *The Northern Star* had become a considerable force within Chartist culture. To his credit, as Marysa Demoor and Laurel Brake observe, O'Connor, in the late 1830s, saw that Chartism would become confusingly diffuse without the uniting force of a national periodical that could regularly reaffirm national goals while recognising local struggles and achievements.[39] Fulfilling this need, the *Northern Star* lived up to its name. Like Polaris, it guided the Chartists. Also like Polaris, it oriented the galaxy of Chartist groups around its own location, ending the London-based leadership of the movement that had flourished under Lovett and the LWMA. Furthermore, the *Northern Star* unleashed a Chartist imagination. It carried not only political news, speech transcripts, and editorials, including by O'Connor (and, incidentally, Engels), but also poetry, reviews, cultural and arts notices, and serial fiction. Moreover, it proved wildly popular. At the height

Fergus O'Connor pictured with Joshua Walmsley, MP, in *Reynolds's Political Instructor.* (Stephen Basdeo's Personal Collection)

of its fifteen-year run, *The Northern Star* outsold all other local papers, including the London *Times*. Read out loud in coffee shops, taverns, and workplaces, its readership is believed to have outnumbered its circulation by at least ten times.[40]

With the *Northern Star* well established, on 20 July 1840, in a Manchester tavern, O'Connor launched the National Charter Association (NCA), which he hoped would live up to his name by directing the movement as the LWMA had tried to do, but from the North. He continued to give speeches at Chartist local meetings and encouraged provincial Chartists to join the NCA and he endeavoured to shape Chartism's strategy in the wake of the 1839 petition's failure. To many, patiently requesting reform seemed an untenable strategy. At the same time, as O'Connor and most of his followers knew, outright violent revolution in the style of 1789 France was also nearly guaranteed to fail. Peterloo and the Bull Ring, among other similar events, warned them of that. So did the Newport Rising. The (L)WMA had a branch in Carmarthen in 1837, and in Newport a year later. That town had 'a long tradition of agitation for municipal reform', which fueled interest in Chartism.[41] There, on 30 October, John Frost, a draper-turned-magistrate, unveiled the Charter at a public meeting. Four days later, Frost led a protest march, to which the authorities reacted by detaining Chartist leaders in a hotel, sparking a confrontation 'entirely unpremeditated', Williams demonstrates, between Chartists and soldiers, and it was not designed to provoke, in the manner of 1789, further physical resistance.[42] In the resulting Newport riot, as it came to be called, ten Chartists were killed and over fifty wounded.[43] Frost and two fellow leaders were promptly arrested and transported to London to face torture and execution, a sentence later commuted to transportation to Australia for life. Was it possible any longer to maintain that all demonstration in support of the Charter would be peaceful? O'Connor thought not.

He resolved that he would get the Charter passed not by resorting to physical force, but by doing something rather more nuanced and also more risky: very publicly threatening to resort to violence should nonviolent means fail. 'Peaceably if we may, forcibly if we must' became O'Connor's catchphrase.[44] In short, observes Chris Vanden

Bossche, 'Chartist discourse made physical force moral by treating it as something that never actually happens, an unrealised potentiality held in check while moral force acts'—this was a strategy that, under O'Connor's leadership, the Chartists deployed.[45] After all, what could guarantee their position as rational beings with a right to political self-determination more persuasively than their abstention from violence in a situation that virtually called for it? In his speeches, O'Connor repeatedly reiterated that if Chartists would risk their lives to get the Charter passed, that was a danger he was willing to accept personally. He soon got the chance to prove he was serious about that. On 11 May 1840, he was imprisoned for seditious libel. He served his eighteen-month sentence in a grim fortress, York Castle. Like Lovett, he wrote from his cell; in his case, primarily for the *Northern Star*.

After O'Connor's release, the Charter was destined to be rejected twice more. A new Chartist petition, probably endorsed by over three million signatories, was paraded to parliament in April 1842, with considerable optimism. O'Brien, for instance, welcomed it with near-prophecy, declaring that the 'worn-out' political order 'must give way'.[46] On 4 May, however, the House of Commons again turned down the petition, with forty-seven votes for it to 287 against. This rejection led to a period of mass dissatisfaction and general strike, which began in mining communities in Staffordshire and continued, spreading throughout Great Britain, across the summer. Because some workers disabled their plants by removing plugs from steam-driven equipment, opponents of the general strike began to call it the 'plug riots' or 'plug plot'. By its suppression in the autumn of 1842, seventy-nine Chartist organisers had been transported and many others suffered lesser sentences. In the following year, O'Connor shared punishment for the strike. On 1 May of that year, fifty-nine Chartists including O'Connor faced trial in Lancashire for seditious conspiracy for having helped to organize or promote the strike.

A technicality prevented O'Connor being sentenced, but the let-downs of 1842–43 seem to have altered his tactics. If the people could not control national politics from the House of Commons, they could build their own microcosmic communities in which they could achieve self-governance and happy subsistence: on collectively farmed land. He argued this point in a series of articles serialised in the *Northern Star* in 1843, entitled *A Practical Work on the Management of Small Farms*. In this tract, O'Connor embeds a Chartist ethos as well as evident despair at the fortunes of the Charter. 'Each man who is willing to work may be independent of every other man in the world for his daily bread'. O'Connor proposes:

> … so that the prosperity of the country shall consist in an aggregate of happy individuals, rather than in a community of a few owners of all its aggregate wealth; and upon whose speculation, whim, and caprice, the poor man must now depend for his bread.[47]

In April 1845, O'Connor followed his theory with practice by establishing the Chartist Co-Operative Land Society. Echoing Lovett's early efforts at co-operative artisanal business and social life, the CCLS was also the ideological successor of generations of utopian collective farming experiments attempted by radical non-farmers, ranging from Samuel Taylor Coleridge and Robert Southey's never-realised undergraduate invention 'Pantisocracy', intended for the banks of America's Susquehanna River in the early 1790s, to Amos Bronson Alcott's 1840s Massachusetts collective 'Fruitlands', featuring the Alcott home at the appropriately named Orchard House.

O'Connor's Land Plan might seem like a shift in philosophical direction for the major promoter of the Charter, but it was in fact a continuation of an established strand of his political thought. During the Irish Potato Famine, the Anglo-Irish O'Connor, long an agitator against the landlords' oppression of the Irish people, characterised the increase of cultivated land as the only solution to mass starvation.[48] Owner-cultivated land offered the industrial population a way out of wage labour, while, by decreasing the competition for urban industrial jobs, giving the remaining urban workers greater leverage.[49] As O'Connor put it, he offered the Land Plan as a solution to 'the landless, helpless multitude now thronging the filthy lanes, courts, and alleys of our cities and manufacturing towns'.[50] With the inauguration of the Land Plan, Joy MacAskill observes, O'Connor raised 'questions which mattered in general to British society' and had always fueled Chartism, especially questions concerning 'man's natural right to the soil'.[51]

In 1846, O'Connor hired, as the auditor of his National Land Company, the Chartist leader, William Cuffay. A Londoner but no fan of the LWMA, Cuffay was a former tailor who had helped to found the Metropolitan Tailors' Charter Association, was elected an officer of O'Connor's National Chartist Association, and then served as President of the London contingent. O'Connor's Land Plan bore fruit—no pun intended—on 1 May 1847 with the foundation of the collective O'Connorville, near Watford in rural Hertfordshire, about fifteen miles outside London. Meanwhile, O'Connor stood for election in Nottinghamshire, which returned him as MP in July. Finally, the Chartists had both land and the privilege previously monopolised by the class of landed property ownership: one of their own in the Commons.

William Cuffay (1788-1870)

The opportunity offered by the National Land Company must have seemed particularly exciting to Cuffay. Born in the Medway Towns region of Kent, Cuffay was of African and English descent. His father, Chatham Cuffay, was born on the island of St Kitts, and began his life in slavery. Chatham Cuffay got away from St Kitts and became a ship's cook. By the time Britain abolished slavery in the last of its Caribbean colonial possessions, William Cuffay was nearly forty years old. In London, he eagerly took part in the culture of mutual improvement and labour politics, just like William Lovett, and applied the lessons he learned to the founding or management of the various trade guild and political organisations that he joined or led. As auditor of the O'Connorville collective, this child of exile, dispossession, and voyaging, nearly sixty years old, had at last found a secure, free home—at least in theory.

In practice, O'Connorville was hardly secure. Its finances were never entirely healthy, and in February 1848, the news was full of not reform but revolution, as

William Cuffay pictured in *Reynolds's Political Instructor*. (Stephen Basdeo's Personal Collection)

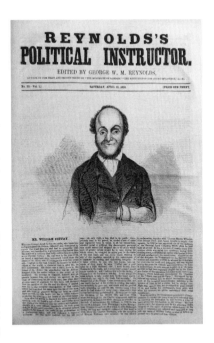

revolts and popular uprisings broke out across Europe. Karl Marx, resident in London and keen observer of the Chartist movement, published the *Communist Manifesto* and in April, the Chartists made another push to persuade parliament to recognize the Charter. The third Chartist petition was signed by over five million people, or so O'Connor claimed. Fraudulent signatures added by opponents seeking to discredit the movement ballooned that figure, but it remains clear that a critical mass had endorsed the petition. The Chartists planned to parade with the carriage bearing the giant roll of signatures but were at the last moment denied permission to gather in such a throng.

Rallying an enormous but orderly crowd at Lambeth's Kennington Common, O'Connor apologised for having agreed to bar them from accompanying the petition to Westminster, but consoled them with the thought that with them, in the petition in the carriage, 'go … the voices of 5,700,000 of your countrymen', who alongside O'Connor and 'the whole world', all 'look to you for good and orderly and citizen-like conduct on this occasion'.[52] With these words, O'Connor did not abandon his belief in physical-force Chartism; he only emphasised, as he often previously had done, that the threat of physical force is most potent as the absolute final resource of a law-abiding, rational community that with Herculean effort had thus far abstained from resorting to it. He then touted the Land Plan and the dream of O'Connorville. With this possibility, 'is not Chartism better worth contending for than ever?' In his view and Cuffay's, the answer surely was in the affirmative. Finally, O'Connor promised the crowd at Kennington Common that he would personally escort the petition to parliament and then, from the floor at Whitehall, 'read the government a lesson inciting you and your resolution, but in telling them of all of your love for order, and your respect for the law', and, even if he is arrested and 'stretched on the rack … smile terror out of countenance'. It was rhetoric like this that made O'Connor both a memorable speaker and, in the view of Lovett and others, a touch too melodramatic or egotistical.

For his part at Kennington Common, O'Connor was neither detained nor tortured, but his adjutant Cuffay found himself under arrest and did in fact smile in the face of very real terror. He was accused of planning a demonstration of physical aggression but not an actual revolt. At its most serious, his plan involved theatre as activism. If this was in fact Cuffay's plan, it seems utterly contradicted by the rhetoric of O'Connor's

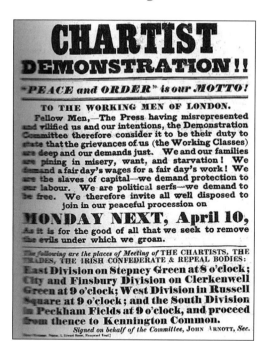

CHARTIST
DEMONSTRATION!!
"PEACE and ORDER" is our MOTTO!

TO THE WORKING MEN OF LONDON.
Fellow Men,—The Press having misrepresented and vilified us and our intentions, the Demonstration Committee therefore consider it to be their duty to state that the grievances of us (the Working Classes) are deep and our demands just. We and our families are pining in misery, want, and starvation! We demand a fair day's wages for a fair day's work! We are the slaves of capital—we demand protection to our labour. We are political serfs—we demand to be free. We therefore invite all well disposed to join in our peaceful procession on

MONDAY NEXT, April 10,

As it is for the good of all that we seek to remove the evils under which we groan.

The following are the places of Meeting of THE CHARTISTS, THE TRADES, THE IRISH CONFEDERATE & REPEAL BODIES:
East Division on Stepney Green at 8 o'clock; City and Finsbury Division on Clerkenwell Green at 9 o'clock; West Division in Russell Square at 9 o'clock; and the South Division in Peckham Fields at 9 o'clock, and proceed from thence to Kennington Common.
Signed on behalf of the Committee, JOHN ARNOTT, *Sec.*

Kennington Common Demonstration Poster, 1848. (Wikimedia Commons).

speech at Kennington Common. His charges were seriously trumped up. He came to trial at the Old Bailey, London's Central Criminal Court, on 30 September 1848, charged with plotting to make war against the queen. Facing the possibility of a sentence of death, imprisonment, or transportation, Cuffay reacted with reserve and Stoic humour. In a moment that has now become famous, he interjected that the *Magna Carta* prohibited his trial by the propertied-class men of the jury, because they were not his 'peers', he being, in his own words, 'only a journeyman mechanic'.[53] Through Cuffay's self-abnegation, it is possible to read a principled assertion of autonomy and dignity. 'Class was a central concept to Cuffay', explains his early biographer Norbert J. Grossman: 'He was proud of his trade'.[54] Reporting on the trial, the *Northern Star* praised Cuffay's rhetoric and his demeanour, affirming him a hero worthy of emulation. 'His protest from first to last against the mockery of being tried a by a jury animated by class-resentments and party-hatred showed him to be a much better respecter of the constitution than either the Attorney General or the Judges on the bench', the *Star* reported, and his testimony in defence of himself and his cause 'should be treasured up by the people'.[55]

Cuffay lost the trial and was sentenced to transportation to Tasmania. His fellow Chartists took up a collection to send his devoted wife, Mary, to follow him across the Equator. They must have been impressed by Mary Cuffay in her own right, for, during her husband's trial, the London *Times* reported, she 'ventured to express her views of the proceeding in too audible terms' and was thrown out of the courtroom by an officer.[56] Fellow Chartists also sent William Cuffay with another consolatory companion: the late Lord Byron, as represented by a copy of the firm of James Murray's 1830s edition of Byron's selected poems. James Grasby, Secretary of the Westminster chapter of the NCA, inscribed it to Cuffay, on behalf of the chapter's membership. The choice of Byron may be read as a reaffirmation of Grasby and colleagues' commitment to Chartism despite the catastrophe of Kennington Common and the failure of the third petition in parliament, which shortly followed that demonstration. Chartists often read Byron in legal and pirated editions, paying attention to the aristocratic poet's often forward-thinking politics as much or more as to his literary style and even

George W.M. Reynolds as pictured in
Reynolds's Miscellany. (Stephen Basdeo's
Personal Collection)

dressing like him.[57] Cuffay may have
found Byron's reactions to the tyranny
of the Peterloo era more powerful than
some of his fellow Chartists, for, born in
1788, he was Byron's exact contemporary,
and so personally witnessed the poet's
meteoric, brief career.

Sadly, Cuffay died impoverished.
His copy of Byron remained in the
Vandemonian prison library. It is an
evidently well-read volume but in good
condition, suggesting it was treasured.
Why it remained in the prison when Cuffay
left is unclear. Perhaps he left it for other
prisoners' consolation. What is clear is that
it is the one and only object associated with Cuffay that now survives. In 2014, it was
donated to Manchester's People's History Museum, where it may be seen today.[58]

George William MacArthur Reynolds (1814-79)

While the Chartists found inspiration in Byron and Shelley, the Romantic poets of
a generation before them, they also consumed reading particularly tailored to their
community and to the Chartist platform. This is the popular Victorian literature
that has been until very recently entirely neglected by the academic literary-critical
establishment from its earliest inception at the end of the nineteenth century. We have
seen that the *Northern Star* carried poetry and serial fiction. It was far from the only
radical periodical to do so. An equally prominent purveyor of Chartist imaginative
literature was George William Macarthur Reynolds. Born into a Royal Navy family in
Sandwich, Kent, on 23 July 1814, Reynolds was raised for a naval career. He briefly
attended Sandhurst, but, orphaned with a small fortune, he became a traveller instead.
In Paris in the wake of the Revolution of 1830, Reynolds became fluent in French
and fascinated by French ideas, especially the idea of the rights of the citizen and the
political doctrine of Republicanism. His disappointment in the British monarchy and
insistence that it both wasted resources and provided no real governance infuses his
publications and those of the writers whom he hired, promoted, or patronised.

Upon Reynolds's return to London in the mid-1830s, he capitalised on his French
experience with *Pickwick Abroad, or, the Tour in France* (1837-8), his contribution to the
Pickwick publishing phenomenon inspired by Dickens's early bestseller *The Pickwick
Papers*, and also in *Alfred, or, the Adventures of a French Gentleman* (1838) and *Robert*

Macaire, or, the French Bandit in England (1839). Reynolds mastered the serial novel format, drawing out epic stories in episodes that, illustrated with enticing woodcuts, encouraged his target audience—working-class families—to seek suspense, adventure, and romance in the following week's issue. Mastering this genre with its endlessly delayed promise of dramatic resolution, he became, arguably, the Scheherazade of working-class London; or, given the proliferation of cheap serial fiction in the late 1830s and 1840s, one of them.

Meanwhile, Reynolds discovered the serial novels of Eugène Sue, an incredibly popular author of serial novels that combined adventure, conspiracy, crime, and romance with progressive political ideas emphatically expressed. Sue's serial *The Mysteries of Paris* (1842–43) was very popular in France and fascinated Reynolds. He paid homage to Sue and promoted recognisably Chartist ideals in his own two most popular and enduring serials, *The Mysteries of London* (1844–48) and its follow-up, the sprawling, multi-volume *Mysteries of the Court of London* (1849–56). In these *tours de force*, Reynolds takes readers on a tour of London criminality, covering the criminality of the poor, which he attributed to social inequities, structural quagmires, and lack of choice or autonomy, and the criminality of the upper classes and, especially, the Hanoverian court, stemming often from egotism, avarice, libertinism, and misogyny. As Stephen Basdeo has shown, while Reynolds acknowledges an urban 'criminal underworld',

he finds it inextricably connected with and enabled by an equally criminal 'upper world'.[59] A particularly haunting character in *The Mysteries of London* is the 'Resurrection Man': a grave-robber (primarily) whose activities highlight the way that London's socio-political *status quo* prevents the majority of the population from ownership even of their own bodies and contradicts its own pretensions to Christian morality or belief in the sacredness of life and death.

The *Mysteries of London* and *Mysteries of the Court of London* inaugurated the 'urban mysteries' genre of Victorian popular fiction, an offshoot of the early nineteenth century Gothic in which the location of enigma, conspiracy, danger, terror, and horror is not a castle in early modern Catholic

The Mysteries of London, no. 1 (1844).
(Stephen Basdeo's Personal Collection)

Europe, as it was for writers such as Ann Radcliffe and the cheap chapbooks of the Regency, but the urban spaces of the relatively recent past and the present, especially in London. While the older Gothic works tended to explore French revolutionary themes displaced to other contexts, the urban mystery concerned itself with the horrors of modern industrial British life. Unlike the older Gothics, with their primarily aristocratic family casts of characters, Reynolds's *Mysteries* tend to depict 'the oppressed' or 'industrious millions' as a conglomeration of the middle and working classes, whom he opposes to the tyrannical royalty and aristocracy.[60] According to literary critic, Rohan McWilliam, with this use of Gothic imagery to illustrate conflict between the people and the oligarchic-monarchic nexus, Reynolds developed a new literary genre: the 'Chartist Gothic'.[61]

Notably, this manifestation of Chartism outlasted the political movement. By the end of 1856, Reynolds's *Mysteries of London* and *Mysteries of the Court of London* together sold over a million copies in only a decade and were frequently reprinted, in entirety and in parts, throughout the rest of the century and beyond, and not only in Britain. They were translated into many languages and sold across Europe and in America and India. A Chicago edition of a section of *The Mysteries of the Court of London,* published circa 1895, is an economical paperback perfect for railway reading and in design looks not unlike a Georgette Heyer or Winston Graham romance of the following century. In looking back to the Hanoverian past to critique his Victorian present, Reynolds proved futuristic.

What followed Chartism, according to some scholars, was an 'Age of Equipoise'. There were fewer mass meetings, wages rose, and the clamour for extension of the franchise receded somewhat. Angelo Calfo takes us through this apparently more peaceful age in the next chapter, in which Reynolds makes an appearance again due to his membership of the National Reform League.

Saliently for this volume's concerns, Reynolds contributed to Chartist political activity sufficiently to play a significant role in the demonstration at Kennington Common. In his urban mysteries, Basdeo observes, 'the rottenness of the English constitution was the cause of crime in nineteenth century London', which certainly militates for the updating of said constitution by the ratification of the Charter.[62] The *Mysteries of London* episode of 4 March 1848, went off on what Chase judges 'a tangent' joyously to celebrate the French Revolution of that year, which deposed King Louis Philippe and established the Second Republic.[63] However, Reynolds's Chartism also comprised direct action. On 6 March 1848, he participated in a demonstration in Trafalgar Square that nominally concerned the impositions of income tax upon the working people but was interpreted by the press as a Chartist demonstration.[64] When the meeting convenor, Charles Cochrane, stepped down because the police had banned a demonstration so close to parliament, Reynolds filled his place, loudly declaring his support for—in his precise words—'the brave Parisians and the People's Charter'.[65] A week later he took to the platform again, at the fateful rally at Kennington Common, where he gave a speech on the unreasonable expense of maintaining the monarchy.[66] It was also Reynolds's idea, apparently, to hold that meeting at Kennington, so as to avoid the problem with proximity to Westminster that had kept Cochrane out of

Trafalgar Square. As Chase notes, the meeting's location sealed the fate of the planned procession of the petition carriage, because the authorities prevented that by closing the bridges that would have allowed the Chartists to cross the Thames after the rally.[67] This decision in turn frustrated the demonstrators already deeply disillusioned to learn that they could not parade with the petition. To get home, they had to cross bridges blocked by policemen. Although many demonstrators insisted they were trying to return home, not go to Westminster, the police attacked them with truncheons. One wounded Chartist was an elderly man. According to the historian Catherine Howe, this conclusion to the day's activities may have helped to turn many demonstrators away from continuing agitation for the Charter. 'The effect upon the people who came to Kennington Common that day is barely imaginable', Howe reflects.[68]

Reynolds proved more effectual as a conductor of periodicals than meetings. He founded, edited, and wrote for many, including *Reynolds's Miscellany* and *The London Journal*. These involved progressive politics, serial fiction, and the talents of writers who shared his political outlook. A notable staff writer at *Reynolds's Miscellany* was James Malcolm Rymer (1814-84), a retiring individual who is not positively known to have attended any Chartist meetings but shared Reynolds's view of the monarchy, wrote fiction that promoted working-class self-determination, and is most famous for the recognisably Chartist 1845-6 serial *Varney, the Vampyre*—an important precursor of *Dracula* and *The String of Pearls* (1846-7), the source of the urban legend of 'demon barber' Sweeney Todd. As the son-in-law from 1859 of William Carpenter, editor of the newspaper *The Charter* (founded 1840), Rymer had his Chartist credentials rather well sewn up. More important for political Chartism than the *Miscellany* was *Reynolds's Political Instructor,* founded in 1849. First appearing at a low point in Chartism's progress, it carried the torch beyond the transportation of William Cuffay and others and the failure of the 1848 petition. In fact, a haunting portrait of Cuffay in his cell, resolutely smiling out at his Antipodean guards or Home Counties admirers, remains the most iconic image of him today.

It was necessary for Reynolds to keep the Chartist dream alive because that dream suffered greatly after Kennington Common. In 1848, not only was the Charter rejected by parliament for the third and final time, but O'Connorville financially failed. Today, its historic site is occupied by a luxury housing development, accessible only to upper-class families and offering zero opportunities for the cultivation of food, collective or otherwise.[69] In 1855, O'Connor, broken by his struggles and suffering from mental health ailments died, at only fifty-nine years old, in a madhouse. In February 1858, the Chartists held a final Convention, a poorly attended shadow of the great meetings of the 1830s and 40s—but, as we will see in the next chapter, the suffrage campaign achieved a partial victory; a stepping-stone to the achievement of some of the Chartists' demands. During the 1850s-70s, Lovett wrote his autobiography, constantly expanding and revising the manuscript, but was virtually uninvolved in politics.

In the 1860s and beyond, Britons continued to enthusiastically contemplate the ideas that the Chartists had put forth—the political rights encapsulated in the Six Points of the Charter. After Chartism, several Leeds Chartists involved themselves in municipal government, as did the Nottinghamshire Chartist, James Sweet, who was still proudly calling himself a Chartist in the 1870s.[70] The Chartist thought tradition contributed to the expansion of male suffrage in 1867 and then, finally, in 1918—ninety-nine years after Peterloo—to the realisation of genuinely universal suffrage. 'The sons of our sons are listening / To hear the Chartists' Cheers', demonstrators sang in a Victorian 'Chartist Hymn' that has survived to be recorded twice, in 1998 and 2003, by the folk-inspired pop band Chumbawamba. There is some truth to this. The London Chartist, George Julian Harney, whose activities are related in the next chapter, lived until 1897, and so was able to gift his personal memory of Chartism to the youth of the twentieth century. In 1918, many middle-aged grandsons and granddaughters of Chartists indeed cast ballots for the first time.

Notes

1. *Victoria, Season One,* written by Daisy Goodwin. Public Broadcasting System (PBS) Distribution, 2017.
2. F.C. Mather, "The Government and the Chartists," in *Chartist Studies,* edited by Asa Briggs, 1959 (London: Macmillan, 1977): 372-405, 372.
3. Copyhold property was land leased or sold from a manorial lord to peasants, who could in turn dispose of the land by selling or leasing it as they saw fit.
4. Jonathan Rose, *The Intellectual Life of the British Working Classes* (New Haven: Yale University Press, 2001), 58.
5. Ibid.
6. Ibid.
7. Rose, *The Intellectual Life of the British Working Classes,* 59.
8. William Lovett, *The Life and Struggles of William Lovett in his Pursuit of Bread, Knowledge, and Freedom, with some short account of the different associations he belonged to and of the opinions he entertained,* introduced by R.H. Tawney. 2 vols. New York: Knopf, 1920, 1, p. 3.
9. Ibid.
10. Ibid.
11. Ibid.
12. Lovett, *Bread,* 1, p. 20.
13. Ibid.
14. Ibid.
15. Lovett, *Bread,* 1, p. 35; Joel Wiener, *William Lovett* (Manchester: Manchester University Press, 1989), 9.
16. Lovett, *Bread,* 1, p. 36; Tawney, "Introduction," vi.
17. Lovett, *Bread,* 1, p. 37.
18. Ibid.
19. Lovett, *Bread,* 1, p. 40.
20. Lovett, *Bread,* 1, p. 43; Wiener, *William Lovett,* 14.
21. Lovett, *Bread,* 1, pp. 58-69.
22. LWMA, 1836, quoted in "Source 3: Minute-Book of the London Working Men's Association," *The British Library,* https://www.bl.uk/learning/histcitizen/21cc/struggle/chartists1/historicalsources/source3/lwma.html [18 May 2020].

23. Ibid.
24. Anna Clarke, *The Struggle for the Breeches: Gender and the Making of the British Working Class* (Berkeley: University of California Press, 1997), 225.
25. Clarke, *The Struggle for the Breeches,* 225.
26. Malcolm Chase, *Chartism: A New History* (Manchester: Manchester University Press, 2007), 9.
27. LWMA, 1836, quoted in "Source 3: Minute-Book of the London Working Men's Association," [18 May 2020].
28. Tawney, "Introduction." 174.
29. Chase, *Chartism,* 19.
30. Lovett, *Bread,* 1, p. 210.
31. Chase, *Chartism,* 43.
32. Chase, *Chartism,* 73.
33. Chase, *Chartism,* 79.
34. "The Queen against Lovett," Reports of State Trials, new series, vol. III, 1831-40, published under the direction of the State Trials Committee, edited by John Macdonell (London: Eyre and Spottiswoode, 1891), 1177-1189, 1179.
35. "The Queen against Lovet," *State Trials,* 1182.
36. Lovett, *Bread,* 1, p. 239.
37. William Lovett, *Chartism, a New Organization of the People, embracing a Plan for the Education and Improvement of the People, Politically and Socially* (London: James Watson, 1840), 77.
38. Friedrich Engels, 'Feargus O'Connor and the Irish People', *Marx and Engels: Collected Works,* 50 vols. (Chadwell Heath: Lawrence and Wishart, 1976-2004), 6, p. 448, 448.
39. Marysa Demoor and Laurel Brake, *Dictionary of Nineteenth-Century Journalism in Great Britain* (Lebanon, New Hampshire: University Press of New England, 2009), 459.
40. Demoor and Brake, *Dictionary of Nineteenth-Century Journalism in Great Britain,* 459.
41. David Williams, "Chartism in Wales," *Chartist Studies,* edited by Asa Briggs, 1959 (London: Macmillan, 1987), 220-49, 224.
42. David Williams, "Chartism in Wales," 229, 241.
43. David Williams, "Chartism in Wales," 234.
44. Chase, *Chartism,* 67.
45. Chris R. Vanden Bossche, "On Chartism," *BRANCH: Britain, Representation, and Nineteenth-Century History,* ed. Dino Franco Felluga. Extension of *Romanticism and Victorianism on the Net.* [17 May 2020].
46. Quoted in Chase, *Chartism,* 207.
47. Feargus O'Connor, *A Practical Work on the Management of Small Farms,* 4th ed. (Manchester: Abel Heywood, 1846), 5.
48. Joy MacAskill, "The Chartist Land Plan," *Chartist, Studies,* 304-341, 306.
49. MacAskill, "The Chartist Land Plan," 307.
50. Feargus O'Connor, *Northern Star,* 21 August 1847, quoted in MacAskill, "The Chartist Land Plan," 322.

51. MacAskill, "The Chartist Land Plan," 306.

52. Feargus O'Connor, Speech at Kennington Common, *The Northern Star* 15 April 1848, transcribed by Tom Collins, *The Kennington Common Project,* 2011, http://www.kenningtonchartistproject.org/wp-content/uploads/2018/06/AUDIO_ TomCollins_FergusOConnor-download.pdf [18 May 2020].

53. Norbert J. Grossman, "William Cuffay: London's Black Chartist," *Phylon* 44, no. 1 (1983): 58–65, 59; see also Chase, *Chartism*, 310.

54. Grossman, "William Cuffay," 59.

55. 'William Cuffay, *The Northern Star* (7 October 1848), facsimile in Mark Gregory, *William Cuffay, 1788-1870* (January 2011), https://cuffay.blogspot.com/2011/01/ reply-at-trial.html [25 May 2020]; see also Chase, *Chartism,* 210.

56. *The Times* (21 August 1848), facsimile in Gregory, *William Cuffay, 1788-1870* [25 May 2020].

57. Dino Franco Felluga, *The Perversity of Poetry* (*Romantic Ideology and the Popular Male Poet of Genius* (Buffalo: State University of New York Press, 2005)*,* 91.

58. Harriet Richardson, "Chartist Leader William Cuffay's Book Donated to People's History Museum," *People's History Museum, Manchester* (6 June, 2014) [2 December 2018].

59. Stephen Basdeo, "That's Business: Organized Crime," in G.W.M. Reynolds's *The Mysteries of London* (1844-8)," *Law, Crime, and History* 1 (2018): 53-75, 53

60. Stephen Basdeo, "The Politics of Victorian England's Vicious Republican: G.W.M. Reynolds," *Geste of Robin Hood: Chronicling the Lives of Robbers, Rogues, and Rebels* (13 February 2019) https://gesteofrobinhood.com/2019/02/13/the-politics-of-victorian-englands-vicious-republican-g-w-m-reynolds-1814-79-stephen-basdeo/ [18 May 2020]

61. Rohan McWilliam, "Sweeney Todd and the Chartist Gothic: Politics and Print Culture in Early Victorian Britain," *Edward Lloyd and his World: Popular Fiction, Politics, and the Press in Victorian Britain*, edited by Sarah Louise Lill and Rohan McWilliam, (New York: Routledge, 2019), 198–215.

62. Stephen Basdeo, "An English Republican's View of Crime and its Causes," *Geste of Robin Hood: Chronicling the Lives of Robbers, Rogues, and Rebels* (19 May 2019) https://gesteofrobinhood.com/2018/05/19/an-english-republicans-view-of-crime-and-its-causes/ [18 May 2020]

63. Chase, *Chartism,* 295.

64. Chase, *Chartism,* 296-7.

65. Chase, *Chartism,* 297.

66. Ibid.

67. Ibid.

68. Catherine Howe, *London Story 1848* (Stourbridge: APS Books, 2020), unpaginated electronic edition. *Google Books.*

69. "Dreamers and Dissenters: Source 10: O'Connorville," The British Library. http://www.bl.uk/learning/histcitizen/21cc/struggle/chartists1/historicalsources/ source10/oconnorville.html [18 May 2020].

70. Asa Briggs, "National Bearings," *Chartist Studies,* 28—304, 292.

Politics in 'The Age of Equipoise'

Angelo Calfo and Stephen Basdeo

On 10 April 1848, Chartist leaders organised a demonstration on Kennington Common in South London, calling for political reform. Their campaign for universal manhood suffrage, vote by secret ballot in elections and other democratic reforms of the parliamentary system, as demanded in the People's Charter of ten years before, enjoyed mass working-class support. The new railway system of 1840 allowed for thousands to make the trek for the demonstration. The idea was that an intimidatingly huge crowd would march from Kennington Common to parliament and deliver a huge petition, demanding the right to vote. The Chartist movement was viewed as a massive threat by the government—the queen was evacuated and thousands of soldiers were recruited to defend the capital against what they feared would be a mass uprising against the government. The events of April of that year were likely the reason behind the passage of a new Treason Felony Act (1848) which held that a person was guilty of treason if they were to:

> Within the United Kingdom or without, compass, imagine, invent, devise, or intend to deprive or depose our Most Gracious Lady the Queen, from the style, honour, or royal name of the imperial crown of the United Kingdom, or of any other of her Majesty's dominions and countries, or to levy war against her Majesty, within any part of the United Kingdom, in order by force or constraint to compel her to change her measures or counsels, or in order to put any force or constraint upon or in order to intimidate or overawe both Houses or either House of Parliament, or to move or stir any foreigner or stranger with force to invade the United Kingdom or any other of her Majesty's dominions or countries under the obeisance of her Majesty, and such compassings, imaginations, inventions, devices, or intentions, or any of them, shall express, utter, or declare, by publishing any printing or writing or by any overt act or deed.[1]

Of course, as Rebecca Nesvet has shown, the British authorities' fear of civil unrest in April 1848 never transpired. And the queen was not in danger; with the exception of G.W.M. Reynolds, G.J. Harney and others, the Chartists were not republicans and did not think of themselves as revolutionaries.

'The Charter and Something More'

To the Chartists, the rejection of their petition in 1848 did not feel as though they were immediately defeated. For many Chartists, as Dorothy George notes, there remained a widespread feeling that there was still something to fight for—that much more was needed to be done to secure voting rights for all men. Some leading Chartist voices, such as George Julian Harney, felt that the Chartists must stay steadfast to their good cause because they were merely 'passing through a period of reaction'.[2] And now the Chartists were widening their aims, looking for 'the Charter and Something More'. The Chartists, of course, did not have our benefit of hindsight; it is clear to us that by the beginning of the 1850s the movement was entering serious decline. Chartism was limping on. The movement had split and the likes of Harney began promoting 'Red Republicanism', while moderate radicals pursued their own agenda and for a time pursued an alliance with middle-class liberals. Finally, after a few years in the political wilderness, the National Charter Association was wound up in 1858.

But where were the disaffected Chartists, who did not wish to affiliate with the Red Republicans or the socialists, to go? As John Belchem notes, after 1848, 'while pragmatic working-class radicals were carried away from Chartist fundamentalism, progressive middle-class radicals began to move in an interventionist direction, abandoning rigid adherence to laissez-faire political economy'.[3] And things seemed to be getting better: there were fewer political mass meetings; wages were rising; the government dropped its hard-line laissez-faire ideology in favour of interventionism; the Ten Hours Bill had been passed, limiting the workday; the Corn Laws—tariffs on imports of grain designed to keep the price of bread high—had been abolished in 1846 and food was cheaper; and the Great Exhibition of 1851 seemed to prove to the government that, after a period of class antagonism, there seemed to be something of a reconciliation between

George J. Harney as pictured in *Reynolds's Political Instructor.* (Stephen Basdeo's Personal Collection)

working people and their 'superiors'.[4] An 'age of equipoise' seemed to have begun—it was an age that witnessed the final political, social, and economic ascendancy of the 'respectable' middle classes.[5]

The next two decades would see two of the Chartists' aims realised: the abolition of the property qualification for MPs was achieved in 1858 and the Ballot Act of 1872 mandated that all voting should henceforth be done in secret. A further extension of the franchise was achieved in 1867 with the granting of household suffrage to members of the 'respectable' working class. The wind was changing and liberals inside and outside of parliament were taking note of the need to extend the franchise. The years between 1841 and 1874 can be justifiably characterised as a period marked by the ascendancy of liberal ideology; the Whigs' ability to garner support from aristocrats, industrialists, the Church of England, artisans, shopkeepers, and relatively prosperous members of the working classes, or 'labour aristocracy' seemed unstoppable. There were also signs that newly-founded apolitical trade unions were moving towards a productive, if not always harmonious, relationship with industrialists. It is telling that the Conservative Party only won two elections between those years while in the 1857 election all of the Radicals lost their seats.[6] So-called 'Lib-Labism' seemed like it was here to stay.

Part of the reason for the Whigs' success was the fact that they modelled themselves as defenders of the constitution while posing as the main means through which the integration of the working classes into the political nation might be achieved. That being said, Lord Palmerston, who served as the Whig Prime Minister twice between 1855–58 and 1859–65 was not personally interested in pursuing a reform agenda. He believed that the Reform Act of 1832 had settled the question of electoral reform once and for all.

It is the second term of Palmerston's tenure as Prime Minister from when we can date the foundation of the new Liberal Party. The new party, under Palmerston's adept management and ability to reconcile opposing factional interests, took under its wing old Radicals, Whigs, 'new' Liberals, and even disaffected former 'Peelites', or, followers of Robert Peel—notable among these former Peelites who joined the new Liberal Party was one William Ewart Gladstone. As Chancellor of the Exchequer in Palmerston's government, Gladstone carried a lot of weight. He privately expressed some sympathy with extending the franchise but while Palmerston was in charge hesitated to publicly avow support for it, and one suspects he was yet to fully make his mind up on the matter when first invited into Palmerston's Liberal government.

But outside parliament pressure groups began making their voices heard. In the same year as the National Charter Association was wound up, the Northern Reform Union was founded by Joseph Cowen the Younger, the proprietor of the *Newcastle Chronicle*. In 1858, the *Newcastle Chronicle* reported that:

> The "Northern Reform Union" seeks the attainment of Manhood Suffrage, and the protection of the vote by ballot, they do so because they are deeply conscious of existing evils, for which it is hoped that an extended and free suffrage may provide a cure.[7]

Cowen's organisation was aiming not just for political reform but also social and moral reform as well. Fired with language reminiscent of that used by reformers in the early nineteenth century, the Northern Reform Union railed against 'a landed and monied oligarchy who, without seeming to do so, rule[d] everything'. Just as vehemently did the union deplore 'the enriching of a few at the expense of the millions'.[8]

Other organisations soon followed. The Manhood Suffrage and Vote by Ballot Association had been formed in 1862. An organisation of working-class men, it had been formed by members of London trade unions and London Trades Council. In the 1850s, the unions had initially wanted to remain politically impartial and concentrate on issues concerning the relations between employers and workmen. But the times were changing. In its inaugural statement, the association proudly declared that:

> Our numbers and our position as skilled artisans of this country give us an influence which, if wisely directed, would greatly advance the interests of the toiling masses of our fellow countrymen in every direction. Hitherto, our efforts have been directed to the removal of one evil only, forgetting, or only partially remembering, that all the evils under which we suffer have a common origin — namely, an excess of political power in the hands of those holding a higher social position … Our object, therefore, is to create an organisation for the purpose of obtaining our rights as citizens; or, in other words, our just share of political power. These objects sought to be obtained by the present organisation are precise and definite — namely, registered manhood suffrage by the ballot. Upon these two great principles we take our stand, and invite the whole of the Trade Unionists of this country to cooperate with us until our agitation is crowned with success.[9]

This association, according to John Belchem, attracted little notice when it was first established but soon the Trades Union movement, in concert with left-wing middle-class radicals, would turn into an internationalist movement by their demonstrations of solidarity with the oppressed working men of Europe. Famous among these early expressions of solidarity with the peoples of other nations was the foundation of the National League for the Independence of Poland. In 1863, the Poles had risen up against their Russian overlords with the aim of securing independence for Poland and social reforms. The revolt was unsuccessful but the Poles won the hearts and minds of middle-class radicals and trade unionists in the United Kingdom who sympathised with the plight of the Poles who were yearning for full nationhood.[10] Meanwhile, the Duke of Sutherland had invited the Italian patriot, nationalist freedom fighter, and hero of Italian Unification, Giuseppe Garibaldi, to stay in London. It was to be a momentous event—there would be processions, banquets, and deputations from various public bodies that would come to honour the great general. Having long admired Garibaldi, representatives of various unions also sent their own delegations—

the Garibaldi Trades Committee—to pay homage to the great freedom fighter. One Mr Hartwell, the Secretary of the Working Men's Committee, declared:

> Illustrious Chief,—
>
> In the name of Britain's sons and daughters of toil, we bid you welcome to this metropolis. We hail you as the representative of a regenerated and united Italy, and for the love we bear to that beautiful land and its noble people, so long oppressed—but, now, thanks to your devoted patriotism and indomitable courage, almost freed from the foreign oppressors, we bid you welcome. Your name is to us a household word, the symbol of liberty, associated with lofty daring, bold enterprise, and unselfish devotion to the cause of human progress.[11]

It was the unions' increasingly 'internationalist' focus that led to the establishment of the International Working Men's Association, whose inaugural address was drafted by two famous German philosophers who shall feature in our history momentarily.

Working men might have the public strength to win the vote because they had organisations through which they could agitate for it. But did 'the powers that were' think they had the *moral* right to be included within the political nation? What did Gladstone think? The perfect opportunity presented itself. It took events across the Atlantic to markedly convince Gladstone that the working classes were morally worthy of the vote: the American Civil War—a war fought over states' rights and slavery. The economy of the southern states depended on slavery while the northern states, under the direction of President Abraham Lincoln, had in 1863 issued the Emancipation Proclamation. When the northern states, or the 'Union', blockaded the ports of the 'Confederacy', or southern states, American exports of cotton to England dropped markedly. However, rather than condemn the Union, factory workers and their unions publicly expressed their solidarity with the Union cause, which unions saw principally as a struggle to eradicate slavery. This impressed Gladstone who declared it 'a shame and a scandal that bodies of men such as these should be excluded from the parliamentary franchise'.[12] Gladstone was ready to publicly support household suffrage. When Edward Baines—a veteran of the Peterloo Massacre in 1819—brought a private members bill to parliament in 1864 which proposed lowering the franchise qualification in boroughs from £10 to £6, Gladstone finally and publicly signalled his willingness to support reform.

Baines's bill failed but that did not stop people organising outside of parliament. John Bright, the stalwart of the Anti-Corn Law League and by this time MP for Birmingham, became one of the most ardent supporters of franchise reform. Bright, indeed, has some claim to being the main figurehead of the movement in the late 1850s and early 1860s. It was at Birmingham in 1858 where he launched his own campaign for manhood suffrage. Later, he penned an essay titled 'Speech on Reform' in which he warned that it would be better for the authorities to extend the franchise in some way, rather than do nothing and risk violent class conflict, the likes of which were feared during the heyday of the Chartist era.[13] Under the direction of one of Bright's associates from his Anti-Corn League days, the National Reform Union was established in 1864.

The union was a broad church composed mainly of middle-class liberals who might hold various views on issues of foreign affairs, intervention, free trade, and religious toleration but who all agreed on the necessity of manhood suffrage. In the words of the Union's own literature they wanted:

1. To obtain such an extension of the Franchise as shall confer the Parliamentary Suffrage, in Counties and Boroughs, on every male person, householder or lodger, rated or liable to be rated, for the relief of the poor.
2. To secure the free exercise of the Franchise, by affording to the voter the protection of the Ballot.
3. To procure an equal distribution of Members of Parliament, in proportion to population and property.
4. To establish more frequent opportunities for the expression of national opinion, by shortening the duration of Parliament to three years.[14]

In spite of the Union holding over 750 public meetings between 1864 and 1867, it remained a thoroughly middle-class affair. It simply seemed unable to draw in former Chartists and other working-class radicals. Instead, these latter groups found a home in the National Reform League, founded in February 1865, with the explicit aim of securing manhood suffrage and vote by secret ballot. Numbering among its ranks the likes of George Julian Harney, Ernest Jones, and firebrand republican journalist G.W.M. Reynolds, under the Chairmanship of Edmond Beales, the League was the true heir of Chartism and succeeded in drawing support from working-class people because it was associated with the London Trades Council and the International Working Men's Association. However, there was little animosity between the Union and the League and the two bodies established a highly productive working relationship. Although both groups' aims were similar to those espoused by the Chartists some thirty years previously, the League and the Union were 'respectable'—it was very important to be deemed thus in the eyes of the establishment—and the extent to which these were 'radical' groups at all is questioned by John Belchem, who argues that they should instead be viewed as 'reformist'.[15] The League was willing to make trade-offs; its members initially agreed to support both household suffrage measures as well as more limited extensions to the franchise similar to those that were proposed by Baines in 1864.

One obstacle remained: Lord Palmerston was still Prime Minister and he fervently believed that the question of suffrage had been settled back in 1832. However, Palmerston passed away and now the floodgates to parliamentary reform were wide open. Lord Russell filled the office left vacant by Palmerston who decided that now was the time to try and get an extension of the franchise through parliament. Besides, the Conservative Party, led by the Earl of Derby, were also coming around to the idea—they had been in the political wilderness so long that they needed to support *something* which might see them returned to office. Thus, in 1865, Russell's Liberals brought a bill to parliament which aimed to enfranchise the 'respectable' working class. Under the terms of the bill, if you paid over £7 per year in rent, if you were a lodger who paid out over £10 per year in rent, or if you had savings of over £50, then you would be entitled to vote.

But the bill failed.

Many liberals were unhappy with the measures while Benjamin Disraeli managed to get enough support from those on the Liberal backbenches, who felt as though their privileges would be eroded were the bill to pass, to oppose the bill.

Russell resigned and Derby's Conservatives took power as a minority administration— Derby governing as Prime Minister from the House of Lords and Disraeli leading the Tories in the Commons as Chancellor of the Exchequer. Disraeli and had got what they wanted: their party was now back in power. But now that the League and the Union felt that, with the Conservatives in power, the need for agitation and public demonstrations was all the more pressing. Protests had accompanied the defeat of Russell's reform bill and, after the Conservatives took power, Bright began touring the country and stirring up people in his audience while hard-line radicals held well-attended public meetings in Trafalgar Square calling for a general strike. The Conservatives *had to* now address the question of political reform.

In the Commons, Disraeli decided to support the extension of the franchise. After all, if the franchise were extended, so Disraeli reasoned, the new voters would be exceedingly grateful to the Conservatives and vote them into power again, hopefully with a majority. Thus, Disraeli introduced a reform bill into the Commons in 1867. Not having a majority in the lower house, the Conservatives had to accept all amendments tabled to the bill (but due to his personal animosity against Gladstone, Disraeli would not accept any that had personally been proposed by him). In the end, because of the several amendments that had been tabled by the opposition Liberals, the second Representation of the People Act that was passed in August was more far-reaching than what the Liberals had proposed back in 1866. Now the vote was accorded not only to 40 shilling freeholders and £10 copyholders but was extended to all renters and lodgers who paid over £10 per year in towns, and to those who were paying £12 in rent per annum in the counties. Some towns containing fewer than 10,000 inhabitants were disenfranchised while some major cities such as Manchester and Leeds were given extra seats in parliament. 'The government,' Gladstone complained, 'bowled us down' by skilfully presenting his measures as household suffrage (even if many working men were still left disenfranchised).[16]

In spite of the fact that it was Disraeli's Conservatives who had introduced the Second Reform Act and got it passed, it was seen by many on the Lib-Lab coalition as a Liberal victory. And reformers quickly began pointing out the bill's flaws, as the Beehive reported in their coverage of a banquet organised by the London Working Men's Association in October:

> What has the Bill done? Has it given manhood suffrage? No. It has given household suffrage, but it has coupled with that the condition that the enfranchised householders are to pay their own rates … What has it done for the working men of London? Do you think that such of you as pay 4s a week for your lodgings will get votes? No. You will not get votes unless you pay 5s a week … It only affects the boroughs … leaving out altogether more than half the whole country.[17]

Disraeli's prediction that new voters would remain grateful to the Conservative Party remained unfulfilled. In the 1868 General Election, the Liberals, now led by Gladstone, won what might now be called a 'landslide' over Disraeli's party, gaining a majority of 100 seats.

Yet it would not be a happy ending for the Lib-Lab coalition. The Reform League was disbanded in 1868. Trade unions had supported the Liberals for the best part of the past decade, and a new Labour Representation League was founded in 1869 which aimed to help promote the electoral success of prospective Lib-Lab MPs. As a result of this partnership, the Liberals accorded full legal recognition and financial support to unions in 1871. But in the same year, the Liberals also passed Criminal Law Amendment Act which:

> Inflicted a punishment of three months' imprisonment, with hard labour, on any one who attempts to coerce another for trade purposes by the use of personal violence; by such threats as would justify a magistrate in binding a man to keep the peace; or by persistently following a person about from place to place, hiding his tools, clothes, or other property, watching and besetting his house, or following him along any street or road with two or more other persons in a disorderly manner. These last clauses were directed against the practice of picketing.[18]

Although intended to protect 'scabs' from violence on picket lines, the bill essentially made it illegal to picket full stop. The leaders of the Labour Representation League were furious with the Liberals and began calling for the establishment of an independent labour party. The establishment of a party especially for labouring men, however, was still two decades away.[19]

The Frightful Hobgoblin

Further extensions to the franchise followed in 1884. This 'Third Reform Act', as it is so-called, enfranchised all male lodgers and householders. It did not matter now whether you rented property, owned property, or were even a servant in a middle-class household—now you could vote. It was halfway between household suffrage and universal male suffrage. A further six million voters were added to the electoral register when the act was passed. But many were still excluded from the political nation, notably women. It would not be until 1918 that *some* women received the right to vote, and their struggle is the story of a subsequent chapter of this book.

Radicals and reformers had been campaigning for an extension to the franchise since the 1850s. While these campaigns were underway in England, something ominous was stirring in Europe. This 'thing' was first noticed in November 1850 when Helen Macfarlane, in G.J. Harney's little-known Chartist periodical *Red Republican*, proclaimed that 'a frightful hobgoblin stalks throughout Europe'.[20] This hobgoblin was frightening the authorities all over the continent. It seemed to Macfarlane that 'all the

201

powers of the past have joined in a holy crusade to lay this ghost to rest,—the Pope and the Czar, Metternich and Guizot, French Radicals and German police spies'.[21]

What was the hobgoblin and why was it stalking Europe? Readers will probably have guessed, of course, that Macfarlane's words were actually a translation of those written by Karl Marx and Friedrich Engels—who were instrumental in drafting the inaugural address of the International Working Men's Association—in a publication of theirs that was published in German two years earlier named *The Communist Manifesto*.

Communism is predicated upon numerous principles, such as common ownership of the means of production and the absence of social classes. However, the idea of common ownership didn't begin with Marx; the foundations of communism can be traced back to the New Testament book of the Acts of the Apostles (2: 45) which states that 'all who believed were together and had all things in common; they would sell their possessions and goods and distribute the proceeds to all, as any had need'. In England, there developed several 'socialisms' independently of Marx and Engels's thinking. Evidence of proto-socialist ideology can be found as far back as 1381, when the radical preacher, John Ball, famously asked: 'When Adam delved and Eve span, who was then the gentleman?' Later, the actions of the Diggers and the Levellers in the English Revolution, along with

Red Republican issue of 9 November 1850, in which the first English translation of Karl Marx and Friedrich Engels's *Communist Manifesto* was published. (Stephen Basdeo's Personal Collection)

Ricardian Socialism and Owenism, demonstrate that the concept of sweeping political and social reform was hardly 'new' when Marx's book first made its appearance in England.

Occurrences in England along with the 1848 revolutions in Italy, France, Germany, Austria, and Denmark had a profound effect on Marx and Engels's writings. With the exception of Britain, most of these countries were ruled by absolute monarchies, the middle classes and the working classes, allied together, sought, in some regions, freedom from foreign rule, along with the right to vote and a free press. The revolutionary movement began in Sicily, Italy, in January 1848. Rebellions then broke out in the capitals of the three great monarchies, Paris, Vienna, and Berlin. The revolution in France, also known as the February Revolution, was the only revolutionary attempt to sustain lasting change. After the February Revolution, the Second Republic and universal manhood suffrage were established. The Revolution was driven by nationalist and republican ideals among the French general public, and the revolution ended the constitutional monarchy of Louis-Phillipe. After the revolution, Louis-Napoleon, in 1852, established himself as a dictatorial emperor of the Second French Empire. In other countries the revolutions were quickly suppressed; thousands of people were killed in the revolution, some were imprisoned, and many more were forced into exile.

Even the most absolutist and reactionary states could not wholly ignore demands for reform and were forced to make some concessions. The abolition of indentured servitude occurred in Austria and Hungary. A representative democracy was established in the Netherlands. However, none of these revolutions were able to bring about a 'new order', paving the way for men by the names of Karl Marx and Friedrich Engels to change the world forever with their writings.

Karl Marx and Friedrich Engels were both born in Germany and founded the Communist Correspondence Society, which, having merged with the League of the Just, became the Communist League in 1847. Founded in London, this organisation was a precursor to the International Working Men's Association. Marx and Engels were inspired by the idea of equality in society. Engels, having written *The Condition of the Working Class in England*, and both of them having been onlookers to the 1848 revolutions, published *The Communist Manifesto* in German which summarised their theories concerning the nature of society and politics, namely that in their own words '[t]he history of all hitherto existing society is the history of class struggles'. It also featured their ideas for how capitalist society would eventually be replaced with a communist society. The final paragraph of the *Manifesto* therefore called for the 'forcible overthrow of all existing social conditions', which served as a call for communist revolutions around the world.[22]

The Communist Manifesto presented a logical approach to the analysis of class struggle and argued that capitalism is unstable. Marx and Engels split the *Manifesto* into four parts:

Part 1: Bourgeois and Proletarians
Part 2: Proletarians and Communists
Part 3: Socialist and Communist Literature
Part 4: Position of the Communists in Relation to the Various Existing
    Opposition Parties.

In a communist society, Marx and Engels argued, the proletariat—the working class—would 'seize the means of production', place them under democratic control, and abolish private property:

> The distinguishing feature of Communism is not the abolition of property generally, but the abolition of bourgeois property. But modern bourgeois private property is the final and most complete expression of the system of producing and appropriating products that is based on class antagonisms, on the exploitation of the many by the few. In this sense, the theory of the Communists may be summed up in the single sentence: Abolition of private property.[23]

Marx and Engels distinguished between private property and personal property. Personal property was that which someone clearly owned through use and was the fruit of their own labour. Besides, the proletariat of most nations had little in the way of property anyway:

> Hard-won, self-acquired, self-earned property! Do you mean the property of petty artisan and of the small peasant, a form of property that preceded the bourgeois form? There is no need to abolish that; the development of industry has to a great extent already destroyed it, and is still destroying it daily.[24]

Marx and Engels called for the abolition of bourgeois private property, which the bourgeoisie owned through exploiting the labour of the working classes, and therefore serves as a means of buttressing the power of one class—the bourgeoisie—over another class, the proletariat:

> You are horrified at our intending to do away with private property. But in your existing society, private property is already done away with for nine-tenths of the population; its existence for the few is solely due to its non-existence in the hands of those nine-tenths. You reproach us, therefore, with intending to do away with a form of property, the necessary condition for whose existence is the non-existence of any property for the immense majority of society ... Communism deprives no man of the power to appropriate the products of society; all that it does is to deprive him of the power to subjugate the labour of others by means of such appropriations.[25]

Although Macfarlane translated the *Manifesto* in the 1850s, it did not immediately pick up much traction in England and its ideas did not become popularised until the 1870s. Eric Hobsbawm identified three reasons for this. The first reason is the leadership role that Marx assumed in the establishment of the International Workingmen's Association, having been a fairly minor figure in Britain prior to this.

Secondly, Marx did not come to prominence among socialists outside of Germany until he expressed his support of the Paris Commune of 1871—which was watched with much interest among socialists in both Britain and Germany—and he elucidated his thoughts on the Paris Commune in *The Civil War in France.* Lastly, and perhaps most significantly, in the popularisation of the *Manifesto*, was the treason trial of Social Democratic Party (SPD) leaders in Germany in 1872. During the trial, prosecutors read the *Manifesto* out loud as evidence which in turn was reported in the press. New editions of the *Manifesto* began to be published in German and English—Macfarlane's original English translation having fallen into obscurity after the *Red Republican* ended its print run in 1852.

The cause of socialism, having hitherto been a fringe ideology in Britain, began to make headway. In 1881, Henry Hyndman founded the Social Democratic Federation in the United Kingdom, which was the first organised explicitly socialist society in the country. Further socialist societies were set up in France and the United States of America. The late Victorian and early twentieth century British and American socialist societies were initially thoroughly bourgeois associations and not in the least dangerous, although this perception among the police would change eventually.[26] And it is to one famous English socialist, who was a member of the Social Democratic Federation, to which Anne Anderson turns in a subsequent chapter as she introduces us to the artist, designer, and communist activist, William Morris.

Notes

1. An Act for the Better Security of the Crown and Government of the United Kingdom, ch. 12. 11 & 12 Victoria (London: HMSO, 1848).
2. G.J. Harney, *Friend of the People* January 18, 1851, cited in Dorothy George, *The Dignity of Chartism* (London: Verso, 2015), 165.
3. John Belchem, *Popular Radicalism in Nineteenth-Century Britain* (Basingstoke: MacMillan, 1996), 102–04.
4. Ibid.
5. See W.E. Burns, *The Age of Equipoise* (London: Unwin, 1964).
6. Ibid., 104; see also Alan Sykes, *The Rise and Fall of British Liberalism: 1776-1988* (Abingdon: Routledge, 2014).
7. "Address of the Northern Reform Union," *Newcastle Chronicle* March 12, 1815, 2.
8. Ibid.
9. "Address of the Manhood Suffrage and Vote by Ballot Association," *Reynolds's Weekly Newspaper* November 23, 1862, 1.
10. John F. Kutolowski, "English Radicals and the Polish Insurrection of 1863–64," *The Polish Review*, 11: 3 (1966), 3-28 (p. 4).
11. Robert Hartwell, "The Welcome to Garibaldi," *Reynolds's Newspaper* April 17, 1864, 2.
12. Asa Briggs, *Victorian People: A Reassessment of Persons and Themes, 1851-67* (University of Chicago Press, 1955), 227.

13. Angus Hawkins, *Parliament, Party and the Art of Politics in Britain, 1855–59* (Basingstoke: Palgrave, 1987), 158.
14. Leaflet issued by the National Reform Union (n.d.) [1866–67] cited in G.D.H. Cole and A.W. Filson, *British Working-Class Movements: Select Documents 1789–1875* (London: MacMillan, 1967), 531–32 (p. 531).
15. Belchem, *Popular Radicalism*, 114.
16. K. T. Hoppen, *The Mid-Victorian Generation: England, 1846–886* (Oxford University Press, 1998), 250.
17. "Reform Fete and Banquet," *The Beehive* October 5, 1867, 1.
18. William Edward Hartpole Lecky, *Democracy and Liberty: Volume II* (Indianapolis: Liberty Fund, 1981), pp. 376-7.
19. Belchem, *Popular Radicalism*, 120.
20. Helen Macfarlane, "Manifesto of the German Communist Party," *Red Republican* November 9, 1850, 1.
21. Ibid.
22. Karl Marx and Friedrich Engels, *The Communist Manifesto*, accessed May 18, 2020. Available at: www.marxists.org.
23. Ibid.
24. Ibid.
25. Ibid.
26. However, separate socialist secret, and in fact, more revolutionary societies formed in London such as the Russian Social Democratic Labour Party in the early 1900s headed by Vladimir Lenin and later joined by Leon Trotsky. Both of these men would later play a larger part in the Russian Revolution and had been exiled from Russia for spreading the idea of communism.

William Morris

Anne Anderson

Following what we would call a mid-life crisis, William Morris (1834-96) was converted to the Socialist cause at the age of forty-nine. His was not a youthful rebellion, but a revolt born out of frustration and despair. He had been a vociferous critic of industrialised society well before he crossed a 'river of fire' to become a revolutionary socialist in 1883.[1] As a radical thinker and energetic doer he is seen as the father of the international Arts and Crafts movement, which promoted 'Unity of the Arts', handicrafts, dress reform, ruralism (the 'Back to the Land' movement), the garden city, the folk-song revival and preservation of rural traditions. All were linked, to some degree, by the ideal of 'the Simple Life', prioritising the quality of life over 'getting on'. Eco-socialist writers see Morris pre-figuring green issues.[2] He expressed many of his radical ideas in his poetry and prose. A prolific writer, he is best remembered for the epic *Earthly Paradise* (1868–70) and his utopian novel *News from Nowhere; or, An Epoch of Rest* (1890). Visiting Red House, Bexleyheath, his first marital home and Kelmscott Manor, Lechlade, his retreat in later life, is for many a pilgrimage, expressing a desire to connect with Morris's spirit; we admire his strength of purpose and sympathise with his underlying anger and unwavering commitment.[3] According to his doctor, his fatal illness was 'simply being William Morris and having done more work than most ten men'.[4]

Art historians, particularly those who see Morris as a pioneer of twentieth century modernism, focus on his art at the expense of his politics, while social and political scholars emphasise his activism rather than his art. This separation impoverishes both sides. In *Pioneers of Modern Design from William Morris to Walter Gropius* (1936), Nikolaus Pevsner highlights Morris's mission to reform the product, condemning the false division between the fine and decorative or applied arts and arguing that even the most humble objects used in daily life could be expressions of beauty as well as utility: 'We owe it to him that an ordinary man's dwelling-house has once more become a worthy object of the architect's thought, a chair, a wallpaper or a vase a worthy object of the artist's imagination'.[5] However, Pevsner maintains Morris's commitment to the handicrafts trapped him in the nineteenth century.

The best Marxist account of Morris, which attempts to cover his entire oeuvre, is E.P. Thompson's *William Morris: Romantic to Revolutionary* (1955). Thompson argues Morris revitalised the philosophies of Thomas Carlyle and John Ruskin, drawing from Carlyle that labour is the basis of life and from Ruskin that labour must be creative.

William Morris as pictured in John William Mackail, *The Life of William Morris*, 2 vols (London: Longmans, Green & Co. 1899). (Anne Anderson Personal Collection)

Having read these writers in his youth, when Morris encountered Socialism in the 1880s, he discovered a shared hatred of modern civilisation and the will to forge a new society. Morris's 'youthful protest, still burning within him' flared; 'Morris, the Romantic in revolt, became a realist and a revolutionary'.[6] Reading Ruskin prepared Morris for Marx's critique of alienated labour; capitalism separated art and work, they could only be reunited under communism. Morris was unique in having a clear vision of the communist organisation of work: 'Nowadays we do not talk about what is going to happen after the revolution. We're always talking about how it is going to be achieved, whereas Morris was always talking about a vision of the future'.[7]

Morris's life can be viewed as a series of awakenings, his radicalisation tracked through his childhood and education, his association with the avant-garde Pre-Raphaelite artists, the founding of his famous firm, Morris, Marshall, Faulkner & Co. in 1861, and his social activism, which came to dominate the 1880s.[8]

Raising a Radical

The eldest son of a successful financier, Morris enjoyed a privileged childhood: his infancy was spent at Woodford Hall, adjacent to Epping Forest, Essex. George Bernard Shaw (1856–1950) considered him spoilt, a little prince in his own land petted and indulged by his two elder sisters. A precocious child, Morris had read all of Sir Walter Scott's *Waverly* novels by the age of nine. Riding around the estate in his own 'miniature' suit of armour, he imagined himself as the hero of Scott's eponymous novel *Ivanhoe* (1819). This enchanted childhood was interrupted by the unexpected death of his father. In later life, Morris cast his father as a capitalist villain, a ruthless speculator who exemplified 'richness was in fact poverty'.[9] However, Morris was in many ways his father's son; a successful businessman who founded an innovative company that was always conscious of its markets.

The fourteen-year-old Morris was sent to Marlborough College. Judging by countless reminiscences, Marlborough's regime crushed the spirit of many boys. With bullying endemic, the only way to survive was by keeping one's distance. Fiona MacCarthy, his biographer, argues Morris was already forming his persona as an 'oddball' or outcast.[10] In November 1851, the college erupted into 'The Rebellion', a series of riots provoked by the headmaster's regimen. Morris's first taste of anarchy instilled his repugnance of mindless 'mob violence. Marlborough also made him aware of class divisions and upper class arrogance. Alarmed by these events many boys were removed, including Morris who spent the next year studying privately for his Oxford entry.

Oxford Days

With Morris falling under the sway of Marlborough's High Church leanings, his first career choice, High-Church Anglican clergyman, was inevitable; drawn by the sensuous beauty of ritualistic worship, Morris also wished for a life devoted to high purposes. The friendships made at Exeter College, Oxford, were rarely broken; it would be true to say Morris was a 'man's man'. His chums in the 'Birmingham Set' included Charles Faulkner (1833-92), a founding partner of Morris, Marshall, Faulkner & Co., and Edward Burne-Jones (1833-98); 'Topsy and Ned', as they were known in this circle, were a perfect pairing, with Morris the energetic 'doer' and Burne-Jones the ethereal 'thinker'.

Reading Scott's *Ivanhoe* (1819), *The Talisman* (1825) and *Quentin Durward* (1823) and Charlotte Yonge's *Heir of Redclyffe* (1853), Morris' view of the medieval world was coloured by modern romance and old-fashioned chivalry. Discovering Sir Thomas Malory's *Morte d'Arthur* (1485), Morris empathised with the gallant quest for the Holy Grail and the camaraderie of a brotherhood bound by a code of honour- loyal, merciful and chivalrous to women. Sir Kenelm Digby, in his eulogy to the Middle Ages, *The Broad Stone of Honour, or Rules for the Gentlemen of England* (1822), claimed Arthur's knights were forerunners of the modern English gentleman. It was a question of character, not birth. Morris was initially steeped in gentlemanly valour and Tory Medievalism.

Carlyle and Ruskin

> Carlyle and Ruskin. The latter, before my days of practical Socialism, was my master … how deadly dull the world would have been twenty years ago but for Ruskin! It was through him that I learned to give form to my discontent, which I must say was not by any means vague. Apart from the desire to produce beautiful things, the leading passion of my life has been and is hatred of modern civilization.
>
> Morris, 'How I became a Socialist' (1896)

Morris was inevitably influenced by the great sages of the era, Thomas Carlyle (1795-1881) and John Ruskin (1819-1900), who constantly compared the past with the present and deemed modern life wanting.[11] Carlyle's *On Heroes, Hero-Worship, and The Heroic in History* (1841) valorised leadership and action: 'the history of the world is but the biography of great men'. *Signs of the Times* (1829) and *Past and Present* (1843), focused on the 'Condition of England Question', the state of the English working class due to industrialisation. The 'mechanical age' was turning people into automatons devoid of individuality and spirituality. Mechanistic thought suppressed human freedom; workers were reduced to slavery, losing the ability to think and act creatively.

According to the architect Augustus Welby Pugin (1812-52), the modern world was filled with ugliness caused by greed: inhuman factories, filthy rivers and appalling housing conditions for the ordinary man. In his famous *Contrasts; or, A Parallel Between The Noble Edifices Of The Middle Ages And Corresponding Buildings Of The Present Day* (1836), Pugin painted a grim picture, the cityscape dominated by chimneys belching out smoke rather than the beautiful spires of medieval churches. It was a Godless age drive by mammon; there was no benevolence, as poverty drove families into the workhouse. The ruling class ignored its obligations to the people, turning their backs on the Condition of England.

Drawn by its 'savage beauty', its variety and naturalism, Ruskin valorised the Gothic as the highest form of architecture. His polemic, expressed in *The Seven Lamps of Architecture* (1849) and *The Stones of Venice* (1851-53), was shaped by Morris into his own 'mission statement'. He would uphold Ruskin's *Lamp of Truth*, the honest use of materials, *Life*, that buildings should be made by human hands allowing the artisan freedom of expression and *Memory*, seeing buildings as living history, with each generation adding to the story.

Morris was a self-confessed sentimentalist; he saw beauty and romance in old buildings. Experiencing England's great medieval cathedrals, 'miracles of art', stirred his imagination allowing him to travel back in time; he identified with the builders, the nameless artisans, masons, woodcarvers and metalworkers, who had created such beauty. The cathedral expressed aesthetic and social harmony, a product of communal effort which united all the different branches of the arts. Ruskin privileged invention over perfection; the medieval craftsman's imagination and creativity was not crushed by standardisation. The modern worker was a slave, every aspect of his work controlled by the machine. Machine-made products were perfect but soulless, as they did not express the human spirit. Although healthy handiwork was by its nature imperfect, it exemplified the 'law of human life ... Effort'; we should always be striving to do better.[12]

Ruskin and Morris's respect for old buildings placed them at odds with the zeal for restoration. Founding the Society for the Protection of Ancient Buildings (1877), Morris endeavoured to save his beloved medieval buildings from the practice of returning them to their original, idealised, state. Conservation, repairing not replacing, and understanding a building as a living entity, its entire evolution worthy of preservation as 'cultural history', are now the norm.

'On the Nature of Gothic Architecture', in *The Stones of Venice*, Ruskin developed his critique of contemporary society. The root of the problem lay in the division of labour but 'It is not, truly speaking the labour that is divided, but the men ... the mass of society is made up of morbid thinkers and miserable workers ... the one envying, the other despising, his brother'.[13] Thought and labour should be united, as they were before the industrial age:

Now it is only by labour that thought can be made healthy, and only by thought that labour can be made happy, and the two cannot be separated with impunity. It would be well if all of us were good handicraftsmen of some kind, and the dishonour of manual labour done away with altogether.[14]

To be a good architect, necessitated working in the mason's yard, gaining an understanding of the properties and practises of working in stone. The distinction between one man and another was down to skill and experience, not birth or class.

Ruskin's thundering prose must have gone far to neutralise Morris's desire to retreat into monastic seclusion: 'What we think, or what we know, or what we believe is, in the end, of little consequence. The only consequence is what we *do*'.[15] Stirred into action, Morris commenced his 'Crusade and Holy Warfare against the Age'.[16]

The Poet and Writer

If a chap can't compose an epic poem while he's weaving tapestry, he had better shut up, he'll never do any good at all.[17]

Morris began writing poetry during his second year at Oxford. His stance, on the relationship between art and society, was mediated through the poems of Alfred Tennyson. In *The Palace of Art* (1832/revised 1842) Tennyson's 'Soul' withdraws from the world into a refuge of beauty (I built my soul a lordly pleasure-house, Wherein at ease for aye to dwell) but locked away, this love of beauty leads to despair, self-loathing and hatred of both death and life. This 'crucial tension between the concept of art as escapist and the belief in art as an incentive to practical commitment' can be found in Morris's *The Defence of Guinevere* (1858).[18] This first volume of poetry, set within a medieval world of chivalric love and the quest for the Holy Grail, dealt with the defeat of noble aspirations and ideals. Through this framework, Morris was really commenting on the impasse of his own times.

While *The Defence of Guinevere* was attacked for its preoccupation with sexuality and death, which went beyond the bounds of Victorian decency, Morris's epic *The Earthly Paradise* (1868) enjoyed popular success. Morris weaves stories from diverse sources, from classical mythology to medieval legends and Icelandic sagas. His powerful descriptions, of buildings and landscapes, transport the reader:

[I] Can see above the green and unburnt fen,
The little houses of an English town,
Cross-timbered, thatched with fen-reeds coarse and brown,
And high o'er these, three gables, great and fair,
That slender rods of columns do upbear
Over the minster doors…Yea, I heard withal,
In the fresh morning air, the trowels fall
Upon the stone, a thin noise far away…[19]

This *picture poesis*, a description of Peterborough cathedral, offers us a 'speaking picture'. Morris used language to describe his experience of art; he could paint with words more effectively than painting on canvas, his descriptions giving us livelier 'Ideas than the Sight of things themselves'.[20] He depicts the building under construction, rather than complete; he was always more concerned with process, the making, rather than the finished work.

In his romances, rather than seeing the Middle Ages as violent and tyrannical, Morris paints a glowing picture of a golden age, when peasants were prosperous and happy, and guilds protected workers from exploitation. His vision of 'Little England' was homely, centred on the lives of ordinary, unnamed folk, who had farmed the land, lived in small villages and built churches. Out of this homeliness came 'an art of peasants, rather than of merchant-princes or courtiers', which 'clung fast to the life of the people'.[21] A sweet, natural, unaffected art that 'lived in many a quaint pattern of the loom and printing block and embroiders needle'.[22] 'English art' was not grand, impressive or pompous but inventive and individual. With no divisions between life, work and art, Morris's agrarian utopia would be fully expressed in *News from Nowhere* (1890)

At his death, Morris was remembered as the author of *The Earthly Paradise*. His politics was dismissed, *The Times* pouring scorn on 'the force that drew him, without much regard for logic, or for the facts of life, into sentimental Socialism'.[23] Morris's Socialistic doctrines had not done much harm, being couched in a poetic language unintelligible to the working man. MacCarthy maintains 'this leading article began a whole tradition of supercilious belittlement of Morris that, a century later, still persists'.[24]

A Pre-Raphaelite Brother

While touring the cathedrals of France in 1855, Morris abandoned the idea of taking holy orders; instead, his life would be devoted to art. Given his love of Medieval buildings, he decided to train as an architect. He briefly entered the offices of the Gothic Revival architect, George Edmund Street (1824-81), best known for the Law Courts on the Strand. Here he befriended Philip Webb (1831-1915), who, much later sagely observed that he designed Morris's first house, Red House (1859) and his last, his tomb in the churchyard at Kelmscott, Oxon. Finding the rigours of architectural drawing tedious, he abandoned this career choice to take up painting. Pursuing this path relatively late in life was risky. Many entered the Royal Academy schools or the National Art Training program at Kensington in their teens. It did not help that his guide and mentor, Dante Gabriel Rossetti (1828-82) was not a dedicated teacher. Morris never received a thorough grounding in either the fine arts or design. Discovering pattern-making was his true calling, Morris learnt by trial and error. Under the influence of Rossetti, Morris took his first step to becoming a rebel; he became a Pre-Raphaelite artist.

Combining revivalism with rebellion, the Pre-Raphaelites are now regarded as 'Britain's first modern art movement'. Founded in 1848, the year of revolution throughout Europe, the Pre-Raphaelite Brotherhood was inspired by the art of the early

Renaissance, the 'art before the time of Raphael' (1483–1520). The key members, William Holman Hunt (1827–1910), John Everett Millais (1830–96) and Dante Gabriel Rossetti (1828–82), challenged the Royal Academy, Britain's premier artistic institution. The Brotherhood was determined to overthrow artistic convention and revitalise British art. They rejected ideal or standardised faces in favour of drawing directly from life. Models were sought on the streets; faces were drawn from people within their circle of family and friends. Landscapes and buildings were carefully recorded, while objects were chosen for their decorative and symbolic meaning. Authenticity became a driving goal; whether the subject was taken from the Bible, Shakespeare or modern life, the characters, their costumes and the setting, had to be accurate. As the Brotherhood fragmented in 1853, a second generation coalesced around Rossetti, who favoured medieval chivalry and courtly love.

Today Pre-Raphaelitism is indelibly linked to Rossetti's romantic medievalism. Themes taken from Dante, Petrarch and Chaucer fuelled Morris's own imagination. Above all Beauty was an antidote to the ugliness of modern life. The first milestone in Morris's career came in 1857, with the decoration of the Oxford Union. Led by Rossetti, a brotherhood of seven eager artists went forth to recreate Italian quattrocento frescoes on the walls of the Union's newly built debating chamber. Inspired by Rossetti's recent illustrations for Tennyson's poems (1857), the topic chosen was King Arthur and his knights. Unfortunately, untutored in the art of fresco painting, the result was bitterly disappointing. Morris abandoned his section, *Sir Palomides' jealousy of Sir Tristram and Iseult*, and began inscribing floral motifs on the ceiling. This was his first attempt at patternmaking.

An unsuitable marriage

A new 'stunner', Jane Burden (1839-1914), modelled for Morris's only known oil painting, *La Belle Iseult* (1858, Tate Britain). Wedded to King Mark when she really loves Sir Tristram, Iseult is the victim of star-crossed love. Life already seemed to be imitating art, as Morris, Rossetti and Jane were to be caught in a complex love triangle. Burden represented a new type of beauty, breaking away from Victorian ideals. She was tall and willowy, with long slender hands; her most distinctive feature was her dark, curly hair. Her facial features were quite course; a heavy jaw, pronounced thick lips and a 'mono-brow'. She was no dainty doll.

Morris is said to have inscribed on the canvas 'I cannot paint you, but I love you', this declaration of love being a marriage proposal. Consciously flouting class boundaries, his family deemed this a highly unsuitable match. Jane was the daughter of a stableman and laundress; with limited prospects, she probably hoped to go into domestic service. An engagement lasting some two years was to prepare her for the role of a gentleman's wife. However, Jane was highly intelligent and embraced her self-education; a voracious reader, she learnt French and Italian and became an accomplished pianist. She was able to converse as an equal with the intelligentsia who passed through her various houses. While Burden recreated herself, a common girl transformed into a society lady,

Miss Jane Burden, later Mrs Jane Morris, after Dante Gabriel Rossetti. (Anne Anderson Personal Collection)

she was not a conventional middle class housewife.

Can this marriage be read as an act of rebellion, a facet of Morris's radicalisation or a form of social experimentation? More likely he was simply following the example of the artists he admired. Rossetti and fellow Pre-Raphaelite painter Ford Madox Brown were involved with working class women. Falling in love, Morris wanted to save Jane from a life of drudgery. This could be couched as an act of chivalry, like saving a damozel in distress. Jane's detractors imply that, motivated by shame, she denied her humble origins, in later life becoming a snob. According to the writer Vernon Lee (pseudonym of Violet Paget, 1856-1935), her husband's 'socialistic doings' made her miserable; she was hostile to 'grubby politics'.[25] This unattractive view of Burden was spread by Shaw:

> I knew that the sudden eruption into her temple of beauty, with its Pre-Raphaelite Priests, of the proletarian comrades who began to infest the premises as Morris's fellow-Socialists, must be horribly disagreeable to her.[26]

Such bias comes from Lee and Shaw's own class consciousness; Lee appropriated Jane's story for her novel *Miss Brown* (1884) which in turn formed the basis for Shaw's *Pygmalion* (1914), with Jane caricatured as Eliza Doolittle. In fact, reading through Jane's letters, her main complaint against Morris's Socialist 'scallywags' was they were all talk, rarely putting words into action. By the 1880s, Jane seems to have been radicalised, judging by her letter to Crom Price, an old friend from Morris's Oxford days: 'I have a new disease called "Socialism on the brain"'.[27] Keenly aware of the plight of working class women, in 1902, she took direct action to assist Ann and Emily Lockyer, seamstresses fined for pawning four pairs of trousers.[28]

Morris's attitude to his marriage has sparked much speculation; even when the affair with Rossetti became quite open, there was no talk of divorce. It has been argued that Morris had to keep up a front of respectability, as one of his main clients was the

Anglican church. Following this line of thought, Kelmscott Manor was leased jointly with Rossetti in 1871, so that Jane and Gabriel could retreat out of the public eye. They may have planned a life together, but disaster struck; in June 1872, Rossetti suffered a mental breakdown from which he never recovered. Tragedy also befell the Morris family, when Jenny, their eldest daughter was diagnosed with epilepsy. During the late 1870s and 1880s, Jane and William increasingly lived separate lives, with Morris taking to the platform and committed to his causes.

Hopes and Fears for Art

Red House, completed for the newly married couple in 1859, enjoyed a relaxed, carefree, spirit. It was both a residential home and a place of work, a gathering place for young dreamers and revolutionaries. From the outset, Morris seems to have envisaged a shared life with his friends, an artistic commune where they could develop and fulfil their artistic potential. Philip Webb even drew up plans for a second wing, to be shared by Burne-Jones and his wife Georgiana and Rossetti and Lizzie Siddal, whom he married in 1860. This ambitious scheme had to be abandoned, as Siddal died.

Red House, Upton and Kelmscott Manor, after a drawing by E.H. New. (Anne Anderson Personal Collection)

215

Masterminding the interior decor, Morris drew on a vast lexicon of influences: Arthurian legend, Chaucer's tales and illuminated manuscripts. Medieval in spirit, Red House is essentially a Pre-Raphaelite 'Palace of Art'. This was a shared endeavour, debated and brought to life with the help of his friends: murals were painted by Burne-Jones and Siddal, the embroideries worked Jane Morris and her sister Bessie Burden, the furniture and glassware designed by Webb. This shared experience led to the founding of Morris, Marshall, Faulkner and Co. in April 1861. The prospectus argued that the smallest work 'susceptible of art beauty' should now be the province of artists. Left in the hands of commercial manufacturers, the decorative arts had declined; inferior design was compounded by poor workmanship. Challenging the accepted status quo, 'with the conceited courage of a young man I set myself to reforming ... and started a sort of firm for producing decorative articles'.[29] The partners, Webb, Rossetti, Burne-Jones, Faulkner and Madox Brown, formed a 'new artistic brotherhood destined to transform the decorative arts and effect a revolution in taste'.[30] Morris argued, the 'true secret of happiness lies in the taking a genuine interest in all the details of daily life, in elevating them by art'.[31] The Firm was to make beautiful objects of everyday use; 'they make our toil happy, our rest fruitful'.[32]

Morris argued in 'The Lesser Arts' (1877) that during the Middle Ages there had been no divisions between the arts.[33] Artists were also craftsmen who turned their skills to different tasks. The separation into higher arts (painting, sculpture, architecture) and 'lesser' (ceramics, glass, textiles and furniture) had been detrimental. The craft system had been gradually destroyed, and with it the basis of a truly popular art. To rectify the problem, the craftsman had to be raised up to work side by side with the artist. However, modern society was dependant on the 'unhappy labour of the greater part of men' who were forced into useless toil by the system of competitive commerce. 'Labour-saving machinery', saved the capitalist the cost of labour, and enabled him to extend the duration of labour to expand profits. Happiness could only be achieved when work was no longer drudgery but free and creative. To be pleasurable work had to offer 'variety, hope of creation, and the self-respect which comes of a sense of usefulness'.[34] Morris asserted such pleasure was 'the birthright of all workmen'; robbed of pleasure they could never be happy.

Morris's position was in part born out of the 'sensuous pleasure' he experienced in making things: he mastered many crafts, embroidery, fabric dyeing and hand-blocked printing, weaving, as well as founding his own printing press. He felt a 'mysterious bodily pleasure' through the 'deft exercise of the bodily powers'.[35] Although Morris enjoyed making things, he realised this was a privilege, as most workers were denied any leisure. Morris's practice as a designer and maker informed his politics; for Morris, the process was as important as the final product. Learning craft practices and struggling to discover techniques lost or abandoned in the course of industrialisation, enabled Morris to understand the relation between the worker and work. Assuming the role of the worker, he crossed from bourgeoisie employer to that of the proletariat employee. Talking man to man about work, Morris bridged a vast social divide; born out of experience, his commitment to the working man was genuine. Moreover, he

The Chintz-printing Room, Merton
Abbey, from a drawing by E.H. New.
(Anne Anderson Personal Collection)

empathised, concluding that if he could not bear to work in a factory for twelve hours a day, how could anybody else. Morris's sense of injustice was compounded by his belief that craftwork was the artistic expression of the common man; 'real art is the expression by man of his pleasure in labour ... art which is made by the people and for the people, as a happiness to the maker and the user'.[36]

Man's genius had flourished during the Middle Ages, when freedom of expression was commonplace but had been crushed by the division of labour and the rigid organisation of the factory which kept the worker chained to a single repetitive task. There are echoes of Ruskin in his rhetoric; 'mere toiling to live, that we may live to toil'.[37] However, while a paternalistic Ruskin called on the ruling classes to reform society, Morris envisaged the overthrow of the capitalist system.

Morris's anti-machine invective has been used to position him as anti-modern, his socialism requiring a return to pre-mechanised modes of production. Modernists, such as Pevsner, focus on the product and not with the process of making; through machinery and mass-production good designs can be made available to all. But Morris was no luddite; at Merton Abbey, his workshops on the outskirts of London, he used Jacquard looms for weaving. He argued for a revival of 'intelligent handicraft', not a return to previous conditions: a society of equals would not tolerate a 'vicarious life by means of machines, that it will in short be the master of its machinery and not the servant, as our age is'.[38] Machinery would help the workman's hand-labour, not supplant it and relieve him from mere drudgery. Morris refined his position in 'The Socialist Ideal' (1891). If art was to become ''the common property of the whole people', then manufactured wares had to keep 'some spirit of the handicraftsman, whether the goods be made by hand, or by a machine that helps the hand, or by one that supersedes it'.[39] Machine production was to be infused with standards of craftsmanship and a spirit of self-expression that had been present in pre-industrial times.

However, although Morris favoured association rather than competition, he did not establish a co-operative or workers guild, such as C.R. Ashbee's Guild of Handicrafts (1888-1907). Morris ran his company in a traditional manner, although much of the revenue from selling his wallpapers and chintzes supported his various causes. As he developed a radical stance, the Firm became a thorn in his side; his detractors charged him with hypocrisy. The comic magazine *Punch* was quick to call him out in 'Sigurd the Socialist':

> Mr William Morris having publicly advocated Socialism, and the division of capital among the labourers, declines an invitation to put his revolutionary theories into practice ... [saying] that he thought on the whole that the time for such deeds was not ripe ... Quoth he, "I'm a Socialist true, but on further reflection, the fact is, The theory's all we should hold, and I won't put the plan into practice.[40]

Although Morris railed against 'ministering to the swinish luxury of the rich', his furnishings were adopted by the intelligentsia, artistic, literary and political, becoming an expression of political correctness or even 'radical chic'. The 'strangely designed wallpapers' and 'sad coloured velveteens' were adopted by the Fabian socialists, as Hubert Bland, one of the founding members of the society, observed.[41] Fabian and social reformer Beatrice Webb (1858–1943) chose Morris papers and furniture, hoping to make her home in Grosvenor Road, London, as beautiful as possible given her 'limited cash and still more limited taste'.[42] Supporter of 'Guild socialism' and the co-operative movement, Fabian G.D.H. Cole (1889-1959) was devoted to both Morris's socialism as well as his wallpapers and fabrics.[43] His wife, Margaret Cole, the Labour party activist, was photographed in an armchair covered in 'Corncockle' chintz.

The Morris aesthetic was also favoured in suffragette and suffragist circles; the Pankhursts were brought up with 'greenery, yallery' wallpapers, while Frances Partridge (1900-2004) recalled the 'dark and jungly' patterns of her family home in Bedford Square.[44] Frances was taken by her mother to a suffragist protest at the tender age of six. Marrying Ralph Partridge, Frances's diaries chronicle the lifestyle of the bohemian Bloomsbury circle of avant-garde artists. In Cambridge, the dining room walls of the family home of John Maynard Keynes (1883–1946), a key figure in the Bloomsbury Group, were clad in deep blue and crimson Morris paper. Aldous Huxley, author of *Brave New World* (1932) also grew up in 'chintz rooms, modern with William Morris'. John Betjeman, joint founder of the Victorian Society, admired the man and his work, hanging his wallpapers in his office and buying 'relics of the great Socialist poet-artist at the Kelmscott Manor sale in 1939'.[45] Betjeman tried to 'bid for such hallowed relics as Morris's French working blouse and his initialled silk handkerchief'. Such memorabilia, alongside Morris's wallpapers and chintzes, was one way of keeping the great man near.

SOWING TARES.

(*With a thousand apologies to Sir John E. Millais, Bart., R.A.*)

John Tenniel, 'Sowing Tares', *Punch or the London Chiavari*, 27 February 1886, Vol. 90, pp.102-103 which was accompanied with the following lines:

'Sowing Tares' (an injurious weed)
Sinister shape that through the shadows steals,
What doest thou? The demon hand that deals
False largesse forth to the deluded throng …
But trust not him he is the enemy.

Taking to the Platform

Having bought out his partners, Morris took on sole ownership of the firm in 1875. At this point he appears to undergo a mid-life crisis; as MacCarthy observes, 'it seems as if Morris, through the late 1870s, was shedding one persona and making himself a new one, deliberately preparing for a new role in the world'.[46] Letters to the press, pamphleteering and lecturing moved Morris into the public eye. Public speaking did not come easily but as with any new craft, he learnt the new skills he needed.

Morris was propelled into action by the Eastern Question Association (EQA), a pressure group advocating resistance to Disraeli's alliance with the Turks; offering to help with funding, Morris became treasurer in November 1876. The EQA was founded amidst panic that the Tory government was heading towards war with Russia. Protest meetings continued into 1878; January saw a 'glorious victory' in Trafalgar Square, 'though I believe some blood was shed (from noses)'.[47] At the Workman's Neutrality Demonstration, held at Exeter Hall, although 'Magnificent: orderly and enthusiastic' it required 'heavy work to keep the roughs out'. This protest had been organised by Trade Union leader, Henry Broadhurst, who asked Morris to provide an inspiring song to open the meeting. Morris obliged with 'Wake, London Lads!' This would be followed by many more rousing radical songs: *Chants for Socialists* (1885) includes 'The Day is Coming', 'All for the Cause' and 'The March of the Workers'.[48] Morris's emotive 'A Death Song' was written for the funeral of Alfred Linnell, who was killed in the aftermath of Bloody Sunday on 13 November 1887. The song sheets, the artwork contributed by Walter Crane, were sold for one penny with the proceeds going to Linnell's orphans.[49]

Morris gave his first public lecture, on 'The Decorative Arts', later published as 'The Lesser Arts', to the Trades Guild of Learning at the Co-operative Hall, Castle Street, off Oxford Street, in December 1877. Many lectures followed; at least eight in 1879 as well as addressing a protest meeting in Oxford over the restoration of St Mark's, Venice. Six in 1880, one delivered to the Annual Meeting of the Woman's Protective and Provident League, at which Morris seconded a resolution on women's rights. The number of engagements escalated following his conversion to Socialism: 91 recorded in 1886, 105 in 1887, 94 in 1888. He also travelled extensively, with 'Art and Labour' delivered eight times in Leeds, Sheffield, Manchester, Newcastle, Glasgow and Bristol during 1884. In Leicester, the birth of Socialism is still attributed to Morris's lecture 'Art and Socialism', delivered at the Secular Society on 23 January 1884. The fledgling architect Ernest Gimson experienced his own conversion, even though his brother Sydney deemed Morris' performance indifferent, his reading of his well-prepared script lacking vigour. Although a 'word spinner', Morris was not a natural orator. Morris was aware of his deficiencies, stemming from repeat performances. He admitted he only gave one lecture: 'after all I have only one thing to say and have to find divers ways of saying it'.[50] However, that evening at the Gimson home the conversation flowed, with Morris taking a real interest in Ernest's future. Armed with three letters of introduction to leading architects, Gimson set off for London; during the 1890s he forged a reputation as the leading architect-craftsman in England.

In Nottingham, he spoke to the Kyrle Society, observing his audience was 'polite and attentive' but he feared 'they were puzzled at what he said; as they might well be, since if they acted on it Nottingham trade would come to an end'.[51] One of the first civic amenity bodies, the Kyrle was founded by Miranda (1836–1910) and Octavia Hill (1838–1912) to 'Bring Beauty Home to the People'; 'to better the life of working people, by laying out parks, encouraging house decoration, window gardening and flower growing'.[52] Thanks to the Kyrle and the Commons Preservation Society, Morris's beloved Epping Forest, the 'cockney paradise', was saved from the 'land grabber'. Morris sought to 'overthrow landlord domination' and to 'get the land back for the people'; 'Commons and heaths of unmatched beauty and wildness have been enclosed for farmers or jerry-built upon by speculators in order to swell the ill-gotten revenues of some covetous aristocrat or greedy money-bag'.[53] A mass demonstration held on Wanstead Flats in 1871, with protestors rallied from the East End of London, alarmed Gladstone's government. Responding to the bad press, the government rushed through a series of acts prohibiting further enclosures. May Morris remembered a Socialist League Picnic in Epping Forest: 'I have a sudden vision of a long train of loaded pleasure-vans with red flags waving, threading their way through the narrow streets of the City eastwards to Epping Forest'.[54]

Morris wrote his lectures in lined exercise books, many of which have survived, demonstrating the evolution of his ideas and growing desperation. Their innocuous titles, 'The History of Pattern Designing' (1879), 'The Lesser Arts of Life' (1882) and 'The Origins of Decorative Art' (1883), belie their true message. He would launch into a passionate analysis of the relevance of art to society and his hopes and fears for civilisation. Although there are echoes of Ruskin, there was an 'approachability that is not bonhomie but something deeper' calling forth fellowship or camaraderie.[55] It was his determination to speak on the most serious of subjects, the quest for a 'happy life for the mass of mankind' that led to his conversion to Socialism.

Conversion

In 'How I Became a Socialist' (1894), looking back at his pre-1883 lectures, Morris argued he was articulating 'socialism seen through the eyes of an artist'. Having joined the Democratic Federation on 17 January 1883, Morris attempted to learn the science and economics of Socialism by tackling Karl Marx: 'I suffered agonies of confusion of the brain'. He confessed he learnt more from continuous conversation with his comrades, 'hard-shell' Marxist economist Ernest Belfort Bax (1854–1926), Austrian socialist Andreas Scheu (1844–1927) and Henry Mayers Hyndman (1842–1921), who founded the Democratic Federation in 1881.[56] From his Anarchist friends, he learned, 'quite against their intention, that Anarchism was impossible'.

From a similar background to Morris, Hyndman was educated at Trinity College Cambridge, read for the bar and then became a journalist. Meeting Marx in the 1870s, he read *Das Kapital* and following his conversion published the optimistic 'The Dawn of the Revolutionary Epoch' (1881); he predicted the Revolution would come in 1889. At the launch of the Democratic Federation, he distributed his pamphlet *England for*

All which became the key text underpinning English Socialism. A plan outlining social reconstruction was sorely needed, as according to anarchist Edward Carpenter (1844–1929), so far Socialism was 'a mass of floating impressions, sentiments, ideals'.[57] However, failing to acknowledge Marx, Hyndman was dismissed by Friedrich Engels as 'an arch-Conservative and an arrantly chauvinistic but not stupid careerist'.[58]

The SDF was a bizarre mix of class and culture, with John Burns, a working-class engineer rubbing shoulders with James Leigh, a disaffected assistant master at Eaton. Shaw first met Morris, 'our acknowledged Great Man', at a social gathering of the SDF. Hyndman recognised Morris's usefulness, as he 'was no needy and greedy proletarian, no embittered revolutionist, no disappointed politician or cynical publicist'.[59] Armed with missionary zeal, Morris took up the Cause with gusto: he was determined to *make* a revolution. The next step was *how* to make a revolution: 'turning neither to the right hand nor to the left till it was done'.[60] Selling the Socialist magazine *Justice*, 'street preaching', lecturing or rallying the crowds at meetings were now necessary to get the job done.[61] The Cause demanded commitment:

> sacrifice to the Cause of leisure, pleasure and money, each according to his means: I mean sacrifice of individual whims and vanity, of individual misgivings … as to the means the organising body may be forced to use; remember without organisation the cause is but a vague dream, which may lead to revolt, to violence and disorder, but which will be speedily repressed by those who are blindly interested in sustaining the present anarchical tyranny which is misnamed Society: remember also that no organisation is possible without the sacrifices … without obedience of the necessities of the Cause.[62]

E.P Thompson, concludes 'this vision of "the Cause" was Morris's special, and his most permanent, contribution to the British Socialist movement'.[63] Thompson also argues Morris was a 'pioneer of constructive thought as to the organisation of socialistic life within Communist society'.[64] Ruth Kinna argues Morris's vision was dependant on the realisation of communism, 'structured by a binding commitment to resist exploitation … and deep sense of fellowship'.[65] Socialism only achieved a change in existing patterns of ownership, a shift from capitalism to socialisation of production. Morris sought the transformation of work, when 'the distinction between work and rest disintegrated' giving way to 'pleasurable labour and productive leisure'.[66]

Morris's vision of a new social order was most eloquently expressed in his poems and prose. His novel *A Dream of John Ball* (1888), which has also been discussed briefly by Stephen Basdeo in this volume, fictionalised the Great Revolt of 1381, popularly known as the Peasants' Revolt.[67] An associate of Wat Tyler, the central figure, the rebel priest John Ball poses the question 'When Adam delved [farmed] and Eve span, who was then the gentleman?' recalling a time when there were no class divisions and all work was equal. In a dream setting, a time traveller tells Ball that feudalism has been swept away by the industrial revolution. Even so, Ball's hopes for an egalitarian society have yet to be fulfilled.

A Dream of John Ball is seen as the forerunner of *News from Nowhere* (1890).[68] Returning from a meeting of the Socialist League, William Guest, the narrator, falls asleep. When he awakens, he finds himself transported to a future agrarian society based on common ownership: no private property, no authority, no monetary system, no divorce, no courts, no prisons, and no class systems. Morris attempts to answer the most frequent objection to Socialism, the supposed lack of incentive to work in a communistic society. Rather than seeing work as a necessary evil that a well-planned egalitarian society could reduce to a minimum, Morris argued that all work should be enjoyable.

Morris yearned for the simple rural life he envisioned in *News from Nowhere*. Visiting Carpenter at Millthorpe, Derbyshire, Morris was envious: 'I listened with longing heart to his account of his patch of ground, seven acres … they grow their own wheat and send flowers and fruit to Chesterfield and Sheffield markets … the real way to enjoy life is to accept all its necessary ordinary details and turn them into pleasures by taking interest in them'.[69] Morris gave up his own dreams of a Simple Life for the Cause; it was 'dastardly to desert'.

The Socialist League

Advice to Socialists
Don't flaunt a red flag before the eyes of John Bull
Punch, February 1886.[70]

With growing conviction, Morris realised that a self-sacrificing organisation of the type he envisioned would not develop under Hyndman's autocratic leadership. This led to an inevitable split, with Morris orchestrating a 'cabal' involving libertarian Socialist Joseph Lane; Sam Mainwaring, whose thinking evolved from revolutionary socialism to anarcho-communism; Edward Aveling and his wife Eleanor Marx; the Scottish radicals Robert Banner and John Mahon, as well as Belfort Bax and Andreas Scheu. At the SDF meeting, held at the end of December 1884, Morris resigned; he led his small group of Socialists 'out into the wilderness'. The Socialist League was formerly inaugurated on 30 December 1884; Morris and Bax hammered out the manifesto on New Year's Day. The new organisation needed its own mouth-piece, *Commonweal* supplanting *Justice*; much of the content was supplied by Morris. Engels's influential 'England in 1845 and in 1885' featured in the second issue. Nevertheless, Engels, 'the *eminence grise* of Marxism in England', concluded 'You will not bring the numerous working class as a whole into the movement by sermons'.[71]

Some argued Morris had damaged the fledging cause by forming a rival body. Rather he should have stayed and fought from within, but from Morris's perspective, Hyndman was already giving Socialism a bad name. Morris's outlook was shaped by the distinguished philosopher, Belfort Bax, the Aveling-Marx household and Engels. However, Engels would have found it difficult to relate to Morris's 'erratic combination of Marxism with visionary libertarianism'.[72] Many of his long-standing friends also

THE POLICE (OF THE FUTURE).

(Vide Letter to " Daily Chronicle," Feb. 15, 1886.)

Alfred Chantry Courbold, 'Police of the Future', *Punch or the London Chiavari*, 27 February 1886, Vol. 90, p. 105.

Explanation: A Light Basket-work Shield (old Hammer-top for instance); B Quarter-staff; C Electric Rattle; D Water-Tank and Hose-Pipe; E Money-Bag to pay for 'Bus rides' (Special Tax in Police Rates); F Neck guard; G Electric Battery; H. Firework, Squibs. &c; J. Mob-persuaders; K Electric wires.

found it difficult to relate to Morris's Socialism, which could no longer be deemed an eccentricity. Even Burne-Jones declined to receive *Commonweal*. 'As a Socialist', Morris wrote, 'I stink in people's nostrils'.[73]

The Socialist League founders numbered literary intellectuals, such as Aveling, exiles like Scheu and 'Chaucerians', self-taught workmen- Joseph Lane, a carter; Frank Kitz, a dyer and the engineer Sam Mainwaring. At last class divisions were being overcome, Morris hearing at first-hand testimonies of working class life. Admiring the 'primitive simplicity' of his East End comrades, Morris was not tempted to join the Fabian Society founded on 4 January 1884. The rarefied nature of the Fabian Society is exemplified by its name, taken from the Roman Republican general Quintus Fabius Maximus Verrucosus, known as 'Fabius the Delayer'. He eventually defeated Hannibal's superior Carthaginian army through dogged persistence. Morris instinctively disliked the society's elite membership: Shaw, H.G. Wells, Annie Besant, Sydney and Beatrice Webb, and Emmeline Pankhurst.[74] However, the Labour Party would grow out of this intellectual milieu.

By the mid-1880s, the police were becoming increasingly heavy-handed in their treatment of Socialists. Meetings were violently broken up, books confiscated, and arrests made. A Defence Club was set up, with Morris as treasurer. In September 1885, 10,000 gathered at Dod Street, Limehouse, to uphold the right of open-air free speech. Both the SDF and the Socialist League addressed the crowd. As the gathering dispersed, the police swooped and made several arrests. At their hearing, the magistrate Thomas Saunders handed down punitive sentences; Lewis Lyons, a poor East-end Jewish tailor. In an ensuing fracas, Morris was arrested for causing disturbance. Brought up before Saunders, he was reprieved. Inevitably Morris was aghast at his preferential treatment, his class sparing him from hard labour. For the authorities, Morris was an annoying embarrassment.

Black Monday and Bloody Sunday

'Song of the Socialist Spouter'
Violence-sweet Violence!
Beautiful brute Violence!
Nice to see the dupes we've maddened to thy practice led.
Nice to see them stealing, smashing,
Shop-fronts wrecking, faces bashing,
Whilst we hung out theories, and hurry-home to bed!
Punch, February 1886[75]

The years 1886 and 1887 were years of political turmoil, the unrest exacerbated by a long trade depression and resulting unemployment. A mass riot which broke out on 8 February 1886 became known as Black Monday. A rally held for the unemployed in Trafalgar Square was appropriated by the SDF. Hyndman and his supporters then headed down Pall Mall towards Hyde Park with some 10,000 people in their wake. Things began to get out of hand, with stones thrown at windows. In Piccadilly looting began. Regrouping at Hyde Park, the rioters headed east towards Oxford Street, smashing windows and looting as they went; Morris's shop was luckily spared. The result was public panic. *Punch's* 'The Great Unemployed: A Song for Scotland Yard', blamed Edward Henderson, chief of the Metropolitan Police, for the unchecked lawlessness: 'Let Roughdom smash and loot, he Stirred not, appeared not, formed no plan'.[76] Morris viewed 'this affair as an incident of the Revolution, and so far, encouraging: the shop wrecking was partly a grotesque practical joke (quite English in manner) at the expense of the upper classes'.[77]

THE TEMPTER.

Spirit of Anarchy. "WHAT! NO WORK! COME AND ENLIST WITH ME,—I'LL FIND WORK FOR YOU!!"

John Tenniel, 'The Tempter', *Punch or the London Chiavari*, Vol. 91, 27 November 1886, p. 105. The caption accompanying the image was as follows:

> Spirit of Anarchy, 'What! No Work! Come and enlist with me,—I'll find work for you!!'

Black Monday was the prelude to Bloody Sunday on 13 November 1887. Organised by the Social Democratic Federation and the Irish National League, a demonstration against unemployment and coercion in Ireland erupted into a violent clash with the police and military forces; 2000 police, four squadrons of cavalry and 400 soldiers, all carrying live ammunition, were deployed. As the protestors marched to Trafalgar Square, they were caught in a trap laid by Sir Charles Warren, the new hard-line chief of the Metropolitan Police who had banned organised processions leading to London's central square. Around 10,000 unemployed workers, Radicals, Anarchists and Socialists assembled across London to begin the march, Morris joining his comrades in the Socialist League at Clerkenwell Green. Also marching were Shaw, Annie Besant, Eleanor Marx and Charlotte Wilson, who co-founded *Freedom* with the Russian anarcho-communist Prince Peter Kropotkin in 1886.[78] Warren had planned a series of ambushes at strategic points, which ensured the procession was broken up before reaching the square. The police charged into the marchers welding their truncheons indiscriminately; three men were killed on the day, hundreds injured. The following Sunday, 20 November, mounted police were stationed in and around Trafalgar Square. They knocked down a young radical lawyer Alfred Linnell who subsequently died from his injuries. His funeral on 18 December provided a focal point for agitators. Morris was one of the six pall-bearers, alongside the radical Scottish nationalist and Liberal MP, Robert Cunninghame-Graham, who was arrested on Bloody Sunday and imprisoned for six weeks. A shield inscribed 'Killed in Trafalgar Square' and three flags, green, yellow and red for the Irish, the Radicals and the Socialists, draped the hearse. The procession grew as the funeral cortege headed east towards the Mile End Road: some claimed the spectacle was comparable to the Duke of Wellington's funeral in 1852. Morris movingly addressed the mourners:

> let them remember for all time this man as their brother and their friend … Their friend who lay there had had a hard life and met with a hard death … They were engaged in a most holy war trying to prevent their rulers … making this great town of London nothing more than a prison … they should begin tomorrow to organise for the purpose of seeing that such things should not happen again.[79]

In the gathering gloom, they sang Morris's 'Death Song', 'the ultimate revolutionary hymn': 'Not one, not one, nor thousands must they slay, / But one and all if they would dusk the day'. The Linnell funeral enhanced Morris's standing in radical circles: he was now venerated as the grand old man of the Socialist cause.

During all this agitation, the Socialist League began to disintegrate. An anarchist faction emerged, sounding its death knell. Even Morris was unable to hold it together. He lost the editorship of *Commonweal*, even though he was still financing it. Bax deserted him, re-joining the SDF. Morris's trip to Paris to attend the International Socialist Working Men's Congress was his swansong. His boredom and frustration, with the machinations of the anarchists, is exemplified by his famous outburst; 'Mr Chairman, *can't* we get on with the business? I want my TEA!' Although Morris retreated to the Hammersmith Socialist Society with his allies, his days of direct activism were largely over. Nevertheless, he continued to lecture and published articles; 'The Socialist Ideal' (1891) and 'Communism' (1893). He also became more pragmatic, retracting his anti-parliamentary position. Morris was now 'prepared to acknowledge the importance of the fight for limited gains, of "steps" on the road to socialism, provided they were fought for with a revolutionary aim kept steadily in view'.[80] It is important to remember that Morris was a 'practical revolutionary socialist'. Morris the utopian is a romantic figure to those 'who would like to commend his vision as an ideal but do nothing to act to bring it about'.[81] Peter Critchley argues, 'For Morris, the utopian imagination served

THE TWO VOICES.

One of the Real "Unemployed,"—"HOW AM I TO MAKE *MY* VOICE HEARD IN THIS BLACKGUARD ROW!!"

John Tenniel, 'The Two Voices', *Punch or the London Charivari*, Vol.93, 29 October 1887, pp.198-9. The caption accompanying the image was as follows:

> 'That this representative body of Working-men, representing the bona fide Unemployed Workmen of the East and South-East of London, beg to place on record their entire want of sympathy, and their utter condemnation of the recent conduct which has been made in the name of the Unemployed'.
>
> Resolution passed at a Meeting of the Representative Workmen, held in Whitechapel, for the purpose of 'considering the present position of the Unemployed Workmen, and the grave events of last week'.

'The Two Voices'
The Unemployed. Well here I stand,
Ave stood for many weary weeks,
With sinking heart and idle hand,
Hunger's white ensign on my cheeks.
I raise no howl
Like yon plump ruffian with the bull-dog jowl;
But the smug swell, with pleasure's honey cloyed,
May see me in the real Unemployed.

Punch made much of the 'real working man' and the 'real unemployed', as opposed to political agitators and 'ruffians' who were giving the working man a bad name.

A demonstration was held in Hyde Park on Tues, Weds and Thurs, 25-27 October 1887 in the name of the unemployed. Although the meeting was allowed, the protestors were not allowed to march to Trafalgar Square.

to locate collective dreams, hopes and aspirations within place and being and both activate and anchor them within a practical project of social transformation'.[81]While Morris may have failed to instigate a revolution or see the birth of a new society, he was about to head an artistic one, with the blossoming of the Arts and Crafts Movement. Morris's ideals inspired a series of visionary craft communities, extolling the virtues of the Simple Life.

In Arcadia

Webb and Morris spent a considerable time looking for the right location for Red House; it had to be in the countryside, as an earthly paradise could not be built in the city, but still within reach of London. Morris started a trend, a 'flight' to the countryside. Those in search of the Good Life or the Simple Life found it in the Lake District, the Cotswolds and East Sussex. The Cotswolds were particularly attractive being within hailing distance of both London and Birmingham. Kelmscott Manor became Morris's retreat, while Crom Price rented Broadway Tower, a folly above the village of Broadway: during the summer of 1876 Morris was 'up at Crom Price's Tower among the winds and the clouds'.

With the collapse of land prices and the agricultural depression of the 1880s, rents were low: Gimson and the Barnsley brothers took Pinbury Park on the Bathurst estate, near Cirencester, on a 'repairing lease'. In return for renovating the property, the rent was minimal. C.R. Ashbee, designer, architect, and social reformer moved the Guild of Handicraft to Chipping Campden in 1902; around a hundred cockneys and their families found themselves in Arcadia. The daily life of the Guildsmen began with morning exercises, labouring in the workshops, tending to gardens and allotments and 'rational recreation' in the evenings, amateur productions and readings. A co-operative society, it was an Arts and Crafts commune. Attracted by the Guild, many artists settled in the area: Frederick Griggs, architectural draughtsman, illustrator and early conservationist, and Paul Woodroffe, illustrator and stained glass artist, arrived in 1904.

Eric Gill moved with his young family to Ditchling, East Sussex, in 1907. Joined by Hilary Pepler and Desmond Chute, The Guild of St Joseph and St Dominic was formally constituted in 1921. Frustrated by friction within the Guild, Gill resigned in 1924. He 'fled to Wales', as he described it, to an abandoned monastery in Capel-y-ffin, in the Black Mountains. These artist-led social experiments often floundered, either due to economic difficulties or friction within the group. Nevertheless, the Arts and Crafts ideal of working within a rural community persists to this day. Although the collective may fail, individual artist-craftsmen have run successful workshops: Gordon Russell at Broadway, Robert Welch at Campden and David Mellor at Hathersage, near Sheffield.

The concept of living and working in the countryside, prioritising quality of life, led first to garden suburbs, such as Bedford Park and Hampstead Garden Suburb in London, and ultimately to the Garden City Movement. Conceived in 1898 by Ebenezer Howard (1850-1928), Garden Cities were intended as self-contained communities, encompassing housing, industry and farming, surrounded by 'greenbelts'. First published in 1898, *To-morrow: a Peaceful Path to Real Reform* was reissued in 1902 as *Garden Cities of To-morrow*. To raise finance, Howard founded the Garden Cities Association, which provided the means to launch the First Garden City, Ltd. in 1899. Howard's original conception of a cooperative ownership scheme had to be dropped. Instead, investors would be paid a dividend, with profits generated through rents. In 1904, architects Raymond Unwin and Barry Parker won the competition to plan Letchworth, the first garden city thirty-four miles outside London. Sharing Howard's vision that the working class deserved better and more affordable housing, Parker and Unwin designed terraces and semi-detached houses in a cottage style along broad boulevards and around open greens.

Nevertheless, it was skilled middle class workers who could afford to make the move, mingling with the many smock-wearing and sandal-shod advocates of 'rational dress', socialists, suffragettes, eccentrics, visionaries and artists also in search of Arcadia. The locally-made sandals, copies of Indian sandals, became known as 'Fabian uniform'.[83] Despite being in the minority, the 'cranks' were highly visible. Francis King paints a vivid picture of the early Letchworthians, 'alighting at Kings Cross station in anything from a toga to a farm labourer's smock and sandals, clutching a shepherd's crook. It was all part of the simple life movement'.[84] 'Crankdom' was serviced by the Simple Life Hotel, which had a vegetarian restaurant and health food shop. The Skittles Inn substituted hot chocolate and Cydrax, a non-intoxicating apple wine, for alcohol; it was backed by a member of the Quaker Cadbury family. The Cloisters, a Theosophical Meditation Centre and open-air school completed in 1907, is one of Letchworth Garden City's more eccentric anomalies

Immediately lampooned, the cranks brought fame to the idealistic new town. In his poems *Group Life: Letchworth* and *Huxley Hall*, John Betjeman painted Letchworthians as earnest free-thinking, health freaks, who 'drink lime-juice minus gin'. George Orwell, who knew Letchworth well, ranted in *The Road to Wigan Pier* (1936): 'the mere words "Socialism" and "Communism" [can] draw with magnetic force every fruit-juice drinker, nudist, sandal-wearer, sex-maniac, Quaker, "Nature Cure" quack, pacifist and feminist in England'. In his memorable tirade against cranks, Orwell singles out 'vegetarians with wilting beards', the 'outer-suburban creeping Jesus' eager to begin his yoga exercises, and 'that dreary tribe of high-minded women and sandal-wearers and bearded fruit-juice drinkers who come flocking towards the smell of "progress" like bluebottles to a dead cat'. Some cranks were a 'hangover from the William Morris period' who propose to 'level the working class *up* (up to his own standard) by means of hygiene, fruit-juice, birth-control, poetry, etc'. All cranks were united by their earnestness: they wanted the world to be a more beautiful place, less cruel and crassly commercial.[85] Their pleasures were wholesome and energetic. Nevertheless, there was widespread disapproval of the 'cohabiters' who lived together and refused to marry.

Written in the 1930s, Orwell's satire was employed in an urgent cause, arguing for non-crankish, common-sense radical politics to combat the threat of Fascism. Cranks were giving socialism a bad name. Moreover, having achieved the Simple Life, they were not really concerned about the plight of the working class. Nowadays vegetarianism and veganism are no longer considered cranky, while environmentalism and ecological anti-capitalism are major causes that unite many political parties.

'Learning by Doing'

Maintaining in the *Commonweal* (1888), he was '*taught-* nothing' at school, 'but *learned* archaeology and romance on the Wiltshire downs', Morris scorned Marlborough College. It was a 'boy farm' with learning by rote and cribbing. MacCarthy claims it was at Marlborough that Morris became a 'de-schooler, an educational anarchist' in the tradition of Enlightenment philosopher William Godwin (1756-1836) and Kropotkin.[86] Godwin insisted education should be a happy experience, not driven by coercion but built on a child's motivation and initiatives. State-sponsored schooling was a form of propaganda; it did not promote enquiry and the search for truth. In 'Brain Work and Manual Work' (1890), Kropotkin bemoaned, that deprived of experience in a workshop, children were driven into a mine or factory; they soon forgot what little they had learned at school. The division of society into brain workers and manual workers prevented the combination of both activities; to remove this pernicious distinction, Kropotkin called for *éducation intégrale*, a complete education. We could add to McCarthy's educational reformers Johann Heinrich Pestalozzi (1746-1827), whose motto 'Learning by head, hand and heart' was appropriated by the Arts and Crafts Movement: 'Head for creativity and imagination, Hand for skill and craft, Heart for honesty and for love'.[87] Pestalozzi's educational methods were child-centred, his aim to educate the whole person. Friedrich Froebel (1782–1852), founder of the kindergarten movement, prioritised 'learning by doing' alongside creativity and socialising.[88] Learning by Doing would become the mantra of the Arts and Crafts movement.

In *News from Nowhere*, Morris's boys and girls learn by doing: observing nature in all its forms, cooking, thatching, making simple furniture, all in an atmosphere of intellectual freedom. The antithesis of Marlborough's regime, Morris looks ahead to the progressive schools of Rudolf Steiner and Bedales, Petersfield, a co-educational school founded by John Haden Badley, a disciple of Ruskin, in 1893. With no chapel, the school's secular stance attracted non-conformists, Quakers, Unitarians, and liberal Jews. The school was also popular within Fabian intellectual circles with connections to the Wedgwoods, Darwins, Huxleys and Trevelyans. Centred on a child's individual needs, two approaches were taken: breadth (Head, Hand and Heart) and character, cultivating intellectual and personal qualities (Intelligence, Initiative and Individuality).

Yet Morris did not champion the teaching of handicrafts to school children, even though he was 'depressed by the mechanical drill' being applied by 'Mr McChoakum-child': 'Capitalism will not allow us the leisure, either for education or the use of it. Slave labour and true education are irreconcilable foes'.[89] In 'Thoughts on education under capitalism', Morris had little sympathy for American educational activist and folklorist Charles Godfrey Leland (1824–1903, aka the writer Hans Breitman) who advocated 'Industrial Art as a branch of education in schools'. In addition to learning the pleasures of making, this would cultivate a demand for 'sound workmanship combined with beauty' compelling manufacturers to change their ways. Morris argued, the substitution of handicrafts for manufacturing was doomed to failure in a capitalist society. With higher labour costs, 'only rich people with a whim for art will be able to buy them'. If handcrafted goods instigated a passing fashion, manufacturers would imitate them using machine production and organised labour leading to degraded products. If the rich continued to demand the genuine article, retailers would exploit the unfortunate handicraftsmen. Taking advantage of those in dire necessity, retailers would drive down wages; cheap art would swell their own purses. This exploitation, requiring little capital or management, would have a 'dash of philanthropy' and 'practical remedy' about it. Such 'sweating' would appear 'an honourable as well as pleasant occupation. Cheap art indeed – and nasty!'[90]

Morris stance explains why he dismissed other well-meaning Art and Crafts interventions as misguided. Leland's handbook *The Minor Arts Porcelain Painting, Wood-Carving, Stencilling, Modelling, Mosaic Work* (1880) inspired Eglantyne Louisa Jebb (1845-1925) to found the Home Arts and Industries Association (1884). Jebb did not support teaching the handicrafts in schools; rather she advocated free craft classes taught by volunteers, delivered during the evening or on Saturdays, in town and country, for 'wage-earning' adults and children.[91] Pupils would learn a skill, furniture making or metalworking, the objects produced would beautify their homes or be sold to augment income, especially during lean times. The handicrafts were lauded as 'rational recreation' aimed at 'rough lads', a hobby comparable to the music concerts, gallery-going and watercolour sketching enjoyed by the upper classes.[92]

However, the Home Arts was more than 'a dash of philanthropy'. In rural areas, it appealed to landowners, whose workforce was easily lured away to the city in search of higher wages. In some cases amateur classes developed into rural craft industries: the Keswick School of Industrial Art founded in 1884 by Canon Hardwicke Rawnsley and his wife Edith as an evening class in woodwork and repoussé metalwork became a fully-fledged village industry. It prospered until 1984. There was often an activist behind the founding of a class: Mary Watts, wife of the artist George Frederick Watts, founded the Compton Potters' Arts Guild (1900), while the Newlyn Industrial Class (1890) was supervised by artist John MacKenzie and financially supported by local MP, Thomas Bedford Bolitho. By 1888, the association boasted 300 classes and 4,000 pupils. This success was due to a centralised administration that trained the largely female instructors and distributed learning materials, designs and models. An annual exhibition, normally held at the Royal Albert Hall, provided a platform for friendly competition and sales. Although this 'practical remedy', could be classed as 'Art for and by the People', it encouraged amateurism, undermining the professional craftsman.

Morris's Legacy: Useful and Beautiful

Morris was surprisingly reserved when the Art Workers Guild was founded in 1884. The Guild's motto 'Unity of All the Arts' stressed the interdependence and equal status of all the arts. The artist-craftsman respected his materials, their capacity and natural limitations, while the outcome was to enhance daily life. Established by young architects, designers and artists, Morris might have regarded this, at the height of his Socialist activism, as a 'gentleman's club'. Morris was not elected until 1888, becoming Master in 1892. His reaction to the founding of the Arts and Crafts

Exhibition Society, which grew out of the Art Worker's Guild, was equally lukewarm; leaving aside works by Burne-Jones and Walter Crane, the remainder 'would tend to be of an amateurish nature ... at the risk of being a wet blanket ... I rather dread the said exhibition'.[93] The first exhibition, held in 1888, provided a platform for designers and craftsmen (and women), working in a wide range of materials, to show their products.

As Morris feared, the Society's exhibitions initiated a fashion, cultivating a sophisticated audience prepared to pay for high-quality goods. As predicted manufactures jumped on the bandwagon, using machine production and factory labour to turn out cheaper replicas. Pandering to the consumer, Liberty of Regent Street, founded by Arthur Lazenby Liberty in 1875, capitalised on the vogue for high-quality handicrafts. Their Cymric silver range (1899) and Tudric pewter range (1902), which appealed to the new tastes, were not made in the Arts and Crafts spirit. The metalwork designed by Archibald Knox in Celtic style was machine made in Birmingham. Worse still Liberty's undercut genuine handcrafted goods, contributing to the demise of Ashbee's Guild of Handicrafts (1888–1907). This had developed from a Ruskin reading class into a craft-based industry, initially as an adjunct to Toynbee Hall, the famous university settlement in the East End of London. By 1890, workshops had been established at Essex House, on the Mile End Road. In 1902, the Guild moved to Chipping Camden in the Cotswold's where around a hundred craftsmen and their families briefly enjoyed the 'Simple Life'. Like many utopias, the idyll was short-lived, as the Guild could not compete in a commercially driven market. Despite such setbacks, the Arts and Crafts evolved into an international movement. The Simple Life was pursued in America, with workshops and colonies established; Gustav Stickley's Craftsman workshop in Eastwood, and Elbert Hubbard's Roycroft campus in East Aurora, New York State. Still a reformist movement, the emphasis shifted to well-decorated middle-class homes. Linked to 'progressivism', simple but refined Arts and Crafts products would encourage a rationale and harmonious society.

Morris's arguments concerning production and work remain relevant in the twenty-first century. John Drinkwater argues Morris's legacy was his fundamental belief that work should be happy, a first step towards 'true dignity and pride of life'.[94] Nevertheless, he is best remembered for his golden rule that would 'fit everybody ... have nothing in your house that you do not know to be useful or believe to be beautiful'.[95] As consumers in a generation more environmentally aware, we are encouraged to have fewer, better things, sustainability is a priority and organic produce is preferred. Many have now opted for a simpler life.

Notes

1. Fiona MacCarthy, *William Morris A Life for Our Time* (London: Faber and Faber, 1994), 461.
2. Derek Wall, *Green History A Reader in Environmental Literature, Philosophy, and Politics* (London: Routledge, 1994) 10.

3. Morris had three principal residences; Red House (1859-65), Kelmscott Manor leased in 1871 and purchased by Jane Morris in 1913 and Kelmscott House, Hammersmith, named after the Manor, leased in 1878, where Morris died.

4. Leslie J. Macfarlane, *Socialism, Social Ownership and Social Justice* (Basingstoke: Macmillan, 1998) 124.

5. Nikolaus Pevsner, *Pioneers of Modern Design from William Morris to Walter Gropius* (Harmondsworth: Penguin, 1960) 22.

6. E.P. Thompson, *William Morris, Romanic to Revolutionary* (London: Merlin Press, 1977) 2.

7. Nicholas Salmon, 'Reclaiming William Morris', *Worker's Liberty, Reason in Revolt*, Submitted on 17 June 2010, www.workersliberty.org>story>2010/06/17.

8. Morris bought out his partners in 1875, the firm becoming Morris & Co. A showroom was opened on Oxford Street in 1877, while the workshops moved out to Merton Abbey in 1881. After his death, W.A.S Benson oversaw the company. Henry Marillier was managing director of Morris and Co. from 1905-1940, when it closed.

9. The family, now dependant on the interest from the shares in Devonshire Great Consolidated Copper Mine Co. .'downsized' from Woodford Hall to Water House, Walthamstow.

10. MacCarthy, *William Morris*, 42.

11. Ruskin's activism was achieved by proxy, through his financing of Octavia Hill's housing projects.

12. John Ruskin, 'On the Nature of Gothic architecture', *Stones of Venice*, Vol 2, 1853, *The Complete Works of John Ruskin* (New York and Chicago: National Library Association, 1905) 171.

13. ibid, 169.

14. Ibid, 169-70.

15. John Ruskin, 'The Future of England', *The Crown of Wild Olive* (1866) lecture IV, section 151, E. T. Cook & A. Wedderburn (eds), *The works of John Ruskin* (London: Longmans, Green & Co, 1905).

16. Elizabeth Luther Cary, *William Morris, Poet, Craftsman, Socialist* (London: G.P. Putnam's Sons, 1902) 22.

17. John William Mackail, *The Life of William Morris*, Vol.1, (London: Longmans, Green & Co. 1899) 186.

18. Amanda Hodgson, *The Romances of William Morris*, Cambridge: Cambridge University Press, 1987, 13.

19. Mackail, *The Life of William Morris*, Vol. II, 314.

20. Joseph Addison; David Marshall, *The Frame of Art Fictions of Aesthetic Experience, 1750-1815*, (Baltimore: John Hopkins University Press, 2005), 47.

21. William Morris, 'The Lesser Arts', *Hopes and Fears for Art, The Collected Works of William Morris*, Vol. 22 (Cambridge: Cambridge Library Collection, 2012) 18. Available at: www.marxists.org.

22. Ibid.

23. MacCarthy, *William Morris*, 672.

24. Ibid.

25. Wendy Parkins, *Jane Morris*: *The Burden of History* (Edinburgh: Edinburgh University Press, 2013) 100.

26. Ibid., 99.

27. Frank C Sharp and Jan Marsh, *The Collected Letters of Jane Morris*, (Woodbridge: Boydell Press, 2012)149, Letter 132.

28. In a letter sent to the Worship-street court, Mrs Morris offered to pay their 10 shilling fine. The trousers belonged to their employer, Shadrac, Schneider and Sons, wholesale clothing manufacturers of Durwood Street, Bethnal Green. http://fannycornforth.blogspot.co.uk/2016/04/the-song-of-trousers.html.

29. Tessa Wild, *William Morris & his Palace of* Art (London: Philip Wilson, 2018) 217.

30. Ibid, 217.

31. Morris, 'The Aims of Art', *Signs of Change* (1886) *The Collected Works of William Morris*, Vol. 23 (Cambridge: Cambridge Library Collection, 2012). Available at: ww.marxists.org.

32. Morris, 'The Lesser Arts', 8.

33. David Gorman, 'Art, Work and Communism: The Vision of William Morris', From *New Interventions*, Vol.10 No.2, 2000, What Next, Marxist Discussion Journal, www.whatnextjournal.org.uk>pages>Newint>Morris, accessed May 2020

34. Morris, 'Art under Plutocracy', *Signs of Change* (1884) *The Collected Works of William Morris*, Vol. 23 (Cambridge: Cambridge Library Collection, 2012), 174. Available at: www.marxists.org.

35. Ibid.

36. William Morris, 'The Art of the People' (1879), *Hopes and Fears for Art*, *The Collected Works of William Morris*, Vol. 22 (Cambridge: Cambridge Library Collection, 2012) 42-44. Available at: www.marxists.org.

37. William Morris, 'Useful Work versus Useless Toil', *Signs of Change* (1884), *The Collected Works,* Vol. 23. Available at: www.marxists.org.

38. William Morris, 'The Revival of Handicraft' (1888) *Fortnightly Review,* November 1888. Available at: www.marxists.org.

39. William Morris, 'The Socialist Ideal: Art' (1891), *New Review,* January 1891. Available at: www.marxists.org.

40. *Punch or the London Charivari*, 15 December 1883, Vol.85, 286. Morris's romance *The Story of Sigurd the Volsung* was published in 1877.

41. Founded in 1884, the Fabians hoped to advance the principles of democratic socialism via gradualist and reformist effort in democracies rather than by revolutionary overthrow.

42. MacCarthy, *William Morris*, 413

43. Related to industrial democracy and worker's self-management, Guild socialism was partly inspired by medieval craftsmen's guilds. In *Restoration of the Guild System* (1906), Arthur Penty argued for a return to artisanal production organised through guilds. Founded in 1907, *The New Age* journal took up Guild socialism, reprinting Penty's work (1914). Samuel George Hobson's *National Guilds: An Inquiry into the Wage System and the Way Out* (1914) followed. This presented

guilds as an alternative to conventional trade union activity. Guilds would not confine their demands to wages and conditions but seek to control industry for the workers. Industrial guilds would serve as the organs through which manufacturing would be organised in a future socialist society.

44. MacCarthy, *William Morris*, 413.
45. Bevis Hillier, *John Betjeman, New Fame, New Love* (London: John Murray, 2002) 242 and 261.
46. MacCarthy, *William Morris*, 382.
47. Ibid., 383.
48. J. Bruce Glasier, *Socialism in song: an appreciation of William Morris's Chants for socialists* (Manchester, National Labour Press,1920)
49. Crane was Morris's most ardent supporter within his artistic circle providing the artwork for much Socialist League propaganda.
50. May Morris, 'Introduction Biographical Note' (1912), *The Collected Works of William Morris with introductions by his daughter May Morris*, Vol. 16 (Cambridge: Cambridge Library Collection, 2012), p. xv.
51. MacCarthy, *William Morris*, 418-19.
52. Anne Anderson, 'The Kyrle Society 1877-1917: 'To the Utmost of our Power... Bringing Beauty Home to the People', Robert Whelan (ed.), *Octavia Hill: Letters to Fellow Workers*, (London: Kyrle Books, 2005), 703. The Kyrle was named for philanthropist John Kyrle (1637-1724), known as 'the Man of Ross'.
53. Owen Holland, *William Morris's Utopianism: Propaganda, Politics and Prefiguration,* (London: Palgrave Macmillan, 2017), 143.
54. MacCarthy, *William Morris*, 15.
55. Ibid.,419.
56. Renamed the Social Democratic Federation in 1883, with Scheu elected president
57. Tony Brown, 'Introduction', Tony Brown (ed), *Edward Carpenter and Late Victorian Radicalism* (London: Frank Cass & Co, 1990) 6. Poet and philosopher, Edward Carpenter is best known as an early activist for gay rights and animal rights, being a noted advocate for vegetarianism and against vivisection.
58. Letter from Engels to A. Bebel; Gotfred Appel, 'Class Struggle and Revolutionary Situation', www.marxists.org>history>erol>denmark>appel-2
59. MacCarthy, *William Morris*, 471.
60. Thompson, *William Morris*, 303.
61. Hyndman started the journal *Justice* with a contribution of £300 from Carpenter.
62. William Morris, 'Art and the People', (1883) *The Collected Works of William Morris*, Vol. 2 (Cambridge: Cambridge Library Collection, 2012), 404-05.
63. Thompson, *William Morris*, 305.
64. Ibid., 682.
65. Ruth Kinna, 'Morris, Watts, Wilde and the Democratisation of Art', Wendy Parkins (ed) *William Morris and the Art of the Everyday* (Cambridge: Cambridge Scholars Publishing, 2010) 88.
66. Ibid.
67. Serialised in *The Commonweal* in 1886–87, published in book form in 1888.

68. *News from Nowhere* was Morris response to Edward Bellamy's *Looking Backward* (1880); Julian West falls into a trance and awakes in the year 2000. Capitalism has been eradicated and all citizens work for the State. Morris had also read Richard Jefferies *After London or Wilde England* (1885), the first dystopian novel.
69. Michael Robertson, *The Last Utopians: Four Late Nineteenth-Century Visionaries and Their Legacy* (Princeton: Princeton University Press, 2018) 5.
70. *Punch or the London Charivari*, 20 February 1886, Vol.90: 90.
71. MacCarthy, *William Morris*, 533.
72. Ibid, 509.
73. Norman Kelvin (ed), *The Collected Letters of William Morris*, Volume II, Part B: 1885-1888 (Princeton: Princeton Legacy Library, 1987) 397, Letter 1069.
74. Annie Besant (1847-1933) socialist, theosophist, women's rights activist, writer, orator, educationist, and philanthropist. Regarded as a champion of human freedom, she was an ardent supporter of both Irish and Indian self-rule.
75. *Punch, or the London Charivari*, 20 February 1886, Vol.90: 93.
76. Ibid., 90.
77. Kelvin, *Collected Letters*, 520, Letter 1211.
78. In exile in England from 1886, Kropotkin was a habitué of Kelmscott House. Sergius Stepniak ('the man of the steppes') was another refugee revolutionary befriended by Morris. Through such contacts, Morris became aware of the international scene. Stepniak's *Underground Russia* (1883) made Morris's 'blood boil'.
79. Thompson, *William Morris*, 496.
80. Ibid.
81. Peter Critchley, *The Ecological Communism of William Morris* [e-book] Available through: Academia website, 2006, 3.
82. Ibid.
83. Carpenter, dubbed the 'Saint in Sandals', began this trend amongst left-wing intelligentsia. Sent a pair of sandals by a friend in India, Carpenter freed his feet from 'leather coffins': 'I soon found the joy of wearing them', Carpenter wrote. 'And after a little time, I set about making them.' Starting as a cottage industry in Derbyshire, Carpenter's sandal making enterprise was moved to Letchworth. In 1883, Carpenter joined the Social Democratic Federation, and in 1885 left to join the Socialist League. He became a founder member of the Independent Labour Party in 1893.
84. Francis King, *Garden City Revels*/northhertsmuseum.org>garden-city-reveals.
85. Paul Laity, 'A Brief History of Cranks', *Cabinet*, www.cabinetmagazine.org>issues>laity
86. MacCarthy, *William Morris,* 29.
87. In was appropriated by Ruskin 'Fine art is that in which the hand, the head, and the *heart* of man go together'. 'The Two Path's, Lecture II: 'The Unity of Art', section 54 (1859).
88. Frobel's ideas were politicised; the Prussian government, suspicious of the socialist views of Froebel's nephew, banned the kindergarten movement in 1851. Frobel

did not live long enough to see this ban lifted in 1860 and witness the subsequent impact of kindergartens.

89. William Morris, 'Thoughts on Education under Capitalism', *Commonweal,* Vol. 4, No. 129, 30 June 1888: 204-205.Available at: www.marxists.org.

90. Ibid.

91. Anne Anderson, 'Victorian High Society and Social Duty: the promotion of `Recreative Learning and Voluntary Teaching', *Journal of the History of Education*, Vol. 31, No.4, July 2002: 311-334.

92. Bernard Bosanquet, 'The Home Arts and Industries Association', *Charity Organisation Review*, Vol. 4, No. 40 (April 1888): 135.

93. MacCarthy, *William Morris*, 595.

94. John Drinkwater, *William Morris A Critical Study* (London: Martin Secker, 1912) 198-99.

95. 'The Beauty of Life' (1880), *Hopes and Fears for Art, Collected Works of William Morris*, Vol. 22. Available at: www.marxists.org.

Radicalism in the British Campaign for 'Votes for Women', 1865-1928

Di Drummond

Introduction

The women's campaign for the right to vote for parliament in Britain was a long, hard-fought, and frustrating one.[1] It took over fifty-two years of near-constant work for women to gain what is now seen as a fundamental civil right; a vote to have a say in the election of the government of the nation you live and work in. In other words, just to be a 'citizen' of their own country. Even then, in 1918, only SOME women were given the vote. Women did not gain voting equality with men until 1928!

The key question of this chapter is whether the campaign to get votes for women in Britain between 1865 and 1928 was a 'radical' one or not? The campaign for women's suffrage certainly started in a very lady-like fashion in 1865, continuing as a highly 'constitutional' movement as the so-called 'suffragists' presented petitions and supported representation of the people bills to parliament (then 'men only' of course). Always obeying the law of Britain in their actions, the suffragists did not appear to be radical in any way. Yet, despite this, radicalism, along with feminism, unquestionably inspired the suffragists' campaign.

In contrast, the other branch of the women's campaign, the Women's Social and Political Union, begun by Emmeline, Christabel and Sylvia Pankhurst in Manchester in 1903, was extreme from

Emmeline Pankhurst. (Wikimedia Commons)

the start. Frustrated by so many years of failure to gain justice in the vote, after 1905, the WSPU resorted to highly militant actions. Starting by merely interrupting politicians' speeches at meetings, the suffragettes went on to hold mass demonstrations, courting arrest for actions like breaking windows in Downing Street and assaulting police officers in 1908. After 1912, the more militant suffragettes of the WSPU escalated their campaign to include arson and bomb attacks. There were even rumours of the leaders of the WSPU calling for revolution. This chapter explores how far, and in what way, the campaign for votes for women in Britain between 1865/6 and 1928, was radical. Before considering this, the meaning of 'radicalism', and a definition of the 'English Radical Tradition', need to be determined, especially in light of the campaign for votes for women.

Defining 'Radicalism' and 'The English Radical Tradition'

Put simply 'radicalism' is, 'The belief in, or expression of, the need for extreme economic and social change'. Radicals believe that only the political transformation of the state, from one ruled by a corrupt elite, to that conducted, 'by the People, for the People', would achieve this. To be a fair, modern state, it is necessary for every adult to enjoy the rights of 'citizenship' in the form of a parliamentary vote. If the government of a state was not based on this, it did not represent the will of 'The People'. For radicals, any state that did not have this was not legitimate. The radical idea of 'popular constitutionalism', held that if a state was not 'the will of the People' because they were not represented politically, it could be overthrown.

Calls for 'citizenship', together with this 'popular constitutionalism', provided radicalism with its key weapons. A mythical history of the rights of the English people was another feature of the radical armoury. This fight for a government that was representative of all 'The People', giving them their liberty, had allegedly occurred throughout English history, creating the 'English Radical Tradition'. But the definition used here, and by the women's suffrage movement, had emerged from radical, revolutionary actions taking place in Europe and America from the 1780s onwards. To qualify as 'radicals', the members of the women's suffrage campaign in Britain, suffragist and suffragette alike, would have to employ these key weapons from radicalism such as 'citizenship', and 'popular constitutionalism', and draw on different aspects of the 'English Radical Tradition' in their fight.

It is little wonder that both men and women in Britain turned to radicalism and radical action towards the end of the eighteenth century. Britain was far from being a democracy during the years that the women's suffrage movement was active. Government was still the monopoly of the aristocracy, seen to represent the interests of everyone in the country because they had property and power. The majority of men, as well as all women, did not have the right to vote for parliament in Britain for most of the Victorian period. Having a vote depended on owning land and property throughout most of the nineteenth century. Until the Great Reform Act of 1832, only males of the British aristocratic elite, three per cent of the population, plus a few women who owned property in their own right, could vote. The act lowered the value of property qualification needed, extending the franchise (the right to vote), to middle-class men. Still, only one out of every seven adult men could.

The few women who previously had the right to vote lost it through the Great Reform Act, because the act stated that only 'male persons' were eligible. The male franchise was extended in 1867 and again in 1884-5, but all men over twenty-one years of age would not have voting rights until 1918. As stated previously, some women gained the vote then, but equal political rights to men only came in 1928. As a result, ordinary people, the majority of the nation, had no say in how they were governed and laws were made.

Extensions to men's rights to vote were won by hard-fought radical campaigns, including violence, riots, and mass demonstrations, where the will of 'The People' was shown by the numbers gathering together. Such actions clearly frightened those in power. They did not just show 'popular sovereignty', 'The People' were also willing to resist the ongoing tyranny of unrepresentative government.

Women were very much part of these various radical movements. Radical political societies, such as those that organised the Peterloo demonstration in Manchester in 1819, were supported by entire families. The 'Peterloo Massacre' that occurred when a local military force, the 'yeomanry', attacked that demonstration resulted in seventeen deaths, including four women, one child and an unborn baby. The Chartists of the 1830s-1840s had significant female support, as did those fighting for the extension of the franchise for men throughout the Victorian period.

Right and overleaf spread: Campaigners for women's voting rights faced a lot of opposition in the press. *Punch* published several comic pieces lampooning the Suffragists and Suffragettes. (Anne Anderson's Personal Collection)

"THE ANGEL IN 'THE HOUSE;'" OR, THE RESULT OF FEMALE SUFFRAGE.
(A Troubled Dream of the Future.)

THE POLITICAL LADY-CRICKETERS.

Lady Cricketer. "A TEAM OF OUR OWN! I SHOULD THINK SO! IF WE'RE GOOD ENOUGH TO SCOUT FOR YOU, WHY SHOULDN'T WE TAKE A TURN AT THE BAT!"

If you do not want to please the man, but only to show your own superiority, it may perhaps be as well to remember that women are better than men, as a rule, in that feelings. Men talk best when they are by themselves, but they are liable to be painfully natural at such times. I had some little difficulty in finding this out, but I thought it my duty to know, and—well, I *do* know.

The correspondence that I have received has not been altogether pleasant. I have had one letter from EYRES aged thirteen) saying that she thinks me a mean sneak for prying into other people's Diaries. I can only reply that I was acting for the public good. I have had a sweet letter, however, from "AZALEA." She has been absolutely compelled, by force of circumstances, to allow the distinct attentions of three different men. She does not give the names of the men, only descriptions, but I should advise her to keep the dark one. She can see the will at Somerset House. "JANE" writes to ask what is the best cure for freckles. I do not answer questions of that kind. I have replied to my other correspondents privately.

REPULSING THE AMAZONS.

(See Cartoon, "Arming the Amazons," Dec. 5, 1891.)

ARMING the Amazons against the Greeks?
That PRIAM SALISBURY tried some few short weeks
Before the present fray. FAWCETTA fair
Had prayed; the question then seemed "in the air,"
And PRIAM proffered then the Franchise- spear,
(A shadowy one, that gave no grounds for fear,
To poor PENTHESILEA.

ROLLITZTUS moves, there's going to be a row,
And lo! the mingled ranks of Greece and Troy
Close 'galnat the Amazons. Her steed, a toy,
A hobby-horse, that any maid may mount,
Is not—just now—of any great account.
Her phantom spear will pierce no stout male mail;
But should ROLLITTUS not—(confound him!)—fail,
A female host, well armed, and set on hobbies,
Might prove as dangerous as a batch of Bobbies.
The fair FAWCETTA then must be thrown over;
PENTHESILEA finds no hero-lover
In either host. PRIAM, shroud, is dumb.
Ah, maiden-hosts, man's love for you's a hum.
Each fears you—in the foeman's cohorts thrown,
But *neither side desires you in its own.!*
The false GLADSTONIUS first, he whom you nourish,
A snake in your spare bosoms, dares to flourish
Fresh arms against you; potent, though polite,
He fain would bow you out of the by-fight.
Civilly shelve you. "Don't kick up a row,
And—spoil my game! Another day, not now,
There's a *dar* creature!" CHAMBERLAINITE, too,
Hard as a nail, and squirmy as a screw,
Sides with the elder hero, just for once;
CHAPLENITE also, active for the nonce
On the Greek side, makes up the Traitorous Three,
One from each faction! Ah! 'tis sad to see
PENTHESILEA, fierce male foes unite
In keeping female warriors from the fight;
Yet think, look round, and—you may find they 're right!

REPULSING THE AMAZONS.

(See Cartoon, "Arming the Amazons," Dec. 5, 1891.)

ARMING the Amazons against the Greeks?
That PRIAM SALISBURY tried some few short weeks
Before the present fray. FAWCETTA fair
Had prayed; the question then seemed "in the air,"
And PRIAM proffered then the Franchise- spear,
(A shadowy one, that gave no grounds for fear,
To poor PENTHESILEA.

ARMING THE AMAZONS.

Priam (loquitur). "ACCEPT NEW ARMS, YE MAIDEN COHORTS! TAKE THE WEAPONS THAT SHALL MAKE ACHILLES SHAKE, AND REINFORCE, AGAINST THE WILES OF GREECE, THE POWERS OF PROPERTY, PRIVILEGE, AND PEACE!"

Satirical pieces from the late nineteenth century mocking the women's suffrage campaign.

Calling for 'universal suffrage', the male-dominated Radical organisations of this period demanded 'votes for women' on only three occasions! They saw no problem with this – women needed no political representation! Not just the radicals, but all other elements of nineteenth century society, many women as well as men, shared similar views about women. These argued that each sex operated in their 'proper' 'separate spheres', God's will and women's biology allotting them roles in the home as wives and mothers. Subordinate to men, women lacked the time, mental abilities, or knowledge of the world (the man's sphere), to be involved in any way in politics. For the campaign for votes for women to be successful the suffragists needed to undermine male authority, not just in the home but in the nation too.

Only men (and for most of the nineteenth century only men who owned property), were seen to be fit for government. However, as the natural protectors of women, men would nobly represent them and vote in their interests! As a result of having no right to be involved in making the law, women had no say in their own lives. Women could not keep their own children in the case of a divorce, which was rare, until after 1839. Women could not sue for divorce on any grounds until after 1857. Women waited far longer for other rights. They could not keep their own earnings if they were married until after 1870, or own property after marriage until 1882. Until the late Victorian period, few women received an education. This improved through feminist pressure during the late nineteenth century.

If the fight for votes for women, and for women's basic rights and equality, was to be won, those campaigning had to put an end to this commonly held belief that women were naturally inferior and subject to men. They had to attack the idea that men naturally always looked after women's interests. Each of these steps was highly radical, and, of course, feminist, bringing fundamental change to British society. If the women's campaign was truly radical, it also had to use radical language and tactics, those women campaigning making the meaning and actions of 'radicalism' their own by giving it a new feminist perspective. The chapter now turns to establish who the suffragists and suffragettes were, and then to determine how far and in what way, both of these groups may be considered to be radicals.

The Women's Campaign for the Vote in Britain: Who were the suffragists and the suffragettes?

So who were the suffragists and the suffragettes? First of all the suffragists were various groups that fought for votes for women, most usually in very peaceful and constitutional ways, from 1865/66, right through to women gaining equal citizenship with men in 1928.

Attempts to reverse the decision that the British parliament had made in 1832 to disqualify women from voting on the basis of their sex began immediately, Orator Henry Hunt of Peterloo fame, putting forward a bill to enfranchise women again. The years between 1832 and 1865 also saw significant developments in feminist ideas. Writers from Mary Wollstonecraft, in her *Vindication of the Rights of* Women (1792), William Thompson in his, *An Appeal of one half of the Human Race* (1825), and Harriet Taylor in her pamphlet on the Emancipation of Women, published in 1851, were defining feminist aims and advancing women's cause. Various organisations such as the Langham Place Group, established in 1857 to pressurise for better female education so that they could enter the professions, had also begun. But it was the fight to reverse the decision made by parliament to exclude women from voting during the Reform crisis of 1865-67 that really kick-started the British Women's suffrage campaign, and the suffragist cause.

During those years radical agitation to widen voting rights for men helped to create a national political crisis. In response first the Liberal government, and then, after this had fallen in June 1866, the Conservatives, proposed new Reform Bills in order to extend the male franchise (right to vote). A group of middle-class ladies who wanted women to be included in this, formed the Kensington Society. In less than a month they had collected nearly 1,500 signatures on a petition to parliament, calling for just that. A small contingent of women from the Society presented the petition to the radical liberal member of parliament, the philosopher John Stuart Mill, at the House of Commons on 7 June 1866. Members of the group included Emily Davies, who campaigned for women to enter universities, Barbara Bodichon, of the Langham Place Group, and Millicent Garrett, later to become Millicent Garrett Fawcett, the future leader of the suffragists. Their range of interests showed that they were intent on gaining the vote in order to improve women's lot in life more generally too.

Mill presented an amendment to the Conservative reform bill in support of the women's petition on 20 May 1867. It simply called for the wording of the bill to be changed from 'man' to 'person'. This, because the law gave a woman's property to her husband on marriage, would have only given the vote to single women who owned property and land.

Defeated in parliament by a vote of 73 to 196, this setback began a national movement for votes for women. Women's suffrage societies, seeking the right to vote on the same property-holding qualifications as men, were formed in London, Birmingham, Bristol, Edinburgh and Manchester. The Manchester National Society for Women's Suffrage brought notable names into the women's movement. These included Dr Richard Marsden Pankhurst, the lawyer who, in 1879, would become the husband of the twenty-year-old Emmeline Pankhurst, future leader of the suffragettes. Lydia Becker, who was the leader of the suffragists' Central Committee of the National Society for women's suffrage, 'lobbying' members of parliament in Westminster from 1881 until her death in 1990, was also a key member of the National Society from its inception.

Wrought with differences and divisions of opinions for many years, suffragist organisations gradually overcame these problems, banding together to form the National Women's Suffrage Societies in 1897. Under the NUWSS, the suffragists became the largest section of the votes for women campaign. The NUWSS maintained this status throughout the years of the militant actions of the suffragettes. Declaring its 'Law Abiding' slogan, a counterpoint to the suffragettes' militancy, the NUWSS had 50,000 members in 1904. By 1914, membership had grown to 100,000 with some 500 branches across Britain. Millicent Garrett Fawcett was their President and was to remain so until 1919.

With such growing support, the NUWSS remained the leading national organisation throughout the women's campaign for the vote, but another important, and often better remembered organisation, the Women's Social and Political Union, was formed in 1903. On 9 October that year, angered by the lack of progress in women gaining the vote, Emmeline Pankhurst, with her daughters Christabel and Sylvia, began the WSPU in their home in Manchester. Their militant campaign commenced in 1905, the supporters of the Union were dubbed 'suffragettes' by Charles Hand, a journalist at *The Daily Mail,* the following year. Coined as a very patronising term for the militant women of the campaign, in effect the word meant 'cute little suffragists', their actions turned the word into one denoting daring, strong, rebellious women.

However, the WSPU was not the only organisation to be referred to as suffragettes because of their militant actions. Some women had started to refuse to pay taxes if they did not have the vote during the 1890s. The Women's Freedom League (WFL) was formed in 1907 by Teresa Billington-Greig and Charlotte Despard, adopting militant but passive resistance as a reaction against the WSPU's increasing violence. The Women's Tax Resistance League (WTRL), which refused to pay taxes without receiving parliamentary representation, was established in 1909.

The number of women in membership of the WSPU was much lower than that of the NUWSS. Initially, there were 2,000 members. This had increased to 5,000 by 1914. But the organisation enjoyed great popularity, one that did however wane when suffragette violence grew too extreme. The WSPU newspaper, 'Votes for Women', founded in 1907, was selling 33,000 copies a week by 1910. Its readership was no doubt much wider.

Other factors suggest that the WSPU was more popular than its membership figures indicate. Having started in Manchester, the Pankhursts and their organisation moved to London in 1906. With branches nationwide, the WSPU's headquarters at Clement's Inn, London, took up twenty-seven rooms by 1912. Another factor that indicates that the WSPU was a much larger organisation was that over a thousand members of the WSPU were arrested and imprisoned between 1908 and 1914, although many women were repeatedly gaoled for their actions. Emmeline Pankhurst remained the leader of the WSPU from its founding through to 1917.

How Radical were the suffragists?

So how 'radical' were the two sections of the Women's Suffrage Movement? At first glance, the suffragists appear to be very poor candidates for the title 'radicals'. Commencing their campaign with the very ladylike presentation of a petition to parliament, the suffragists continued in this same 'constitutional' manner for the further fifty-two years of the campaign to win the vote for women in Britain.

Carefully following the processes laid down by parliament, between 1866 and 1918, the suffragists presented 16,000 petitions. They also canvassed members of parliament to support bills for women's right to vote, winning over male electors to their cause, and persuading them to only elect MPs who wanted the female franchise. Despite the NUWSS officially being non-party political in position until it switched to supporting Labour and universal suffrage in 1912, many Liberal MPs were in favour of votes for women. Liberal governments, and Conservative ones, did not. Between 1870 and 1914, some twenty-eight bills for votes for women were considered in parliament. Two of them actually received a majority vote, but they failed to be passed as acts because no government would give them enough time to receive a final ratifying vote in 'The House'.

Another highly constitutional way that the suffragists tried to regain the vote for women was by appealing, under law, against their own personal disqualification under the Reform Acts of 1832 and 1867. In 1867, one woman in Manchester, Lilly Maxwell, took her case to a special court to prove that she, as a property owner in her own right, should still have the vote. Maxwell won and was allowed to cast her vote in a parliamentary election. However, a further court case fought by Dr Richard Marsden Pankhurst on behalf of over 5,000 women with property in Manchester was lost in November 1868, proving that women had lost their parliamentary votes under the Reform Act of 1867.

Constantly thwarted by parliament and the law, how could the suffragists not rebel against so many years of disappointment and male betrayal in their fight for votes for women? The suffragists were closely allied with the Liberal party. They believed in the liberal philosophy that advancement in government, and in society, was a gradual, 'improving' process. It was just a matter of time before they would change male politicians' minds to see that it was only logical to extend liberal policies of 'equality' and 'freedom', gaining votes for women.

'Radical' change did not appear to be in the suffragists' thoughts, yet they were. At this time even the idea of women being equal to men, or females speaking in public was radical. There was also an extremely strong tradition of radicalism amongst members of the women's suffrage campaign, one historian on the subject arguing that from 'the 1860s onwards the [women's suffrage cause] emerged as a liberal radical initiative'. The suffragists were also strongly feminist, although their feminism was not extreme, seeking equality between men and women and nothing more. Their campaign was also most important in undermining fundamental ideas in society that led to women being refused the vote for so long. The suffragist campaign eventually made feminism a key dimension of English Radicalism. But how far were British suffragists radical, and to what degree did their feminism became an integral part of English radicalism?

The first indication that the suffragists were radical lay in their own personal histories. Leading members had a radical inheritance from the earliest days of the movement. Women who presented the petition in 1866, such as Barbara Bodichon (her grandfather was a radical supporting the abolition of slavery), and Millicent Garrett Fawcett (her father was a convert to Gladstonian Liberalism), claimed a radical background. JS Mill, the MP who presented the women's petition in parliament, along with his colleague, Henry Fawcett, husband of Millicent, were leading liberal radicals of their era. There was a rich strain of radicalism in the history of other women's suffrage campaigners too. Lydia Becker had such a background, as did Barbara Bodichon of the Langham Place Group. Those who were suffragists in the nineteenth century, turning to being suffragettes in the twentieth, also had long-established radical roots. Emmeline Pankhurst's parents were nonconformist in religion and radical in their politics, while her husband Richard was known as 'The Red Doctor', as much for the extremism of his politics, (he was an anti-royalist and anti-imperialist), as for his red hair and ruddy complexion.

Another way that the suffragists were radicals lay in their use of one traditional strategy of radicalism. It has already been noted that radicals in England used two weapons, those of 'popular constitutionalism', and 'citizenship', in their fight to gain the political representation of 'The People'. The first idea argued that any parliamentary system that was not elected by the popular sovereignty of all, 'The People', was tyrannical and should be defied, even overthrown. Proving that women were 'of The People' was fundamental to the women's suffrage cause. Defiance and revolution were resorted to by only one wing of the movement, that was the extreme militants in the WSPU.

In contrast, the suffragists always stopped well short of standing against government. However, at times, certain sections of suffragists did denounce government for being unjust and unconstitutional. Some suffragists had given their support to Josephine Butler's Ladies' National Association for the Repeal of the Contagious Diseases Acts. A campaign running from 1869, the Association damned the British government as dictatorial for passing laws against prostitution that denied women basic human rights. (Women could be locked up without trial if they were thought to be on 'the game'. Wrongful imprisonment had been banned under the legendary 'Magna Carta'. This was seen as a key event in the English Radical Tradition. Butler's campaign was highly controversial, both because of its association with 'fallen women', and this strategy of denouncing the government. However, the majority of the suffragists, unlike their later suffragette sisters, were unwilling to take that next radical step, that of resisting the government, either passively or physically.

While the suffragists were usually totally unwilling to adopt this first radical strategy, the second, that of arguing for women's rights of citizenship, lay at the very heart of their policy and actions. From the beginning of their campaign, one of the key aims of the suffragists was to prove that women were just as worthy of citizenship as men. That women should actively demonstrate that they qualified for the vote was Millicent Garrett Fawcett's focus throughout her long leadership of the NUWSS. In a speech made at the outbreak of the Great War in 1914, she called women to work for the nation with the cry of, 'Let us prove ourselves worthy of citizenship'.

However, right from the start of their campaign suffragists had realised that if not just a parliament of men, but also the British nation were to consider women worthy of citizenship they would have to completely redefine the definition of 'worth' in contemporary society, As early as the 1860 and 70s, suffragists Millicent Garrett Fawcett, and Lydia Becker, noted that certain men saw women's rights 'as the very incarnation of all that is repulsive', one MP actually saying that the idea of women speaking in parliament made him feel sick! Women were seen to be men's subordinates because of their 'natural' 'disabilities', 'their biology' that not only kept them in the 'domestic sphere', but also ensured that they did not have the intellect necessary to function in politics and the wider world. This required the suffragist to employ highly feminist strategies to challenge such widely held and fundamental ideas, adding feminism to liberal radical ideologies in the process.

The suffragist movement led the way in arguing that women were worthy of citizenship from its start. JS Mill, MP, was not just the leading liberal radical philosopher of the Victorian age, he also published *The Subjection of Women,* in 1869. This argued consistently for women's rights on grounds of equality with men, Mill compared women denied the franchise with slaves because of their lack of freedom. Mill had developed his ideas after many years of collaboration with Harriet Taylor (he was to marry her in 1851). In her pamphlet, 'The Enfranchisement of Women', Taylor Mill argued against the 'separate sphere' idea. This was the key argument used to prevent women from having the vote for so long. Maintaining that women's role in life should not be dictated by their biology, Taylor Mill supported equality between the sexes, stating that the only 'proper sphere for all human beings is the largest and highest they can attain'.

Women had begun making speeches and publishing them before the suffragists started their campaign in 1866, but the suffragists put forward key feminist ideas (highly radical in nature), that seriously undermined the arguments that contemporary society used to deny women the vote. They skilfully pointed out the 'double standards' of these! Millicent Garrett Fawcett did this in a speech that she made in 1872, 'The Electoral Disabilities of Women'. For instance, men denied women a means of cultivating their intellect, and then declined to give women the vote because they did not have the intelligence. They also argued a wife having a vote would just cause rows at home, and that women did not need the vote, as men, and national legislation, would gallantly protect them. The young suffragist (she was only twenty-five) pointed out that the fact that men made such fatuous objections to women receiving justice in the form of equal citizenship demonstrated their total lack of concern for them!

Garrett Fawcett arguments not only totally undermined male objections to women having the vote, they also went much further, stating that women's political representation was not only essential for women, it was necessary for men too. In this suffragists were radical and highly feminist. Harriet Taylor Mill had argued in her pamphlet of 1851 that women should have the vote as they were a vital civilising force in British society, pacifying and quietening men. Garrett Fawcett took this feminist idea further. Political representation of women was for the good of the nation and for the Empire (Garrett Fawcett held a very imperialist position). A female perspective, gained from the roles in life that God and Nature had allocated women, was needed to improve everyday life, making it more civilised than when men only had political control. The suffragists had cleverly, and very radically, turned the tables on deeply traditional, negative views of women held by Victorian society.

The suffragists also actively demonstrated the radical strategy that women were worthy of citizenship in the way that they organised and ran their long-standing campaign. This showed that women were well able to deal with political matters, being good administrators, indefatigable in their efforts, highly intelligent in how they worked. Always respectful of parliament, the suffragists became skilled in engaging with the parliamentary process. This was seen in the Central Committee's and then the NUWSS' constant work in seeking MPs support of their bills and amendments. Garrett Fawcett's knowledge of parliamentary procedure was second to none. She was vital to her husband's role as an MP, Henry having been blinded in a hunting accident seven years before he became a member and nine years before they were married. Women's suffrage societies were well organised from the outset, becoming one of the largest political organisations in Britain by the outbreak of war in 1918.

Women were also proving themselves worthy of citizenship in other areas of contemporary politics, the inclusion of women in certain areas of local government being the result of various organisations, such as the Langham Place Group, pressuring for representation in matters that were naturally within the woman's 'sphere'. From 1870, women were allowed to be members of boards that managed state elementary schools. In 1875, they were permitted to be elected as administrators of the Poor Law. This provided workhouses and hospitals for the needy. Many suffragists, and future suffragettes, 'cut their teeth', gaining essential experience in such roles. Emmeline Pankhurst, for instance, was elected a Poor Law Guardian in part of Manchester in 1894. There, as a woman and a mother, she could do far more than any man, discovering the level of neglect that the earlier appointed Guardians allowed in their workhouse. Pregnant women and girls as young as eight were made to scrub cold stone floors, while Pankhurst discovered that the children were given no underwear by the penny-pinching Guardians. Pankhurst said that it was this experience that made her a militant. A vote for women was vital if the poor, young and elderly in British society were to be protected.

Other campaigns mounted by organisations allied to the suffragist cause also demonstrated that women had other very good reasons why they needed the vote. Barbara Bodichon had published a pamphlet in 1854 that outlined the laws of England

and how they penalised women, beginning to pressurise for acts to change married women's property-holding rights as a result. The fact that the Married Women's Properties Acts were passed many years later, in the 1870s and 1880s, demonstrated that an all-male parliament was neglectful, and not protective, of women and their fundamental interests.

This widening of government, to include matters that were seen to be key concerns of women, happened not just because of the suffragists' campaigns, but as societal views changed. During the later nineteenth century, national government introduced legislation into areas, such as education, care of the poor, and health. This trend in 'progressive' politics was to increase in the early twentieth century as the Liberals recast their policies to improve the welfare of the British people, and after the Labour party was established in 1901. By 1912, the NUWSS had become so involved with these new progressive forms of politics that the organisation abandoned its established policy of backing the Liberal party, demanding an equal vote for men and women based on property qualification, in favour of supporting Labour and a vote for all British citizens. The work of the NUWSS had not only brought recognition of the need to award women the parliamentary vote by the early years of the twentieth century, it also extended the definition of 'citizenship' to include women.

This radical work of the suffragists, feminising politics by demonstrating that women were worthy of citizenship, continued into the twentieth century. A further change in politics during the early twentieth century that made the NUWSS rather more radical in the way it pressed for women's citizenship came with the foundation of the Women's Social and Political Union in 1903. Having presented examples of women acting as citizens in many different capacities for so long, the NUWSS both followed and set the example of the WSPU. They held large-scale public demonstrations to prove that women were worthy citizens.

As already seen, the suffragists had held deputations to parliamentary candidates, MPs, government ministers and the Prime Minister throughout their history, but the WSPU, together with other suffragette organisations, started to do this in a spectacular way from the 1900s onwards. It was the NUWSS that staged the first mass demonstration in favour of votes for women. In February 1907, some 3,000 women and their supporters from forty different local national and provincial organisations processed through London, demonstrating that women wanted the vote. This became known as the 'Mud March' because of the conditions the suffragists walked through. In April 1909, the NUWSS organised a 'Pageant of Women's Trades and Professions' demonstration. Led by Garrett Fawcett, this saw female doctors, nurses, teachers, factory and mill workers, claim themselves worthy of citizenship because of the essential jobs they performed for the nation.

The suffragists often joined forces with the suffragettes in forming important deputations to parliament, as in the case of their support of the Conciliation Bills, proposals put forward by all political parties to give women the vote in 1910, 1911 and 1912. However the suffragists, unlike the suffragettes, were determined to act peacefully and did not try to get arrested in order to gain publicity for their cause. They still wanted to show that women were calm and rational, worthy of citizenship.

Anxious to distance themselves from the excesses of the WSPU and other suffragettes, especially after the WSPU began their extremely radical militant campaign of arson, bombing, and hunger strikes in 1912, the NUWSS's staged 'The Women's Pilgrimage' on 26 July 1913. Using a religious term for the demonstration's title, the suffragists hoped to convey the seriousness of their campaign. Some 50,000 women came to Hyde Park from all corners of the country, their sheer numbers showing that women did indeed want votes for themselves; their good behaviour indicated that it was time for them to be promoted to citizenship. Garrett Fawcett addressed the crowd under a banner that proclaimed to be 'law-abiding'.

Surprisingly, therefore, while the NUWSS endeavoured to be constitutional in its actions, it was radical in constantly upholding the demand that women should have equal citizenship with men. Their case against men's refusal to give women that right was liberal, radical and feminist in character. They had made 'radicalism their own', proving that women were as much 'of the People' as men. But the suffragists did not even contemplate the highly radical tactic of resisting government that they considered unrepresentative because women did not have the vote. In contrast, the suffragettes resisted government both passively and actively, at times even advocating revolution against an unrepresentative government that showed itself to be cruel and tyrannical in its treatment of suffragettes. The next question is, 'How radical were the suffragettes?'

How radical were the suffragettes?

Remembered today for the drama and often, the apparent desperation of their often very violent actions, the 'suffragettes' are often seen to be the militant, radical winners of the vote for women in Britain. Starting off by simply asking the question, 'Will the Liberal government give women the vote?' of the Liberal politicians, Sir Edward Grey and Winston Churchill, in a meeting at the Free Trade Hall in Manchester in 1905, the WSPU campaign escalated into resistance, even terrorism, and martyrdom. Above all the suffragettes sought publicity for their cause, fed up with a media that failed to address women's plight. Yet many of the policies and actions of the WSPU, as well as those of the WFL and WTRL, drew on radical thought and protest, adding a clearly stated feminism to this. Their actions were modelled on those of past male radicals fighting for their rights to citizenship and the vote. In many senses, the suffragettes became the epitome of radicalism, not simply because of the level of militancy and violence they were prepared to resort to, but because of their beliefs.

Surprisingly, suffragettes were also, in effect, suffragists. They shared constitutional tactics with the suffragists, but demonstrated also staged militant actions to hammer home their point. In 1907, the WSPU started to hold 'Women's Parliaments' when bills for votes for women were being introduced into the House. By holding a parallel parliament for women they wanted to emphasise that women could conduct political business, often more effectively than men. They, like the suffragists, sent deputations to parliament to lobby the House. The WSPU and WFL held twenty-four of these in 1909 alone.

The suffragettes were also keen to prove that women were worthy of citizenship, a key radical and feminist strategy that they did share with the NUWSS. Although, as already seen, the suffragists had begun holding demonstrations, it was the WSPU that made this tactic their own, gaining huge publicity for the cause as they did so. They held massive processions in 1908, 1909, 1910 and 1911. These were most beautiful spectacles, demonstrating the nobility, grace and fortitude of women, as well as the huge numbers who were in favour of votes for women.

In June 1909, the Women's Sunday Procession in London brought some 300,000 to Hyde Park. It was led by a suffragette dressed as Joan of Arc, a brave fighting woman who defended her country, (that women did not do this was another reason many said that they could not have the vote for parliament).

In June 1911, the year that King George V was crowned, all suffragists and suffragette organisations held a joint 'Women's Coronation Procession'. The two-mile-long demonstration proclaimed female worth as women of different essential professions and trades, such as doctors (a few), nurses, mill and textile workers, walked through London. A multitude of banners not only displayed suffragist and suffragette slogans, but also historical women of national fame like Florence Nightingale, a leading innovator in the nursing profession in the 1860s.

However, the suffragettes not only demonstrated women to be worthy of the vote, they also literally 'staged' the meaning of their exclusion from citizenship, not just for women, but men too! In this, they were providing an image of what feminists such as Harriet Taylor had been arguing since the 1850s. Suffragette theatre was both prolific and popular, plays being produced in London's West End by key female playwrights and members of the 'Actresses' Franchise League'. In 1909, for instance, a play by Cicely Hamilton and Christopher St John (a woman), 'How the Vote was won!', was staged at the Royalty Theatre, London. In protest at, once again, not been given the vote, the play had women call a national strike. Horace Cole, a clerk living in Brixton, finds himself surrounded by spinster aunts and cousins who have come to live with him, their nearest male relative, while they are striking. The maid has left, and Horace's wife refuses to do any housework. Plagued by so many dependent women, and without anything decent to eat, Horace rapidly sees the error of his ways and canvasses the government to give women the vote!

This same story of women's worth, and male injustice in denying them the vote, was told by other areas of the Arts where the suffragettes worked tirelessly. Posters produced by a special division of the WSPU, the D'Ateliers, a 'collective' of female artists, depicted women of worth, who were denied the vote, contrasting them with male drunkards, 'white slavers' ('pimps'), and prisoners, who, despite their exceedingly bad characters, kept theirs. The women's suffrage movement, especially, but not exclusively the WSPU, also did much culturally to raise women's confidence as individuals so that they saw themselves worthy of citizenship in the nation. Suffragette publications and posters portrayed women as active, able and beautiful. Emmeline Pankhurst was most insistent that suffragettes should present themselves as well-dressed ladies as they worked for the cause (Pankhurst always looked elegant). Being a suffragette became a fashion statement as they sported the WSPU colours of green (for hope), white (purity), and purple (dignity). This was not just in their clothing and jewellery, but in household items like tea services too.

While it is true that the suffragettes often tried to get arrested during their demonstrations, certain mass protests staged by suffragists as well as suffragettes demonstrated the injustice and excesses of men, and of the liberal male state. Excessive force was used against the women, not just by the police, but by members of the public too. This showed that the anti-suffragists' argument that women did not need the vote because men and the law protected them, was a false one. This was clearly a radical and feminist position. Black Friday, an incident that resulted from a deputation of suffragettes attempting to take a petition of support for the Conciliation Bill of 1910, provided evidence of this. Prime Minister Asquith refused to meet the women, while 300 of their supporters were prevented from approaching the Houses of Parliament by a police cordon. The ensuing 'battle' went on for six hours. In all, 115 female suffrage protestors, and four men, were arrested. They were released without charge the next day. Many suffragettes had been assaulted, some twenty-nine of them sexually. Two women died later as a result of the injuries they sustained that day.

Other suffragette demonstrations also resulted in the shaming of male politicians, and the state because of their maltreatment of women. This won sympathy from many male voters. In 1914, Emmeline Pankhurst was arrested while attempting to lead a deputation to meet the king, a constitutional right. The world-famous photograph of Pankhurst, a slight woman still recovering from hunger strike in gaol, being forcibly carried by the burly Chief Inspector of Police, Rolfe, damned government and monarch alike.

This same radical and feminist strategy of shaming the punitive British state, illegitimate because of its refusal to make women citizens of their own country, had also been used very effectively by the suffragettes of the WSPU who went on hunger strike. Refusing food, and sometimes water, because the Liberal government would not accept the suffragettes as political prisoners, WSPU posters showed women in prison tied down and fed through tubes forced down their throats in order to prevent their martyrdom through starvation. The poster proclaimed, 'Electors! Stop this torture by voting against the Prime Minister!'

In many of these protests, the suffragettes identified key elements of the English Radical Tradition that inspired them. One of the first WSPU hunger strikers, Marion Wallace Dunlop, had been arrested in the precincts of parliament in 1909 after stencilling a passage from the Bill of Rights of 1668/9, a key document in the English Radical Tradition. The famous Conspiracy Trial of leading WSPU figures, Emmeline and Christabel Pankhurst, and Emmeline and Frederick Pethick Lawrence, in 1912, gave the suffragette defence in court the opportunity to state why they had organised mass window-breaking in London's West End the previous year. In her closing statement, Emmeline Pankhurst argued that they were following their radical forefathers, such as the Chartists, who only found justice from the British state when they were prepared to resort to violence. Emmeline Pankhurst identified this same suffragette radical inheritance in 1913 when making the speech, 'Why we are Militant?' in New York City while raising funds for the British suffragette cause.

The suffragettes were willing to take that step to the highest level of radicalism, the one that the suffragists would not even contemplate, that of breaking the law because it was made by a tyrannical government, unrepresentative of 'The People' because of women's continued exclusion from the vote. At times, it has been argued, the WSPU even proposed revolution against the state. Many instances of suffragette law-breaking made on this basis took the form of passive resistance, especially on the part of the two suffragette organisations, the Women's Freedom League and the Women's Tax Resistance League. 'No taxation without representation' was the slogan that suffragists used. In 1911, women of these two organisations, and the WSPU, refused to be included in the national census. If they did not count as citizens so they would not be counted by the state. Most famously the suffragette, Emily Wilding Davison, who was to later die as a martyr for the women's suffrage cause, hid herself away in a cupboard in the Palace of Westminster in order to avoid the census.

The WSPU is most famous for the extreme violence that it turned to. Violent action against property began in the WSPU in 1908 with stones being used to break windows on Downing Street when government was slow to meet suffragette demands for the vote. Women took to mass shop window-breaking, not just on Oxford Street, but elsewhere in Britain (my grandmother remembered seeing a woman shouting, 'Votes for Women!' and then taking out a shop window in Chesterfield in Derbyshire). This had a clear radical aim, information sheets given to the shopkeepers affected argued that if they wanted such outrages to end, they simply needed to use their vote to put the Liberal government out of power because it refused to give votes to women.

Suffragette violence escalated. Cabinet ministers were physically attacked. Winston Churchill was horsewhipped by a suffragette in 1909, while Prime Minister Asquith was assaulted on numerous occasions. There was an attempt to kill him with an axe in Dublin in July 1912, and to firebomb a theatre he was to speak on the same day. From then until the outbreak of the Great War, suffragette bombing and arson campaigns caused between one and two billion pounds worth of damage in current day values. Politicians houses, such as that of Lloyd George at Walton-on-Thames, public buildings, including government locations, railway stations, and churches, were subject to attack or attempted attacks. It could be argued that the suffragettes were keen to leave a deep impression on men, as they committed arson in sports pavilions, while also placing bombs in men's lavatories. While it is true that no one died as a result of the suffragettes' actions, some people did suffer minor injuries. Suffragette violence would be seen as terrorism under the British Terrorism Act of 2000. This is because its aim was to coerce government.

While a blind eye should not be turned to some of the suffragettes' terrorism, the motives of the extremists of the WSPU had a deeply radical logic. They argued that they had a moral duty to resist the tyranny of government made unrepresentative by not giving women the vote. A correspondent to *The Times* newspaper summarised this truly radical argument that was at the heart of the suffragettes' campaign in 1906; 'The real responsibility for these sensational methods lies with the politicians, misnamed statesmen, who do not attend to demands of justice unless they are accompanied by some form of violence'.

Conclusion

With the outbreak of the First World War in September 1914, the women's campaign for the vote came to a temporary end for 'the duration'. So near to gaining votes for women between 1910 and 1913, both the NUWSS and the various suffragette organisations, most notably the WSPU, declared a truce.

The leader of the NUWSS, Millicent Garrett Fawcett, stated that her supporters would demonstrate that women were worthy of citizenship by serving the British war effort. NUWSS members worked at home and abroad, staffing field hospitals in France and Serbia, and founded a military hospital in London.

Emmeline and Christabel Pankhurst of the WSPU also called a truce to their battle with the British government, declaring their new aims to be 'victory, national security and progress'. Highly patriotic, their organisation became 'The Women's Party' in 1917. Their followers took to awarding any man who was not in military uniform a white feather of cowardice, quite often without any justification, while they gave a kiss to men serving in the Forces.

It was argued that the gift of citizenship that all adult men, and certain women, received in 1918 was a reward for war work. It would appear from this that the very long-fought campaign for women's suffrage in Britain, and the English radicalism that inspired it, had little to do with women getting the vote. My grandma certainly felt that way, still dismissing the suffragette who had smashed the shop window in Chesterfield for the women's cause as 'a right daft cat' when speaking about the incident in the 1980s.

However, there is no doubt that the women's campaign for the vote was vital, not just in women gaining the vote, but in transforming British society's attitudes to women and their place. Without this the vote would not have been won. Both the suffragists and the suffragettes could claim a radical identity and legacy. The women's suffrage campaign also made feminism central to the English Radical Tradition.

Many remember Emmeline Pankhurst and the suffragette fight for votes for women. A statue to her was erected near parliament in Tower Hill Gardens in 1930, two years after her death. The work of the suffragist leader Millicent Garrett Fawcett was not to be celebrated until 2018 when her statue was erected in Parliament Square. Only vaguely remembered for so many years, Millicent Garrett Fawcett and the suffragists are now in their rightful place in the story of how the vote was won. Hopefully, the role of radicalism in that fight is also restored.

Note

1. Recommended further reading for this chapter: Laura E. Nym Mayhall, *The Militant Suffrage Movement: Citizenship and Resistance in Britain, 1860-1930* (Oxford University Press, 2003) and Helen Rogers, *Women and the People: Authority, Authorship and the Radical Tradition in nineteenth century England* (New York: Routledge, 2016).

Epilogue

The electoral reform acts of 1867 and 1884 made members of the male working classes a force to be reckoned with. We saw how, during the 1870s, there was a so-called 'Liberal-Labour' coalition, in which trade unions offered qualified support to the Liberal Party. Yet the relationship increasingly came under strain as unions watched with horror how Liberal governments placed restrictions on strike activity. It soon became clear that a party of the people was needed who would work in conjunction with the unions. The answer to this was the Independent Labour Party (ILP) which was founded in 1893, having grown out of the Scottish Labour Party (established in 1888), and which boasted the firebrand Keir Hardie as its first chairman. The ILP then affiliated themselves to the Labour Representation Committee, which was later renamed as the Labour Party, when that party was founded in 1900.

Entire volumes have been written on the lineage of the Labour Party. Some scholars trace its lineage back to the Chartists; an obvious part of the party's heritage is the trade union movement, while some early Labour activists such as Keir Hardie were confirmed socialists. Others have noted the influence of Methodism on the formation of the Labour Party. The party, when it was first founded, was truly a broad church.

The inclusion in this volume of a brief history of the rise of the Labour Party, however, should not be taken to mean that the whole of English radical history throughout the ages was progressing to a single point, or *telos*, in the formation of the Labour Party—far from it. In the early twentieth century, the Liberal Party was still a force to be reckoned with in spite of the rise of the Labour Party. Although Labour today can be assured that in any election it will either emerge as either the party of government or the opposition, the Labour Party's rise as one of the two main political parties in the United Kingdom was by no means assured in the early 1900s. The Liberals were changing their own approach to governing in the early part of the twentieth century; it was clear even before the First World War began that Victorian laissez-faire ideology was dying and the Liberals were abandoning Gladstonian Liberalism in favour of increasing government intervention into the economy. David Lloyd George's Liberal Party proposed, in 1909, a People's Budget which would have seen pensions paid to older citizens and, among other things, unemployment insurance for workers. All of this was to be funded through general taxation—the budget contained measures that would have been unthinkable to politicians of a century before (although to give Lord Liverpool some credit, he ensured the passage of the Poor Employment Act in 1817 to curb unemployment after the end of the Napoleonic Wars). In 1909, Lloyd George declared that he was at war:

This is a war Budget. It is for raising money to wage implacable warfare against poverty and squalidness. I cannot help hoping and believing that before this generation has passed away, we shall have advanced a great step towards that good time, when poverty, and the wretchedness and human degradation which always follows in its camp, will be as remote to the people of this country as the wolves which once infested its forests.[1]

The passage of this bill was certainly a battle for the Liberals—a battle with the predominantly Conservative House of Lords, who blocked the bill's passage. By convention, the House of Lords could reject, but not amend a financial bill, although the house had not used this power for over a century. The king had urged the lords not to reject the budget but they did; as a great number of the Lords were landowners, they probably objected to the Land Tax contained in the bill, although some of the lords admitted that they would pass the bill provided that Lloyd George obtained an electoral mandate for it. Another election was called, then, in January 1910.

The result of the 1910 election was actually a hung parliament and the Liberals had to rely on the newly-formed Labour Party and the Irish Home Rule bloc for support. One measure that the Irish bloc demanded was the removal of the Lords' veto powers and, in December 1910, another election was held. The result was another hung parliament, with the Liberals again relying on the support of the other parties. But the coalition succeeded in curbing the Lords' veto power with the passage of the Parliament Act in 1911, which *just* made it through the upper chamber on a fairly slim majority of 131 votes in favour and 114 against.

A turning point in the Liberals' fortunes was the First World War. A significant proportion of Labour supporters, who classed themselves as socialists and internationalists, were against the war. They were 'disgusted' with the Liberals' tacit support of conscription—a measure which flew in the face of ideas of liberty.[2] Yet the Liberals were not yet a spent force. In 1918, the Liberals, in coalition with the Conservatives, passed the Representation of the People Act which granted voting rights to all men over the age of twenty-one and all women over the age of thirty. And the result of the 1918 election, held after the passage of the 1918 act, resulted in a landslide victory for Lloyd George's coalition.

The coalition fell in 1922 when the Conservatives, under Andrew Bonar Law, outright won a general election. But Bonar Law died in October 1923 and, feeling that he needed a fresh mandate from the people, the new leader, Stanley Baldwin, again went to the polls in December 1923. The result was a hung parliament. Unable to govern without the support of another party, Baldwin told the king to send for Ramsey MacDonald, the leader of the Labour Party, who could govern as a minority government. MacDonald accepted the king's invitation to form a government: this was the first time that Labour was in government. The government lasted but a year, but the important thing about the Labour Party was that they proved themselves as 'fit to govern'. The next election at the end of 1924 saw the Conservatives returned to power, winning a total of 412 seats, with Labour's share of seats reduced from 191 to 151, and the Liberals were dying; H.H. Asquith's Liberals garnered but 118 seats.

It was clear that the Labour Party was cementing its support among a significantly enlarged electoral base. Slowly the two-party system, recognizable to Brits in 2020, was beginning to take shape: elections were becoming a contest between the Conservatives and the Labour Party. Nowhere was this more apparent than in the General Election of 1929 when Labour won 287 seats, with the Conservatives winning only 260, while the Liberals won a pitiful fifty-nine.

While during the Second World War the parties came together in coalition, in the General Election of 1945, Labour, under Clement Attlee, won a landslide majority and the party began building a welfare state under what might be called a 'one nation' vision of the future, which included a programme of slum clearances and house building, the creation of a nationalised health service, and a planned economy which appealed to both the middle and working classes. As *New Statesman* remarked in 1948:

> During the war the conception of planning had stirred the minds of all, whether in the Forces or in industry. By 1944, the discussion on the need for planning in order to rebuild and re-site industry, to create new towns and demolish slums and to extend social services, was widespread. The middle classes, nodding their heads over their wireless sets, reading their Penguins or looking at *Picture Post*, were on the side of the planners. Many voted Labour.[3]

Labour's success, or otherwise, has always depended upon its ability to reconcile the interests of the middle classes, and win enough votes from them, with those of the working classes, whose interests the party was founded to represent.[4] In appealing to the middle classes, Labour was obviously successful, and it should be noted that voters did remember the fact that some prominent Tory politicians had expressed support for the Nazis before the war, and as the aforementioned *New Statesman* article remarked, voters remembered this and accordingly voted against the Conservatives.

Was there, then, a space for radical politics driven by the people at a grassroots level after the rise of the Labour Party?

Continuing the work of the suffragists and suffragettes were the 'Second Wave' feminists. Beginning in the United States in the 1960s, Second Wave feminism's appearance in the United Kingdom is generally marked by the foundation of the British Women's Liberation Movement in 1970, when the organisation held its first conference between 27 February and 1 March. The BWLM then made headlines in November of the same year for organising a protest outside a Miss World beauty competition in London.[5] Although some women gained the right to vote in 1918, with further extensions of the franchise occurring in 1928, the BWLM felt that women's position had not changed much for the better. As Florence Binard points out, British society's attitude to women's roles was still very 'Victorian' and patriarchal—men were viewed as the breadwinners and women rarely entered high-status professions; women could not obtain mortgages without the support of a male guarantor; and until the passage of the Equal Pay Act (1970) women could legally be paid less than men for the same job. Two factors convinced the government of the need to pass this act: in the first place, the US Government had passed a similar act in 1963 and in 1968, women workers at the Ford factory in Dagenham went on strike because management informed them that they would receive fifteen per cent less pay than male workers. When the second reading of the Equal Pay Act came before the Commons, the MP Shirley Summerskill remarked that the heroes of the Dagenham strike had played '[a] very significant part in the history of the struggle for equal pay'.[6] In spite of the Equal Pay Act, women still faced struggles in other areas of life. Women's rights campaigners since the 1960s have fought hard to combat what they see as the demeaning stereotypes of women in the media, while others continue to fight for an end to the gender pay gap. In politics, women have faced struggles for representation, even in, surprisingly, the Labour Party. Although women comprised over forty per cent of the membership of the Labour Party, and whose members had always been strongly committed to campaigning for the party at a grassroots level, by 1970, the number of female Labour MPs was a very low twenty-nine.[7]

With the rise of the Cold War, a lot of radical activity was focused upon what might be called 'single issue' concerns. The rise of nuclear disarmament groups in Britain and across the Western world might be classed as one such example of radicalism. Or perhaps they are not radical at all—at least not by Turner's definition given in the beginning of this volume whereby radicalism is predicated upon changing the political constitution of the nation. Although the historian E.P. Thompson did highlight the lack of democratic accountability in nuclear war planning in his pamphlet *Protest and Survive* (1980).[8] More recently grass-roots green activism has taken prominence over anti-nuclear campaigns. In the UK, Extinction Rebellion became famous in 2019 for their street protests, although there are certain commentators who do not see this group as radical at all but reactionary who attempt to subvert democratic processes.[9]

It might be asked—with radical activism seemingly focused on these 'single issue' concerns, was there any further need to campaign for changes to the British political system once all people had the vote?

In the nineteenth century, as we have seen, radicals' energies were focused upon changing *how* the British people were governed—that is, campaigning for changes to the constitution. This involved not only fighting for universal suffrage but also ending 'Old Corruption'—a system whereby members of an unelected oligarchy, in receipt of pensions and sinecures, lived upon the toil and taxes of the industrious classes. Perhaps the anti-Old Corruption spirit was alive in some of the 'Eurosceptics' who, since Britain's entry into the European Economic Community (EEC) in January 1973, campaigned tirelessly to wrench the United Kingdom out of what they saw as an undemocratic organisation. They feared that democratic accountability in Britain would be sidelined to the wishes of a group of unelected commissioners in Brussels. Much of the criticism of the EEC came from the left. To observers such as Tony Benn, another stalwart of the Labour Party, it was the democratic deficit of the EEC which was most troubling:

> When the economic and other arguments are melted away, I feel strongly about it because, at bottom, this [membership of the EEC] erodes the importance of the vote. For people in this country who don't have money or power in industry it is the vote that is their main safeguard for the

future and common market membership devalues and downgrades the vote because it prevents people using the ballot box to adopt policies, change policies, change men who adopt policies, and thus change taxes and laws, because in future, if people vote yes on Thursday, then whatever the outcome of the general elections may be, much real power will rest in the hands of those who will not be affected by our elections. Now there are men who give their lives for the right to self-government, independence, democracy; there are many men in the world today in prison for those rights, and we are being invited to give up those rights for whatever purposes we shall be discussing.[10]

Membership of the EEC was not, in the eyes of left-wing Eurosceptics, 'internationalist' in any way. The 'Red Queen' Barbara Castle, a stalwart of the Labour Party, criticised the faux-internationalism of EEC supporters by asking them:

What kind of internationalism is it that says that henceforth this country must give priority to a Frenchman over an Indian, a German over an Australian, an Italian over a Malaysian? This isn't the language of internationalism ... it is Euro-jingoism.[11]

To Castle, it seemed as though Britain was turning its back on the multi-racial Commonwealth and joining an exclusive organisation of (predominantly white) European nations that saw itself as superior to other countries.

Not all Labour politicians and activists shared Castle and Benn's views, of course; the Labour Party was in fact divided on the question of EEC membership. Heath could only get the European Communities Bill passed with the support of pro-EEC Labour politicians. Roy Jenkins (1920–2003) was the leader of a group of sixty-nine pro-European Labour politicians who supported Heath's entry into the Common Market in the Commons in 1971. Jenkins and fellow Labour EEC supporters did this in spite of having been 'whipped', and in defiance of the Labour Party's conference motion to reject Heath's plans for entry. Where Castle and Benn saw in EEC membership the erosion of hard-won democratic rights, Jenkins saw EEC membership as an extension of the great progressive measures of the past. As Jenkins stated:

I was convinced that it was one of the decisive votes of the century, and had no intention of spending the rest of my life answering the question of what did I do in the great division by saying "I abstained." I saw it in the context of the first Reform Bill, the repeal of the Corn Laws, Gladstone's Home Rule Bills, the Lloyd George Budget and the Parliament Bill.[12]

Those on the left of the Labour Party denounced Jenkins and his supporters as 'traitors' and wanted them out. As one correspondent in *The Times* remarked: 'The unconcealed objective of the Left now is either to humiliate Roy Jenkins and his allies into submission—or drive them from the party'.[13]

Epilogue

In October 1974, the Labour Party won a General Election under Harold Wilson (there had been an election earlier in February which resulted in a hung parliament). To ease some of the divisions in his party, and in recognition of the fact that membership of the EEC was controversial among the general public as well, Wilson agreed, for the first time in history, that the government would ask the British people directly whether Britain should remain as a member of EEC. Thus, on 5 June 1975, the first-ever referendum in British history was held. The question the people were asked was 'Do you think the United Kingdom should stay in the European Community (the Common Market)?' The result was a resounding yes—seventeen million people voted in favour of continuing Britain's membership of the Common Market. Sitting atop the queen, Lords, and Commons of the British constitution was now another layer of government: a European Commission. The Commission was elected by no one but was able to initiate legislation that had to be complied with among all member states of the EEC, renamed in 1993 as the European Union (EU).

The question seemed settled. Under the Labour Prime Minister ,Tony Blair, Britain seemed to be transforming itself into a cosmopolitan European nation. 'Cool Britannia' was multicultural and welcomed freedom of movement of capital and labour into its borders as a condition of 'single market' membership. Mainstream opinion was, so it seemed, decidedly with Europe. For a majority of those on the left of British politics—who often claimed to be heirs to Victorian radical traditions—Castle's earlier warnings seemed to have been completely disregarded; membership of the EU fit well with the left's internationalist ideals; the EU, with its labour rights and regulations, also seemed to offer protection from a Conservative Party which since Thatcher's days seemed intent on cutting 'wasteful' public spending and rolling back the state.

Yet Euroscepticism never went away, on the left or the right, although it became more prevalent on the right from the 1990s onwards. A large majority of the media characterised Eurosceptics as cranky 'Trots', militant trade union bosses, or even, in the early twenty-first century, racists; 'fruitcakes and loonies' was another characterisation given by David Cameron to the United Kingdom Independence Party (UKIP) who campaigned for withdrawal from the EU. UKIP appealed to the poorer sections of British society in former industrial towns who were 'left behind' as a result of globalisation—of which EU membership was a part—and steadily they eroded the power of both Labour and the Conservatives, first at a local level in council elections and thereafter at a national level. It is also safe to say that criticism of the EU by the right-wing UKIP was, in some respects, also tinged with xenophobia. UKIP and other Eurosceptics on the right, and of course the 'fringe' left of British politics, much like those who railed against Old Corruption in times gone by, attributed poorer people's problems to the fact that they were subject to the diktats of an unelected and faraway elite who they could not vote out. Meantime, it seemed as though the EU, with its token parliament, seemed to be building a new superstate; ever more legislative powers seemed to be given over to the Commission, with issues coming to a head over the Lisbon Treaty, which seemed, so Eurosceptics thought, to be a tool for the creation of an EU constitution by stealth. The only answer, in the Eurosceptics' view, was to get out of the EU.

The Eurosceptics always had allies in the main party—Jeremy Corbyn was once known for his staunch anti-EU views, while members of the European Research Group in the parliamentary Conservative Party had always advocated for leaving the EU. The Conservative Prime Minister, David Cameron, seeking to reconcile the pro- and anti-EU factions in his own party—especially after the defection of two MPs to UKIP—agreed to offer voters an 'In/Out' referendum on EU membership at the General Election in 2015. This would also, he hoped, bring back to the Conservative fold former Conservative voters who had defected to UKIP as well as attracting disillusioned Labour voters. Cameron did not want to leave the EU himself; growing pressure within and without his party had forced him to offer a referendum. Besides, Cameron had overseen the 'once in a generation' Scottish Independence referendum in 2014 and held the United Kingdom together—he assumed, probably, that the same would hold true for a referendum on EU membership and that people would vote for the *status quo*.

When the referendum was held on 23 June 2016 the turnout was huge—seventy-two per cent of voters turned up at polling stations to cast a ballot. The result was a majority of fifty-two per cent in favour of leaving the EU. Having supported remaining in the EU, David Cameron decided to resign. A new Conservative leader, Theresa May, was appointed by the party to lead Britain through what was certainly going to be a turbulent time. Almost immediately did people on the losing side sign up *en masse* to a petition calling for a second referendum. Affluent lawyers and academics, who overwhelmingly supported Remain,[14] mounted petition after petition,[15] legal case after case, to try and overturn the result. At the level of high politics, May's situation was not helped by the fact that, seeking a mandate for her Brexit policies, Theresa May lost her majority in 2017 and had to rely on the DUP for support. May's Tory government was at the mercy of a predominantly 'Remain' parliament on the one hand, and the staunch Eurosceptics in the European Research Group (ERG) in her own party on the other (it is unclear the amount of 'research' that was actually conducted by the ERG; their main remit was to act as an internal opposition within the Tory party). Although an able politician, May's hands seemed tied and it seemed as though the parliamentary implementation of Brexit was stalling. Sensing that the Conservatives might be backsliding on Brexit, the former leader of UKIP, Nigel Farage, founded the Brexit Party in 2018 which he would lead into the EU parliament elections in 2019. Farage was careful to disassociate himself from UKIP at the time; his former party and himself having faced accusations of racism, he selected a number of ethnically and politically diverse candidates to field in the European elections. The Brexit Party eventually 'crushed' Labour and the Tories.[16] With the Brexit Party promising to field candidates in the next UK General Election, May's position as prime minister was now in question and she was quickly persuaded to resign.

May's replacement was Boris Johnson, a man who had always dreamed of being prime minister. Although his parliamentary majority was exactly the same as May's when he became prime minister, he took a gamble and went to the polls in December 2019 in what was to be a 'Brexit Election'. Labour under the traditionally Eurosceptic Corbyn decided to support a second referendum while Johnson campaigned to 'Get Brexit Done'. Johnson's gamble paid off: he won an eighty seat majority. Brexit day was set for 31 December 2019. After this Britain would enter a 'transition' period of one year, following all relevant European Union rules, and the 'full' Brexit occurred at 11 p.m. on 31 December 2020.

Time will tell of the political, social, and economic consequences that will ensue from Brexit—whether it was a wise decision or the wrong one is a task that future historians will have to assess. Although the left has usually been the side to pursue radical constitutional change, with Brexit, it was the Conservatives who, although usually favouring gradual political reform, pursued the most far-reaching political change in a generation.

Notes

1. David Lloyd George, *Better Times* (London: Hodder & Stoughton, 1910), 143.
2. Belchem, p. 184.
3. Maurice Edelman [online], "Labour and the middle classes," *New Statesman* June 12, 1948, accessed November 19, 2020. Available at: www.newstatesman.com.
4. Belchem, p. 186.
5. Florence Binard, "The British Women's Liberation Movement in the 1970s: Redefining the Personal and the Political," *Revue Française de Civilisation Britannique / French Journal of British Studies* XXII Hors-série: The United Kingdom and the Crisis in the 1970s (2017), 2.
6. "Equal Pay No 2 Bill (1970)". House of Commons. Historic Hansard. 9 February 1970. c976. Retrieved 29 April 2020.
7. Ina Zweiniger-Bargielowska, *Women in Twentieth-Century Britain* (Harlow: Longman, 2001), 87, 197.
8. E.P. Thompson, "Protest and Survive," in *Protest and Survive*, ed. E.P. Thompson and Dan Smith (London: Penguin, 1980), 26.
9. Austin Williams [online], 'Extinction Rebellion: the new millenarian cult', *Spiked* August 19, 2019, accessed August 20, 2020. Available at: www.spiked-online.com.
10. Tony Benn [online], 'Tony Benn on Sovereignty', accessed August 19, 2020. Available at: www.youtube.com
11. Barbara Castle, Oxford Union Debate, accessed August 17, 2020. Available at: https://www.youtube.com.
12. Roy Jenkins, *A Life at the Centre* (London: Politico, 2006), 329.
13. John Campbell, *Roy Jenkins: A Well-Rounded Life* (London: Penguin, 2014), 380.
14. John Morgan [online], "EU referendum: nine out of 10 university staff back Remain," *Times Higher Education* June 16, 2016, accessed November 23, 2020. Available at: https://www.timeshighereducation.com/
15. Parliament UK [online], "EU Referendum Rules triggering a 2nd EU Referendum," accessed November 23, 2020. Available at: https://petition.parliament.uk/archived/petitions/131215.
16. Anon. [online], "European elections 2019: Brexit Party dominates as Tories and Labour suffer," *BBC News* May 27, 2019, accessed August 20, 2020. Available at: www.bbc.co.uk.

Select Bibliography

For further references please see the individual reference lists at the end of each chapter.

Acheson, R.J. *Radical Puritans in England 1550-1660.* London: Longman, 1993.

Aldridge, Alfred O. *Man of Reason: The Life of Thomas Paine.* Philadelphia: J. B. Lippincott, 1959.

Anderson, Anne. "Victorian High Society and Social Duty: the promotion of `Recreative Learning and Voluntary Teaching." *Journal of the History of Education* 31 no. 4 (2002): 311-334.

Aston, Margaret. "Corpus Christi and Corpus Regni: Heresy and the Peasants' Revolt." *Past & Present* no. 143 (1994): 3-47.

Atlas, Jerrold. "The Black Death: An Essay on Traumatic Change." *Journal of Psychohistory* 36 no.3 (2009): 249-259.

Barker, Juliet. *England Arise: The People, the King, and the Great Revolt of 1381.* London: Abacus, 2014.

Basdeo, Stephen. *The Life and Legend of a Rebel Leader: Wat Tyler.* Barnsley: Pen and Sword, 2018.

Belchem, John. *Popular Radicalism in Nineteenth-Century Britain.* Basingstoke: MacMillan, 1996.

Braddick, Michael. *The Common Freedom of the People, John Lilburne and the English Revolution.* Oxford: Oxford University Press, 2018.

Bradstock, Andrew. *Radical Religion in Cromwell's England.* London: Tauris, 2011.

Brailsford, H.N. *The Levellers and the English Revolution.* Ed. Christopher Hill. Nottingham: Spokesman, 1983.

Brown, Tony. Ed. *Edward Carpenter and Late Victorian Radicalism.* London: Frank Cass & Co, 1990.

Burchell, Kenneth. *Thomas Paine in America.* London: Pickering Chatto, 2009.

Chase, Malcolm. *Chartism: A New History.* Manchester: Manchester University Press, 2007.

Chiu, Frances, *The Routledge Guidebook to Paine's Rights of Man.* New York: Routledge, 2020.

Claeys, Gregory. *Thomas Paine: Social and Political Thought.* London: Unwin Hyman, 1989.

Clarke, Anna. *The Struggle for the Breeches: Gender and the Making of the British Working Class.* Berkeley: University of California Press, 1997.

Clayton, Joseph. *The Rise of the Democracy*. London: Cassell, 1911.

Cole, Margaret. *The Story of Fabian Socialism.* Stanford University Press, 1961.

Dart, Gregory. *Metropolitan Art and Literature, 1810-1840: Cockney Adventures.* Cambridge: Cambridge University Press, 2012.

Dunn, Alastair. *The Peasants' Revolt: England's Failed Revolution of 1381*. Stroud: Tempus, 2004.

Dyer, Christopher. *An Age of Transition? Economy and Society in England in the Later Middle Ages*. Oxford: Clarendon Press, 2005.

Evans, R.J.W. and Hartmut Pogge von Strandmann, ed. *The Revolutions in Europe, 1848–1849: From Reform to Reaction*. Oxford University Press, 2000.

Gordon, Lyndall. *Vindication: A Life of Mary Wollstonecraft.* New York: HarperCollins, 2005.

Harvey, I. M. W. *Jack Cade's Rebellion of 1450*. Oxford: Clarendon Press, 1991.

Hill, Christopher. *The World Turned Upside Down: Radical Ideas During the English Revolution.* Harmondsworth: Penguin, 1975.

Hunt, Henry, *Memoirs of Henry Hunt Esq.*, 3 vols. London: 1820-22.

Jobson, Adrian. *The First English Revolution: Simon de Montfort, Henry III and the Barons' War*. London: Bloomsbury, 2012.

Justice, Steven. *Writing and Rebellion: England in 1381*. Berkeley and Los Angeles: University of California Press, 1994.

Kaufman, Alexander L. *The Historical Literature of the Jack Cade Rebellion*. Farnham: Ashgate, 2009..

Maddicott, J.R. *Simon de Montfort*. Cambridge: Cambridge University Press, 1994.

Oman, Charles, and E. B. Fryde. *The Great Revolt of 1381*. Oxford: Clarendon Press, 1969.

Paine, Thomas. *Complete Writings of Thomas Paine.* Ed. Philip Foner. New York, Citadel Press, 1945, 1969.

Riding, Jaqueline, *Peterloo: The Story of the Manchester Massacre*. London: Head of Zeus, 2019.

Robertson, Geoffrey. *The Levellers: The Putney Debates*. London: Verso, 2018.

Rose, Jonathan. *The Intellectual Life of the British Working Classes.* New Haven: Yale University Press, 2001.

St. Clair, William. *The Reading Nation in the Romantic Period.* Cambridge: Cambridge University Press, 2004.

Thompson, E.P. Thompson, E. P., *The Making of the English Working Class*, 2nd edn. Harmondsworth: Penguin, 1968.

———, *William Morris, Romantic to Revolutionary*. London: Merlin Press, 1977.

Todd, Janet. *Mary Wollstonecraft: A Revolutionary Life.* New York: Columbia University Press, 2000.

Turner, Michael J. *Independent Radicalism in Early Victorian Britain*. Westport, CT: Praegar, 2004.

Wiener, Joel. *William Lovett.* Manchester: Manchester University Press, 1989.

Index of Names

Index of Names

Index of Names